SVEC

2001 : 08

Manuscripts (two copies with a brief summary) should be prepared in accordance with
the *SVEC* stylesheet available on request and at the Voltaire Foundation website
and should be submitted to the
Voltaire Foundation
99 Banbury Road, Oxford OX2 6JX, UK

Pastel portrait of Rousseau by Maurice Quentin de La Tour
(*Bibliothèque publique et universitaire, Neuchâtel*)

RAYMOND BIRN

Forging Rousseau

Print, commerce and cultural manipulation in the late Enlightenment

VOLTAIRE FOUNDATION

OXFORD

2001

ISBN 0 7294 0770 5
ISSN 0435-2866

Voltaire Foundation
99 Banbury Road
Oxford OX2 6JX, UK

A catalogue record for this book
is available from the British Library

The correct reference for this volume is
SVEC 2001:08

This series is available on annual subscription

For further information about *SVEC*
and other Voltaire Foundation publications see
www.voltaire.ox.ac.uk

Printed and bound by CPI Group (UK) Ltd, Croydon, CR0 4YY

Table of contents

Acknowledgements

As might be expected with a book that has taken shape over ten years, my debts of gratitude are enormous. Released time at Washington University's Center for the History of Freedom, the Newberry Library in Chicago, the Ecole des Hautes Etudes en Sciences Sociales in Paris and the University of Oregon's Humanities Center allowed me to press forward with the project at just the right moments. An NEH Travel-to-Collections grant and a University of Oregon summer fellowship helped me reach libraries in France and Switzerland; and I have addressed my topic at conferences in Austin, Cleveland, Bristol, Totnes (UK), Lyon, Paris and elsewhere.

My personal obligations are even greater than my institutional ones. Colleagues at the University of Oregon – Cynthia Brokaw, Matthew Dennis and Stanley Pierson – read an entire manuscript in its penultimate draft. So did Eric Birn, while William Ray of Reed College read an earlier one. Robert Darnton of Princeton University read pieces of a yet more primitive version. Roger Chartier of the Ecole des Hautes Etudes en Sciences Sociales in Paris offered me the opportunity to share my research with him and his students, while Daniel Roche of the Collège de France and Bronislaw Baczko of the University of Geneva have inspired me through deed and word. As a cultural historian I wish to note my warm appreciation for the work of two incomparable scholars: the late Ralph Leigh, editor of the correspondence by, to and about Rousseau; and Jo-Ann E. McEachern, bibliographer of the eighteenth-century Rousseau editions. The publications of Professors Leigh and McEachern made mine possible. A friend and colleague who is no longer here, Robert Lang, helped me through all sorts of muddles; and Joyce Hatch, who is very much present, has done the same and more. For the unswerving companionship of the latter two I shall be forever thankful.

Raymond Birn

Introduction

THIS book is about image marketing, cultural discipleship and the economics of literary canonisation. It reveals how, in a pre-copyright age, Rousseau, the quintessential 'shy star' of literature, asserted his authorial uniqueness by challenging the claims of legitimate publishers and book pirates alike to ownership of his printed texts.[1] Subsequently, for the decade following the writer's death, it illustrates how his closest disciples manipulated the meanings of *rousseauisme* with the publication of the Master's massive testament, the *Collection complète des œuvres de J.-J. Rousseau*. The stated function of the *Collection complète* was to house Rousseau's life and works in an authoritative edition. Yet the deeper purpose of the edition was both exemplary and didactic. Readers were invited to sort through Rousseau's theories of politics and education, his fiction, and his autobiographical writings and correspondence. They were asked to appropriate as they saw fit, aware that the texts they absorbed might change their lives.[2] During the mature stages of the French Revolution, however, particularly the years of the Jacobin dictatorship and early thermidorian reaction, the mythologising of Rousseau shifted focus. The fluid autobiographical lessons of the *Collection complète* gave way to a static political symbol: Rousseau as *père de la patrie* and eventually as an embalmed corpse lying in state in the Panthéon, revered at a distance but rarely interrogated.

The publishing history of Rousseau's major works, particularly the commercial tribulations of the posthumous *Collection complète*, serves as the narrative bridge connecting my analysis of cultural discipleship with that of image marketing. Rousseau advertised himself as an *écrivain de vocation*, the moral

1. The term 'shy star' pertaining to Rousseau ('the person who desires to be spiritually public and physically private') was employed by Leo Braudy in his very useful survey, *The Frenzy of renown: fame and its history* (New York 1986), p.375.

2. In a recent collective work, *La Notion d'œuvres complètes*, ed. Jean Sgard and Catherine Volpilhac-Auger, *SVEC* 370 (1999), Professor Sgard distinguishes among 'œuvres diverses', 'collections complètes' and 'œuvres complètes' in the eighteenth century. The idea of 'œuvres complètes', writes Sgard, 'suppose l'exhaustivité et l'achèvement présumé du travail de l'écrivain'. It assures the author, 'sous la forme d'un "monument" ou d'un "tombeau", une sorte d'éternité' ('Des collections aux œuvres complètes, 1756-1798', p.1-12, at p.1-2). On the other hand, again according to Sgard, the late eighteenth-century 'collection complète' was primarily a publisher's economic speculation, a pulling together of a writer's available work from wherever it might be found. In Jean Sgard's view the selling points of a 'collection complète' were its novelty, stylishness and the polemics it might contain. In evaluating the publication of the *Collection complète des œuvres de J.-J. Rousseau* I shall suggest some nuance to Sgard's hypothesis. Those who prepared the Rousseau volumes were at least as interested in offering readers the sourcebook of an exemplary life as they were in producing a commercial success. Furthermore the edition was not intended to be Rousseau's sepulchre, but rather his gospel message. Robert Darnton has analysed the dialogue between Rousseau and his 'active' reader in 'Readers respond to Rousseau: the fabrication of romantic sensitivity', in *The Great Cat massacre and other episodes in French cultural history* (New York 1984), p.215-56, 279-82.

sage, whose earnings from his pen were secondary to the messages he delivered. Nevertheless, his initial decision to prepare a definitive edition of his collected works seems to have been based as much upon concerns over amassing sufficient retirement income as it was upon a need for leaving an authorised literary legacy. Persecution and exile aborted Rousseau's edition, the writer died without finishing it and it was left for the embattled disciples to combat book pirates, would-be heirs and one another in the production of the *Collection complète*. Their efforts clearly stimulated 'the business of Rousseau' in western Europe during the late eighteenth century, further commodifying the cultural icon – even as piracies, non-paying booksellers and misguided decisions provoked spectacular financial losses for original investors. Though it introduced the *Rêveries*, *Confessions* and Rousseau's most exemplary correspondence to the world, the original edition of the *Collection complète* proved to be a commercial disaster. Exploring the reasons for this calamity is integral to my story and to an evaluation of late eighteenth-century book-publishing practices.[3]

Part I of what follows is an exploration of Rousseau's author-centred interpretation of literary property. In particular it surveys the writer's dialogue with his publisher of record, Marc-Michel Rey of Amsterdam, over ownership of the corpus. Like Rousseau, Rey was an expatriate from Geneva, a hard-headed businessman who sensed that his mercurial author could make him rich. Between 1754 and 1762 Rey paid Rousseau for manuscripts of the *Discours sur l'origine de l'inégalité*, the *Lettre à d'Alembert*, *La Nouvelle Héloïse* and *Du contrat social*; but the pair never was able to reach an accord concerning ultimate title to the works, particularly as it affected re-publication rights and rights to an edition of collected works, and no body of international copyright law adequately defined matters for a Swiss author publishing in the Netherlands for an overwhelmingly French readership.

Accusing Rey of having underpaid Rousseau for manuscripts of his works, the writer's friends the maréchale-duchesse de Luxembourg and C.-G. de Lamoignon de Malesherbes persuaded him to bypass the Amsterdam publisher when it came to producing his masterpiece, *Emile*, in 1762. The Paris bookseller Nicolas-Bonaventure Duchesne offered Rousseau an unprecedented 6000 *livres* for the treatise, nearly three times what Rey had paid for *La Nouvelle Héloïse*. Included in the contract with Duchesne were first publication rights to an edition of collected works, though it remained unclear whether this edition would be the authorised one which Rousseau anticipated. Once *Emile* appeared, of course, debates with publishers over property rights became moot. Agencies of church and state in France outlawed the book.

---

3. While indebted to Robert Darnton's *The Business of enlightenment: a publishing history of the 'Encyclopédie' 1775-1800* (Cambridge, Mass. 1979), I am less inclined than Darnton to ascribe overwhelmingly material motivations to publishers and editors. Those behind the *Collection complète* believed themselves to be disseminating Rousseau's moral vision. Their conflicts had more to do with competing interpretations of that vision than with ways of stimulating profits. For a full discussion of Darnton's views see *The Darnton debate: books and revolution in the eighteenth century*, ed. Haydn T. Mason, *SVEC* 359 (1998).

Regimes in Holland, Switzerland and the Austrian Netherlands condemned it as well. At nearly the same moment Malesherbes, director of the French monarchy's censorship and book-trade agency, was ordered to seize Rey's edition of *Du contrat social*. Rousseau had to flee France. Unwelcome in his native city of Geneva, the fugitive found a temporary haven in the village of Môtiers, located in the principality of Neuchâtel, Swiss territory nominally ruled by Frederick the Great of Prussia.

While in Neuchâtel Rousseau encountered the individual who, over the next quarter-century, would serve as his most faithful disciple and literary advocate: the millionaire Pierre-Alexandre Du Peyrou. Du Peyrou's wealth derived from slave-maintained plantations in the New World; he saw no conflict, however, between his commercial interests and propagation of Rousseau's message of universal freedom. In 1764 Du Peyrou agreed to subsidise an edition of Rousseau's writings and correspondence, overseen by the author. As payment he would guarantee Rousseau a lifetime annuity, thereby assuring maintenance for the writer and his companion, Thérèse Levasseur. Meticulously edited and graciously presented, the edition was envisioned as a weapon directed at the piracies which had emerged over the past decade and which drove Rousseau to distraction.

Unfortunately, the moment for such an edition was ill-timed. New persecutions forced the writer to flee Môtiers for England and Du Peyrou had to set aside his plans. He packaged up and stored away the manuscripts which Rousseau had assembled or was preparing. While in England Rousseau abandoned the edition of his collected works and sought to justify his life via the *Confessions*. Occasionally he sent Du Peyrou packages of papers which the dutiful disciple conserved, safe from light and dampness. One day, Du Peyrou hoped, the packages would be opened in Rousseau's presence and the edition of collected works revived. But this never occurred. Following Rousseau's return to France in 1767 it remained out of the question, even though piracies and cobbled collections were undertaken throughout Europe without the writer's participation.

In the morning of 2 July 1778 Rousseau died at Ermenonville, north of Paris, on the estate of his last host, marquis René-Louis de Girardin. Six weeks earlier Voltaire had finished his days in the French capital. Neither writer had validated the totality of his career with an authorised edition of his collected works. It was left to disciples and entrepreneurs to fix the heritages in print. During his lifetime Voltaire certainly had come closer than Rousseau to presenting an ensemble, co-operating with the Dresden publisher George Conrad Walther for a nine-volume set of *Œuvres* (1748-1750), inquiring after the Paris *libraire* Michel Lambert for an eleven-volume set in the mid-1750s, and working closely with Geneva's Gabriel Cramer over a *Collection complète* in seventeen volumes in 1756.[4] In 1777 the Paris press lord Charles-

---

4. René Pomeau, *Voltaire en son temps*, vol. iii with Christiane Mervaud, *De la cour au jardin, 1750-1759* (Oxford 1991), p.261-63; vol. iv *'Ecraser l'infâme', 1759-1770* (Oxford 1994), p.262-63.

Joseph Panckoucke had discussed publication of a definitive edition with the aged Voltaire, but the Patriarch died before progress could be made. Suspecting correctly that Rousseau had left unpublished manuscripts behind, particularly the *Confessions*, Panckoucke toyed with the notion of an edition of the Genevan's corpus as well. But the 'Atlas de la librairie française' overestimated his financial liquidity. Both the Voltaire and Rousseau projects passed to others. Beaumarchais undertook the Voltaire, and the result was the Kehl edition of 1784-1789.[5] The story of the Rousseau canonical edition is the subject of Parts II and III of what follows.

Constructing Rousseau's shrine at Ermenonville and appointing himself guardian of Thérèse Levasseur, Girardin considered it a sacred duty to revive the aborted project of 1764/65 and oversee what was to become the *Collection complète des œuvres de J.-J. Rousseau*. He persuaded Du Peyrou to open the packages in Neuchâtel and added the Genevan Paul-Claude Moultou as a third editor. In his pan-European quest for manuscripts, letters and other documentation, Girardin charmed, cajoled and browbeat Rousseau's one-time admirers and correspondents. Sequestered on the marquis's estate and denied what she considered her rightful inheritance, Thérèse Levasseur bitterly resented being thrust aside except when cast as a tourist attraction for entranced disciples and curious visitors. Eventually Thérèse fled Ermenonville in the company of Girardin's *valet de chambre*, and for more than twenty years would fight for her share of Rousseau's literary property. Meanwhile Girardin's image of Rousseau as political and literary martyr and his eagerness to alter Rousseau's texts to support his vision clashed with Du Peyrou's insistence upon presenting Rousseau faithfully. Furthermore, by hiding and withholding the second part of the writer's unpublished *Confessions*, Girardin betrayed the great project and was forced to abandon his role in its completion. Meanwhile he egged on Rousseau cousins, residing as far away as London and Iraq, to stake their claims to the inheritance.

In the end, however, as he attempted to extract the significance of the writer's corpus from his mountain of documentation, not even Du Peyrou was able to resist fabricating *his* Rousseau. Du Peyrou's strategy in editing Rousseau's correspondence, his tactical placement of materials in the edition, his choice of which polemics would enter the supplementary volumes of the *Collection complète* and his ultimate decision to publish an unexpurgated edition of the entire *Confessions*, produced Rousseau the thundering warrior, still employing print to berate encyclopedists and privileged enemies from

See as well *Voltaire, lettres inédites à son imprimeur Gabriel Cramer*, ed. Bernard Gagnebin (Geneva 1952). Cramer undertook a new edition of Voltaire's works in 1768. By 1777 it had reached thirty volumes, and he produced an 'édition encadrée' in 1775 (forty volumes).

5. *Œuvres complètes de Voltaire*, 70 vols in-8° and 92 vols in-12° ([Kehl], Société littéraire typographique 1784-1789). The history of the Kehl Voltaire is treated in the following: P. H. Muir, 'The Kehl edition of Voltaire', *The Library* 3 (September 1948), Fifth Series, p.85-100; Giles Barber, 'The financial history of the Kehl Voltaire', in *The Age of the Enlightenment: studies presented to Theodore Besterman*, ed. W. H. Barber *et al.* (London and Edinburgh 1967), p.152-70; Brian N. Morton, 'Beaumarchais et le prospectus de l'édition de Kehl', *SVEC* 81 (1971), p.133-47.

the grave. As moulded by Du Peyrou, who would replace the disgraced Girardin as workhorse editor, the *Collection complète* assumed the unique literary form of a 'total' moral autobiography, one shaped by Rousseau's memoirs, essays, fiction, music, polemics and, most especially, by the *Confessions* and selected and edited correspondence.

The anticipated popularity of the *Collection complète* proved its undoing. Printed in Geneva by a consortium of young, largely inexperienced investors, banded together as the Société typographique de Genève, the edition obtained tacit permissions to circulate in the tiny republic and in France. These permissions, however, were no guarantee of exclusivity. At least eight piracies were made of the Geneva edition, in less expensive formats than the in-quarto and in-octavo of the original. Priced out of the market, sets of the original edition collected dust in the warehouses of the STG or else were peddled at deep discounts to more than 140 European booksellers. As a final blow, dealer after dealer defaulted on invoices. An editorial triumph, the project proved to be a financial disaster.

Nevertheless, during the 1780s the publishers and pirates of the *Collection complète* codified rousseauism in print. With the *Confessions* and correspondence as essential discursive supports, the *Collection complète* was intended to record an exemplary life and works, and readers derived their individual inspirations from the 'total' moral autobiography. During the pre- and liberal-revolutionary decade (1782-1792) complementary images of Rousseau were to be located in biographical essays, poems, engravings, theatrical representations and folk festivals. Pilgrimages to the burial site on the île des Peupliers at Ermenonville became obligatory. Commanding Rousseau's bones, Girardin still insisted upon his role as keeper of the flame.

During the radical phase of the French Revolution, however, everything changed. A new edition of Rousseau's works undertaken in 1788 subsequently turned from autobiographical parable to high politics. Meant to replace the *Collection complète*, after November 1792 each volume of this 'revolutionary' edition, as it appeared, was offered to the presiding officer of the French Republic's National Convention.[6] In the meantime the older generation of Rousseau's disciples either disappeared, became isolated or found themselves genuinely endangered. Moultou died in 1787. Du Peyrou survived in Neuchâtel until November 1794. Girardin wound up losing everything – his fortune, Ermenonville and even Rousseau's remains, which were ceremonially disinterred and borne to the Panthéon in Paris. Though she never obtained her full inheritance, Thérèse Levasseur achieved moral redemption. Revolutionaries transformed her from an *ancien régime* harridan into a woman-of-the-people. While she was thus extolled, Jacobin and thermidorian governments alike rejected the intimate rousseauisms of the *ancien régime* and early revolutionary period. Politicians created a unitary theology for the cult, one

---

6. Jean-Claude Bonnet, 'L.-S. Mercier et les *Œuvres complètes* de Jean-Jacques Rousseau', in *La Notion d'œuvres complètes*, ed. Sgard and Volpilhac-Auger, p.111-24.

promoted by officially sanctioned essay contests and controlled commemorations. The object of personal devotion emerging from the autobiographical *Collection complète* was thus converted into a distant *père de la patrie*, to be honoured regularly with minutely defined ritual observances.[7]

What follows is an account of the icon construction in print of the eighteenth century's most controversial literary personality. Image marketing and cultural discipleship, what constitutes an edition, what constitutes a piracy, competing definitions of intellectual property and literary heritage reappear as working themes throughout my story. Intensely possessive about literary property and frustrated by the avalanche of unauthorised piracies which appeared in his own lifetime, Rousseau had renounced all editions of his writings except the very first, that is those which he originally contracted with a publisher. Rousseau's disciples, however, believed that the first editions had poorly served his reputation; and worse yet were the piracies and unauthorised editions that, over the years, had made publishers' fortunes and brought embarrassment to the writer. The disciples believed that posthumous redemption could derive only from the magisterial volumes of an authorised set of Rousseau's books. A detailed commercial history of their edition unveils their cultural strategies.

For Girardin, Du Peyrou and Moultou, discipleship conveyed authority. With varying degrees of presumption this trio of *amis de Rousseau* assumed responsibility over what Michel Foucault has labelled an 'author-function'. Through classification, ordering and distribution they came to exercise control over Rousseau's texts.[8] In the *Collection complète* the *amis* had Rousseau speak the language of autobiography, inviting readers to respond actively to their idol, be manipulated by him and even 'convey how that [manipulation] ought to be done more expertly'.[9] What the *amis* failed to foresee, however, was the rapid politicisation of culture, shaped by revolution, that would devalue a flexible and intimate interpretation of texts, and in its place offer up Rousseau as a remote republican prophet – the severe ghost of the Panthéon.

7. Carol Blum has shown how Robespierre and Saint-Just transmuted Rousseau's myth of virtue into a justification for Jacobin politics in 1793/94. See Blum, *Rousseau and the republic of virtue: the language of politics in the French Revolution* (Ithaca 1986), ch. 7, *passim*.

8. Michel Foucault, 'What is an author?', in *Textual strategies: perspectives in post-structuralist criticism*, ed. Josué V. Harari (Ithaca 1979), p.147-53. See Roger Chartier, 'The chimera of the origin: archaeology, cultural history, and the French Revolution', in *Foucault and the writing of history*, ed. Jan Goldstein (Cambridge, Mass. and Oxford 1994), p.168.

9. Braudy, *The Frenzy of renown*, p.381.

I

Rousseau and intellectual property rights

1. Up to and including *La Nouvelle Héloïse*

Rousseau, Marc-Michel Rey and literary property

ROUSSEAU always expressed understandable irritation over unauthorised editions of his books. He considered them to be encroachments upon his literary property rights and betrayals of what he believed to be a legitimate text, namely one which he personally had reviewed or revised. On the other hand, long before the French book-trade reforms of 1777 and 1778, which facilitated authors' use of publication permits (the *privilèges*), Rousseau had announced his writer-centred interpretation of literary property. He insisted upon his moral right to renegotiate the sale of any individual work as many times as he saw fit. This position customarily placed him at odds with publishers of his first editions.[1]

Prior to the *arrêts* of 1777 and 1778 registered booksellers or bookseller-printers in France controlled the use of royal *privilèges*. Generally, the king awarded the *privilège* to a publisher (*libraire* or *libraire-imprimeur*). If, on rare occasion, an author obtained the *privilège*, regulations or custom inhibited his or her direct marketing and distribution of the books concerned, forcing sale of the permit to a publisher. In effect, therefore, authors usually forfeited property rights to their works. Obtaining *privilège* renewals or continuations, publishers might enjoy a monopoly over a given work and its re-editions for a decade or longer.[2] Because Rousseau's publisher of record, the Amsterdamer

1. It was not until 1777 and 1778 that royal legislation in France redefined literary property rights in favour of the author. Thereafter the publisher would no longer be the dominant party in the use of royal *privilèges*. As a consequence of the reforming *arrêts*, an author who acquired a *privilège* for his or her work was encouraged to keep and use it, holding the permit as long as was needed and serially renegotiating contracts with different publishers over time. An author's heirs gained the same right. On the other hand, a publisher who acquired a *privilège* from the king or purchased it from an author faced a temporal limit of ownership: either ten years or the lifetime of the author concerned. Once the stipulated period of ownership expired, the work entered the public domain. Furthermore the publisher might renew the *privilège* only if the text of the work concerned was augmented by at least one-quarter. See Paris, BNF, f.fr. 22180, no. 80, 81, 82, 87, 91 (*arrêts du Conseil* of 30 August 1777); no. 175 (amendment of 30 July 1778). See Raymond Birn, 'The profits of ideas: *privilèges en librairie* in eighteenth-century France', *Eighteenth-century studies* 4 (1971), p.131-69; and 'Rousseau and literary property', *Leipziger Jahrbuch zur Buchgeschichte* 3 (1993), p.13-37.

2. On the other hand, a few authors and their heirs successfully challenged publisher monopolies during the 1750s and 1760s. In 1752 the playwright Prosper Jolyot de Crébillon regained a surrendered *privilège* for his collected works. A decade later the granddaughters of Jean de La Fontaine obtained the *privilège* for the *Fables* which the writer had surrendered in his lifetime. And in 1769/70 Pierre-J.-F. Luneau de Boisjermain won the right to keep the *privilèges* and oversee the sale of three of his works. In 1763 Diderot's 'Lettre sur le commerce de la librairie' energetically defended authors' literary property rights, winning support for his position among royal administrators of the Librairie. See Birn, 'The profits of ideas', p.150-57; and Raymond

Marc-Michel Rey, was a foreigner he was ineligible for obtaining a *privilège* for each of the writer's books. Instead Rey was obliged to apply to the French Bureau de la Librairie for a *permission tacite*. With the *permission tacite* Rey might acquire exclusive rights to sell, through a local distributor, Rousseau's books in France over a brief period, rarely more than a few months. Unlike the *privilège*, the *permission tacite* served as no long-term guarantee against piracies or eventual rival editions. Furthermore the Bureau de la Librairie might encourage a French publisher to produce a rival edition, or even withdraw Rey's *permission tacite*. Because of the risks he took, Rey insisted that his payment to Rousseau for a manuscript restrained the author from selling the same manuscript to a second publisher, particularly a French one. But long before the book-trade reforms of 1777/78 liberalised property rights of authors, Rousseau disagreed.

For example, in October 1758 an unidentified Parisian bookseller approached Rousseau, offering to publish the *Lettre à M. d'Alembert* 'sur son article "Genève" dans le VIIe volume de l'*Encyclopédie*', which Rey had printed for the first time only a few weeks earlier. Rey had paid Rousseau 720 *livres* for the *Lettre*. Rousseau informed Rey that he was unlikely to concur with the request from Paris, at least not without letting the Amsterdamer know ahead of time. But Rousseau also emphasised: 'quoiqu'en livrant un Manuscrit à un Libraire, je ne prétende pas m'ôter le droit après la prémiére édition de la réimprimer de mon côté toutes les fois qu'il me conviendra'.[3]

Rey's response to Rousseau's proprietary claims was characteristically forthright. He was not surprised by the Paris bookseller's desire to hire the author for a new edition of the *Lettre à d'Alembert* and he appreciated Rousseau's unwillingness to be associated with what Rey considered a piracy. Nevertheless Rey did express shock at Rousseau's assertiveness in negotiating terms with another publisher, particularly because the Amsterdamer's own first edition had not yet sold out: 'Mais mon Cher Rousseau, pour quoi vous aige payé? n'est ce pas pour acquerir le droit que vous y aviez? Vous ne voulez pas vendre 2 fois le meme ouvrage?' Rey asked. Rey acknowledged the existence of creative agreements among European publishers who bartered in literary properties as though they were woollens or acreage. But according to him the liberty to arrange such transactions did not apply to authors. Once an author had given or sold a manuscript to a publisher, he forever alienated rights to whatever it might become. By virtue of the agreement the manuscript was converted from an abstract piece of intellectual property into a concrete commodity of exchange: 'ou en seroit notre comerce s'il n'y avoit pas des raigles?' Rey added self-righteously.[4]

Birn, 'Lettre sur le commerce de la librairie' and 'Luneau de Boisjermain', in *Dictionnaire de Diderot*, ed. Roland Mortier and Raymond Trousson (Paris 1999), p.283-84, 300.

3. Rousseau to Rey, 24 October 1758, *Correspondance complète de Jean-Jacques Rousseau*, ed. R. A. Leigh, 52 vols (Oxford 1965-1998), v.186. Hereafter cited as *CC*.

4. Rey to Rousseau, 31 October 1758, *CC*, v.198-200.

But what rules? No pan-European agreement on literary property existed. Nor was there anything resembling an international copyright code. Authors and booksellers sought their printing privileges from governments; but only the bookseller customarily possessed the capital to make use of privileges through publication and sale. Furthermore, most continental regimes administered a national censorship apparatus which was tied to the process of awarding publication privileges. For example, when the director of the French Bureau de la Librairie awarded a *privilège* to a publisher, not only did the *privilège* affirm the publisher's right to print the book, but it also certified a censor's approval of the book's religious, moral and political orthodoxy.[5]

As a foreign publisher Rey was disqualified from applying for a French royal *privilège*. He had to request a *permission tacite*, which increased chances of piracy or even seizure. In eighteenth-century France, where different jurisdictions such as the Royal Council, parlements and episcopacy competed for the authority not only to approve books but also to burn them, the *permission tacite* offered Rey flimsy copyright protection. The quasi-legal character of a tacitly permitted work, which tempted a hungry author to re-market his manuscript, also encouraged an unscrupulous French bookseller-distributor to delay or even neglect paying his Dutch publisher-supplier.[6] It is no wonder that Rey so vigorously protested Rousseau's claim to ownership of the *Lettre à d'Alembert*.

Rousseau's decision in the first place to look abroad for his publisher of record was not particularly unusual. Mid-eighteenth-century French publishers were better known for their sharp dealings or ingenuity as book pirates than for their honourable treatment of authors. Moreover, unlike France, the Dutch Netherlands lacked a centralised board of preventive censorship control, and the States General there possessed the best record on the continent for tolerating heterodox ideas in print. As Rousseau later would learn to his dismay, inside the Netherlands machinery repressing the printed word certainly could be set in motion, but its parts were scattered among the Dutch provinces and corporate bodies. Then, too, Rousseau believed that a book originally published in the relatively tolerant climate of the Netherlands stood a better chance of obtaining a *permission tacite* than one published in

5. Wallace Kirsop, 'Les mécanismes éditoriales', in *Histoire de l'édition française*, vol. ii *Le Livre triomphant, 1660-1830* (Paris 1990), p.15-34; see also in the same volume, Daniel Roche, 'La censure' and 'La police du livre', p.88-109; Henri-Jean Martin, 'La prééminence de la librairie parisienne', p.331-57; Christiane Berkvens-Stevelinck, 'L'édition française en Hollande', p.403-11.

6. Though unrecognised in formal legislation, *permissions tacites* were tolerated in fact and the Bureau de la Librairie maintained registers of many of them. For example, BNF, f. fr. 21990-94 contains *permissions tacites* for the period 1718-1774: 'Registres des livres d'impression étrangère présentés a monseigneur le chancelier pour la permission de débiter [...]'. The title of the registers is misleading, because French publishers often requested *permissions tacites* under assumed foreign names and false addresses. See Chrétien-Guillaume de Lamoignon de Malesherbes, *Mémoires sur la librairie; mémoire sur la liberté de la presse*, ed. Roger Chartier (Paris 1994), p.209. For the period 1772-1789, see the registers in BNF, f.fr. 21983-88.

Paris. This flexibility might hold true even for a book known to have been printed in France but bearing a false Dutch imprint. Finally Rey, Genevan by birth, had gained the writer's trust. By the time the two first had met in 1754 Rey possessed an international reputation. He had to his credit an edition of Racine's theatre (1750) and Diderot's unacknowledged *Apologie de l'abbé de Prades* (1753). He had been a member of Amsterdam's corporation of bookseller-publishers since 1746 and was married to the daughter of the respected Huguenot bookman, Jean-Frédéric Bernard. His sales catalogue for 1754 contained 2685 titles covering an imposing variety of subjects.[7]

As Rousseau's publisher of record, Rey was taking risks. On the other hand Rey suspected that the writer might make him rich. Should purchasers in France, captivated by Rousseau's growing celebrity, buy Rey's first editions, the Amsterdamer would take his profits before French publishers obtained their own *permissions tacites*. Furthermore, armed with his original *permission tacite*, Rey hoped he would be in a position to secure quick renewals and therefore print and distribute re-editions. Everything depended, of course, upon decisions made in the French government's Book-trade Office. While not particularly indulgent towards publishers like Rey who enjoyed their profits abroad, the office's director, C.-G. de Lamoignon de Malesherbes, was sympathetic towards Enlightenment writers and encouraged limited press freedom where he could.[8] Like Rousseau, Malesherbes understood that a potentially controversial first edition produced by a foreign publisher stood a better chance of avoiding condemnation in France than one made by a Parisian.

Malesherbes, however, was as much an economic nationalist as a cultural liberal, and for Rey such a combination was fraught with danger. Malesherbes possessed the authority to injure Rey in at least three ways: (1) Even before Rey's edition had sold out, the *directeur de la Librairie* might award French publishers non-exclusive *permissions* for cheap versions of the same book. (2) Malesherbes might choose to tolerate concurrent French-produced piracies of Rey's edition. (3) He might hold up the distribution of Rey's edition in order to give French publishers a competitive edge. And in each instance, appealing to Rousseau's moral title to literary property, Malesherbes might encourage the writer to seek compensation from the French publishers

7. *Catalogue des livres françois de Marc-Michel Rey, libraire* (Amsterdam 1754). Albert Schinz, *Jean-Jacques Rousseau et le libraire Marc-Michel Rey. Les relations personnelles* (Geneva 1916); K. R. Gallas, 'Autour de Marc-Michel Rey et de Rousseau', *Annales de la Société Jean-Jacques Rousseau* 17 (1926), p.73-90; Max Fajn, 'Marc-Michel Rey: boekhandelaar op de bloe[m]mark (Amsterdam)', *Proceedings of the American philosophical society* 117 (1974), p.260-68; Jeroom Vercruysse, 'Marc-Michel Rey, imprimeur philosophe ou philosophique?', *Literaturgeschichte als geschichtlicher Auftrag: in memoriam Werner Krauss* (Berlin 1978), p.149-56; Raymond Birn, 'Marc-Michel Rey's enlightenment', in *Le Magasin de l'univers: the Dutch republic as the centre of the European book trade*, ed. C. Berkvens-Stevelinck *et al.* (Leiden 1992), p.23-32.

8. Raymond Birn, 'Malesherbes and the call for a free press', in *Revolution in print: the press in France, 1775-1800*, ed. Robert Darnton and Daniel Roche (Berkeley and Los Angeles 1989), p.50-66.

involved, as he indeed would do in 1760. Rey needed to forestall any potential co-operation between Rousseau and Malesherbes by informing the writer of his own property claim to books he was publishing, however much it clashed with Rousseau's alleged moral right.

Publishing the two *Discours* and the *Lettre à d'Alembert*

By 1758 Rousseau's writings had brought him notoriety but little income. Apparently the Paris publisher G.-F. Quillau had paid him nothing for the *Dissertation sur la musique moderne* (1743), graced though it was with a royal *privilège*.[9] As an unpublished essay, Rousseau's prizewinning contribution to the Dijon Academy's contest of 1750 had been highly controversial and likely to be condemned. Noël-Jacques Pissot of Paris, who undertook publication of the essay, withheld the name of its author. As further protection, on the title page of the *Discours* Pissot falsely identified a pair of deceased Geneva book-sellers, Jean-Louis Barrillot and his son Jacques-François, as the publishers. Asserting the corruption of morals caused by the arts and sciences, the *Discours* appeared with a *permission tacite* and the false address in January 1751.[10] Pissot offered Rousseau no compensation for the first edition or for two subsequent reprintings. The *Discours* sold well, provoking retorts by Rousseau's critics and rejoinders from himself, and affirming the writer as a controversialist who had touched a sensitive nerve among readers. Following Pissot's editions the Genevans Claude and Antoine Philibert published theirs, at last identifying Rousseau as author of the *Discours*,[11] and Marc-Michel Rey printed the essay in the May 1751 number of his Amsterdam edition of the *Journal des savants*.[12] In none of these instances did Rousseau receive any compensation. As a matter of fact, until Pissot gave him 300 *livres* in cash and 200 *livres* worth of books for publication rights to his opera, *Le Devin du village* (January 1753), Rousseau remained an unpaid writer.[13]

Yet Rousseau also had become a public figure, contributing to Diderot's *Encyclopédie*, writing for France's leading literary magazine, the *Mercure*, composing tracts that responded to critics of the first *Discours*, and engendering controversy over musical taste. Reaction to his *Lettre sur la musique française* (1753) was so fierce that it nearly drove him from the country; the controversy only energised him, however, contributing to his self-realisation as an *écrivain de vocation*, not an *écrivain de métier*. In 1754 Rousseau composed a new essay for

9. In-8°, xvi + 101 pages. Its sales appear to have been poor.
10. *Note explicative* c, *CC*, ii.140. For the bibliographical analysis see Jean-Jacques Rousseau, *Œuvres complètes*, ed. Bernard Gagnebin and Marcel Raymond, 5 vols (Paris, Bibliothèque de la Pléiade 1964-1995), iii.1854-55. Hereafter cited as *OC*.
11. *OC*, iii.1857.
12. *Note explicative* c, *CC*, ii.140.
13. Contract between Rousseau and Pissot [2 January 1753], *CC*, ii.322. The royal perform-ance of *Le Devin*, 18 October 1752, brought Rousseau 3600 *livres* from Louis XV and Mme de Pompadour, however, and the directors of the Paris Opéra awarded him 1200 *livres* for perform-ance rights.

the Dijon Academy's latest competition. On this occasion he was not named winner, but the piece eventually became the *Discours sur l'origine et les fondements de l'inégalité parmi les hommes*.[14] Rousseau offered his essay to Pissot for publication, now insisting upon an honorarium of 600 *livres*.[15] The Parisian paid it, but unable to adhere to the printing schedule Rousseau had insisted upon and possibly sceptical about whether he would obtain even a *permission tacite*, Pissot withdrew and returned the manuscript to its author.

When he travelled to Geneva during the summer of 1754 Rousseau possibly encountered Rey who also was visiting the republic. Following Pissot's return of the manuscript of the *Discours sur l'inégalité*, the writer contacted Rey and offered him the essay. Rey reimbursed Pissot for the 600 *livres* awarded Rousseau and the Parisian agreed to serve as Rey's French distributor. Between November 1754 and March 1755, with Malesherbes's office serving as a mail depot, Rey and Rousseau exchanged sheets, and the surviving correspondence between them splendidly exemplifies the give-and-take between author and publisher in the late years of the hand-press era. Rousseau was not the sort of writer to leave publishing details to professionals. Rey had to endure an unending stream of recriminations over alleged typographical errors, unsatisfactory fonts, incorrect line spacing, sloppy punctuation and maddening delays.[16]

Rousseau was convinced that Rey's packages to him containing the sheets for the *Discours sur l'inégalité* were being opened in the mails.[17] He worried whether Rey would be able to obtain a *permission tacite* from Malesherbes. At the same time Rousseau urged Rey to forswear smuggling his edition into France, for he had no wish to become an underground author. Time and again Rousseau gave Rey unsolicited advice on how the book should be distributed. Fearing potential piracies, he urged the publisher to instruct Malesherbes not to let out of sight the sheets coming through the director's office; and he scolded Rey for requesting a written *permission tacite* rather than an oral accord.[18] Addressing the question of ownership of the *Discours*, Rousseau was scrupulous in distinguishing between Rey's 'édition' and 'mon ouvrage'.[19]

14. For a detailed discussion of the publication of the *Discours* see Raymond Birn, 'A certain place for memory: Rousseau, *Les Confessions* and the first edition of the *Discours sur l'origine de l'inégalité*', in *Le Livre et l'historien. Etudes offertes en l'honneur du professeur Henri-Jean Martin*, ed. Frédéric Barbier *et al.* (Geneva 1997), p.557-70.

15. Rousseau to François Mussard, 9 June 1754, *CC*, ii.267-69.

16. Rousseau to Rey, 17 November 1754, *CC*, iii.50-51; Rousseau to Rey, 12 December 1754, *CC*, iii.69; Rousseau to Rey, 3 January 1755, *CC*, iii.85-87; Rousseau to Rey, [20 February 1755], *CC*, iii.100-102; Rousseau to Rey, 23 March 1755, *CC*, iii.113-14.

17. Rousseau to Rey, [20 February 1755], *CC*, iii.100.

18. Rousseau to Rey, [20 February 1755], *CC*, iii.100; Rousseau to Rey, 29 May 1755, *CC*, iii.128-30. It is probable that Malesherbes used his office as an intermediate station for Rey's sheets to Rousseau so as to eliminate postage costs for both publisher and author – they took advantage of the director's franking privileges. Sheets for the *Lettre à d'Alembert*, *La Nouvelle Héloïse*, *Emile* and *Du contrat social* also passed through Malesherbes's office.

19. Rousseau to Rey, 23 March 1755, *CC*, iii.113.

Rousseau's proprietary interest in the *Discours sur l'inégalité* proved all-encompassing. He initially worried more about unauthorised piracies than about being refused a *permission tacite*.[20] When Malesherbes permitted Rey to distribute one hundred advance copies of the *Discours* in Paris, but hesitated over allowing the release of the main shipment of 1500 books, the Amsterdam publisher panicked.[21] With such a small consignment available, the *Discours* was bound to be pirated and his investment lost. Late in May 1755, the *permission tacite* still not in hand, Rousseau exploded in frustration and anger.[22] He expressed dissatisfaction with all of Rey's procedures and threatened to open negotiations with publishers in London. At last, in mid-June, Malesherbes sent Pissot a verbal *permission tacite* to distribute Rey's edition.[23]

The authorisation did come extremely late, and piracies quickly cut into sales of Rey's edition. Rey had selected an in-octavo format, but the book pirates opted for cheaper, smaller size versions.[24] Rey accused Pissot himself of piracy, and in 1756 the Parisian acknowledged publishing the *Discours* in a pocket-sized in-24°, which he incorporated into volume ii of an edition of Rousseau's *Œuvres diverses*: the sort of unauthorised collection that horrified the writer.[25] Much to Rousseau's dismay, Rey printed two subsequent inexpensive in-12° editions of the *Discours*. They partially compensated him for losses incurred by the in-8°.[26]

During the next two years Rousseau and Rey neglected their relationship, and in December 1757 the writer informed Sophie d'Houdetot that he had no wish to sell to the Amsterdamer the large new novel he was preparing.[27] Early in 1758, however, he did propose a much shorter piece to Rey, the *Lettre à d'Alembert*, written in response to the encyclopedist's scandalous article 'Genève' and vigorously opposing establishment of a theatre in Rousseau's (and Rey's) native city. More than a mere work of circumstance, the *Lettre* was yet a new weapon in Rousseau's arsenal confronting the Enlightenment's cultural conventions. Insisting upon absolute secrecy, Rousseau promised Rey a best-seller for his pains.[28] He requested 30 *louis*, or 720 *livres*, for the first edition of the book, held out the promise of a short piece on the legality of warfare and added that, in the event of his death, he wished to have his unpub-

20. Rousseau to Malesherbes, [5 May 1755], *CC*, iii.125.
21. Rey to Malesherbes, [22 May 1755], *CC*, iii.126-27.
22. Rousseau to Rey, 23 March 1755, *CC*, iii.128-30.
23. Rousseau to Rey, 19 June 1755, *CC*, iii.134-35.
24. *OC*, iii.1862-63.
25. *OC*, p.1863. Théophile Dufour, *Recherches bibliographiques sur les œuvres imprimées de J.-J. Rousseau, suivies de l'inventaire des papiers de Rousseau conservés à la bibliothèque de Neuchâtel*, introduction by Pierre-Paul Plan, 2 vols (Paris 1925; New York 1971), i.55-56, ii.1. Pissot also published the *Œuvres diverses* in-8° and in-12°. The Parisian's volume i contained the *Discours* of 1750, Rousseau's responses to critics of the *Discours* and his play *Narcisse*. Volume ii contained the *Lettre sur la musique française*, *Le Devin du village* and the *Discours sur l'origine de l'inégalité* (*Œuvres diverses de M. J.-J. Rousseau de Genève*, 2 vols, in-16° and in-12°, Paris, Pissot 1756).
26. Dufour, *Recherches*, i.58-59.
27. Rousseau to comtesse Sophie d'Houdetot, 5 December 1757, *CC*, iv.384.
28. Rousseau to Rey, 9 March 1758, *CC*, v.51.

lished writings passed on to Rey for incorporation into a 'general edition'. Indeed Rousseau already was thinking about posterity. His greatest fear was a mountain of posthumous editions of his *œuvres complètes* posing as authoritative. Therefore he needed to legitimise a single one and acknowledge it publicly.[29]

Aside from Rousseau's customary complaints over Rey's manuscript corrections and the quality of his proofs, printing the *Lettre à d'Alembert* went smoothly. In May 1758 Rousseau sent Rey the manuscript from his retreat on the maréchal de Luxembourg's estate at Montmorency.[30] Rey insisted upon receiving his *permission tacite* directly from Malesherbes and urged Rousseau to assist him in acquiring a year's exclusive sales rights in Geneva. He anticipated a print run of 3000 copies and promised to have the book ready by the end of July.[31] Earlier that month Rey had sent two-thirds of the sheets of the *Lettre* to Malesherbes and arranged, once the time came, to have the Paris bookseller Laurent Durand distribute the work.[32] As he received the last of the sheets, Malesherbes forwarded the text to d'Alembert himself for approval. By appointing as censor the very person against whom the *Lettre* was specifically directed, Malesherbes possibly wished to short-circuit potential trouble; and the tactic worked.[33] Despite Rousseau's advocacy of views he abhorred, d'Alembert graciously urged Malesherbes to allow the *Lettre*'s admission into France.[34] Yet three more weeks passed without Rey's receiving any official word from the director of the Book-trade Office. Fretting over a possible last-minute hitch, the publisher also was concerned that d'Alembert's proofs were being recopied. Still lacking a *permission*, he nevertheless took the chance of shipping 1600 *Lettres* to France.[35]

At length, on 4 September 1758 Rey could inform Rousseau that a *permission tacite* was in hand and an additional 500 copies of the *Lettre* had been sent to Geneva. So optimistic was Rey of the *Lettre*'s potential success that he informed Rousseau of his intention to prepare a new printing of the work, fattening the volume with the *Discours sur l'inégalité*, the *Discours* on science and the arts and the *Lettre sur la musique française*. Believing these pieces to comprise the core of the 'general edition' Rousseau had been mentioning, Rey asked the writer for fresh manuscripts of them. He even stated his intention of purchasing Dutch publication rights to Rousseau's opera, *Le Devin du village*, from the Hague bookseller Pierre Gosse.[36]

At this point, however, several contentious issues threatened the budding collaboration. Rousseau grew upset over the fact that copies of the *Lettre à*

29. Rousseau to Rey, 9 March 1758, *CC*, v.51.
30. Rousseau to Rey, 14 May 1758, *CC*, v.78.
31. Rey to Rousseau, 24 May 1758, *CC*, v.80.
32. Rey to Malesherbes, [3 July 1758], *CC*, v.105.
33. D'Alembert to Malesherbes, [8 July 1758], *CC*, v.112-13. D'Alembert stated that, if appointed censor, he would grant his approval in advance.
34. D'Alembert to Malesherbes, [22 July 1758], *CC*, v.120.
35. Rey to Rousseau, 21 August 1758, *CC*, v.131-32.
36. Rey to Rousseau, 4 September 1758, *CC*, v.140-41.

d'Alembert had circulated in Paris prior to the arrival of Rey's large shipment. He wrote to Rey, 'Cependant il me revient de toutes parts que beaucoup de gens ont lû mon ouvrage et qu'il est comme public à Paris. De sorte que quand vos exemplaires arriveront, il sera déja usé et personne ne s'en souciera plus.'[37] Rousseau blamed Rey for getting the proofs of the *Lettre* into d'Alembert's hands too soon (even though their allocation and the delay over the *permission tacite* were Malesherbes's fault), and he criticised Rey for selecting Durand (Diderot's publisher and therefore considered an enemy) as distributor for the book. Worried about his reputation, however, and desirous of producing the authorised edition of collected works before it was too late, Rousseau agreed to offer Rey fresh texts of his two *Discours* and the *Lettre sur la musique française*. The writer was puzzled by Rey's neglect of two other favourites of his, the response to king Stanislas's critique of the first *Discours* and the preface to his unperformed play *Narcisse*. Concerned lest Rey still might pursue the edition of collected works without his participation, Rousseau proposed that they wait and add future writings to it: 'Vous savez que mon dessein est de faire une Edition générale, d'y joindre plusieurs piéces nouvelles que j'ai en manuscrit et plusieurs additions que j'ai faites à ce qui est déja imprimé.' The writer estimated that everything would fit into four volumes induodecimo, and he proposed to spend the winter of 1758/59 putting texts in order.[38]

Rousseau noted that, should Rey prefer to pursue the publisher's less comprehensive project, the small incomplete edition, he would not stand in the Amsterdamer's way. Ever worried about the accuracy of the edition, Rousseau even agreed to proofread it. Nevertheless, should Rey not wish to undertake the larger investment, the writer insisted upon pursuing the complete general edition as he saw fit, even if it meant negotiating with another publisher for the same material Rey would be printing.[39] Rousseau knew that such a prospect would undoubtedly displease Rey, who questioned the writer's proprietary claims to the corpus. But, it turned out, Rousseau was bluffing. Recognising that Rey's efforts to produce the *Lettre à d'Alembert* had been generally commendable, Rousseau had no wish to track down a new publisher. So the writer tossed an additional piece of bait in Rey's path. He laconically informed the publisher that a new work, one ostensibly familiar to Rey, was finished: 'il est en six parties, et si vous aimiez mieux commencer par celui-là, cela dépendra de vous'.[40] The book was *La Nouvelle Héloïse*. At the time, mid-1758, neither he nor Rey had an inkling that each was a step away from producing the publishing sensation of the century.[41]

At this delicate stage, however, nearly everything unravelled. Rousseau received his offer from Paris to renegotiate the sale of the *Lettre à d'Alembert*,

37. Rousseau to Rey, 13 September 1758, *CC*, v.144.
38. Rousseau to Rey, 13 September 1758, *CC*, v.147.
39. Rousseau to Rey, 13 September 1758, *CC*, v.147.
40. Rousseau to Rey, 13 September 1758, *CC*, v.147.
41. To maintain its epistolary character, the novel was called *Lettres de deux amants, habitants d'une petite ville au pied des Alpes*, and Rousseau assumed the fictive role of collector of the letters.

and Rey challenged his right to do so. At the same time Rousseau spelled out his terms for Rey's modest edition of collected works: 60 *louis* (1440 *livres*) to recopy and, if need be, revise earlier manuscripts; plus 90 additional *louis* (2160 *livres*) for *La Nouvelle Héloïse*. In the margin of Rousseau's letter offering his services and *La Nouvelle Héloïse*, Rey jotted down some figures of his own: 1320 *livres* (payment already made for the first editions of the *Discours sur l'iné-galité* and *Lettre à d'Alembert*); plus the 1440 and 2160 *livres* requested by Rousseau. Total potential disbursement: 4920 *livres*.[42] Mulling over the sum, Rey decided it was too much. He balked at granting Rousseau 60 *louis* for the older works, even if they were to be revised. He wrote: 'Je Comptois que vous m'auriez fourny vos ouvrages, revu & Corrigé, gratis. S'il y a des pieces nouvelles rien de plus juste que de les payer, mais une fois payée tout est dit. Vous voyé que nous somes éloigné de Compte.'[43]

Once again correspondence between Rousseau and Rey lapsed, for the two shared no common ground over the essential nature of intellectual property. Custom and law in both France and the Netherlands demanded that an author relinquish claim to his manuscript once a publisher acquired a *privilège* and compensated him; but the quasi-legal circumstances surrounding French *permissions tacites* and the failure of international agreements even to consider the existence of these non-exclusive permits left little basis for negotiating. Rey expected Rousseau to yield up claims to his manuscripts as though they were fully privileged works. After all, he would argue, businessmen who obtained *permissions tacites* were taking a far greater risk with their investment than publishers who were protected by *privilèges*. For his part, Rousseau had no desire to base sale of his works upon traditional commercial practice. He understood that none of his books could ever hope to pass normal censorship controls of most European states and thereby receive a *privilège* or its equivalent. Therefore he refused to understand how restrictions imposed upon authors who alienated their *privilèges* to publishers could possibly apply to him. Implicit in his claims to free-market authorship was the fact that, dependent as his books were upon extra-legal censorship formalities, they ought therefore to be subject to novel proprietary ones.[44]

Undertaking *La Nouvelle Héloïse* with Rey[45]

In February 1759 Rey broke his silence. He informed Rousseau that he had just reprinted the *Lettre à d'Alembert* and was putting an in-duodecimo re-edition of the *Discours sur l'inégalité* in the press. As a token of peace he offered

42. *Notes explicatives* f, g and h, *CC*, v.188.

43. Rey to Rousseau, 31 October 1758, *CC*, v.200.

44. This view would appear to be close to Foucault's position, linking proprietorship to transgression – or at least to the probability of transgression.

45. The standard narrative publishing history of the first three editions of *La Nouvelle Héloïse* is by Jo-Ann E. McEachern. See her *Bibliography of the writings of Jean-Jacques Rousseau to 1800*, vol. i *Julie, ou La nouvelle Héloïse* (Oxford 1993), p.13-145.

30 *louis* for the first two parts of *La Nouvelle Héloïse* and tried to revive discussion of the now dormant edition of collected works.[46] Rousseau shrugged off Rey's overtures and made a counter-offer. He proposed purchasing Rey's alleged rights to the *Lettre à d'Alembert* and *Discours sur l'inégalité*.[47] Rousseau was hoping to negotiate a new edition of the *Lettre* with his Geneva friend Jacques-François Deluc, to whom he had just sent a highly distorted view of Rey's position on literary property.[48]

When nothing came of Rousseau's project with Deluc, the writer indicated to Rey a desire to get on with *La Nouvelle Héloïse* and Rey considered it worthwhile to lay aside their recent disagreement. Opting for reconciliation, the publisher wrote: 'Voici la reponse a ce que vous me demandez, c'est de faire com̃e vous le jugerez a propos, je n'exige de vous que votre amitié, je voudrois qu'elle ne soufrit aucune atteinte; je ne me plaindrai point de tout ce que vous ferez [...]. J'ay gagné avec L'Impression de vos ouvrages, je suis content.'[49] Also seeking accommodation, Rousseau skirted the literary property issue and addressed Rey's reluctance to pay for revisions to the edition of collected works: 'Vous avez raison de ne vouloir pas payer deux fois les mêmes ouvrages; mais moi je n'ai pas tort de ne vouloir pas vous faire présent de deux ans de mon tems; car je n'ai de ressource pour vivre que mon travail, et tandis que je revois mes écrits, il faut que je dine.'[50] Still desiring 60 *louis* for reviewing any projected edition of collected works, Rousseau proposed adding new pieces to it. The most pressing issue at hand, however, was *La Nouvelle Héloïse*; further discussion of the general edition was suspended.

During the remainder of 1759 Rousseau's correspondence with Rey centred upon *La Nouvelle Héloïse*. The details largely concerned issues of payment, Rey's printing calendar and the publisher's dismay over the unequal sizes of the novel's sections. Yet literary property issues remained close to the surface. Rousseau still wished to start working on the general edition and remained eager to settle the question of ownership of his previously published work. In November Deluc, who hoped to oversee the general edition himself, responded to Rousseau's request to research the legal issues involved. As a consequence of his findings Deluc wrote: 'dès qu'un libraire a débité la première édition d'un livre; l'auteur a le droit des éditions suivantes, à moins qu'il n'y ait nommément renoncé'.[51] On the basis of eighteenth-century continental publishing practice, Deluc's conclusions were highly dubious; but they were exactly what Rousseau wished to hear. The writer responded that though he would honour Rey's claim to the *Lettre à d'Alembert*, he also would request Deluc's assistance with the edition of collected works at the appropriate time. Rousseau informed Deluc of his certain moral right to negotiate the *édition*

46. Rey to Rousseau, [19 February 1759], *CC*, vi.36-37.
47. Rousseau to Rey, 22 February 1759, *CC*, vi.40-41.
48. Rousseau to Jacques-François Deluc, 9 February 1759, *CC*, vi.23-24.
49. Rey to Rousseau, 27 February 1759, *CC*, vi.41.
50. Rousseau to Rey, 14 March 1759, *CC*, vi.44.
51. Deluc to Rousseau, 7 November 1759, *CC*, vi.187.

générale as he saw fit; but because Rey also was interpreting the ownership question as a matter of conscience, the author assumed that it had to be dealt with delicately. For the moment he would not press the issue.[52]

La Nouvelle Héloïse proved to be Rey's most ambitious undertaking with Rousseau. It was a major investment, and Malesherbes's office again served as a mail bureau for uncorrected proofs and corrected sheets.[53] Initially Rey foresaw a press-run of 6000 copies in six volumes in-duodecimo and complained about having inadequate amounts of type font.[54] From his cottage at Montmorency Rousseau scrutinised minutely every detail of the novel's production: corrections of proof, ornaments, headpieces, page makeup, choice of paper, whether or not to use the author's motto on the frontispiece. Rousseau informed Rey when he was pleased with the progress of the work, but more frequently he despaired of it: 'Vous m'envoyez des epreuves pleines de fautes horribles, sur du papier qui boit si fort qu'on n'y sauroit écrire.'[55] Fearing that the slow pace of production would delay publication until spring 1761, Rey urged Rousseau to correct more rapidly.[56] Meanwhile, getting wind of the novel, rival publishers tempted Rousseau with offers for the manuscript. On 18 May 1760 the writer mischievously informed Rey:

Dimanche un M. de la Bastide que je ne connois point mais qui publie a Paris des feuilles périodiques [*Le Nouveau spectateur* (1758-1760), 8 vols, *Le Monde comme il va* (1760), 2 vols] vint me voir et m'offrir deux cents loüis du manuscrit de la nouvelle Héloïse si je voulois m'en defaire. Je lui dis que ce manuscrit n'étoit plus à moi, qu'il vous appartenoit, mais que j'avois lieu de croire que vous n'y étiez pas fort attaché. Là-dessus il me demanda vôtre adresse et mon consentement si vous etiez d'humeur de faire affaire avec lui; je lui dis que quant à moi je ne m'y opposerois point. Il repartit là-dessus paroissant disposé à vous écrire.[57]

Bastide did write to Rey, asking the Amsterdamer to name his price for *La Nouvelle Héloïse*,[58] but Rey would not part with the novel. During the publishing process an affinity evolved between the hypersensitive author and his plodding bookseller, and in Rey's half-calculating, half-heartfelt correspondence with Rousseau flashes of perceptiveness shined through:

la seule chose dont vous devez etre persuadé, c'est que je veux faire tout au monde pour meriter votre Estime, que S'il m'arrive de faire quelque chose contraire, ne l'attribuez point au Cœur mais au manque de réflexions; j'ay le malheur pour le Siecle où nous vivons d'etre trop franc, de dire ce que je pense d'une façon trop crue, pour le premier je ne veux pas m'en départir et pour le Second c'est manque de Sçavoir mieux, vous n'en avez que trop de preuves par mes lettres [...] je voudrois come Mᵣ de Volmar & Julie pouvoir vivre retiré & que la providence me mit a même de faire du bien aux malheureux, toute mon ambition seroit remplie, en attendant je tâche de rendre mes

52. Rousseau to Deluc, 2 December 1759, *CC*, vi.216.
53. Malesherbes to Rousseau, 19 April 1760, *CC*, vii.74.
54. Rey to Rousseau, 3 May 1760, *CC*, vii.79.
55. Rousseau to Rey, 11 May 1760, *CC*, vii.86.
56. Rey to Rousseau, [10 May 1760], *CC*, vii.85-86.
57. Rousseau to Rey, 18 May 1760, *CC*, vii.95.
58. J.-F. de La Bastide to Rey, [19 May 1760], *CC*, vii.97-98.

enfans plus honnet home que leur pere, & j'ay lieu d'esperer que Dieu benira mes Soins.[59]

For the time being, however, Rey worried about his investment in *La Nouvelle Héloïse*. He had borrowed 13 000 *livres* to produce the book and needed to ship it to France before the Dutch canals froze solid during the winter of 1761. If that proved impossible and distribution was delayed until spring, Rey foresaw overdue payments to his creditors, increased interest charges and deep cuts in his profits.[60] The use of Malesherbes's office for exchanging proofs and sheets saved postage costs, but it also resulted in delays and misplaced mail.[61] The fact that Rousseau insisted upon receiving both first proofs and corrected sheets slowed matters yet further.[62] Nevertheless Rey considered it his duty to cheer up Rousseau whenever the writer despaired over what he believed to be the inferior literary quality of *La Nouvelle Héloïse*, and the publisher offered to send his author additional money should Rousseau need it.[63] If all went well Rey envisioned a net profit of 10 000 *livres*. He reduced his original press-run to 4000 copies: 2000 for France, to be purchased by an agent in Paris, the Palais-Royal bookseller Etienne-Vincent Robin, who probably represented a wealthier one, Jean-Augustin Grangé; 300 for the Netherlands; and approximately 550 apiece for London, Geneva and Germany. Rey planned to charge his distributors 8 *livres* per volume. Everything depended upon Malesherbes, who was to decide whether the novel ought to be admitted to France in the first place. As late as October 1760, however, Rey had not received a word from the director.[64]

There was an understandable reason for Malesherbes's silence. Rousseau had been eager to manoeuvre the director into undertaking the role of unofficial censor, reading the page proofs addressed to his office by Rey before forwarding them to the writer. Rousseau hoped that Malesherbes's admiration of the text might imply approval of it; or else, should he discover incriminating material, the director might discreetly request revisions.[65] But Malesherbes felt uncomfortable playing censor;[66] indeed Jo-Ann McEachern wonders whether he actually even read the proofs and sheets.[67] In all likelihood he did for, as events proved, Malesherbes betrayed discomfort with what he found in the novel.

For their part both Rousseau and Rey worried that someone in Malesherbes's office might copy the proofs received by the director and sell them clandestinely to a publisher in Paris. A piracy or tacitly permitted edition then would emerge, perhaps even before the arrival of Rey's books, and the

59. Rey to Rousseau, 12 September 1760, *CC*, vii.234-35.
60. Rey to Rousseau, [22 May 1760], *CC*, vii.105.
61. Rey to Rousseau, [1 June 1760], *CC*, vii.120.
62. Rousseau to Rey, 10 April 1760, *CC*, vii.69-70.
63. Rey to Rousseau, [6 October 1760], *CC*, vii.249.
64. Rey to Rousseau, 23 October 1760, *CC*, vii.264.
65. Rousseau to Malesherbes, [6 March 1760], *CC*, vii.54-55.
66. Malesherbes to Rousseau, 10 March 1760, *CC*, vii.56-57.
67. McEachern, *Bibliography*, i.36-38.

authorised version would be gravely compromised. To avoid such a contingency Rousseau sought assurance from Malesherbes that no French-produced edition of the novel would be countenanced until Rey's had run its course.[68] The director, however, had no wish to protect Rey's investment against all comers. As a matter of fact Malesherbes's interpretation of literary property rights did not assure Rey of anything in France. The director stated unequivocally that the laws of no country prohibited reproduction of a book originally published beyond its frontiers. Because they were Europe's leading book pirates, he wrote, the Dutch should be the last to complain. In other words, in Malesherbes's view *La Nouvelle Héloïse* remained the property of Rousseau in France, and the director urged the author to cut a deal with a Paris publisher:

Le gouvernement de France veut que vous ayés le même avantage Sur les Editions qui se feront en France que Sur celles de Hollande. C'est un Benefice qui vous appartient, qui est le prix de votre travail et qui ne fait aucun tort a Rey puisque cette Reimpression, qu'il appelle contrefaction, Se feroit de même Sans votre consentement.[69]

The position taken by Malesherbes might have pleased Rousseau a few years earlier; in current circumstances, however, it presented the writer with a dilemma. Before Rey's edition even had arrived in the capital, the Paris bookseller-printer H.-L. Guérin offered to find a French publisher for another edition of *La Nouvelle Héloïse*.[70] Rousseau proved to be a reluctant client, for he had no wish to see Rey lose money. In fact he already was discussing plans with the Amsterdamer for a new book on political theory.[71] Rousseau therefore tried to hold off Guérin, first stating that a new preface he was preparing for the novel was not yet ready and later adding, more forthrightly, that he did not wish to cause harm to Rey's investment.[72] Rousseau sent Malesherbes a long, convoluted letter in which he tried to indicate how the tolerant publishing practices existing in Holland benefited the circulation of ideas in France, how Dutch reimpressions did little harm to the French book trade, but how French reimpressions would grievously injure Dutch publishers. Then Rousseau sought to prove that Rey's Paris distributor, not the Amsterdamer himself, would be the one to suffer from a new French edition of *La Nouvelle Héloïse* – Rey would get paid anyway – and therefore Malesherbes's policy really was injurious to the kingdom's trade balance. Rousseau insisted that, should he be responsible for Rey's financial loss, he would owe his publisher damages. The writer concluded by refusing to consent to a French reimpression of his novel or to accept compensation for one.[73]

68. Rousseau to Malesherbes, 22 October 1760, *CC*, vii.261.
69. Malesherbes to Rousseau, 29 October 1760, *CC*, vii.270.
70. Guérin was interested himself in publishing an album of engravings based upon *La Nouvelle Héloïse*'s text. For the detailed history of the *Recueil d'estampes* see McEachern, *Bibliography*, i.133-41.
71. [Missing letter, Rousseau to Rey, 21 September 1760], *CC*, vii.238-39.
72. Rousseau to H.-L. Guérin, [30 October 1760], *CC*, vii.271-72; Rousseau to Guérin, [*c*. 3 November 1760], *CC*, vii.283.
73. Rousseau to Malesherbes, 5 November 1760, *CC*, vii.297-302.

Rousseau's protest hardly resolved the matter. Malesherbes responded that Rey was fully aware of the likelihood of a French edition of *La Nouvelle Héloïse*.[74] Guérin informed Rousseau that Rey would have two months to sell his book without competition. Then a Paris publisher (Nicolas-Bonaventure Duchesne) intended to produce the French edition of the novel, preferably one enlarged with a new preface by Rousseau and garnished with illustrations, and Duchesne would be happy to pay the writer for publication rights. But even this was not all. Duchesne was prepared as well to undertake an updated version of Rousseau's collected works, with Malesherbes's blessing and, he hoped, with the author's collaboration. Pissot would be involved too.[75]

Before this onslaught of a consortium of influential Paris publishers, all conniving with the director of the royal Book-trade Office, Rousseau's scruples melted. Once he convinced himself that Rey was aware of Duchesne's projected edition of his novel and had not protested, Rousseau agreed to a Paris printing. He would make some unspecified corrections to the text; he would add his new preface (the *préface dialoguée*) to the work; and he would commission a young friend, François Coindet, to arrange for the illustrations. The writer worried about the need for textual changes in a French-produced edition. He reminded Malesherbes that the young correspondents of *La Nouvelle Héloïse* were not French Catholics, but rather 'des protestans et des républicains', and therefore bound to hold unorthodox opinions.[76] The director tried to alleviate Rousseau's concerns and guaranteed that Rey's edition of the novel would be tolerated in Paris.[77]

The true and false 'Rey' editions of *La Nouvelle Héloïse*

Convinced that Duchesne's anticipated general edition of Rousseau's works would be undertaken with or without his participation, the author reckoned that his only choice was to co-operate with the Paris publisher. Duchesne's general edition was to include everything Rousseau already had published, and it also was to add items still in manuscript. Because Rousseau doubted whether French authorities would tolerate, even tacitly, the educational treatise he presently was writing, the author considered Duchesne's general edition to lie far in the future.[78]

74. Malesherbes to Rousseau, 13 November 1760, *CC*, vii.312-13.
75. H.-L. Guérin to Rousseau, [19 November 1760], *CC*, vii.320-21.
76. Rousseau to Malesherbes, [17 November 1760], *CC*, vii.316.
77. Malesherbes to Rousseau, 13 November 1760, *CC*, vii.312-13.
78. Rousseau to Guérin, 21 December 1760, *CC*, vii.363-65. The maréchale-duchesse de Luxembourg assumed responsibility for selling the manuscript of *Emile*. Although she obtained an unprecedented 6000 *livres* from Duchesne, Rousseau would have preferred that the duchess negotiate with Rey. Like Malesherbes, however, she believed that Rey had exploited the writer, and Rey never was given the opportunity to bid for the manuscript (see Rousseau to Madeleine-Angélique de Neufville-Villeroy, maréchale-duchesse de Luxembourg, 12 December 1760, *CC*, vii.348). Meanwhile, failing to obtain *Emile* for J.-F. de La Bastide's new periodical, *Le Monde comme il est*, Charles Pinot Duclos persuaded Rousseau to send his extract of the abbé de

I. *Rousseau and intellectual property rights*

As yet unaware of how seriously his edition of *La Nouvelle Héloïse* was threatened, Rey expressed concern about the very whereabouts of the volumes he had sent to the kingdom. In mid-December he travelled to Paris to receive his shipment personally. The crates had not yet arrived, but half a dozen advance copies of *La Nouvelle Héloïse* intended as gifts for Malesherbes seemed to be making the rounds of the French capital.[79] Rey worried: how much longer would it take before a pirate reproduced one of them? At last Malesherbes assured Rey orally that the Amsterdamer's books would be permitted to enter the kingdom, but rough seas were delaying their safe passage. Unable to secure an exclusive sales monopoly of six months for his edition, and learning that Malesherbes indeed was going to award second edition rights to a Paris publisher, Rey understandably became nervous. He asked Malesherbes not to award preference for the Paris edition of *La Nouvelle Héloïse* to his rival Duchesne, but rather to the Dutchman's distributor Etienne-Vincent Robin.[80]

Rey's nomination of Robin to take charge of a French edition was a clever tactic. As its distributor, the Palais-Royal bookseller, or at least his backers, already had a significant financial interest in Rey's own edition. Rey therefore believed that Robin would wait until the Amsterdam books had sold out before marketing a Paris imprint. Rey's nomination of Robin also put Malesherbes in a tight spot. The director suspected that Rousseau would agree to the choice of Robin. Moreover, for Malesherbes to snub Rey was tantamount to attacking the Amsterdamer's investment and was likely to commit the Dutchman to a career in piracies. Since Robin was not even a member of the elite Paris guild, the Community of Booksellers and Printers, and lacked essential capital, he was incapable of undertaking the French edition alone. J.-A. Grangé, an upstanding member of the guild and not on the best of terms with Guérin and Duchesne, was willing to back Robin and do the printing. Rey asked Rousseau to concur with his nomination of Robin. Grangé and Robin offered the author 720 *livres* for their edition, and Rousseau reluctantly accepted the money. Soon thereafter Malesherbes persuaded Grangé to raise Rousseau's honorarium to 1000 *livres*.[81]

Meanwhile, where were Rey's books? On 20 December a shipment to London arrived in the English capital, and within a week travellers were carrying their copies of *La Nouvelle Héloïse* to Paris.[82] This opened yet another route for potential piracy. Rousseau considered it likely that the British navy

Saint-Pierre's *Projet de paix perpétuelle* to Bastide. The essay was read by a censor and appeared as a volume in-12° in 1761. Rousseau received 12 *louis* (268 *livres*) for his pains. See Dufour, *Recherches*, i.113.

79. Charles Pinot Duclos to Rousseau, [*c.* 20 December 1760], *CC*, vii.361; Rey to Rousseau, 31 December 1760, *CC*, vii.380.
80. Rey to Rousseau, [26 December 1760], *CC*, vii.377-78.
81. Robin to Rousseau, [21 February 1761], *CC*, viii.145.
82. Orlando de Lorenzy to Rousseau, 22 December 1760, *CC*, vii.366. An English translation already was underway under the auspices of Thomas Becket and Pieter Abraham de Hondt, who later would undertake *Emile*, the *Social contract*, the *Letter to Christophe de Beaumont* and the *Miscellaneous works of M. J.-J. Rousseau* (1767) in five volumes.

had seized Rey's transport to France on the high seas and 'qu'au lieu d'ennuyer les dames de Paris, la *Julie* ennuie actuellement les dames de Londres'.[83] At last, on 9 January 1761, Rey's books reached the French capital. In the meantime Robin and Grangé were instructed to prepare their edition.[84]

At this point the strange publication history of *La Nouvelle Héloïse* took its most bizarre twist of all. Rey's books languished in the sealed warehouse of the royal customs service. Neither Robin nor Grangé hurried to retrieve them, and Rey must have wondered whether he was being set up after all. It shortly became apparent to him that Malesherbes intended the Robin–Grangé edition to *precede* his on the market. Was his edition to be ruined after all? At this critical juncture Rey behaved unusually. He packed his bags and returned home to Amsterdam.[85] Considering the fact that he already had taken a month of his life to travel to Paris and assure the arrival of his books, his decision to abandon them at a critical time was peculiar. Jo-Ann McEachern surmises that Rey's hasty departure was predicated upon his discovery that the Robin–Grangé edition was not to be an exact replica of his after all. Instead, it was a censored version of it. McEachern interprets the censor's intervention to signify that, despite Malesherbes's previous assurances, Rey's unexpurgated edition was deemed unacceptable for French tastes. The Paris-produced version thus leapfrogged to priority and there was little reason for Rey to remain in France.[86]

This conjecture has considerable merit. On the other hand, none of Rey's correspondence in January–February 1761 betrays much desire to bargain for the release of his books. He seems to have interpreted what was occurring as a commercial decision rather than a censorship issue. He believed that his edition would be circulating very shortly, and it is likely that Malesherbes counselled patience. Nevertheless the Robin–Grangé edition indeed was expurgated. Though no 'improvements' were made to it, the censor had insisted on cuts. Whatever he told Rousseau and whatever Rey believed, Malesherbes had become alarmed by the Amsterdamer's proofs of *La Nouvelle Héloïse*, and the director worried that he would be powerless to prohibit an unexpurgated first edition from being challenged and seized.[87] Therefore,

83. Rousseau to Marie-Madeleine de Brémond d'Ars, marquise de Verdelin, 28 December 1760, *CC*, vii.379.
84. Rey to Rousseau, [9 January 1761], *CC*, viii.6.
85. Rey to Rousseau, [17 January 1761], *CC*, viii.9-10.
86. McEachern, *Bibliography*, i.106.
87. Well might Malesherbes express concern. Following Damiens's attempt to assassinate Louis XV early in 1757, a monstrous royal declaration decreed the death penalty for anyone caught writing or publishing works deemed seditious or hostile towards religious authority. Though the act never was enforced, it inspired campaigns against the printed word. Among the best publicised was the attack of the Parlement of Paris upon Claude-Adrien Helvétius's *De l'esprit*, a work which possessed a royal *privilège*. The *Encyclopédie* also was threatened: on 5 March 1759 it was placed on the Catholic Church's index of forbidden books and three days later a royal decree revoked its *privilège*. At this point Malesherbes delicately undermined the royal order by permitting labour on the *Encyclopédie*'s plates to continue unabated; and even more significantly, the director privately advised Diderot to continue editing the text. The concluding ten volumes

rather than risk sacrificing Rey's edition, Malesherbes decided to offer up Robin–Grangé's to the censor. Excisions were requested from their proofs. They were accepted and Robin–Grangé's book was quickly released for sale. There was one final irony. The Robin–Grangé edition did not bear a Paris imprint. Rather it falsely announced: '*A AMSTERDAM*, Chez MARC MICHEL REY'![88]

Malesherbes hoped that within a few weeks Rey's genuine edition might be released quietly. Labelled a re-edition, it stood a better chance of passing a censor's perusal than it would have as the original. Malesherbes knew that Rousseau never would acknowledge an expurgated edition, so he told the writer nothing about the censor's cuts to Robin–Grangé's and Rousseau initially believed that its text was identical with Rey's. Meanwhile Guérin informed Rousseau that Duchesne still was interested in publishing a third edition. Rousseau touched up the *préface dialoguée* and on 25 January Coindet wrote that Duchesne had acquired publication rights for *La Nouvelle Héloïse*'s plates, the manufacture of which had not much interested the writer.[89]

When Robin and Grangé naively presented Rousseau with a copy of their hurriedly published *La Nouvelle Héloïse*, the author was aghast. The censor's cuts and, nearly as bad, an unending stream of typographical errors, persuaded him to disown the volumes altogether. He informed Coindet: 'je n'y reconnois plus mon manuscrit. Mon dessein est de desavoüer hautement cette édition, et même publiquement dans les journaux et gazettes; il n'est point juste qu'on ose publier sous mon nom un monstre ainsi difforme et un livre ainsi mutilé.'[90] For Rousseau the product of seven months' intense labour with Rey had been supplanted by a hash concocted in fewer than four weeks, and probably lifted from copies of Rey's own edition.[91] The writer asked Coindet to return, via Malesherbes, the 1000 *livres* that Robin and Grangé had given him.[92]

Malesherbes failed to share Rousseau's dismay. Conceding that the author was probably justified in renouncing the Robin–Grangé edition because he never had examined the book's page proofs, the director nevertheless reminded Rousseau of the latter's assent to the edition. Then Malesherbes observed that Rousseau's repudiation would have little effect upon the sales

would appear six years later, without incident, and bearing the false address of Samuel Fauche of Neuchâtel. Nevertheless, as Rousseau would learn to his dismay, in 1761 and 1762 the temperature of repression remained high.

88. 6 vols, in-12°. Dufour, *Recherches*, i.87-88.

89. Coindet to Rousseau, [25 January 1761], *CC*, viii.25.

90. Rousseau to Coindet, [26 January 1761], *CC*, viii.29.

91. The source for the Robin–Grangé edition of *La Nouvelle Héloïse* remains somewhat of a mystery. It was probably printed from one of the half-dozen sets that Rey had brought to Paris in December 1760. Malesherbes accepted three of the sets and passed them round among friends. Rey did the same with the other three sets. McEachern believes that Malesherbes's circulation of his sets is evidence that he had not read the uncensored copies of *La Nouvelle Héloïse* brought to Paris by Rey (*Bibliographie*, i.102, note 305).

92. Rousseau to Coindet, [26 January 1760], *CC*, viii.29-30.

of *La Nouvelle Héloïse*. Only the public would decide which edition, Robin–Grangé's or Rey's, was preferable. Furthermore, Malesherbes advised Rousseau, publishers were interested in their profits and nothing more. All, including Rey, were indifferent to the aesthetic and literary concerns of authors. Malesherbes advised Rousseau to concentrate upon the potential third edition of his novel, which Duchesne would prepare in Paris under the author's own eyes. For the time being the director advised Rousseau to swallow his pride and accept the Robin–Grangé gratuity.[93] To placate Rousseau he said he would release the sixty author's gift copies of Rey's genuine edition. He assured the writer that the entire lot would be on sale shortly.[94]

In all of this Malesherbes seemed to be saying that literary property was a highly fluid commodity. In his view Rey certainly did not 'own' *La Nouvelle Héloïse*. Nor, of course, did Robin–Grangé. Once he concluded his contract with Rousseau for the third edition, Duchesne might have a claim. Because he eventually would publish his version under the false address 'Neuchâtel', however, even his ownership seemed doubtful.[95] For the director, publishers always were testing the waters; authors simply should swim with the tide.[96] And this is precisely what Rousseau did. His indignation notwithstanding, the writer decided to keep Robin–Grangé's 1000 *livres*; and, conscience-stricken, he tried unsuccessfully to compensate Rey with half of it.[97] Subsequently Rousseau accepted 50 *louis* from Duchesne for the projected third edition of the novel, ostensibly as payment for the *préface dialoguée*.[98] Rey's own edition was released and placed on sale in February. Fortunately for him and Robin, Duchesne's was delayed until 1764, by which time piracies of *La Nouvelle Héloïse* were flooding Europe.[99]

Just how badly did the Robin–Grangé edition distort *La Nouvelle Héloïse*? In the *Confessions* Rousseau complained that more than a hundred pages had been torn from his novel.[100] He was exaggerating. Still, Robin–Grangé was hardly the sort of edition to engender pride in such a fastidious author as Rousseau. With her customary thoroughness Jo-Ann McEachern has studied

93. Malesherbes to Rousseau, [*c.* 28 January 1761], *CC*, viii.33-34.
94. Malesherbes to Rousseau, 29 January 1761, *CC*, viii.36-37.
95. Dufour, *Recherches*, i.100; McEachern, *Bibliography*, i.288-97.
96. Malesherbes's position, contrasting the rights of authors with those of publishers, would be justified in the Librairie rulings of 1777 and 1778. Interestingly enough, it also does not appear at odds with modern copyright law, particularly in the United States, where freelance writers or authors under contract may lay claim to their work after publication of the first edition. See Alvin Kernan, 'Literature and the law: the moral rights of artists', in *The Death of literature* (New Haven 1990), p.93.
97. Rousseau to Malesherbes, [19 February 1761], *CC*, viii.132-36; Rousseau to Malesherbes, 19 February 1761, *CC*, viii.137-38; Rousseau to Malesherbes, [*c.* 10 March 1761], *CC*, viii.235-38.
98. Abbé de Graves to Malesherbes, [2 February 1761], *CC*, viii.49.
99. Duchesne published the *Préface de la nouvelle Héloïse* as a discrete work in February 1761 (see Dufour, *Recherches*, i.90-92 and McEachern, *Bibliography*, i.148-50). Shortly thereafter Rey's own edition of the *Préface* appeared (see Dufour, *Recherches*, i.88-90 and McEachern, *Bibliography*, i.152-54).
100. *OC*, i.512.

both the Rey and Robin–Grangé editions, noting typographical errors as well as the excisions demanded by the state censor, Christophe Picquet.[101] McEachern concludes that nearly every page of Robin–Grangé contained errors in spelling or punctuation, wrong words and lacunae.[102]

What did the censor dislike about *La Nouvelle Héloïse?* On 16 February Malesherbes sent Rousseau a list of the excisions that Picquet had made.[103] The director subsequently informed Rousseau that Picquet's cuts for the Robin–Grangé edition would not necessarily be requested for a potential third edition.[104] Barbara de Negroni suggests that the excisions amounted to around twenty-five printed pages of the 1976 contained in the Rey edition.[105] For de Negroni the cuts fell into three categories. The first had to do with Rousseau's notes, whose suppression had no effect upon the novel's text; the second concerned entire paragraphs or ends of paragraphs, which impaired comprehension of Rousseau's chain of thought while not necessarily changing his meaning; the third set of cuts was the most insidious, eradicating sentences within paragraphs or words within a single sentence, modifying completely what Rousseau had meant to say.[106] Picquet inserted nothing of his own into the text. Concentrating upon politics and religion, he limited himself to expurgating. For example, a scornful reference to boudoir government was removed because it might bring to mind Mme de Pompadour, and an analysis of royal boredom was stricken for allegedly conjuring up Louis XV's reputation. Above all Picquet excised criticisms of Roman catholicism: suggestions of sensuality located in mystical texts, harsh commentary on Jansenist theology, accusations of clerical hypocrisy, sacramental abuses or idolatry lurking in the cult of saints. Finally Rousseau's benevolent treatment of Wolmar disturbed the censor, for Rousseau appeared to assure salvation to his upright atheist.[107]

Malesherbes insisted that he was sending the censor's remarks so that Rousseau could adjust his text for the proposed third edition. Contemplating the disappearance of his own words, the writer resisted all negotiation. He protested that the views he had published in the *Discours sur l'origine de l'inégalité* and the *Lettre à d'Alembert* were far bolder than the ideas articulated by his fictional characters in *La Nouvelle Héloïse.* Why, he pleaded with Malesherbes, did his novel have to submit to continued persecution? Rousseau suspected several reasons.

---

101. Picquet was a professional administrator, a lawyer who had been serving as *inspecteur de la Librairie* for a few weeks. In 1763 he would translate Henry Fielding's *History of Jonathan Wild* into French.

102. 'La Nouvelle Héloïse et la censure', in *Rousseau and the eighteenth century: essays in memory of R. A. Leigh,* ed. Marian Hobson, J. T. A. Leigh and Robert Wokler (Oxford 1992), p.83-99.

103. Malesherbes to Rousseau, 16 February 1761, *CC*, viii.117-26.

104. Malesherbes to Rousseau, [*c.* 26 February 1761], *CC*, viii.177-78.

105. *Jean-Jacques Rousseau/Chrétien-Guillaume de Lamoignon de Malesherbes: correspondance,* ed. Barbara de Negroni (Paris 1991), p.88. De Negroni lists the excisions in notes 34-60, p.316-22, of her edition.

106. *Rousseau/Malesherbes: correspondance,* p.97-98.

107. Malesherbes to Rousseau, 16 February 1761, *CC*, viii.117-26.

First of all, the writer maintained that *La Nouvelle Héloïse* was turning him into a moral preceptor for the young, replacing church and family. And he claimed not to relish this role one bit: 'Je ne me soucie pas qu'on me lise en France, s'il faut employer pour cela six volumes de fadeurs, uniquement à servir de secretaire d'amour à la jeunesse, et à donner aux lecteurs l'érudition du coucher'. Second, he accused the French critical establishment of hostility towards *La Nouvelle Héloïse*'s enlightened feminism. Preferring female characters who commence as libertines and finish by taking lessons from their confessors, critics could not abide a young woman who was 'à la fois aimable, dévote, éclairée et raisonnable [...] un objet plus nouveau et selon moi plus utile'. Third, Rousseau considered his novel to be the victim of religious bigotry. He wrote that his characters bore a Protestant piety and the censor was trying to mould them into Catholics: 'L'Eglise Romaine n'exige point une piété éclairée, elle éxige une piété aveugle, et quant à l'Eglise protestante, c'est précisément parce qu'elle exige une piété éclairée qu'elle laisse à chacun l'usage de sa raison.' Rousseau concluded that he would prefer not to participate in any third edition if it meant whitewashing over his text:

J'ai pensé aux changemens proposés, et j'ai vu que je ne pouvois rien substituer aux choses retranchées sans changer aussi l'objet de ce livre et sans le gâter, ce que je ne veux pas faire [...]. Je remercie très humblement Monsieur de Malesherbes de sa bonne volonté, mais je ne sais ni veux apprendre comment il faut préparer un livre pour le mettre en état d'être imprimé à Paris.[108]

When Rey's uncensored volumes went on sale without incident in mid-February, Rousseau no longer felt the need to accede to a manipulated text, even though Duchesne's anticipated edition promised the *préface dialoguée* and illustrations by Gravelot. Robin urged Rousseau not to co-operate at all with Duchesne; he predicted that Rey would fail to be paid if Duchesne's projected volumes impeded sales of the Amsterdam edition.[109] Rey also asked Rousseau not to participate in the proposed third edition.[110] The writer, however, already had pocketed Duchesne's 1200 *livres*, and he was feeling less responsible than earlier for the success of Rey's investment. Believing that Rey had known everything about the Robin–Grangé edition, including the cuts to the text, and had not shared his information with him, Rousseau was disinclined to protect his publisher.

Concerning his earlier views on literary property, Rousseau ought to have felt vindicated. He had collected income for *La Nouvelle Héloïse* from three different publishers: Rey (2160 *livres*), Robin–Grangé (1000 *livres*) and finally Duchesne (1200 *livres*). The eventual spectacular success of the novel ought to

108. Rousseau to Malesherbes, [19 February 1761], *CC*, viii.132-34.
109. Etienne-Vincent Robin to Rousseau, [21 February 1761], *CC*, viii.145-47. Robin maintained that three hundred sets of his edition remained unsold and that sales of the Amsterdam edition had slowed down. He blamed this on rumours of the projected third edition, purportedly under Rousseau's supervision. The rumour spread that the author's text would be expanded, accompanied by illustrations and reduced in price.
110. Rey to Rousseau, [2 March 1761], *CC*, viii.200-202.

have guaranteed the writer steady revenue, at least as long as he was willing to supply would-be publishers with a stream of amended prefaces, corrections and additions. By spring 1761, however, Rousseau had lost interest in *La Nouvelle Héloïse*, even though fawning correspondents would urge him to explain and expand upon his text.[111] Ever concerned about his mortality, Rousseau primarily felt the need to get new manuscripts into print in authorised editions. Therefore he turned once more to Rey. During Rey's visit to Paris Rousseau had offered the Amsterdamer *Du contrat social* for 3000 *livres*, and subsequently lowered the price to 1000 *livres*.[112] Meanwhile he permitted Malesherbes and the duchesse-maréchale de Luxembourg to negotiate the sale of *Emile* to Duchesne. This treatise brought him a record sum: 6000 *livres*.[113] Indeed Rousseau seemed to be undergoing a conversion. Increases to his income were transforming him from an *écrivain de vocation* into an *écrivain de métier*. However much he might scorn the literary commercialism of Diderot or Voltaire, whom he believed to be writing for the market rather than for the moral regeneration of humanity, he was beginning to resemble them more than he was willing to admit.[114]

111. *CC*, viii.256-65.
112. Charles Duclos to Rousseau, [*c.* 20 January 1761], *CC*, viii.18; Rousseau to Rey, 18 February 1761, *CC*, viii.128-29.
113. Text of contract with Duchesne for *Emile*, 4 September 1761, *CC*, ix.371.
114. On Rousseau's income and 'conversion' see Benoît Mély, *Jean-Jacques Rousseau. Un intellectuel en rupture* (Paris 1985), p.114-18.

2. *Emile* and the *Œuvres complètes*

Rousseau's minuet with Rey

OWING to his near disastrous experience with *La Nouvelle Héloïse*, Rey became more convinced than ever that the sale of a manuscript by Rousseau eliminated whatever proprietary claim the writer might have to that work. Conversely, in February 1761 the publisher informed his author that he felt free to reprint any of Rousseau's books whose manuscripts he once had purchased.[1] In June Rey went yet further. First he notified Rousseau that he soon would republish *La Nouvelle Héloïse*, 'quoi qu'on ay contre fait *Julie* par tout'. Rey requested whatever modifications Rousseau might wish to make. The publisher noted the appearance of William Kendrick's English translation of Rousseau's novel. Then he hinted that he shortly would start reprinting the writer's entire corpus: 'Je suis obligé de réemprimer vos autres ouvrages, on les demande & si je ne les execute pas, d'autres le feront come on l'a déja fait ici en partie & en France pour le tout.'[2]

Rousseau did not reply immediately. Once Rey's announcement of the *Œuvres diverses de M. J.-J. Rousseau citoyen de Genève* appeared later that summer, however, the writer exploded:

Puisque vous avez fait, Monsieur, sans ma participation une édition de mes ouvrages, même de ceux qui ne vous appartiennent pas, et que par un privilége obtenu vous m'avez dépouillé autant qu'il étoit en vous du droit de les faire imprimer où il me plairoit, vous devez vous soucier tout aussi peu de mon agrément pour l'exécution que pour l'entreprise; et, que l'édition me paroisse bien ou mal faite, c'est ce qui surement vous est très égal.[3]

What Rey intended to make was an in-octavo patchwork edition, which he could fill with overstocked copies of Rousseau's books that he already had published, such as the *Discours sur l'inégalité* and the *Lettre à d'Alembert*. What particularly dismayed Rousseau, however, was Rey's intention to add pieces which had not cost the publisher anything. These were works that other publishers had purchased or for which they had been granted first edition rights. They included the *Discours sur les sciences et les arts*, Rousseau's responses to that essay's critics, *Narcisse*, the *Lettre sur la musique française*, *Le Devin du village*, the article 'Economie politique' from the *Encyclopédie* and Rousseau's extract of

1. Rey to Rousseau, [25 February 1761], *CC*, viii.172.
2. Rey to Rousseau, [1 June 1761], *CC*, ix.1. On 13 October Rousseau's cousin Jean, writing from London, noted that the English edition was a blockbuster success. Excerpts were appearing in London's leading magazines (Jean Rousseau to J.-J. Rousseau, [13 October 1761], *CC*, ix.156-57; see as well *note explicative* f, *CC*, ix.160).
3. Rousseau to Rey, 9 August 1761, *CC*, ix.90.

abbé de Saint-Pierre's *Projet de paix perpétuelle*.[4] At no time had French authorities awarded Rey a *permission tacite* for these latter items, though the Amsterdamer did obtain a Dutch privilege for the *Œuvres diverses* themselves. Rousseau indignantly claimed that he was being despoiled. He lamented that the public would wrongly associate him with an inevitably flawed product: 'et l'on m'en imputeroit les fautes; on supposeroit que je n'ai pas voulu corriger les endroits qui demandent correction'.[5]

Unmoved by Rousseau's protests, Rey went ahead with the *Œuvres diverses*. He published three volumes in 1762 and two years later cobbled together a nine-volume collection in-octavo.[6] For Rousseau's benefit Rey prepared a spirited defence of his practices. The Amsterdamer claimed to have deferred publishing the writer's older works as long as he could, despite the fact that publishers with no relationship whatsoever to Rousseau had printed the first Dijon *Discours* and *Le Devin du village*. Rey maintained that Rousseau had agreed to the Amsterdamer's publication of the *Lettre sur la musique française*; and he insisted that the essay 'Economie politique', originally written for Diderot's *Encyclopédie*, was part of the *Encyclopédie*'s corpus, not Rousseau's. Suggesting that Rousseau's recent sales of *La Nouvelle Héloïse* were ethically tainted and aware of the impending purchase of *Emile* by Duchesne, Rey considered it perfectly appropriate to take advantage of the writer's celebrity.[7] Once more he requested Rousseau's editorial assistance in the re-publication of *La Nouvelle Héloïse* and proposed a sanitised abridgment of the novel targeting younger readers.[8]

Rousseau's recent misfortunes over censorship of *La Nouvelle Héloïse* and the writer's insistence upon the integrity of his texts left him cool to any condensation of his novel for Europe's youth.[9] He characteristically misrepresented Rey's position on literary property, interpreting the publisher's desire to

---

4. All of these latter pieces did appear in volume i of Rey's *Œuvres diverses* (1762).

5. Rousseau to Rey, 9 August 1761, *CC*, ix.90.

6. *Œuvres diverses de M. J.-J. Rousseau citoyen de Genève*, 3 vols, in-8° (Amsterdam, Marc-Michel Rey 1762). With the addition of *La Nouvelle Héloïse*, *Emile* and the *Lettres écrites de la montagne* in 1764, the *Œuvres diverses* reached nine volumes. Five years later Rey published his *Œuvres de J.-J. Rousseau, de Genève*, nouvelle édition, revue, corrigée et augmentée de plusieurs morceaux qui n'avaient point encore paru, 11 vols, in-8° (Amsterdam, Marc-Michel Rey 1769); and in 1772 there appeared his *Œuvres de J.-J. Rousseau, de Genève*, nouvelle édition, revue, corrigée et augmentée de plusieurs morceaux qui n'avaient point encore paru, 11 vols, in-8° (Amsterdam, Marc-Michel Rey 1772). Dufour, *Recherches*, ii.2-3, 15-16; McEachern, *Bibliography*, i.362-66, 390-97.

7. Jean Sgard's definition of 'œuvres diverses' to a large extent confirms what Rey was trying to accomplish. 'Visiblement, les œuvres "diverses" ou "mêlées" constituent des ensembles provisoires, de moyenne dimension (une dizaine de volumes au plus), publiés par différents libraires en compétition, à un moment où l'œuvre totale est encore en cours d'élaboration: ce sont des *œuvres* occasionnellement réunies' ('Des collections aux œuvres complètes', p.1).

8. Rey to Rousseau, 17 August 1761, *CC*, ix.97-100.

9. Much to Rousseau's grief, the Prussian academician and ex-pastor J.-H.-Samuel Formey would make a career of sanitising *La Nouvelle Héloïse* and *Emile*. See Formey's *Anti-Emile* (1762), *Emile chrétien, consacré à l'utilité publique* (1764) and *L'Esprit de Julie, ou Extrait de la Nouvelle Héloïse, ouvrage utile à la société et particulièrement à la jeunesse* (1763).

widen the public domain as a mask covering a contrary notion, namely the acquisition of exclusive publication rights over the writer's entire corpus. At heart Rousseau preferred Rey to any other potential publisher of a general edition and he conceded Rey's claim to republish first editions which the Amsterdamer originally had paid for. Nevertheless Rousseau insisted upon his own moral right to revise and subsequently resell his books, particularly those to be incorporated into a general edition. He informed Rey: 'Quoique des ouvrages mêmes dont j'ai traitté avec vous j'aye eu toujours soin de me reserver le droit d'en faire une édition générale et d'y faire entrer tous ceux que je vous ai cedés.'[10]

Rousseau would have preferred to save his canonical edition for later in life, as a means of assuring retirement income for himself and his companion, Thérèse Levasseur. During the summer of 1761, however, the actions of others had forced him to consider undertaking it sooner than anticipated. In the first place, he feared that disreputable publishers throughout Europe would seize upon his popularity, pirate one another's books and produce botched collections misleadingly labelled as authorised. Secondly, he had to cope with the well-meaning interference of the maréchale de Luxembourg and Malesherbes. Both believed that Rey always had underpaid the writer, and the contract they drew up with Duchesne for *Emile* was about to bring Rousseau an unprecedented 6000 *livres*. The contract did award Rousseau the right, after three years, to renegotiate the sale of *Emile* for an edition of collected works. Most significant of all, however, Duchesne was to obtain preference in publishing that edition.[11]

Financially speaking, the contract negotiated by Malesherbes and the maréchale treated Rousseau generously. Believing, however, that the preferential clause concerning Duchesne and the edition of collected works had been forced upon him, the writer sought ways of amending or cancelling it. Once Duchesne began putting together his volumes for the general edition, Rousseau's participation would be hesitant and half-hearted, and the writer simultaneously dangled the prospect of competing editions before other publishers. In fact, two days prior to signing the contract with Duchesne, as he huffily accused Rey of usurping his rights, Rousseau tempted the Amsterdamer with the following:

Cette édition [générale], Monsieur, me tient fort au cœur, soit pour ma réputation, à cause de l'exactitude et de la correction que j'espère y mettre; soit pour mon aisance, étant ma derniére ressource pour avoir du pain quand mes infirmités me laissent hors d'état d'en gagner. Si dans le tems, vous voulez entrer dans les arrangemens qui se

---

10. Rousseau to Rey, 2 September 1761, *CC*, ix.114.
11. 4 September 1761, *CC*, ix.371: 'je Compte donner La préference audit sieur Duchesne de La vente de Cette edition generale si Lorsque nous en traitterons dans le tems nous sommes d'accord sur les Conditions'. This is a copy made around 1778 of the original contract between Rousseau and Duchesne. It is in the Rousseau archive at Chaalis. Leigh has reproduced early drafts of the contract: *CC*, ix.107-108, 111-12, [28 August 1761, 29 August 1761]. These can be found in Paris, BNF, n.a.fr. 1183, f.51, 53.

prendront pour la faire je vous y verrai concourrir avec plaisir et j'espére que vous vous en trouverez bien.[12]

It is tempting to interpret Rousseau's longwinded hint at an offer simply as part of a double game. It is more likely that the writer considered his proposal to be a sincere effort to reassert control over his corpus. After all, in recent months leading Paris publishers, the state's *directeur de la Librairie*, the writer's latest patron and a royal censor had been telling Rousseau what he could print and who ought to do the printing. Each actor in the drama claimed to be guided by solicitude towards a literary genius unpractised in the ways of the world. For an author whose proprietary interest in the printed word was as all-encompassing as Rousseau's, however, such benevolence proved suffocating. Indeed he considered it to be nothing less than a siege attack upon his intellectual autonomy. Above all else the writer desired to negotiate his literary property as he saw fit. That is why he dealt concurrently with Duchesne and Rey.

While he would treat Duchesne crudely, Rousseau stroked Rey. He informed the Amsterdamer that by delaying co-operation with Duchesne over the Parisian's projected *La Nouvelle Héloïse* he was doing all he could to protect Rey's original investment. In fact, even while refusing to abridge *La Nouvelle Héloïse* for youth ('il n'est point destiné pour les jeunes gens'), he did agree to send to Rey a corrected copy of the novel for the Amsterdamer's projected new edition of it. Then Rousseau noted that if Rey still intended to publish the writer's recently completed manuscript on political theory he would send a courier to Amsterdam bearing the piece. Rousseau requested a publication date of March 1762: 'A l'égard du Manuscrit [*Du contrat social*] il est tout prêt et vous le ferez retirer quand il vous plaira, rien ne presse. Je vous Salüe, Monsieur, de tout mon cœur, et souhaite que nous nous entendions mieux à l'avenir que par le passé.'[13]

During the next several months Rousseau and Rey cemented their accommodation. Aware of Rey's disappointment over the sale of *Emile* to Duchesne, Rousseau was heartened by the Amsterdamer's gracious acceptance of that bad news.[14] For his part Rey appreciated Rousseau's gift of the fresh manuscript of *La Nouvelle Héloïse*.[15] Despite a tense moment when the manuscript for *Du contrat social* nearly was seized by French customs officials while being carried out of Paris by the Dutch ambassador's chaplain, Jean-Jacques Duvoisin, the text arrived safely in Amsterdam.[16] There were few delays over composition and correction. Rousseau continued to promise Rey an edition of collected works and in January 1762 divulged to the Amsterdamer his intention of revising his contract with Duchesne. He would ask the Parisian to

12. Rousseau to Rey, 2 September 1761, *CC*, ix.115.
13. Rousseau to Rey, 2 September 1761, *CC*, ix.115.
14. Rousseau to Rey, 31 October 1761, *CC*, ix.217.
15. For Rey's new edition see Dufour, *Recherches*, i.99; Jo-Ann E. McEachern, *Bibliography of the writings of Jean-Jacques Rousseau to 1800*, vol. ii *Emile, ou De l'éducation* (Oxford 1989), p.282-86.
16. Pastor Jean-Jacques Duvoisin to Rousseau, [24 November 1761], *CC*, ix.273-74. For Rousseau's description of the incident in the *Confessions* see *OC*, i.560.

substitute publication rights to the *Dictionnaire de musique* for the contractual clause granting him preference for the edition of collected works. Should Duchesne insist, however, upon undertaking the edition, Rousseau advised Rey to join the Parisian as a partner.[17] The writer clearly was trying to distance himself from his French benefactors and draw closer to Rey. Once it became evident that Duchesne would experience difficulty getting volumess iii and iv of *Emile* past French censors, Rousseau would propose a complicated scheme to have the entire treatise transferred to Rey.[18]

For his part Rey was pleased with the evolution of his relationship with Rousseau and he could afford to be magnanimous. His original edition of *La Nouvelle Héloïse* had brought him a profit of 10 000 *livres* after all, and he invited the writer to Amsterdam so that the two might co-operate closely upon the anticipated general edition.[19] Rey urged Rousseau to place at its head the 'Mémoires sur votre vie', a clear indication that the writer already was contemplating his autobiography (for which the publisher offered him 1000 *livres* sight unseen).[20] Rey's benevolence towards Rousseau attained a deep personal level. He offered a lifetime annuity of 300 *livres* for Thérèse Levasseur and wished to name Rousseau godfather of the child he and his wife were expecting.[21] Such a strategy of merging the personal with the professional bore fruit and Rousseau addressed Rey with uncharacteristic charity: 'J'aime à penser que mes écrits et mon nom ont contribué à vous en faire un, et à commencer vôtre fortune.'[22]

Publishing *Emile*

From the start Rousseau's relations with Duchesne and the Parisian's business associate Pierre Guy were cooler and more businesslike than those with Rey. They began cordially enough; publication of *Emile*, however, proved to be a complicated and contentious affair. Worried about the French censor's eventual reading of the treatise, Duchesne and Guy chased after ways of easing *Emile*'s passage through the bureaucratic machinery of the royal Book-trade Office. Above all else they wished to obscure the fact that *Emile* was being published in Paris at all. Assisted by Guérin, Duchesne and Guy therefore arranged with the distinguished and aged Amsterdam bookseller, Jean Néaulme, to place Néaulme's name and address on the title page of

---

17. Rousseau to Rey, 23 January 1762, *CC*, x.49.
18. Rousseau to Rey, 18 [11] February 1762, *CC*, x.92-95.
19. Rey to Rousseau, 7 December 1761, *CC*, ix.299.
20. Rey to Rousseau, 31 December 1761, *CC*, ix.368-70; Rey to Rousseau, [18 January 1762], *CC*, x.141. Concerning the autobiography, Rousseau already worried that his own justification would compromise others. Rousseau to Rey, 6 January 1762, *CC*, x.15: 'Mais pour ma vie il est difficile qu'elle soit mise en état de paroitre, parce qu'elle est mêlée de beaucoup de faits qui en sont inséparables et qui compromettroient le secret d'autrui.'
21. Rey to Rousseau, 31 December 1761, *CC*, ix.368; Rey to Rousseau, 6 March 1762, *CC*, x.141.
22. Rousseau to Rey, 29 November 1761, *CC*, ix.284.

their edition. The purpose of this ruse was the hope of acquiring a *permission tacite* and the censor's indulgence for examining a work allegedly produced in Holland's tolerant printing climate. In return for the use of Néaulme's name and address, the Parisians agreed to send him revises so that the Dutchman could make his own edition of the educational treatise, one intended largely for the Dutch, English and German markets.[23] Though Néaulme and Duchesne were not necessarily on intimate terms, their formal contract awarded to each the right to print whatever future manuscript of Rousseau's the other might acquire, and that right included the collected works, 'avec les augmentations que l'Auteur jugera à propos d'ÿ faire'.[24]

Pleased as he might have been with the high price offered for his manuscript, Rousseau nevertheless endured several disputes with Duchesne over *Emile*. It was agreed that the Paris edition would appear in two formats, in-duodecimo and in-octavo. The writer wanted Duchesne to place the major part of his investment in the in-octavo, 'qui surement est le plus convenable à l'ouvrage et sera, selon moi, le plus recherché'. For his part, however, Duchesne preferred concentrating upon the cheaper in-duodecimo. Rousseau believed that Duchesne's timetable for sending proofs was far too slow and he suspected that the publisher was passing round the manuscript to others without his knowledge.[25] Haggling over the volume divisions for the various parts of *Emile* caused additional delays and Rousseau nourished suspicion of Guérin's (and, by implication, Duchesne's) involvement in an alleged Jesuit plot to suppress the treatise altogether and release a thoroughly distorted version after the writer's death.[26]

Rousseau therefore looked for ways to amend his contract with Duchesne and on 30 November offered the Parisian several alternative proposals. He asked Malesherbes to pass them on to the publisher. A characteristic pronouncement on literary property introduced the recommendations. First Rousseau insisted that Duchesne was entitled solely to the profits of a single edition of *Emile*. The writer regretted conceding even this, however, and tried to have his manuscript restored to him. He accused Duchesne of delaying everything and therefore not holding to the original terms. If Duchesne returned the manuscript, Rousseau agreed to remit to the Parisian the 3000-*livre* advance he had received. Should Duchesne not concur, Rousseau was willing to exchange the manuscript of his *Dictionnaire de musique* for *Emile*. If Duchesne still insisted upon keeping *Emile*, either he was to set a firm publication deadline and adhere to it, failing which Rousseau could find a replacement for him, or else the publisher was to cancel his agreement with Néaulme. This would permit Rousseau to locate another publisher for production and distribution of copies of the book intended for sale outside France. If this latter

23. Jean Néaulme to Rousseau, [4 January 1762], *CC*, x.11-14.
24. Contract between Nicolas-Bonaventure Duchesne and Jean Néaulme, [early November 1761], *CC*, ix.372.
25. Rousseau to Duchesne, 19 October 1761, *CC*, ix.184-86.
26. Rousseau to Malesherbes, 18 November 1761, *CC*, ix.245-46.

edition beat Duchesne's to the draw and found its way into the kingdom, the Parisian would have to accept the consequences.[27]

As Rousseau's intermediary with Duchesne, Malesherbes elected not to hand over to the publisher the writer's ultimatum of 30 November. Instead the director appointed one of his police inspectors of the book-trade (probably Joseph d'Hémery) to monitor Duchesne's progress weekly. Then Malesherbes himself tried to alleviate Rousseau's mistrust of Duchesne and counselled the writer to be patient.[28] Solicitous though Malesherbes might have been towards Rousseau, what he failed to comprehend was the genuine reason lying behind the writer's concerns, namely a deep-seated sense of having lost control of *Emile* to others. Initially Rousseau had sacrificed his book to the maréchale de Luxembourg and Malesherbes, negotiators of the manuscript sale to Duchesne; then to Duchesne and Néaulme, who seemed to be treating the writer's masterpiece as a chunk of merchandise to be split apart and traded off; finally to the suspected Jesuit conspiracy which, in Rousseau's mind, sought to destroy his work and malign his posthumous reputation. When all was said and done, for the writer the core issue, as always, was the need to maintain the integrity of his most treasured possession, his intellectual property.

Néaulme became aware of Rousseau's mistrust of Duchesne and sought to take advantage of it, for the Dutch publisher was not enthralled by the prospect of collaborating with the Parisian on a future edition of collected works. He therefore approached Rousseau and sought the writer's co-operation in a luxurious in-quarto *collection complète* which he hoped to publish on his own.[29] Rousseau responded favourably to Néaulme's feeler.[30] The writer hinted at extricating himself from his commitment to Duchesne who, in Rousseau's view, lacked basic common sense. Rousseau felt certain that Duchesne's edition of collected works never would see light of day.[31] He therefore agreed to assist with Néaulme's edition of *Emile*, the one projected for sale outside France. At the least it would give him the opportunity to observe Néaulme's work habits.[32] However, for the moment unknown to Rousseau or, for that matter, Néaulme, Duchesne had negotiated for yet a third edition of Rousseau's treatise. His partner in the project, who would do the printing, turned out to be the Lyon bookseller Jean-Marie Bruyset. Since Bruyset was a notorious pirate and also adept at smuggling illicit works in and out of France, Duchesne's transaction represented a sort of insurance policy in the event of

27. Propositions of Rousseau to Duchesne, [30 November 1761], *CC*, ix.290-91.
28. Malesherbes to Rousseau, 7 December 1761, *CC*, ix.297-99; Malesherbes to Rousseau, [16 December 1761], *CC*, ix.323-28.
29. Néaulme to Rousseau, [4 January 1762], *CC*, x.11-14.
30. Rousseau to Néaulme, 13 January 1762, *CC*, x.32.
31. Rousseau to Rey, 13 January 1762, *CC*, x.32.
32. In the *Confessions* Rousseau claimed to be less amenable than he appeared to be in his correspondence: 'Durant tous ces essais je vis bien que l'ouvrage s'imprimoit en France ainsi qu'en Hollande, et qu'il s'en faisoit à la fois deux éditions. Que pouvois-je faire? Je n'étois plus maitre de mon manuscrit' (*OC*, i.563).

his own possible difficulties with censorship. Bruyset sought a *permission tacite* for his edition, so as to gain limited legitimacy for what Néaulme certainly considered an outright piracy.[33]

By February 1762 all of Rousseau's concerns crystallised. Duchesne had nearly completed first proofs for volumes i and ii of *Emile* when Malesherbes asked the writer to make some revisions of them. Fearing worse trouble once the director examined the rest of his treatise, especially the 'Profession de foi du vicaire savoyard' slated for volume iii, Rousseau requested Malesherbes to negotiate the return of the entire manuscript to him.[34] Malesherbes refused to co-operate and Rousseau started to doubt whether Duchesne's edition (despite the cover of Néaulme's name and address on its title page) would be tolerated in France after all. He was certain that the as yet unprinted part of the treatise contained material that powerful interests in the kingdom were bound to find objectionable.

Insisting once more upon his absolute rights as author, Rousseau informed Rey of his desire to annul his contract with Duchesne for volumes iii and iv. To replace it he proposed a new agreement with Rey, who would be invited to publish the volumes in Amsterdam. Then, as Rousseau saw it, two final pieces would fall into place. Duchesne would be forced to break *his* agreement with Néaulme. Rey then could establish contact with Néaulme, take advantage of his fellow Dutchman's ingrained timidity and religious scruples and obtain control over Néaulme's publication and distribution privileges. To be sure, by replacing Néaulme Rey still would have to share distribution of volumes i and ii with Duchesne. Concerning these volumes, the Parisian would continue to have the French market while Rey would have Holland, Germany, England and elsewhere. Of greatest importance, volumes iii and iv, the most interesting and controversial parts of *Emile*, would be Rey's alone.[35]

As he pondered Rousseau's strategy, Rey no doubt perceived the desperation lurking behind it. Though the Amsterdamer wondered about the wisdom of becoming involved at all, the temptation of publishing what promised to be the most desirable parts of *Emile* intrigued him. Rey therefore proposed an alternative to the plan Rousseau had suggested. He urged the writer to revise his contract with Duchesne, limiting their arrangement to volumes i and ii of the treatise. If Rousseau were successful in getting Duchesne to agree, Rey would extricate Néaulme from any responsibility for volumes iii and iv. Rey wanted clearcut and exclusive rights to publish these volumes, sell them outside France and, above all, distribute them among Paris's most distinguished booksellers on an exchange basis (which they

33. Néaulme would learn about Bruyset's edition in February, and he would inform Rousseau of it (Rousseau to Duchesne, 16 February 1762, *CC*, x.101-102). The Lyon edition was published in four volumes in-12°. Part of the edition falsely cited Néaulme, Amsterdam, as publisher. See McEachern, *Bibliography*, ii.96-100.
34. Rousseau to Malesherbes, 8 February 1762, *CC*, x.87.
35. Rousseau to Rey, 18 [11] February 1762, *CC*, x.92-95.

preferred to a cash transaction). Confronting these favourable terms, so hoped Rey, the Paris Community of Booksellers would pressure Malesherbes to admit the Amsterdamer's books, via a *permission tacite* or oral arrangement. Rey insisted, however, that his volumes iii and iv of *Emile* should appear with a new title, as a work totally distinguished from volumes i and ii, whose ownership Duchesne and Néaulme would continue to share.[36]

Meanwhile Néaulme was doing his best to produce his edition of *Emile*. His version was based upon the revises that Duchesne was supposed to supply from Paris. But fearful lest Néaulme's edition appear prior to his own, Duchesne took his time forwarding the corrected sheets to the Dutchman. From the start Néaulme betrayed nervousness over Rousseau's critiques of religious orthodoxy in the treatise, and Rousseau became understandably furious when Néaulme's reader began making unauthorised changes to the text.[37] Yet preoccupied as he was with correcting two sets of proofs simultaneously (Duchesne's for *Emile* and Rey's for *Du contrat social*), Rousseau found it nearly impossible to devote as much attention as he wished to yet a third set, Néaulme's. Still he valiantly plunged ahead, seeking to allay Néaulme's concerns.[38] Even with his fears of a Jesuit conspiracy momentarily behind him, Rousseau was convinced that at the last minute French authorities would suppress Duchesne's edition, and he wished to get Néaulme's into Rey's hands.

Any hope Rousseau might have had of cancelling or amending his agreement with Duchesne was shattered by a letter that the Parisian's associate, Pierre Guy, wrote to Rey early in March. Vigorously denying that he and Duchesne ever had pirated *La Nouvelle Héloïse* at Rey's expense, Guy added that he could find no reason for treating the Dutchman with any special consideration. As 'master' of *Emile*, Guy claimed the right 'de le Communiquer à qui il m'a plu, et je n'etois pas obligé d'avoir des Egards pour vous, puisque vous [...] n'en avés pas eu pour moy'.[39] Meanwhile, in one of his habitual misconstructions of Rey's meaning, Rousseau interpreted the Amsterdamer's lukewarm response to the writer's strategy for obtaining publication rights to *Emile* as a refusal to recognise those held by Néaulme.[40] Subsequently Rey tried to clarify his position. He was open to taking on *Emile*, but he preferred to have Néaulme drop out voluntarily. If this were done, Rey certainly was interested in dealing.[41]

---

36. Rey to Rousseau, 6 March 1762, *CC*, x.139-42.

37. Néaulme to Rousseau, [*c*. 20 January 1762], *CC*, x.45-46; Rousseau to Néaulme, 29 January 1762, *CC*, x.70-72.

38. Rousseau to Néaulme, [*c*. 22 February 1762], *CC*, x.113.

39. Pierre Guy to Rey, 4 March 1762, *CC*, x.139.

40. Rousseau to Rey, 18 March 1762, *CC*, x.159-61.

41. Rey to Rousseau, [25 March 1762], *CC*, x.167.

Disaster

Meanwhile Rey progressed with publication of *Du contrat social*. On 15 April 1762 he informed Rousseau that two bales containing the in-octavo pages of the work had been shipped by sea to Dunkerque. From there they were to be transported by land to Paris.[42] In the meantime the Amsterdamer already had published the first volumes of his *Œuvres diverses* and sent three sets to Rousseau via Malesherbes. Characteristically angry over this unauthorised edition, the writer informed Rey that he had not taken the trouble to examine it; he had, however, given two of the sets to the maréchale de Luxembourg who, he noted, 'les ont trouvés pleins de fautes épouvantables'.[43]

Rey was publishing 5000 copies of *Du contrat social*: 2500 in-octavo and 2500 in-duodecimo. Though Rousseau preferred the larger format, Rey despaired that pirates would destroy it by making their own cheap in-duodecimos. He saw fit, therefore, to challenge the inevitable competition with his own modest format. He was optimistic about the treatise's sale in France and arranged with the Paris booksellers Laurent Durand, Jean Desaint and Charles Saillant to distribute his volumes;[44] however, he took a significant risk. As he had done with the *Lettre à d'Alembert* four years earlier, he shipped his copies to France prior to obtaining the *permission tacite* for them. He was counting upon Rousseau's intimacy with book-trade director Malesherbes to assure toleration of *Du contrat social*.

This proved to be a lamentable miscalculation. By 9 May Malesherbes had received his gift copy and was reading it. Rousseau failed to share Rey's optimism over easy admission to France and suspected trouble: 'M. de M. est bon et bienfaisant, mais malheureusement il ne peut pas toujours écouter son bon cœur et ses lumiéres, ni faire toujours ce qu'il voudroit bien.'[45] The writer's fears proved justified. On 12 May Desaint and Saillant informed Rey that, reading his advance copy of *Du contrat social*, Malesherbes had decided to prohibit the book's distribution.[46] On the following day Desaint and Saillant wrote to Rey again and expressed deep worry about Rousseau's physical safety at Montmorency. An unnamed magistrate (Malesherbes?) was requesting that Rey immediately order the removal of Rousseau's name from *Du contrat social*'s title page, for the principles enshrined in the book were capable of causing its author grave trouble in France. In a reproachful tone, the Paris booksellers lectured Rey: 'nous ne pouvons pas concevoir comment vous avez pu vous persuader que l'on pût jamais tolerer L'Entrée et l[a] distribution d'un pareil ouvrage'. They doubted whether Rey's copies would be returned to Amsterdam. Most likely they would be destroyed. Orders had been sent to the French provinces gravely warning individuals not to circulate the book.[47]

42. Rey to Rousseau, [15 April 1762], *CC*, x.196-97.
43. Rousseau to Rey, 23 April 1762, *CC*, x.205.
44. Rey to Rousseau, [28 April 1762], *CC*, x.216-19.
45. Rousseau to Rey, 9 May 1762, *CC*, x.235.
46. Jean Desaint and Charles Saillant to Rey, [12 May 1762], *CC*, x.240-41.
47. Desaint and Saillant to Rey, [13 May 1762], *CC*, x.241.

As soon as he heard from Desaint and Saillant, Rey wrote back indignantly. He was certain that Malesherbes's suppression of *Du contrat social* had been forced upon him by unknown parties. The Amsterdamer doubted whether his books would be burned and predicted that two weeks after their return to him piracies would appear in Lyon and Rouen. As a consequence, 'on ruinera un homme qui cherche à gagner sa Vie en Contribuant autant qu'en Lui est à rendre Ses semblables, meilleur'.[48]

Around 25 May Rousseau heard from Rey about the suppression of *Du contrat social*. Meanwhile the Paris edition of *Emile* was ready and Duchesne had just distributed the author's gift copies. The maréchale de Luxembourg, Charles Duclos, Alexis-Claude Clairaut and Charles-Marie de La Condamine acknowledged receiving theirs, and the latter pair offered lame excuses for having turned directly to the 'Profession de foi du vicaire savoyard', which they praised.[49] A few days earlier Jean Néaulme also was reading the 'Profession de foi' in the revises supplied to him by Duchesne. But the old Huguenot bookseller was much less enamoured of what he had found than were the academicians of Paris. In fact he was appalled. He wrote to Rousseau: 'Il faut que je vous ouvre mon Cœur [...] j'ai Senti dans mon Cœur que ce Livre, tel qu'il est aujourd'huy Sans rétranchements (qui n'i nuioroit pas) feroit plus de mal que de bien.' Néaulme claimed to have shown the 'Profession de foi' to fairminded acquaintances, 'D'honnete gens nullement Bigot, ni Enticheés d'un Esprit de critique [...] et il leur à parut comme à moy que l'ouvrage tombe dans la Classe des *Livres Prohibé* & déffendue par nos ordonnances & nos placard: ainsi que je courre grand risque de me faire des affaires les plus Serieuses, Si ce qui est dit Contre la Revelation y restoit Ainsi; & Si foiblement déffendu.' Néaulme pleaded with Rousseau to remove the 'Profession de foi' from the treatise. He then suspended publication of his edition.[50]

But it was too late for Néaulme to do anything about Duchesne's edition. By the time Rousseau received Néaulme's letter, the in-octavo version of Duchesne's edition was on sale in Paris. Its title page, disguised in the red and black ink which identified a Dutch edition, bore the false imprint: 'A la Haye, Chez Jean Néaulme, Libraire. M. DCC. LXII. Avec Privilège de Nosseign. les Etats de Hollande & de Westfrise.'[51] Faced with this *fait accompli* Néaulme decided to complete his own edition after all; however, he purposely made his title page resemble a crudely produced piracy. Néaulme's identifying marks – his name and address, headpiece, publisher's foreword and Dutch privilege – were noticeably absent. He disguised his edition, using black ink

48. Rey to Desaint and Saillant, [18 May 1762], *CC*, x.249. Malesherbes honoured Rey's request that the seized pages of *Du contrat social* be returned (Rey to Malesherbes, [7 June 1762], 17 June 1762], *CC*, xv.391-92; Malesherbes to the officers of the Paris Booksellers' Guild, 1 July 1762, *CC*, xv.393).

49. Alexis-Claude Clairaut to Rousseau, [24 May 1762], *CC*, x.286-87; Charles-Marie de La Condamine to Rousseau, 24 May 1762, *CC*, x.287-88.

50. Néaulme to Rousseau, 22 May 1762, *CC*, x.278-80.

51. McEachern, *Bibliography*, ii.72-81.

only, and even considered printing the false imprint: 'A Paris, Chez Duchesne'! Fearful of being caught in the spirit of vengeance, however, he dismissed the ploy in favour of printing the vaguer and more innocuous: 'Selon la Copie de Paris, Avec Permission tacite pour le Libraire'.[52]

As literary property, the status of *Emile* now was ambiguous to say the least. The two publishers who had acquired the book either were denying or veiling possession of it. Furthermore the work's author would shortly become a fugitive from French justice. On 1 June police lieutenant for Paris A.-R. de Sartine sent orders for Duchesne to cease distributing *Emile* and to take back the copies he already had sold.[53] On 7 June the syndic of the Sorbonne's Faculty of Theology declared Rousseau's treatise to be impious and a threat to public order. Two days later the Parlement of Paris condemned *Emile* and on 11 June the book was ritually destroyed at the foot of the grand staircase of the Palais de Justice.[54] Officers were sent to Montmorency to arrest Rousseau,[55] but he already had fled.[56] Malesherbes denied that *Emile* ever had obtained a *permission tacite* based upon the report of a censor.[57] Both *Emile* and *Du contrat social* were condemned in Geneva.[58] Despite their own privilege gracing the title page of Duchesne's edition, the Estates of Holland and West Friesland suppressed the treatise as well.[59]

Just prior to the Dutch condemnation Néaulme sold his publication rights to Rey, who immediately found himself possessing a worthless privilege.[60] Worse luck for Néaulme, the old man was summoned before Amsterdam's police magistrate, before whom he explained that he had nothing to do with the edition condemned in Paris and bearing his name.[61] With the Dutch police watching him, Néaulme had little incentive to publicise his true edition.[62] Meanwhile in France the Duchesne–Guy edition (with Néaulme's name on the title page) and Bruyset's Lyon version (published alternatively as 'A Amsterdam, Chez Jean Néaulme' or as 'A Leipsick, Chez Hérit. de M. G. Weidmann & Reich') went underground.[63] Concerning *Du contrat social*, most of Rey's copies were returned to him and subsequently made the rounds

---

52. McEachern, *Bibliography*, ii.88-95.

53. Antoine-Raymond de Sartine to Malesherbes, [1 June 1762], *CC*, xi.7-8.

54. 'Arrest *de la Cour* de Parlement, *qui condamne un imprimé ayant pour titre*, Emile ou de l'Education, par J.J. Rousseau, *imprimé à La Haye* [...] M.DCC.LXII. *à être laceré & brulé par l'Exécuteur de la Haute-Justice*', 9 June 1762, *CC*, xi.262-70.

55. 'Extrait des Registres de Parlement', 9 June 1762, *CC*, xi.272-73.

56. Guillaume-François-Louis Joly de Fleury to Chancellor Guillaume de Lamoignon de Malesherbes, 10 June 1762, *CC*, xi.56-58.

57. Malesherbes to his father, Chancellor Guillaume de Lamoignon de Malesherbes, 10 June 1762, *CC*, xi.59.

58. Judgement of Geneva's public prosecutor, 19 June 1762, *CC*, xi.301-302.

59. The Estates of Holland and West Friesland to the municipality of Amsterdam, [23 June 1762], *CC*, xi.302-303.

60. Rey to Rousseau, [17 June 1762], *CC*, xi.102.

61. Néaulme to Rousseau, 28 July 1762, *CC*, xii.123-25.

62. Rey to Rousseau, [22 July 1762], *CC*, xii.85-86.

63. McEachern, *Bibliography*, ii.96-103, 114-17.

as an illicit book. Rousseau's publisher of record treated all the horrific events stoically. He wrote to his best-selling author, now a fugitive from French, Genevan and Dutch justice: 'Nous vivons dans un Siecle où L'honnêthoᵐe n'est pas a couvert de la malice des hommes. Il faut prendre Son parti & Se roidir contre L'Infortune.'[64]

Rousseau eventually found physical refuge in the Swiss village of Môtiers, part of the principality of Neuchâtel, territory nominally ruled by Prussia's Frederick II. While authorities in Geneva and France considered the author a fugitive, Duchesne and Néaulme (co-publishers of his *Emile*) escaped with mere reprimands. Duchesne set to work upon his general edition, the *Œuvres de M. Rousseau de Genève*, eventually to reach nine volumes, placing the false address, 'Neuchâtel', on each volume's title page. The Parisian and his associate Pierre Guy had the good sense to omit *Emile* from their edition; they did, however, place into their set other books of Rousseau's that either were condemned or else soon would be: the *Lettre à Christophe de Beaumont* (volume vi), *Du contrat social* (volume viii) and the *Lettres écrites de la montagne* (volume ix).[65] For his part Néaulme was contrite. Claiming to have been duped by Duchesne, he divested himself of his edition of *Emile*, apparently turning what he had printed over to Rey, and he negotiated with J.-H.-S. Formey for a 'cleansed' version of the educational treatise that had brought him grief.[66] But the old bookseller's name was thereafter inextricably associated with the condemned *Emile* and over the next decade illicit edition after illicit edition would bear one or another false address, 'Néaulme, Amsterdam' or 'Néaulme, La Haye'.[67]

By virtue of their condemnations of *Emile*, *Du contrat social* and, later on, the *Lettres écrites de la montagne*, governments actually confirmed Rousseau's unwavering opinion concerning intellectual property. In their view he, as author, was accountable for books declared illicit. Indeed the Rousseau case endorses Foucault's interconnections among property, transgression and punishment. Once Rousseau was recognised as an owner of his transgressive texts, he was subject to appropriate punishment for alleged literary sins.[68] Police authorities considered Rousseau's publishers to be merely his agents and they emerged relatively unscathed. After June 1762, however, the author feared setting foot in France, Geneva, Bern, Holland and the Austrian Netherlands, even as Duchesne, Rey and innumerable pirate publishers profited from his notoriety. Not even the authority of Frederick the Great would prove sufficient to prevent the writer's virtual expulsion from Môtiers in 1765.

64. Rey to Rousseau, [21 June 1762], *CC*, xi.122.
65. For the bibliographical analysis of Duchesne's edition see Dufour, *Recherches*, ii.6-15. The arrangement between Duchesne and Rey concluded very badly. See Guy to Rey, 26 June 1764, *CC*, xx.216-18.
66. *Projet de souscription pour un livre intitulé: le véritable Emile consacré à l'utilité publique, rédigé par M. Formey* (1763); *CC*, x.320-25.
67. See McEachern, *Bibliography*, ii.439-40.
68. Foucault, 'What is an author?', p.148-49.

At the same time the condemnations of *Emile* and *Du contrat social* affected Rousseau's marketability. First editions of whatever he might undertake became risky investments, and publishers of record would be reluctant about paying the writer sums comparable to Duchesne's 6000 *livres*. Rey would offer Rousseau the paltry sum of 500 *livres* for the *Lettre à Christophe de Beaumont* (1763) and another 1500 *livres* for the *Lettres écrites de la montagne* (1764). On the other hand, the tumultuous events of late spring and early summer 1762 bore one additional irony. Even though publishers would be reluctant about paying Rousseau very much for first edition rights, demand for the author's banned books became overwhelming. Piracies now were the rule. As a consequence any exclusive claim to Rousseau's individual titles was derisory, and he shuddered at what was being produced in his name. In 1774, four years before his death, the writer desperately denounced as unauthorised every edition of his works except the very first.[69] Of course the disavowal was toothless. Like Jean-Jacques himself, the corpus had entered the public domain.

The *Œuvres complètes* of Rousseau[70]

By 1769 Duchesne–Guy's edition of the *Œuvres de M. Rousseau de Genève* had appeared in nine volumes, overseen by abbé Joseph de La Porte and bearing the false address of Neuchâtel. Because Duchesne intended to include in his edition *Du contrat social*, the *Lettre à Christophe de Beaumont* and the *Lettres écrites de la montagne*, works officially condemned in France, the false address was a necessary precaution.[71] Furthermore, the Paris publisher commissioned Rey to print the condemned pieces in Amsterdam, thereby resulting in the Amsterdamer's subversion of his own first editions.[72] This formulaic semi-clandestinity worked, for the French book police did not appear to disturb sales of Duchesne's set. For his participation, which was cranky, sporadic and half-hearted, Rousseau earned only 1200 *livres*. Furthermore, the writer never considered the Duchesne edition to be the authorised one he had anticipated. In fact, lacking *Emile* and *La Nouvelle Héloïse*, it was not even complete.

In truth Rousseau would have much preferred working with Rey than with Duchesne. The Amsterdamer's editorial techniques were familiar and Rousseau believed that Rey had paid him fairly for his manuscripts. In May 1764

69. 'Déclaration relative à différentes réimpressions de ses ouvrages', 23 January 1774, *OC*, i.1186-87.

70. Two recent articles discuss the history of Rousseau's *œuvres complètes*: Raymond Birn, 'Les "œuvres complètes" de Rousseau sous l'ancien régime', *Annales de la Société Jean-Jacques Rousseau* 41 (1997), p.229-62; and Jean-François Perrin, 'Ceci est mon corps. J.-J. Rousseau et son "édition générale"', *SVEC* 370 (1999), p.85-94.

71. Abbé Joseph de La Porte to Duchesne, [1 December 1762], *CC*, xiv.148-49. Duchesne's edition was entitled *Œuvres de M. Rousseau de Genève*, nouvelle édition, revue, corrigée et augmentée de plusieurs morceaux qui n'avaient point encore paru, 9 vols, in-12° and in-8° (Neuchâtel [Paris and Amsterdam] 1764-1769).

72. Guy to Rey, 18 [November] 1764, *CC*, xxii.82-83.

the writer wrote to Rey from Môtiers, proposing that the pair collaborate upon a fresh edition of complete works. Rousseau desired an in-quarto of six volumes with eighteen to twenty plates and he agreed to concede to Rey an inexpensive in-duodecimo if the publisher so desired. The order of presentation was important to Rousseau: volume i was to contain his works on politics and morals; volumes ii and iii would contain *La Nouvelle Héloïse*; volumes iv and v would hold *Emile* which, despite its near-universal condemnation, was being pirated regularly; volume vi would contain 'les piéces de theatre, ouvrages de litterature, lettres et mémoires'.[73] At this point, however, the prospect of a costly edition of collected works authorised by Rousseau and publicised throughout Europe made Rey uncomfortable. The recent condemnation of *Emile* by the Estates of Holland remained fresh in his mind and he worried about investing any further in the treatise. Awaiting calmer days, Rey therefore rejected Rousseau's offer and concentrated upon his own hodgepodge edition, the *Œuvres diverses*, which reached nine volumes in-octavo.[74]

Rey had good reasons for distancing himself from Rousseau. In mid-1764 the writer's livelihood surely was compromised. For a publisher sensitive to the censorship whims of an unsympathetic government, even one as relatively benign as Holland's, Rousseau was a risk. Moreover, book pirates throughout Europe were taking advantage of Rousseau's international notoriety by publishing their own faulty editions based upon whatever texts were at hand. They charged cut-rate prices and the public bought them up.[75] All of this dismayed Rousseau immensely, and two professional goals crystallised in his mind. The first was justification of his career and the second was assurance of economic survival for himself and Thérèse Levasseur. Rey advised Rousseau that the most appropriate means of achieving these objectives was to get on with his memoirs, not add to the flood of editions of collected works.[76] The writer believed, however, that gathering the documents necessary for his autobiography would consume precious time, and he needed income. For the moment at least, he doubted the wisdom of publishing another potential *succès de scandale*. He therefore opted for a canonical edition. But condemned as several of his books were in so many places, how and where could this be accomplished?[77]

The answer turned out to be in Môtiers itself, so Rousseau hoped. There the Neuchâtel publisher Samuel Fauche proposed establishing a printshop for the purpose of working with the writer on an authorised *collection complète*. Rousseau sought counsel and material assistance for the project from his new

73. Rousseau to Rey, 13 May 1764, *CC*, xx.56-59.

74. Rey to Rousseau, [15 June 1764], *CC*, xx.194-97.

75. This was alluded to by the Lyon bookseller Jean-Baptiste Réguillat in a letter to Rousseau. Réguillat proposed, obliquely, an edition of collected works with Rousseau's co-operation. There is no recorded reply (Jean-Baptiste Réguillat to Rousseau, 8 June 1764, *CC*, xx.166-68). On the unauthorised general editions see Dufour, *Recherches*, ii.2-6.

76. Rey to Rousseau, [15 June 1764], *CC*, xx.195.

77. Rousseau to Charles Pinot Duclos, 2 December 1764, *CC*, xxii.147-49.

Neuchâtel friend, the millionaire shipper-planter Pierre-Alexandre Du Peyrou, to whom he wrote: 'Cette entreprise doit m'assurer du pain, sans lequel il n'y a ni repos, ni liberté parmi les hommes: ce recueil sera d'ailleurs le monument sur lequel je compte obtenir de la postérité le redressement des jugemens iniques de mes contemporains.'[78] Du Peyrou was generous with advice and financial backing for Fauche, whom he believed correctly to lack the necessary capital for such an ambitious undertaking. The playwright-engraver Claude-Henri Watelet agreed to supervise the illustrations.[79] Rousseau envisioned an edition of six volumes in-quarto or in-octavo for collectors and a more modest version of fifteen volumes in-duodecimo for serious readers. He foresaw three or four years of work and requested an honorarium of 12 500 *livres* or a guaranteed lifetime annuity of 1200 *livres*. Confidently he predicted that the project would bring investors between 50 000 and 100 000 *livres* of profit.[80]

In order to pacify Duchesne and Guy, who were producing their own 'Neu-châtel' set with Rousseau's ostensible co-operation, the writer emphasised the need to be physically proximate to the publisher of any definitive edition. Therefore, he insisted, the authorised one could only be published in Môtiers. Rousseau also stated his conviction that the French government would not soon lift its ban on publishing openly either *Emile* or *Du contrat social* in the kingdom. Aware that a Môtiers edition might well injure Duchesne–Guy's and feeling sheepish about his treatment of the Parisians, Rousseau offered them first crack at his *Dictionnaire de musique*. He requested 4800 *livres* (or a down payment of 2400 *livres* and an annuity of an additional 300 *livres*) for what he maintained to have represented sixteen years of work.[81] Meanwhile Du Peyrou settled with Rousseau for the Môtiers edition, guaranteeing the writer an annuity of 1600 *livres*, with Thérèse inheriting 400 *livres* per year at the writer's death.[82] Rousseau accepted Du Peyrou's offer, further agreeing to let the financier serve as his literary executor. Next he supplied Du Peyrou with a list of titles for each of the six volumes intended to comprise the Môtiers edition.[83]

Unfortunately, once Rousseau set about revising his manuscripts, the roof fell in. The writer's latest response to his enemies in Geneva, the *Lettres écrites de la montagne*, was condemned not only in his birthplace but also by regimes in

78. Rousseau to Pierre-Alexandre Du Peyrou, 29 November 1764, *CC*, xxii.130.
79. Claude-Henri Watelet to Rousseau, [10 December 1764], *CC*, xxii.205-206.
80. Rousseau to Du Peyrou, 13 December 1764, *CC*, xxii.226-28.
81. Rousseau to Duchesne, 16 December 1764, *CC*, xxii.242-44; Rousseau to Duchesne, 30 December 1764, *CC*, xxii.326-28.
82. Du Peyrou to Rousseau, [20 January 1765], *CC*, xxiii.161.
83. Rousseau to Du Peyrou, 24 January 1765, *CC*, xxiii.179-83; Rousseau to Du Peyrou, [31 January 1765], *CC*, xxiii.241. Thirteen years later, once Part I of the *Confessions*, *Rêveries du promeneur solitaire*, *Rousseau juge de Jean-Jacques* and correspondence were added to the œuvre, Du Peyrou would interpret Rousseau's organising principle of 1765 as the basis for his 'total' moral autobiography, the canonical *Collection complète des œuvres de J.-J. Rousseau*.

Holland, Bern and Neuchâtel.[84] Shortly thereafter the Parlement of Paris would have the *Lettres* ritually destroyed.[85] Worse still, the Small Council of Neuchâtel, under whose political jurisdiction Môtiers lay, ordered Fauche to suspend publication of the general edition.[86] In explaining to Frederick II why it had withdrawn Fauche's permission to print, Neuchâtel's Council of State wasted no time revealing the public danger it perceived in Rousseau's corpus: 'Nous craignons, Sire, que la publicité de ces écrits dans lesquels n'est pas observée la moderation necessaire sur les dogmes de la foy, ne produise des éffets dangereux parmi Nous, ou le Laboureur qui semble n'être né que pour les ouvrages grossiers de la Campagne, est naturellement speculatif et occupe son loisir à la lecture de toutes sortes de livres.'[87]

The Fauche edition was now impossible, and Rousseau contemplated flight from Môtiers. Needing income, the writer again turned to Rey, offering to travel to Amsterdam and, despite the fact that three of his books were prohibited in Holland, work on the edition of his corpus there. Rousseau dangled before Rey the prospect of the *Confessions* and requested a survival income of between 600 and 1000 *livres* per year. The autobiography, he wrote, now was crucial:

Il reste la grande entreprise de ma vie et des piéces qui S'y rapportent. Entreprise qui doit être séparée de la précédente; parce que quand même ma vie seroit écrite, on ne peut la mettre sous la presse qu'au bout d'un nombre d'années dont on conviendra, à cause des choses importantes qu'elle contiendra, surtout depuis quelques années en ça, et des personnes en place qui seroient compromises, ce que je ne veux pas faire et que celui qui se chargera de cette entreprise doit éviter pour lui-même.

L'Ouvrage est déja commencé et je vois à vue de pays que ce sera un ouvrage aussi considérable que singulier. Car jamais homme n'aura fait une entreprise semblable et ne l'aura executée comme je me propose de le faire; j'ai dequoi, et l'abondance de mes matériaux m'étonne moi-même.[88]

Rey offered financial assistance to the writer, but remained reluctant about taking on the grand project. Instead he continued to produce his less costly in-octavo editions, borrowing whenever he could from earlier sets and individual works.[89] In August 1765 he mentioned to Rousseau that he intended to publish a fresh edition, and sought guidance.[90] He had no intention, however, of paying Rousseau for revised texts. Instead he borrowed freely from Duchesne–Guy's edition. While omitting most texts not from Rousseau's quill, Rey did include the principal refutations of the first *Discours*,

84. 'Resolutien van den Hove van Holland', 11-17 January 1765, *CC*, xxiii.377-78; 'Déclaration de nos magnifiques & très honorés seigneurs, sindics et conseil' [Geneva 1765], 12 February 1765, *CC*, xxiii.369-72; *note explicative* c, *Gazette de Berne*, 23 January 1765, *CC*, xxiii.204; Charles-Guillaume de Montmollin to a Genevan, 18 February 1765 and *note explicative* c, *CC*, xxiv.40-41.
85. 'Arrest de la Cour de parlement', Paris [19-20 March] 1765, *CC*, xxiv.348-49.
86. *Note explicative* b, 18 February 1765, *CC*, xxiv.7.
87. The Conseil d'état of Neuchâtel to Frederick II of Prussia, [4 March 1765], *CC*, xxiv.141.
88. Rousseau to Rey, 18 March 1765, *CC*, xxiv.235-36.
89. Rey to Rousseau, 31 May 1765, *CC*, xxv.360.
90. Rey to Rousseau, 19 August 1765, *CC*, xxvi.232-34.

d'Alembert's response to Rousseau's *Lettre* on the theatre and the archbishop of Paris's condemnation of *Emile*.

Therefore, on the eve of Rousseau's departure from Môtiers in September 1765, aside from outright piracies, Europe knew two so-called editions of his collected works: one published in Paris with the false address 'Neuchâtel', the other emerging from Amsterdam and patching together various individual volumes. Neither edition was complete or in any way truly authorised; Rousseau's participation in each had been minimal. Meanwhile the writer still was collecting 1600 *livres* per year from Du Peyrou for an aborted *collection complète* and he had left his friend in Neuchâtel sealed packages of books, letters and manuscripts which one day, the pair hoped, might be put to use.

During Rousseau's exile in England (January 1766 to May 1767) the possibility of an authorised edition of the writer's complete works still existed, and now Rey showed interest. Preoccupied with his quarrel with Hume, however, and busy with early drafts of the *Confessions*, Rousseau paid little attention to Rey's inquiries. He informed the Amsterdamer of his disgust over Rey's business squabbles with Duchesne and urged him not to request any revised manuscripts for future publication. If Rey desired to make a more authoritative edition than the one he presently was compiling, Rousseau advised him to contact Du Peyrou.[91] Rey did this; however, Du Peyrou refused to dispose of the manuscripts in his safekeeping – certainly not without Rousseau's express consent.[92]

There matters stood. Though Rousseau's reputation remained formidable between 1766 and 1775, during these years no European publisher collaborated with the writer upon an authorised edition of his collected works. Plenty of pirates were at work, however. Either they imitated the Duchesne–Guy and Rey editions or else they strung together scattered volumes haphazardly, to peddle them as sets. For example, in October 1766 Rousseau's friend Toussaint-Pierre Lenieps informed Guy that a Marseille correspondent was offering him 'la petite Edition des œuvres de Rousseau Lyon toute reliée pour 24^{H} que j'en prenne 3 Exemp^{es}'.[93] Guy angrily responded that it was fantasy to believe that an acceptable edition could sell for so little: 'Ce n'est certainement pas notre édition; il peut bien se faire que ce soit quelque mauvaise compilation de province ou de pays Etrangers, ou peut etre bien n'entend t'on que les œuvres diverses [of Rey].'[94]

Once Rousseau had returned to France in 1767 and was living at the prince de Conti's country house at Trye, Du Peyrou visited him. Becoming very ill,

---

91. Rousseau to Rey, 3 March 1766, *CC*, xxix.9-11.

92. Du Peyrou to Rousseau, 23 April 1766, *CC*, xxix.138-41; Du Peyrou to Rousseau, 6 July 1766, *CC*, xxx.11-15.

93. Toussaint-Pierre Lenieps to Guy, 10 October 1766, *CC*, xxxi.23-24.

94. Guy to Lenieps, 11 [October] 1766, *CC*, xxxi.26-27. Another edition, probably pirating Duchesne's, also circulated in Paris in 1772. In a letter probably addressed to police lieutenant-general Sartine, Rousseau denied having received any compensation for alleged participation in its publication (Rousseau to Antoine-R. de Sartine[?], 15 January 1772, *CC*, xxxix.11-16). See also Dufour, *Recherches*, ii.16-17, 23.

Du Peyrou turned delirious and accused the writer of trying to poison him. Stunned and hurt, Rousseau abandoned any hope of reviving the Môtiers project. On the day following Du Peyrou's accusation, the writer composed an 'Etat de mes affaires' abrogating the agreement he had made with Du Peyrou three years earlier. Rousseau went further. He stated his hope of restoring to Du Peyrou 2400 *livres* already advanced to him as the annuity.[95] In this way Du Peyrou's literary role shifted. Instead of serving as executor of Rousseau's papers, he became mere guardian of them. As for the papers themselves, which now included revisions of published works and more than three manuscript chapters of the *Confessions*, Rousseau wrote to his former benefactor:

Quant à mes écrits et papiers qui sont entre vos mains, ils y sont bien; permettez que je les y laisse, résolu de ne les plus revoir et de ne m'en remêler de ma vie. Ce recueil S'il se conserve deviendra précieux un jour; S'il se démembre, il S'y trouve suffisamment d'ouvrages manuscrits pour en tirer d'un libraire le remboursement des avances que vous m'avez faite.[96]

During Rousseau's final years in Paris disillusionment and a desire to avoid trouble with the authorities persuaded him not to co-operate in the republication of his works in any form. Responding to Rey's query about possible revisions to *Emile* for a reprint of the *Œuvres de J.-J. Rousseau* that the Amsterdamer was preparing, the writer noted:

Je n'ai nul changement à faire ni à l'Emile ni à aucun de mes écrits. Ne reconnoisant pour mienne que la prémiére édition de chacun d'eux je ne prends aucun interest aux éditions postérieures et n'ai pas même le tems d'éxaminer celles que je suis à portée de voir. J'ai pourtant toujours recommandé les vôtres par préférence, persuadé que vous êtes incapable de vous prêter à aucune infidelité. Au lieu que toutes celles qui se font et se feront en France portent tous les caractères de perfidie et de réprobation qui m'assurent qu'elles sont infidelles, falsifieés, et faites avec les plus sinistres intentions.[97]

Particularly tormenting to Rousseau were his suspicions of false editions commissioned by his enemies, which, he believed, would disfigure his texts and destroy his credibility as an author. For Rousseau, even Rey's 1772 reprint of the Amsterdamer's collective edition of 1769 proved to be disreputable. Therefore, in order to demonstrate the illegitimacy of similar publications, in a circular letter placed in the *Gazette de littérature, des sciences et des arts*, Rousseau publicly disavowed all editions of his works except the very first.[98]

The major reason for Rousseau's denial was the impending appearance in 1774 of a newly conceived *Collection complète des œuvres de J.-J. Rousseau*.[99] Though announced as a London imprint, the work actually was being

95. Rousseau to Du Peyrou, [10 November 1767], *CC*, xxxiv.174-76.
96. Rousseau to Du Peyrou, 10 June 1768, *CC*, xxxv.306.
97. Rousseau to Rey, 14 June 1772, *CC*, xxxix.66.
98. *Gazette de littérature, des sciences et des arts* 12 (19 February 1774), *CC*, xxxix.305-307.
99. (1774-1776) 9 vols in-4°. Dufour, *Recherches*, ii.18-19.

published in Brussels by the Belgian bookseller J.-L. de Boubers. This was the sort of unauthorised edition that Rousseau had most feared: one intended for collectors, in-quarto, carefully printed, and luxuriously illustrated by a well-known artist, J.-M. Moreau the younger.[100] According to the writer's paranoid entry in *Rousseau juge de Jean-Jacques*, posthumously published by Thérèse Levasseur in the *Journal de Paris*, Boubers had sought Rousseau's participation in his edition; however, Rousseau wrote, the publisher's trick of passing a correct text under the author's nose, while intending to print false and injurious ones for public consumption, failed to work. Nevertheless, Rousseau added that he was unable to prevent the appearance of Boubers's first four volumes.[101]

When Guillaume Olivier de Corancez, editor of the *Journal de Paris*, sent Rousseau a complimentary copy of the first instalment of Boubers's edition, the writer refused to examine it.[102] Nevertheless, such a cold reception failed to inhibit the Brussels publisher. Boubers's volumes, sold largely on a subscription basis, appeared regularly and claimed to be a canonical edition. Following Rousseau's death the Belgian staged a genuine coup by acquiring for his edition the writer's early letters to his first mistress, Mme de Warens. Boubers published them in volume viii.[103]

Boubers was not the only publisher preparing an edition of Rousseau's collected works in 1774. On 14 January 1775 the *Supplément* to the *Gazette de Berne* contained an announcement by the bookseller Emmanuel Haller of the availability of a *Collection complète des œuvres de J.-J. Rousseau*, in eleven volumes, 'grand 8° 1775, ornés de très jolies figures & planches en taille-douce, beau papier & caractere'.[104] The publisher, it turned out, was none other than Samuel Fauche of Neuchâtel, attempting to capitalise upon the opportunity lost ten years earlier when, in light of Rousseau's persecution, his Môtiers edition had been abandoned. This time Fauche completed his set, which soon was selling openly in Geneva and Lausanne despite the fact that it included *Emile*, *Du contrat social* and the *Lettres écrites de la montagne*.[105] At first blush it might be suspected that Fauche indeed was offering an authorised revision, based upon the contents of the packages Rousseau left with Du Peyrou when the writer fled Môtiers and the papers he had sent his then literary executor

---

100. Philip Stewart, 'Rousseau, Boucher, Gravelot, Moreau', *LIT* 5 (1994), p.261-83.

101. *Rousseau juge de Jean-Jacques*, in *OC*, i.958-59; letter from Marie-Thérèse Levasseur [11 May 1779] to the *Journal de Paris* 136 (16 May 1779), p.545-46, *CC*, xliii.265-67. Boubers eventually would admit publicly to having solicited Rousseau's participation in his edition (letters from J.-L. de Boubers to the *Gazette de Leyde*, 6 July 1779, p.4, and to the *Gazette d'Amsterdam*, 23 July 1779, p.3-4, *CC*, xliii.348-50).

102. Rousseau to Guillaume Olivier de Corancez, [August/September 1774], *CC*, xxxix.269.

103. R. A. Leigh, 'Jean-Jacques Rousseau and Mme de Warens: some recently discovered documents', *SVEC* 57 (1969), p.165-75.

104. *Remarque* ii, *Gazette de Berne*, *Supplément* (14 January 1775), *CC*, xl.1-2.

105. Dufour, *Recherches*, ii.20-21. *Collection complète des œuvres de J.-J. Rousseau, avec figures en taille-douce*, nouvelle édition, soigneusement revue et corrigée, 11 vols, in-8° (Neuchâtel, Samuel Fauche 1775).

from England. No such luck. Except for a few letters by Rousseau, Fauche's edition contained nothing new. It depended heavily upon Rey's editions of 1769 and 1772.

Fauche's *Collection complète* failed to satisfy the hunger of readers desiring an accessible and genuinely revised edition, one enriched with heretofore unpublished manuscripts and correspondence. For example, one disciple, Jean Ranson of La Rochelle, asked F.-S. Ostervald, director of the Neuchâtel publishing house, the Société typographique, to persuade Rousseau to authorise an edition of complete works before it was too late.[106] When Ostervald was visiting Paris in 1777, however, Rousseau refused even to see him. The writer held firm to his strategy of denying the correctness of all editions of his books save the very first. On 2 July 1778 Rousseau's fatal stroke while a guest at the château of Ermenonville ended all hope that an authorised edition might appear in his lifetime.

106. *Remarque* ii, 8 March 1777, *CC*, xl.130.

II

The *trois amis* and the widow Rousseau

3. Girardin, Moultou and Du Peyrou

In Book XI of the *Confessions* Rousseau reflected upon his literary legacy. The plots against him notwithstanding, he wrote: 'je mourrai beaucoup plus tranquille, certain de laisser dans mes écrits un témoignage de moi, qui triomphera tôt ou tard des complots des hommes'.[1] Rousseau believed in the achievement of immortality through print, and a canonical edition remained his great hope. False starts and censorship problems had aborted the author's efforts during his lifetime, and it was left to literary disciples to produce the *Collection complète*. The faithful became certain that turning out the Master's texts was a sacred mission; they interpreted the edition as the essential means of assuring his redemption.

The forty-two days of Ermenonville

Chief inspirer of the *Collection complète* was the writer's last host, marquis René-Louis de Girardin (1735-1808), seigneur of Ermenonville. Inspired by *La Nouvelle Héloïse*, Girardin's estate, near Senlis north of Paris, was to represent Clarens reborn. It contained a concoction of laboriously designed ruins and weepy English gardens, reputedly the most carefully contrived in all of France. Patronising dilettante that he was, Girardin in 1777 published an ambitious advertisement for the landscape concepts behind Ermenonville and urged other property-owners to emulate his accomplishment.[2]

Concerning Rousseau, Girardin was a textbook disciple and his children were reared according to the principles of *Emile*. Dressed *à l'anglaise* for their autumn excursions to Paris where, as objects of bemusement for urban sophisticates, they frolicked in the Tuileries, the little Girardins would then be left on their own to trek the forty kilometres home.[3] One of them, twelve-year-old Amable-Ours-Séraphin, became Rousseau's companion during the writer's plant-collecting strolls at Ermenonville. In his imperious way Girardin

---

1. *OC*, i.568.
2. *De la composition des paysages, ou Des moyens d'embellir la nature autour des habitations, en joignant l'agréable à l'utile* (1777). Michel-H. Conan has edited a reprint (Paris 1979). Daniel Malthus, father of the economist, translated *De la composition des paysages* into English as *An essay on landscapes* (London 1783). A reprint of the translation exists: (New York 1982). A guidebook for Ermenonville, probably written by Girardin, accompanies Conan's edition. It is known as the *Promenade ou itinéraire des jardins d'Ermenonville*, p.119-94. The *Promenade* was translated into English and published by T. Becket in 1785. The only full-length work on Girardin is hagiographical, composed by the sometime priest of Ermenonville: A. Martin-Decaen, *Le Marquis René de Girardin (1735-1808). Le dernier ami de Jean-Jacques Rousseau* (Paris 1912). A more recent and better balanced study is R. B. Rose, 'The marquis René-Louis de Girardin: the perfect Rousseau revolutionary', *Australian journal of French studies* 20 (1992), p.131-52.
3. Martin-Decaen, *Le Marquis René de Girardin*, p.64-66.

claimed to have done all he could to assure Rousseau's comfort during the six weeks of the philosopher's retirement on the estate. While the marquis was constructing a cottage for his celebrated guest, Rousseau participated in his host's family concerts and entered peasant archery contests. At least one moonlit country ball was staged in his honour. If Girardin were to be believed, the strains of Rousseau's bucolic *Le Devin du village* might be imagined echoing from beyond the garden gate.[4]

Whether or not Rousseau's retirement at Ermenonville had been as idyllic as later described by Girardin, the stay nevertheless concluded abruptly with the philosopher's fatal stroke of 2 July 1778. For his part Girardin immediately recovered from the catastrophe to seize control of the legend. First of all the marquis theatrically (and untruthfully) informed his likely rival torchbearer Du Peyrou and Du Peyrou's successor as literary executor, the Genevan Paul-Claude Moultou: 'M. Rousseau vient de mourir dans nos bras.'[5] Aware that Du Peyrou held important manuscripts for the aborted 1765 edition of collected works, as well as papers that the writer had sent from England two years later, and rightly suspecting that Moultou possessed even more interesting manuscripts handed over by Rousseau just prior to the writer's departure for Ermenonville in May 1778, Girardin compounded deception by informing Du Peyrou of the Master's alleged instructions: 'il m'a Chargé Monsieur, de réclamer votre amitié et Votre parole de ne jamais Laissé sortir de vos mains aucune de ses pensées, et de ne jamais remettre ce dépot sacré qu'à Sa malheureuse femme'.[6]

Though Rousseau had requested no such thing, neutralising both Du Peyrou and Moultou was an essential piece of Girardin's strategy. Assuming command over the interests of Rousseau's widow was another. Among enemies and disciples alike Thérèse Levasseur had a terrible press. Her sexual loyalty was questioned, she was blamed for Rousseau's paranoia, and amidst the rumours concerning the writer's sudden death, a tale of suicide provoked by her reputed secret sale of the manuscript of the *Confessions* was making the rounds.[7] The facts of the matter were quite different. Barely literate, nearly sixty years old, thoroughly dependent upon Rousseau for three-and-a-half decades, Thérèse in July 1778 was cast adrift in an alien environment, and Girardin assumed the role of her rescuer. Hours following Rousseau's death, the marquis gained access to his guest's study, emptying it of

4. Draft, Girardin to Marie-Françoise Le Danoise de Cernay, comtesse de La Marck, [23 August 1778], *CC*, xli.204-30.
5. Girardin to Moultou, 3 [2] July 1778, *CC*, xl.231; Girardin to Du Peyrou, 2 July 1778, *CC*, xl.232.
6. Girardin to Du Peyrou, 2 July 1778, *CC*, xl.232-33. Girardin's first draft of the letter to Moultou read: '[Rousseau] m'a chargé de reclamer votre amitié, et votre parole de ne jamais remettre qu'à sa malheureuse femme Le Depot qu'il vous a Confié' (3 [2] July 1778, *CC*, xl.231-32).
7. See, for example, the letter of Denis Fonvizine to his sister, [5 July 1778], *CC*, xli.4-6; published in Joseph Suchy, 'Les *Confessions* à la mort de Rousseau', *Œuvres et critiques* 3 (1978), p.126-27.

papers and money that Rousseau had brought from Paris.[8] Then Girardin announced that he was Rousseau's choice to protect the widow and her inheritance.[9]

Another means of legitimising himself as chief disciple was for Girardin to create the myth of Rousseau's death and turn Ermenonville into a shrine. The background was banal enough. As early as February 1777 Rousseau had sent a circular letter to acquaintances, indicating a desire to leave Paris and locate a party willing to accept him and an ailing Thérèse as paying guests.[10] For more than a year nothing came of the request. In spring 1778 the writer's friend Olivier de Corancez offered his cottage at Sceaux to Rousseau and Thérèse for a few months. Subsequently, speaking for Girardin, Rousseau's physician Achille Lebègue de Presle made the counter-offer of a permanent arrangement at Ermenonville. The Girardins, who previously had hired Rousseau to copy music for them, came to Paris and personally extended the invitation. On 20 May, accompanied by Lebègue de Presle, Rousseau travelled to Ermenonville to examine the site. Three days later he instructed Thérèse to pack their bags.[11]

Lebègue de Presle's account of Rousseau's forty-two days at Ermenonville notes the writer's satisfaction with the Girardins' hospitality, his pleasure at renewing his plant collecting and his enjoyment of the company of little Amable-Ours-Séraphin. The doctor did not add much more. While awaiting construction of their cottage, Rousseau and Thérèse occupied a small pavilion facing the marquis's country house. According to Lebègue de Presle, on 2 July Rousseau arose early, as was his custom, took his coffee with milk and asked Thérèse to help him dress since he intended to visit the Girardins that morning. Preparing to leave, he complained of weakness, of a tingling in his feet, of chills, chest pains and a severe headache. Lebègue wrote: 'Ce fut dans un de ces accès que sa vie se termina; & il tomba de son siege par terre. On le releva à l'instant, mais il etoit mort.'[12]

Initially Lebègue de Presle's detached narrative was not the standard public announcement of Rousseau's death. Rather an anonymous notice, probably written by the jurist François-Joseph de Foulquier to the *Journal de Paris* and circulating eventually as a brochure, served that purpose.[13] Visiting

8. Just how much gold Rousseau had left is unclear. It possibly was worth as much as 14 000 *livres*. Girardin's objective was to dole out 700 *livres* per year to Thérèse.

9. Girardin to the comtesse de La Marck, [23 August 1778], *CC*, xli.213-15. For Thérèse's interpretation of Girardin's intentions see her letter to Du Peyrou, [6 March 1780], *CC*, xliv.174-80.

10. 'Mémoire écrit au mois de février 1777, et depuis lors remis ou montré à diverses personnes', *CC*, xl.243-44; subsequently published in the *Journal de Paris* (20 July 1778) and the *Mercure* (25 July 1778), p.356-57.

11. [Achille-Guillaume Lebègue de Presle], *Relation ou notice des derniers jours de M. Jean-Jacques Rousseau [...] et quels sont les ouvrages posthumes qu'on peut attendre de lui [...] avec une addition [...] par J.-H. de Magellan [...]* (1778); *CC*, xl.327-33.

12. *CC*, xl.331.

13. Manuscript version, 13 July 1778, *CC*, xli.38-44; printed as the *Lettre sur la mort de J.-J. Rousseau écrite par un de ses amis, aux auteurs du J.al de Paris. Paris le 12 juillet 1778* (*CC*, xl.359-65). On

Ermenonville during the week following Rousseau's death, Foulquier inter-
viewed both Girardin and Thérèse. He was impressed by the widow's story,
filled as it was with conjugal sentimentality, implicit denials of Rousseau's
alleged suicide and the writer's deathbed allusions to a new dawn. Foulquier's
account acknowledged the Girardins' hospitality; what stood out, however,
was an emotionally charged dialogue between Rousseau and Thérèse. Girardin is not present at the scene, and the marquise, summoned by Thérèse, is
quite brusquely dismissed by Rousseau. 'Ma chère femme, ne pleurez pas',
the dying philosopher instructs his companion, 'vous avez toujours Souhaité
de me voir heureux, et je vais l'être [...]. Ne me quittez pas un Seul instant; je
veux que Seule vous restiez avec moi, et que Seul[e] vous me fermiez les yeux.'
Once Rousseau keels over, Thérèse tumbles with him and their bodies inter-
mingle. Girardin's role is purely utilitarian. He arranges for the autopsy,
embalming and burial. True, Rousseau had requested to be interred on Ermenonville's grounds; according to Foulquier, however, he had no special wishes
as to location. It is with Rousseau cold that Girardin truly takes charge,
burying the writer on the île des Peupliers and measuring out the site for the
tomb.[14]

Concerning its rehabilitation of Thérèse, Foulquier's account pleased Girardin; for, after all, the widow now was the marquis's charge, and his intention
was for her to serve as mouthpiece for his wishes. But Girardin obviously felt a
need to amend the secondary role attributed to himself in Rousseau's last
weeks and especially during the final hours. The marquis therefore invented
his own account of Rousseau's stay at Ermenonville, the 'Lettre à Sophie comtesse de ***', which first circulated in manuscript and whose elaborate description of the supposed events of 1 and 2 July would be published in 1779 by Jean-
Antoine Roucher. From Girardin's pen the 'Lettre à Sophie' serves as a model
of myth construction.[15]

18 July Foulquier sent to Girardin a copy of his account, which the marquis rewrote to his own
advantage (see *CC*, xli.53-57). During the following month, in private correspondence Girardin
elaborated yet further upon the story of Rousseau's death (see Girardin to the comtesse de La
Marck, [23 August 1778], *CC*, xli.213-15). The definitive version of Girardin's re-inventions was
the so-called 'Lettre à Sophie comtesse de ***', backdated July 1778 and published in part by
Jean-Antoine Roucher (*CC*, xl.334-54). When the *Journal de Paris* failed to print Foulquier's
original letter, he published it himself, anonymously. It was reprinted at least twice, late in
1778 and again in 1779.

14. [Foulquier], *Lettre sur la mort*, *CC*, xl.360-62.

15. 'Lettre à Sophie comtesse de *** par René Girardin, sur les derniers momens de
J.-J. Rousseau à Ermenonville, juillet 1778', *CC*, xl.334-54. Leigh's edition notes the editorial
changes made by Girardin's son Stanislas nearly half a century after the letter's composition.
Abridged versions of the 'Lettre à Sophie' appeared in correspondence sent by Girardin to Du
Peyrou, to abbé François Rozier, to the comtesse de La Marck and others (see *CC*, xli.58-65, 78-
80, 204-30). Though Girardin never printed the 'Lettre à Sophie' on his own account, Leigh is
certain that it was intended for publication. Jean-Antoine Roucher's version of Girardin's
account of the events of 1 and 2 July appeared as an appendix to his poem *Les Mois* (1779),
ii.307-11. Stanislas Girardin's corrected and abridged version of his father's 'Lettre' was printed
in his own *Lettre de Stanislas Girardin à M. Musset-Pathay, sur la mort de J.-J. Rousseau* (Paris 1824),
p.31-48, and in two subsequent volumes (1825, 1829).

The 'Lettre à Sophie' is divided into three sections. The first portrays Rousseau's purported ecstasy at his last residence. According to the marquis, from the moment he descended from his carriage to walk the final mile and throw himself into the arms of the Girardins, Rousseau rediscovered the joys of his adolescence: 'Je vis ses yeux se mouiller de larmes, et sentis bien avec quelle sensibilité son cœur se rappellait en ce moment le souvenir des délices de Son pays, et le bonheur pur de sa jeunesse.'[16] Ermenonville's romantic and literary allusions were infectious. Girardin had carved a cave into the cliffs, called by his family 'le Monument des anciennes amours', and he labelled other sites 'L'Autel de la rêverie', 'La Prairie arcadienne' and 'Le Tombeau de Laure'. It is no wonder that Girardin had Rousseau sigh, recalling the hallowed sites from *La Nouvelle Héloïse*: 'Je trouve ici les jardins de ma Julie.' What truly mattered for Girardin, however, was that the marquis himself should be the source of Rousseau's newly found happiness: 'Je lui donnai alors une clef générale; il fut chez lui partout, et il y fut plus le maître que je n'étais chez moi; car il pouvait être seul tant qu'il voulait.'[17] At the same time, according to Girardin, Rousseau eagerly participated in family activities, mingling with the household in the orchard after dinner and pulling the oars for the Girardins on the estate's moonlit pond. While the marquis manipulated the strings, Rousseau at Ermenonville was portrayed as assimilated into a human and natural paradise.

According to Girardin, the one blemish upon this delightful image concerned tales emanating from the smoke-filled streets of Paris. Rumour had it that Rousseau's 'mémoires', excerpts of which he had read publicly in 1770 and 1771, were in the hands of some unscrupulous publisher and would soon see the light of day.[18] Girardin claims to have mentioned to Rousseau the possible appearance of the *Confessions*, but received a serene reply. According to the marquis, Rousseau stated that 'il avait remis l'unique exemplaire de Son écrit en pays étranger, dans des mains Sur les quelles il croyait devoir compter; que par conséquent l'ouvrage dont on parlait à Paris, ou n'existait pas, ou qu'il n'était pas de lui'. Girardin stated that it was Rousseau's wish not to have the *Confessions* appear until long after the writer's death and the deaths of those mentioned in them.[19]

The second part of Girardin's 'Lettre à Sophie' related the marquis's account of Rousseau's death. The purpose of this section was to provide a corrective to Foulquier's report. Girardin wished to render Thérèse incapable of playing a central role in the melodrama;[20] he himself was to take her place.

16. 'Lettre à Sophie', *CC*, xl.337.
17. 'Lettre à Sophie', *CC*, xl.338.
18. 'Lettre à Sophie', *CC*, xl.340. Boubers had just printed heretofore unpublished letters from Rousseau to Mme de Warens in volume viii of his *Œuvres de J.-J. Rousseau*. In April 1779 he promised Rousseau's 'mémoires'. See *Gazette littéraire* 33 (23 April 1779), p.4, *CC*, xliii.234-35.
19. 'Lettre à Sophie', *CC*, xl.341.
20. On the 'democratic' aspects of the melodramatic literary form see Sarah Maza, 'Stories in history: cultural narratives in recent works in European history', *The American historical review* 101 (1996), p.1510-12.

During Girardin's description of the death scene, Thérèse either appears hysterical or else is made to fill a commonplace function such as opening the shutters for her husband to perceive the greenery of Ermenonville for the last time. The dying Rousseau reveals his serenity by consoling Thérèse: ' "Ma chère femme", lui répondit-il, avec une grande tranquillité, "j'ai toujours demandé à dieu, de mourir Sans maladie et sans médecin, et que vous puissiez me fermer les yeux. Mes vœux vont être exausés".' The pair offer one another mutual forgiveness, and Girardin makes certain to have Rousseau assure Thérèse that the marquis will protect the integrity of the writer's papers. Next Girardin reduces Thérèse to infant status by having Rousseau request that the marquis and marquise adopt her: ' "Je vous laisse entre leurs mains, et je compte assez sur leur amitié pour emporter avec moi, la douce certitude qu'ils voudront bien vous Servir de père et de mère".'[21]

As this section concludes, Girardin (man of action) replaces Thérèse (passive widow). The marquis creates Rousseau's final words to Thérèse, words which themselves would become canonised as the myth unfolded: ' "Voyez comme le ciel est pur […] il n'y a pas un seul nuage, ne voyez vous pas que la porte m'en est ouverte et que Dieu m'attend." '[22] As in Foulquier's account, Rousseau falls head first to the ground, pulling Thérèse with him; but this time the image is of chaos, not convergence. Thérèse screams for help; Girardin comes to the rescue. At first his efforts at resuscitation appear to bear fruit, but it is too late: 'Soins Superflus! Hélas! Cette mort si douce pour lui, et si fatale pour nous; cette perte irréparable était déjà consommée, et si Son exemple m'a appris à mourir, il ne m'a pas appris à me consoler de Sa mort.'[23] While Thérèse clings to the corpse, Girardin prepares Jean-Jacques's immortality. He arranges the autopsy, guaranteeing reports of a natural demise; he hires the sculptor Houdon to carve the death mask; he has the coffin built according to his specifications; he assures a proper Protestant burial on Ermenonville's île des Peupliers; and he erects a tomb graced by an epitaph which he himself composed:

> Ici, sous ces ombres paisibles,
> Pour les restes mortels de Jean Jacques Rousseau
> L'amitié posa ce tombeau:
> Mais c'est dans tous les cœurs Sensibles,
> que cet homme divin, qui fut tout Sentiment,
> doit trouver de son cœur l'éternel monument.[24]

Girardin consecrates the île des Peupliers: 'C'est une espèce de sanctuaire, qui semble formé par la nature même pour recevoir Son favori dans Son Sein.'[25] The ground is covered with verdant lawn, wildflowers grow beneath the poplars, the pond surrounding the island is calm and transparent. Rousseau's

21. 'Lettre à Sophie', *CC*, xl.343.
22. 'Lettre à Sophie', *CC*, xl.344.
23. 'Lettre à Sophie', *CC*, xl.344.
24. 'Lettre à Sophie', *CC*, xl.345.
25. 'Lettre à Sophie', *CC*, xl.345.

tomb itself is simple and starkly classical, in keeping with the occupant's character and morals. While Thérèse stalks the pond's outer banks, grieving and attempting to converse with Rousseau's ghost, Girardin recalls the sentiment of the dying Julie concerning the transmigration of souls: 'Et en effet il Semble que cette âme dont le dernier soupir fut celui de la bienfaisance et de l'amour, erre encore autour de ces ombrages épais pour s'y confondre dans celles de tous ceux qui viennent y rêver à la tendresse et à l'amitié.'[26]

Having laid claim to Rousseau's last days, mortal remains and shrine, Girardin concludes his 'Lettre à Sophie' with an interpretation of Jean-Jacques's life and work. Hoarding the unpublished manuscripts sequestered from Rousseau's study and writing desk, the marquis grants himself special licence to dig to the core: 'Les œuvres de génie rendent un homme immortel', Girardin writes, and it is the obligation of discipleship to transmit such messages to anticipating humanity. In time, publishing the *Collection complète* will provide Girardin with his opportunity. As preliminaries, a pithy explanation of Rousseau's literary legacy and moral genius will suffice.

For Girardin, Rousseau, more than any other writer, embodied what he created. He signed nearly everything, and as his persecutions woefully attest, he was held responsible for it all. 'Malheureusement pour lui son Style tout puissant, le rendit trop célèbre pour qu'on put lui pardonner dans un siècle où tout est esprit de parti, De n'être du parti de personne; ne voulant être d'aucune secte, tous les sectaires se mirent contre lui.'[27] Jealousy, and the despotism of both academicians and encyclopedists, dogged him. Unable to destroy his writings, his enemies tried to wreck his reputation. He was accused of practising the opposite of what he advocated; his simplicity was interpreted as affectation, his modesty as vanity, his poverty as pride. In other words, he was forced to endure a career whose meaning was at best misunderstood, at worst considered hypocritical. Fleeing churches and governments alike, Rousseau for Girardin was society's archetypal victim.

Why was this so, the marquis asks? Girardin locates the key in Rousseau's singular androgyny which made him appear incomprehensible to women and men alike. 'Il a été un être unique, que la nature n'avait pas encore présenté, et qu'elle ne représentera jamais; il réunissait en lui toutes les qualités morales des deux Sexes, jamais homme n'eût un jugement plus Sain, un génie plus profond, et une âme plus Sublime.'[28] The moral combinations working inside Rousseau produced what ordinary men could only consider puzzling and

---

26. 'Lettre à Sophie', *CC*, xl.346. See *La Nouvelle Héloïse*, sixième partie, lettre xiii, *OC*, ii.745.
27. 'Lettre à Sophie', *CC*, xl.346.
28. 'Lettre à Sophie', *CC*, xl.349. As time would reveal, Girardin's insights into Rousseau's character were hardly original and in fact were borrowed from the *Confessions*, which the marquis was surreptitiously reading. For example, in Book 1 of the *Confessions* Rousseau wrote: 'Telles furent les prémiéres affections de mon entrée à la vie; ainsi commençoit à se former ou à se montrer en moi ce cœur à la fois si fier et si tendre, ce caractére efféminé mais pourtant indomptable, qui flottant toujours entre la foiblesse et le courage, entre la mol[l]esse et la vertu, m'a jusqu'au bout mis en contradiction avec moi-même, et a fait que l'abstinence et la jouissance, le plaisir et la sagesse, m'ont egalement échappé' (*OC*, i.12).

contradictory traits.[29] Timid as a woman in returning injury, proud as a hero in refusing to betray his ideas, he was slow to respond and therefore was considered uncommunicative. His anger at times erupted in the manner of an impetuous male; but the slightest alarm sufficed to extinguish it, as would a tender female. As stormy as Rousseau's passions seemed, they were the consequence of his natural virtues. Irreconcilable contrasts of strength and weakness, violence and gentleness, defiance and confidence, boldness and timidity, laziness and energy, anger and *bonhomie* – according to Girardin, all churned within Jean-Jacques.

The marquis concludes that Rousseau argued in a manner Socrates would never have condoned. While the cool reason of the Athenian philosopher might reduce his antagonist to confusion, the petulant Jean-Jacques would use conviction to bombard his adversary. Then he would plead as a jealous lover who realises that he has unjustly offended his mistress. Rousseau's gifts were intuitive, not reasonable. Sentiment and passion were his guides:

C'est Sans doute à cette merveilleuse réunion dans le même individu d'une âme male et un cœur femelle, qu'est due cette magie de Son Style qui entraine par une attraction invincible et de laquelle aucun orateur n'a jamais approché, parce que le Sentiment de Son cœur brulant Sans cesse du feu de toutes les passions aimantes, ajoutait à l'énergie Sublime et majestueuse de Son âme, Cette persuasion pénétrante qui ne cherche point à convaincre, mais qui entraine; charme divin que possèdent Si bien les femmes, et qui est presque réfusé aux hommes.[30]

The mission of the *trois amis*

Girardin's analysis established the tone for *rousseauisme* as a moral challenge, inexplicable according to the rational game plan of male Paris intellectuals.[31] In other words, Rousseau's androgyny rendered him incomprehensible to the likes of Voltaire, Diderot, d'Alembert and Grimm. How could Hume, engulfed by the exclusively masculine atmosphere of whisky and tobacco smoke, ever have hoped to perceive anything but contradiction and malevolence in Jean-Jacques, the Scotsman's initial good intentions notwithstanding? Meanwhile Rousseau's female lovers, friends and acquaintances were no better prepared for understanding him than Hume. It would take a new generation, attuned to its own androgyny, to grasp intuitively the moral revolution offered by its epicene prophet.

This of course was asking for a good deal; and in securing his role as chief interpreter, Girardin resorted to baser tactics of control, vengeance and

29. This accusation of paradox, dominant in Rousseau's lifetime, has had a long critical history. See, for example, how it is employed in the virulently hostile interpretation of J. H. Huizinga, *The Making of a saint: the tragi-comedy of Jean-Jacques Rousseau* (London 1976).

30. 'Lettre à Sophie', *CC*, xl.350. On the androgynous romantic personality see Diane L. Hoeveler, *Romantic androgyny: the woman within* (University Park, Penn. 1990), p.1-23.

31. See Mark Hulliung, *The Autocritique of enlightenment: Rousseau and the philosophes* (Cambridge, Mass. 1994).

manipulation. Aware that Du Peyrou and Moultou might have claims to discipleship better honoured by time than his own, the marquis sought to head off their advantage by reminding potential rivals of Rousseau's alleged last words. For Du Peyrou's benefit, Girardin repeated the supposed instructions for Thérèse: ' "Ecoutés moi ma Chere femme ... Mes amis fidèles m'ont promis de ne point disposer de mes papiers sans votre aveu. M. de Gerardin voudra bien reclamer Leur parole et leur amitié; j'honore et je remercie M. et Mᵉ de Gerardin, je vous Laisse entre leurs mains, et je suis sur qu'ils vous serviront de pères".'[32] And from Thérèse's own hand, no doubt guided by the marquis: 'Non, ge noublierai gamais Ce que dieu ma oté, g'ai pardu en luy tout omonde mai il ma laissé a monsieur de Geraden Comme aun pere et sincere ami.'[33]

Initially Girardin's attempt to co-opt the heritage enjoyed success. Around 26 July F.-S. Ostervald of the Société typographique de Neuchâtel (STN) wrote to Du Peyrou, offering to publish a new edition of Rousseau's corpus, including the 'Seconde partie d'Emile & les mémoires de cet homme célèbre' reputedly still in manuscript. Noting that powerful people wished to prevent publication of the 'mémoires', Ostervald stated his belief that both works were in Du Peyrou's hands, or in the hands of others known to Du Peyrou. The publisher concluded by promising to make Thérèse a worthwhile offer for the manuscripts.[34] Ostervald failed to mention that standing behind him was the Paris press lord C.-J. Panckoucke, ostensibly prepared to offer Thérèse 30 000 *livres* for her inheritance.[35] Du Peyrou replied that he was ignorant of Rousseau's intentions concerning the writer's manuscripts, that the papers rightfully belonged to Thérèse and that Girardin was the one authorised to pass on to the widow whatever proposals the STN wished to make.[36] Ostervald followed up by addressing his offer to Girardin.[37]

Concerning Moultou, Girardin's tactics were much cruder than those he had employed with Du Peyrou. The marquis was aware that just prior to the move to Ermenonville, Rousseau had given Moultou some manuscripts, and Girardin suspected that these included the *Confessions*. All of literary Europe knew that the *Confessions* existed somewhere. In 1770 and 1771 Rousseau had provided a foretaste of what to expect with his public readings of them in Paris and at the comtesse d'Egmont's country house, until Mme d'Epinay asked the police to bring those sessions to an end.[38] Even before that, fears of their

32. Girardin to Du Peyrou, 22 July 1778, *CC*, xli.62.
33. Marie-Thérèse Levassur to Du Peyrou, [22 July 1778], *CC*, xli.65.
34. Frédéric-Samuel Ostervald to Du Peyrou, [26 July 1778], *CC*, xli.71-73.
35. Charles-Joseph Panckoucke to the STN, 21 July 1778, *CC*, xli.50.
36. Du Peyrou to Ostervald, 27 July 1778, *CC*, xli.74-75.
37. The STN to Girardin, [28 July 1778], *CC*, xli.82-85.
38. Charles-Joseph Dorat to Marie-Anne-Françoise Mouchard, comtesse de Beauharnais[?], [early December 1770], originally published in the *Année littéraire* 4 (20 July 1771), p.210-14, and later in the *Journal de Paris* (9 August 1778), *CC*, xxxviii.154-58; Sophie-Jeanne de Vignerod Du Plessis de Richelieu, comtesse d'Egmont, to King Gustav III of Sweden, 8 May 1771, *CC*, xxxviii.227-28; Louise-Florence de La Live d'Epinay to Antoine-Raymond de Sartine, 10 [May

publication had persuaded David Hume to print his ill-advised *Concise and genuine account of the dispute between Mr Hume and Mr Rousseau* (1766).[39] Immediately following Rousseau's death the *Mémoires secrets* attributed to Bachaumont mentioned the concerns of one-time encyclopedists over possible publication of the *Confessions*; for, invaluable as they might be as Rousseau's ultimate psychological striptease, they also were thought to contain terrible indictments of those who had wounded him.[40] For their scandal value if for nothing else, there was significant public interest in having them printed.[41] Girardin considered it imperative that he alone decide when and where that might be accomplished.

The marquis's strategy when addressing Moultou was to adopt an aggressive, even belligerent, air. In an angry letter Girardin accused the society-loving former pastor of near infidelity towards the Master. According to Girardin, Moultou had never acknowledged the marquis's original announcement of Rousseau's death, and while in Paris had failed to visit Ermenonville. Alluding to the manuscripts that Rousseau had given Moultou, Girardin threatened: 'Le depot ne vous a eté confié qu'a La Condition expresse qu'il ne [put] etre jamais rendu Public que longtems après La mort de celuy qui vous l'a confié et après celle de toutes les personnes Interessées. Si vous etes jamais Capable d'y manquer ce seroit a moy depositaire de ses derniers moments a venger sa memoire.'[42]

Though Girardin thought better of mailing his stern warning, he most probably sent a toned-down version (now lost), which excluded the caution concerning the *Confessions*. Around 26 August Moultou contritely responded that he had not visited Ermenonville while in Paris because he had been called back precipitously to Geneva. He showered Girardin with exaggerated flattery: 'C'etait un hoᷡe, c'etait le dernier protecteur du grand & malheureux Rousseau que je Souhaitais surtout de coñaitre, c'etait dans Son Sein que je voulais pleurer un ami que j'aimerai jusqu'a mon dernier Soupir.'[43] Reviewing what he claimed to know of Rousseau's manuscripts, Moultou refused to acknowledge that he possessed the *Confessions*. He wrote that Rousseau had remitted 'ses memoires', along with the 'Dialogues' [*Rousseau juge de Jean-Jacques*], to a Paris academician, of whose name he was unaware.[44]

1771], first published in [Louis-]Pierre Manuel, *La Police de Paris dévoilée* (1791), i.97-98, *CC*, xxxviii.228-30.

39. See, for example, Hume's explanation to the comtesse de Boufflers, 15 July 1766, *CC*, xxx.94-97.

40. [Attributed to Louis Petit de Bachaumont], *Mémoires secrets pour servir à l'histoire de la République des lettres en France depuis M.DCC.LXII jusqu'à nos jours, ou Journal d'un observateur*, 36 vols (1780), xii.65 (1 August 1778).

41. Jean Ranson to Ostervald, 1 August 1778, *CC*, xli.108-109.

42. Draft, Girardin to Moultou, [2 August 1778], *CC*, xli.113-14.

43. Moultou to Girardin, [26 August 1778], *CC*, xli.235.

44. Rousseau had sent a copy of *Rousseau juge de Jean-Jacques*, but not the *Confessions*, to abbé de Condillac.

Less than a month after Rousseau's death it became clear to Girardin that the most appropriate means of propagating the philosopher's message and codifying his cult was through the medium of print: namely by publishing an edition of Rousseau's collected works that would consign to the ash-heap all the unauthorised ones which had appeared over the previous two decades.[45] Because he still possessed Rousseau's manuscripts for the aborted Môtiers edition of 1765 and because he held papers that Rousseau subsequently had sent to him, Du Peyrou was a necessary collaborator. Though Girardin distrusted Moultou, who was far too comfortable in the company of aristocratic Frenchwomen and Paris encyclopedists, the Genevan had been identified by Rousseau as his last literary executor and therefore could not be ignored. As a front for obtaining manuscripts which were scattered from Poland to England, Thérèse would be essential as well.

There was little time to lose. Besides Panckoucke and the STN, Marc-Michel Rey also was trying to track down the *Confessions*.[46] Boubers of Brussels was after them, and soon too would be Marie-Antoinette Duchesne, widow of the Paris bookseller who had bought *Emile* for 6000 *livres* in 1762 and had undertaken the mislabelled 'Neuchâtel' edition of collected works during Rousseau's lifetime. In addition journalists, considered by Girardin as models of literary irresponsibility, were seizing upon leaks. On 20 July editor Guillaume Olivier de Corancez had published in his *Journal de Paris* Rousseau's circular letter to his friends, dated February 1777, stating his desire to seek a new home. Corancez appended to the letter the coroner's report of the writer's death.[47] This angered Girardin, who protested the publication of private documents without Thérèse's permission.[48] But the marquis's irritation was nothing compared to his fury upon reading the preface to Rousseau's *Confessions* themselves in the 30 July number of Corancez's newspaper.[49] Exploding, Girardin prepared a complaint to Paris police lieutenant J.-C.-P. Le Noir, but then thought better than to send it.[50] Instead he wrote hurt notes both to Corancez and to the journalist's father-in-law, Jean Romilly, Rousseau's old acquaintance.[51] And he began his own quest for manuscripts.

---

45. In his work on *rousseauismes* Roger Barny has ignored the *Collection complète*. Years ago Bernard Gagnebin introduced the history of the edition as worthy of further study. See 'L'héritage littéraire de Rousseau', in *Rousseau after 200 years: proceedings of the Cambridge bicentennial colloquium*, ed. R. A. Leigh (Cambridge 1982), p.151-81. See as well Raymond Birn, 'Rousseau et ses éditeurs', *Revue d'histoire moderne et contemporaine* 41 (1993), p.127-36; 'Rousseau senza frontiere', *Rivista storica italiana* 107 (1995), p.575-613; and 'Les "œuvres complètes" de Rousseau', p.229-62.

46. Marc-Michel Rey to Girardin, [16 July 1778], *CC*, xli.31-33.

47. *Remarque* ii, *CC*, xli.48-49.

48. Draft, Girardin to Guillaume Olivier de Corancez, [*c*. 25 July 1778], *CC*, xli.70-71.

49. François Moureau, 'Les inédits et la campagne de presse de 1778', *Dix-huitième siècle* 12 (1980), p.411-23.

50. Incomplete draft, Girardin to Jean-Pierre-Charles Le Noir, [*c*. 1 August 1778], *CC*, xli.112-13.

51. Girardin to Guillaume Olivier de Corancez, 2 August 1778, *CC*, xli.114-15; Girardin to Jean Romilly, 2 August 1778, *CC*, xli.115-16.

II. *The 'trois amis' and the widow Rousseau*

As a consequence of interrogating Thérèse, Girardin tracked down several copies of *Rousseau juge de Jean-Jacques*, the savage semi-autobiographical dialogues whose manuscript the writer had unsuccessfully tried to deposit on the altar of Notre-Dame cathedral on 24 February 1776. Rousseau knew at the time that publishing the dialogues was out of the question, but he had made several manuscript copies and distributed them. Etienne Bonnot, abbé de Condillac, possessed the original; Charles-Claude Flahaut de La Billarderie, comte d'Angiviller, director general of royal buildings, had another copy; a young Englishman, Brooke Boothby, who had visited Rousseau in April 1776, held part of a third manuscript ('Dialogue I'). What Girardin did not yet know was that a fourth copy was in the hands of Moultou.

Early in August Girardin wrote to Condillac, d'Angiviller and Boothby, stating that he had been authorised by Rousseau to look after Thérèse's interests, which included publication of her husband's manuscripts; and he urged his correspondents to forswear printing on their own any that they might be holding.[52] Girardin was particularly worried about Boothby. For the Englishman's benefit, in his fractured English, the marquis invented the tale of Rousseau's 'Constant Intentions and any man who would presently Intend to print any writing of him without the formal consent and Interest of his widow would be the rob[b]er of the widow's penny.'[53] For his part Boothby ignored Girardin's plea as well as the marquis's claims to exclusive discipleship. In June 1780 the Englishman published his manuscript, nearly two years before the complete *Rousseau juge de Jean-Jacques* appeared in the *Collection complète*.[54]

Meanwhile Girardin sought out other items, including Rousseau's music, for which he hoped to open a separate subscription on Thérèse's behalf. This led him to correspond with Rousseau's English hosts of 1766/67, especially Count George Simon Harcourt and the Davenport family. The marquis asked Harcourt to make certain that *Les Muses galantes* and other pieces of music remained secure until it was time to send them to Ermenonville to be engraved.[55]

Faced with Girardin's seizure of Rousseau's literary heritage, Du Peyrou initially abandoned any claim he once might have had to it. In a letter to Moultou, dated 5 August, the Neuchâtel millionaire recalled the particularly poignant moments of his fourteen-year association with the writer. The most tragic event, Du Peyrou's delirious accusation of attempted murder at Trye in 1767, had tolled the knell of their intimacy. Rousseau cooled towards his disciple and benefactor; and though their relationship remained correct in the

52. Draft, Girardin to Charles-Claude Flahut de La Billarderie, comte d'Angiviller[?], [early August 1778], *CC*, xli.122-25; draft, Girardin to Etienne Bonnot, abbé de Condillac[?], [early August 1778], *CC*, xli.125-26; draft in English, Girardin to Brooke Boothby, [early August 1778], *CC*, xli.126-28.
53. Girardin to Boothby, *CC*, xli.126.
54. *Rousseau juge de Jean-Jacques, dialogues, premier dialogue*, d'après le manuscrit de M. Rousseau, laissé entre les mains de M. Brooke Boothby, à Lichfield, chez J. Jackson, aux dépens de l'éditeur, et se vend à Londres chez Dodsley, Cadell, Elmsley, et Strahan, in-8° (1780).
55. Girardin to George Simon Harcourt, 30 July 1778, *CC*, xli.101-103.

years that followed, the passion which had heretofore accompanied it was gone. Most significantly, according to Du Peyrou, because of the Trye incident, the earlier arrangement he had made with Rousseau to publish the writer's collected works for an annuity of 1600 *livres* had been abrogated.[56] In his letter to Moultou, Du Peyrou abandoned rights to the papers in his possession, or to any other of Rousseau's works. Crippled by gout and depressed by a hearing disability, Du Peyrou blamed his estrangement from the Master upon Rousseau's misfortunes, the writer's mistrust and Thérèse's jealousy. But he was willing to join Moultou and Girardin in the *Collection complète* project and proposed a meeting of the three collaborators, 'pour prendre des mesures convenables à la memoire de Rousseau et à l'avantage de sa Veuve'.[57]

The third of the *amis*, Paul-Claude Moultou of Geneva, had known Rousseau the longest. Moultou had initiated their correspondence in 1758 and become an intimate friend in the early 1760s. Their relationship was closely linked to Genevan politics and cooled during the years immediately preceding Rousseau's death, owing largely to Moultou's courtship of encyclopedist acquaintances whom Rousseau detested. Nevertheless, Moultou's visit to Paris in spring 1778 had produced a reconciliation of sorts, and Rousseau handed the one-time Protestant minister several packages of manuscripts for safekeeping, just prior to the journey to Ermenonville. While Girardin seized command over the proposed edition of Rousseau's works and Du Peyrou lamented what might have been, Moultou appeared uncomfortable as a partner in the project. His reluctance was based, at least in part, upon his social pretensions, his aristocratic lady friends no longer needing to consider the dead Rousseau as an embellishment to their households or reputations. Girardin himself would have preferred not to associate Moultou with the sacred enterprise. Fearing, however, that the Genevan might make unacceptable use of the papers confided to him by Rousseau if left out, the marquis knew that he had to collaborate with Moultou. As the writer's remaining acknowledged literary executor, Moultou agreed to compose a eulogy for the edition. Though unaware of exactly what pieces Moultou held, Girardin nevertheless dropped broad hints to Du Peyrou that the former pastor was fondling the most valuable manuscript of all, that of the *Confessions*.[58]

The *trois amis* concurred that they must meet shortly to take inventory of the manuscripts, select a publisher and decide upon Thérèse's compensation. They accepted Du Peyrou's invitation to gather at his newly constructed mansion in Neuchâtel early in September 1778. Then delays ensued. Moultou begged to wait until mid-month because he was entertaining the duchesse d'Anville.[59] Girardin claimed that the French government was

56. See 'Etat de mes affaires avec M. du Peyrou', [16 November 1767], *CC*, xxxiv.174-76.
57. Du Peyrou to Moultou, 5 August 1778, *CC*, xli.135.
58. Girardin to Du Peyrou, 11 August 1778, *CC*, xli.158-59; Girardin to Du Peyrou, 5 September 1778, *CC*, xli.259-60.
59. Moultou to Girardin, [26 August 1778], *CC*, xli.234-36.

withholding his passport.[60] Plans to have Thérèse and the marquise accompany him were scrapped on account of the advancing season, and then Girardin decided that he could not leave the women at home by themselves. Subsequently the marquis requested postponement of the meeting until the following spring, and he sought to neutralise Moultou by dropping upon Du Peyrou the not very subtle hint as to what the Genevan was holding: 'L'unique et precieux dépôt dont il est chargé Conformément aux Intentions de L'ami qui Le luy a remis avec La plus extreme Confiance.'[61] Meanwhile, as he began opening the packages which he had held in safekeeping for Rousseau over the past dozen years, Du Peyrou made a startling discovery. He informed Moultou (but not Girardin): 'Un des paquets renferme le 1er volume de ses *Confessions*, contenant les 3 premiers Livres et le commencement du 4me ainsi que les liasses des piéces justificatives.'[62]

During the next twelve months the dynamics of the edition took shape. From Ermenonville, where he was holding Thérèse under virtual house arrest, Girardin established his court, transforming his property into the shrine, accompanying visitors to the hallowed tomb, editing Rousseau's papers according to his fancy and scouring Europe for additional manuscripts. In Neuchâtel an ailing Du Peyrou laboured through the papers in his possession, attempting to make sense of Rousseau's corrections, erasures and emendations, guided by a self-proclaimed principle of utter editorial fidelity to the writer's intent. In Geneva Moultou concentrated upon locating investors. In the ensuing correspondence Du Peyrou sensed that the irrepressible Girardin was creating a personal and distorted image of Rousseau, and he conveyed his concerns to Moultou. Meanwhile Girardin tried to frustrate the coalescing of a Moultou–Du Peyrou alliance by warning the Neuchâtel businessman of the Genevan's affinity for encyclopedists, Paris high society and other enemies of the project.

All through the drama the issue of the *Confessions*, as well as their place in the proposed edition, assumed larger proportions. It was in September 1778 that Du Peyrou revealed to Moultou the existence of Books I to III and part of Book IV; shortly thereafter Moultou would confide to Du Peyrou that he possessed Books I to VI. Yet was that all there was? It was common knowledge that Rousseau had written more of his 'mémoires' than was being acknowledged and Girardin doubted Moultou's candour as to what the Genevan was holding. And what of the marquis himself? With his invention of Rousseau's last words, detention of Rousseau's widow and obsessive appropriation of the heritage, how far could he be trusted?

60. Girardin to Du Peyrou, 29 August 1778, *CC*, xli.242-43.
61. Girardin to Du Peyrou, 5 September 1778, *CC*, xli.259-60.
62. Du Peyrou to Moultou, 2 September 1778, *CC*, xli.249. In a letter to Moultou, dated 5 December, Du Peyrou described his manuscript: '[Il] est in 4° cartonné en papier marbré, et contient 182 p. d'écrites' (see *CC*, xlii.191). This is the so-called 'manuscrit de Neuchâtel', which, after Du Peyrou's death in 1795, entered the municipal library of that city: Ms. R. 17. Its introduction is more developed than that of the definitive edition. Théophile Dufour published the entire Neuchâtel manuscript in the *Annales de la Société Jean-Jacques Rousseau* 4 (1908), p.1-276.

Publishing wars

While the proposed meeting of the *trois amis* continued to be postponed, a considerable amount of time was spent manoeuvring with potential publishers. Back in July Marc-Michel Rey, Rousseau's much abused publisher of record, had written to Girardin acknowledging the marquis's report of the author's death and stating his interest in the 'mémoires'.[63] Rey then inquired of Thérèse as to which manuscripts she might be holding.[64] On 8 August Girardin responded on Thérèse's behalf, informing Rey that he, Girardin, was gathering Rousseau's papers, scattered as they were throughout Europe, with the intention of publishing a comprehensive edition for the widow's benefit. Cagily Girardin wrote: 'vous devés etre bien persuadé Monsieur, que ses sentiments pour vous aussi que les miens, nous porteront bien volontiers a vous donner touttes sortes de preference'. Girardin added: 'Quant à L'ecrit particulier dont vous nous parlés [the *Confessions*] il est en paiis etranger si tant est qu'il existe encor.' Then the marquis repeated what would become his litany concerning the *Confessions*: 'L'intention formelle de M. Rousseau a été que dans aucun Cas il ne put paroitre que longtems après sa mort et Celle de touttes Les Personnes interessées.' Girardin underscored that this was Rousseau's 'Condition expresse'. The marquis concluded that he knew the identity of the possessor of the manuscript in question: 'et Si jamais il venoit a trahir La Confiance de L'amitié Ce Seroit une Infamie de la quelle j'aime encor à penser qu'il n'y a point d'homme qui fut Capable'.[65]

Although Du Peyrou eventually would consult Rey on publication strategies and offer him Dutch distribution rights for the *Collection complète*, the publisher who had built his fortune upon the first editions of the second *Discours*, the *Lettre à d'Alembert*, *La Nouvelle Héloïse*, *Du contrat social*, the *Lettre à Christophe de Beaumont* and the *Lettres écrites de la montagne*, as well as several unauthorised editions of collected works, was in no mood to undertake the grand project. In 1778 he was mourning the recent deaths of his wife and daughter; the latter was Rousseau's godchild, whom the writer had never seen. Rey was tired, his career was nearly over and he had no wish to follow up his initial inquiries aggressively.[66]

On the other hand, a second name from Rousseau's past now surfaced: Marie-Antoinette Duchesne, widow of Nicolas-Bonaventure who had undertaken the ill-fated *Emile* and begun the nine-volume *Œuvres* in-duodecimo and in-octavo.[67] Shortly after Rousseau's death veuve Duchesne contacted Lebègue de Presle in Paris. She informed the physician that, by virtue of an agreement with Rousseau made by her husband and his late associate, Pierre

---

63. Marc-Michel Rey to Girardin, [16 July 1778], *CC*, xli.31-32.
64. Rey to Marie-Thérèse Levasseur, 28 July 1778, *CC*, xli.77-78.
65. Girardin to Rey, 8 August 1778, *CC*, xli.144.
66. Rey would die in June 1780.
67. Dufour, *Recherches*, ii.6-13. Duchesne died in 1765. His associate Pierre Guy and his widow completed publication of the *Œuvres*.

Guy, the Duchesne heirs had first preference to all published and unpublished works of the author.[68] When notified by Lebègue of the Duchesne ultimatum, Girardin began an immediate search through the correspondence left by Rousseau for any reference to its source. He found nothing. Intimidated by the widow Duchesne, however, Lebègue created a scenario whereby he imagined being hauled into court and charged with breach of contract. His reasoning was as follows. For fourteen years the Duchesnes had provided Rousseau with a pension of 300 *livres* per annum. According to Lebègue, this represented a sort of guarantee for rights to all the collected works. Now, at Girardin's behest, the doctor had just persuaded veuve Duchesne to transfer the sum to Thérèse. Therefore, Lebègue concluded, to deny veuve Duchesne the definitive collective edition, especially when her house had published the most nearly authorised one during Rousseau's lifetime, smacked of betrayal. The doctor believed that Thérèse's greed lay behind Girardin's reluctance to honour veuve Duchesne's claim, and he insisted that Rousseau's widow possessed moral title to nothing.[69]

Girardin responded with a flat rejection of veuve Duchesne's demand. According to the marquis, while ceding his individual manuscripts to publishers, Rousseau never renounced rights to an edition of his collected works. Alluding to a mysterious secret that he and Lebègue alone possessed, Girardin added that he would pursue a strategy of responding vaguely to publishers' inquiries concerning the anticipated general edition, that he would gather the scattered manuscripts and then would decide what to print separately or together.[70] In practice the marquis played the game of encouraging all interested parties and of anticipating a bidding war among them. Aware that piracies of the edition, or of the heretofore unpublished parts of it, were a certainty, he felt no need to be overly scrupulous.[71] When the Société typographique de Neuchâtel inquired about the manuscripts reputedly in Thérèse's hands, stretching veracity to its limit by asserting Du Peyrou's recommendation and announcing a wish to publish,[72] Girardin responded in

68. In Lebègue's view Rousseau's sale to N.-B. Duchesne of *La Nouvelle Héloïse* with the 'préface dialoguée' back in 1761 appeared to give the Paris publisher first printing privileges to a general edition. Such claims were alluded to ambiguously when Rousseau sold the manuscript of *Emile* to Duchesne (see above, chapter 2, p.33). By no means, however, did Rousseau ever consider them to represent an iron-clad agreement.

69. Achille-G. Lebègue de Presle to Girardin, 14 [August 1778], *CC*, xli.170-77. In attempting to recreate Rousseau's dealings with the Duchesnes, Girardin apparently obtained the original contract for *Emile* and had his secretary copy it (see *CC*, ix.371). The marquis interpreted the contract as leaving Rousseau free to renegotiate the sale of *Emile* for an edition of collected works after a three-year period, with N.-B. Duchesne having first bidding privileges.

70. Girardin to Lebègue de Presle, 20 August 1778, *CC*, xli.189-93.

71. Frédéric-Samuel Ostervald, director of the STN, reminded Du Peyrou of his own intentions quite clearly if he were unable to secure a role in publishing the collective edition: 'Au reste Si nous arrivons à tard, il nous restera une ressource; nous contreferons bravement & pour rien. Cependant nous aimerions mieux pour une aussi bonne affaire, aller devant les autres & payer' (Ostervald to Du Peyrou, [28 July 1778,] *CC*, xli.81).

72. STN [F.-S. Ostervald] to Girardin, [28 July 1778], *CC*, xli.82-85.

an encouraging though non-committal manner. As for the *Confessions*, the marquis noted that Rousseau's intentions were to keep them from being printed, that Thérèse intended to honour her husband's wishes and that the work probably was in a foreign country.[73] As director of the STN, F.-S. Ostervald shared Girardin's letter with Du Peyrou. Ostervald expressed surprise at the marquis's reluctance to see the *Confessions* published, since this represented the work of Rousseau's which the public was most curious to read. Ostervald doubted whether Thérèse could hope to reap much profit from any sale of Rousseau's manuscripts which excluded the *Confessions*, and he did not believe that a publisher would undertake an edition without them.[74] After all, in 1778 there already were half a dozen so-called editions of Rousseau's collected or 'diverses' works circulating, not including piracies.[75] Ostervald's observation had an immediate effect upon Du Peyrou, who, the following month, proposed to Girardin the incorporation of Books I to VI (Part I) of the *Confessions* in the edition proposed by the *trois amis*. He of course was addressing the manuscript in Moultou's possession. Du Peyrou kept the Genevan's confidence, refusing to identify him to Girardin as holder of the *Confessions*, Part I. Instead he simply informed the marquis that a third party had offered the manuscript under condition that it be restored to its anonymous owner following publication: 'Vous Sentés vous mème Monsieur, combien ce morceau haussera lés offres á recevoir dés Entrepreneurs de l'Edition, et le danger que refusé par nous, le possesseur anonyme ne se determine á le faire paroitre lui mème.'[76]

Girardin raised no objection to Du Peyrou's proposal, though again he could not resist hinting that he knew the identity of the manuscript's possessor. His surprising co-operation allegedly was based upon Du Peyrou's assurance that Part I of the *Confessions* concluded with Rousseau's arrival in Paris in 1742 and therefore was unlikely to injure any living person. Furthermore, Girardin feared that a publisher unknown to him might gain access to Moultou's manuscript or, what was yet worse, to a manuscript of which the *trois amis* were unaware. For example, a rumour circulated that Samuel Fauche of Neuchâtel had acquired the *Confessions* and was about to publish them.[77] A more likely

---

73. Girardin to the STN, 8 August 177[8], *CC*, xli.142-43. Girardin's reply assuredly contained a touch of irony. Ostervald, the STN's director, had been no ally of Rousseau's during the Môtiers persecution in 1765. In subsequent years all of Ostervald's attempts at reconciliation with Rousseau were shunned. See R. A. Leigh, 'Une balle qu'il eût fallu saisir au bond. Frédéric-Samuel Ostervald et l'édition des *Œuvres* de Rousseau (1778-1779)', in *Aspects du livre neuchâtelois*, ed. Jacques Rychner and Michel Schlup (Neuchâtel 1986), p.89-90.

74. F.-S. Ostervald to Du Peyrou, [20 August 1778], *CC*, xli.197-98.

75. These included four by Rey (1762, 1767, 1769 and 1772); one by Duchesne and his widow (1764-1769); one by Samuel Fauche of Neuchâtel (1775); and one by J.-L. de Boubers of Brussels (1774-1776). The most accurate editions were the *Œuvres de J.-J. Rousseau, de Genève* (Amsterdam, Marc-Michel Rey 1769); the *Œuvres de M. Rousseau de Genève* (Neuchâtel [Paris and Amsterdam, Duchesne] 1764-1769); and the *Collection complète des œuvres de J.-J. Rousseau* (London [Brussels, J.-L. de Boubers] 1774-1776).

76. Du Peyrou to Girardin, 27 September 1778, *CC*, xli.300.

77. Barthélemy Chirol to the STN, 4 August 1778, *CC*, xli.130.

culprit than Fauche was Boubers of Brussels, who had recently placed heretofore unpublished letters from Rousseau to Mme de Warens in the eighth
volume of his *Collection complète*.[78] Boubers had few scruples about how he
might acquire Rousseau documents and he was not beyond lying in print
that he was also holding a manuscript of the *Confessions*.[79]

Once the STN became aware that Part I of the *Confessions* would appear in
the edition proposed by the *trois amis*, Ostervald initiated an all-out campaign
to secure publication preference.[80] His tactics, however, were crudely inept
and cost him the goodwill of both Du Peyrou and Girardin. On the one hand
he behaved as though he had no competition, and on the other he played the
role of a bully dealing with inexperienced amateurs. First Ostervald wanted
public guarantees from Thérèse and the *trois amis* that all remaining Rousseau
manuscripts (even those not in their possession) would be remitted to the
STN. Then he demanded that the most valuable piece of all, 'la partie des
mémoires qu'on ne juge pas convenable de publier présentement', be sealed
and placed with Du Peyrou for safekeeping, so as to prevent Thérèse or
anyone else from selling it.[81] Finally Ostervald stated the price he would pay:
10 000 *livres* or an annual pension for Thérèse of 600 *livres*.[82]

It is instructive to note that the STN's price was 6700 *livres* less than what
Rousseau had received for the seven manuscripts he had sold between April
1755 and December 1764; it was 9000 *livres* less than what the Lyon publisher
Réguillat and the STN itself had offered Rousseau in 1764 for an edition of
collected works; and it was 6000 *livres* less than what Du Peyrou had proposed
the following year.[83] Furthermore, Du Peyrou's revised honorarium for
Rousseau, the pension he had paid the writer in 1766 and 1767, had come to
2400 *livres* per annum.[84] Aware of this history, Girardin considered Ostervald's offer to be inadequate. As Thérèse's self-designated representative, the
marquis believed that, excluding the *Confessions* (Part I) and correspondence,
the collection was worth at least 24 000 *livres*.[85]

---

78. Girardin to Du Peyrou, 8 October 1778, *CC*, xlii.8.

79. See, for example, Boubers's announcement in the *Gazette de Leyde* 33 (23 April 1779), p.4, of
the appearance of Rousseau's *Confessions*, correspondence, 'ouvrage sur la Pologne' and other
pieces in the Brussels publisher's forthcoming *Œuvres posthumes*. Of course what Boubers was
alluding to was no rare manuscript discovery but rather his anticipated piracy of the *trois amis*
edition (*CC*, xliii.234).

80. Around 20 October Du Peyrou sent the STN a draft of the proposed contents of the
edition of collected works. Among the unpublished pieces were '3me. Sur la Constitution de
Pologne, 4°. Les 6 premiers Livres dés *Confessions*, 5me. Quatre lettres à Mr de Mallesherbes,
[...] 7me. Les Reveries de promeneur Solitaire' (Du Peyrou to the STN, [20 October 1778], *CC*,
xlii.46.

81. STN [F.-S. Ostervald] to Du Peyrou, [*c.* 21 October 1778], *CC*, xlii.49-50.

82. STN [F.-S. Ostervald] to Du Peyrou, [*c.* 23 October 1778], *CC*, xlii.53.

83. Girardin to Du Peyrou, 13 November 1778, *CC*, xlii.116-23; Du Peyrou to Moultou,
28 November 1778, *CC*, xlii.168-72.

84. Rousseau to Du Peyrou, [10 November 1767], *CC*, xxxiv.174-76.

85. Girardin to Du Peyrou, 13 November 1778, *CC*, xlii.118.

Girardin's views notwithstanding, Ostervald continued to behave as though he held all the cards. He doubted whether negotiations could proceed until it was confirmed that Thérèse actually possessed a manuscript of the *Confessions*.[86] The STN's attitude infuriated Du Peyrou, who at the same time worried about unknown manuscripts getting into the hands of unscrupulous publishers, especially those who had made general editions of their own in recent years; 'je crains la piraterie des Libraires, dont l'avidité fomente lés infidélités les plus odieuses', Du Peyrou wrote to Girardin.[87] Of all the existing publishers, Boubers was the one preferred by Du Peyrou, who considered the Belgian's in-quarto edition to be the most attractive presently on the market. The Neuchâtel millionaire also believed, however, that it was essential to proceed cautiously rather than rush into a financially unsatisfactory project forced upon the *trois amis* by an avaricious publisher. Du Peyrou wrote to Moultou: 'Il me semble donc que le seul parti à prendre, est celui de nous rendre maitres de l'Edition generale, soit pour le choix des piéces, soit pour celui du tems, sans nous mettre à découvert, et sans compromettre lés interets de la Veuve.'[88]

For once taking the initiative, Du Peyrou proposed a strategy to Girardin. Because so many publishers were trying to complete their own general editions with whatever manuscripts they could lay their hands on, it was imperative to beat them to the draw, without, however, committing oneself to a hastily conceived and unsound project. Du Peyrou suggested, therefore, that the *trois amis* precede their grand edition with a limited one of two volumes, subscribed to for Thérèse's profit. It was to contain the works most likely to be pirated from circulating manuscripts, namely the *Confessions* (Part I) and the *Considérations sur le gouvernement de Pologne*. Manuscripts of the *Considérations* in fact were in the hands of both Girardin and Moultou. To these pieces Du Peyrou would add the *Discours sur la vertu la plus nécessaire aux héros*, also in Moultou's hands, in order to counter the unfaithful published versions circulating.[89] Finally, a preface to the small edition should announce the larger general one. This would be the most appropriate means of advertising the *Collection complète* and of buying time for careful negotiations with potential publishers of it.[90]

Occupied with his own manuscript hunt, with a separate edition of Rousseau's music that he wished to engrave, and obsessively worried about the emergence of Rousseau's blood relatives who might challenge Thérèse's claim to the literary heritage, Girardin greeted Du Peyrou's proposal coolly. Within a week, however, there appeared on the scene a fresh element: a trio of

---

86. STN [F.-S. Ostervald] to Du Peyrou, [27 October 1778], *CC*, xlii.58-59.
87. Du Peyrou to Girardin, 29 October 1778, *CC*, xlii.65.
88. Du Peyrou to Moultou, 4 November 1778, *CC*, xlii.95.
89. 'Discours […] qui n'a point encore été imprimé, sur cette question: quelle est la vertu la plus nécessaire aux héros, et quels sont les héros, à qui cette vertu a manqué?', *Année littéraire* 7 (14 October 1768), p.4-27; republished without Rousseau's permission (Amsterdam [Lausanne] 1769). See *OC*, ii.1262-74.
90. Du Peyrou to Girardin, 12 November 1778, *CC*, xlii.111-13.

potential publishers who would lay to rest Du Peyrou's spectre of losing the project to cunning, seasoned money-grubbers, all prepared to soil this noblest of testaments with their naked greed. By way of contrast, the partners in the freshly established Société typographique de Genève (STG) were young, inexperienced and enthusiastic. One was the twenty-one-year-old François d'Ivernois (1757-1842), whose father, a veteran of Geneva's *représentant* political party, had been one of Rousseau's champions during the 1760s. The second was the twenty-three-year-old lawyer Pierre Boin (1755-1815), who stemmed from a Genevan family of artisans and achieved bourgeois status during the mass promotion of June 1770. The third, Jean-François Bassompierre (1748-after 1794), at the age of thirty, was senior partner. Descended from a family of Liégeois booksellers, Bassompierre was the most seasoned of the trio.

The Société typographique de Genève had been founded on 1 October 1778, acquired printing equipment from the de Tournes publishing family and only became officially registered as a corporation in January 1779.[91] It was probably Moultou who proposed the Société to Du Peyrou and Girardin. Its lack of experience was both worrisome and a blessing. As publisher of the *Collection complète*, however, it could guarantee that the *trois amis* would not lose control over their project. Moultou could keep an eye on the activity of the Société and the young publishers were not inclined to haggle over the price of the manuscripts. Then too there was the delicious irony of having Genevans undertake the edition. The veteran bookseller Gabriel Cramer (Voltaire's 'caro Gabriele') was willing to advise the Société typographique de Genève and invest in its project. Moultou and possibly Du Peyrou would sink money into it as well. Best news of all was that Geneva seemed prepared at last to atone for the injustices and persecutions it had inflicted upon its most celebrated son. The city government promised the Société a *permission tacite* prior to publication and Du Peyrou was ecstatic. Dropping his idea of publishing the small edition, he informed Moultou of the pleasure he felt that Geneva would be the site of the *Collection complète*: 'Certainement c'est de tous les lieux, celui que pour l'honneur de la memoire de nôtre ami, je prefererois.'[92]

But the STN refused to withdraw gracefully. Learning of Girardin's terms of 24 000 *livres* minimum, it suddenly reversed position and offered that sum without argument, removing every one of its impossible demands in the process. The STN simply asked Du Peyrou to do all he could to prevent a rival publisher from printing Part II of the *Confessions* while Part I still was on sale, and it urged diligence during the production period.[93] But the Neuchâtel offer came too late and it was left to Girardin to break the bad news to Ostervald.[94] In response the STN pretended that Girardin's original answer of 8 August had suggested preliminary acceptance, and with consider-

91. *Remarque, CC*, xlii.171-72.
92. Du Peyrou to Moultou, 28 November 1778, *CC*, lxii.169.
93. Copy prepared by Du Peyrou's secretary and inserted into a letter from Du Peyrou to Girardin, STN to Du Peyrou, [November 1778], *CC*, xlii.182-86.
94. Girardin to F.-S. Ostervald, 22 December 1778, *CC*, xlii.258-59.

able bitterness Ostervald complained of having been treated unfairly. For example, he argued, when Du Peyrou had asked the STN to state a price for the edition of collected works, he ought to have known that the offer of 10 000 *livres* was intended only as a starting point for negotiation. By way of contrast, in dealing with the STG, Girardin was accused of presenting straight away the rock-bottom price he was prepared to accept, 24 000 *livres*, thereby rendering negotiation unnecessary. Then Ostervald launched into additional accusations of bad faith on the part of Girardin, Du Peyrou and Moultou.[95]

Girardin took several weeks to reply. Once he did, he characteristically denied having promised the Neuchâtelois anything. On the contrary, he wrote, they had their excessive demands and parsimony to blame for having lost the project.[96] When all was said and done, the only satisfaction the STN derived from Girardin's response resulted from an indiscretion on the marquis's part. Girardin mistakenly inserted with his letter to the STN another one intended for Du Peyrou. It contained confidential strategies regarding production of the edition as well as an accusation that Moultou was secretly holding Part II of the *Confessions*.[97] Ostervald must have relished reading this, as well as Girardin's suggestion to Du Peyrou that one day Part II might bring its owner and publisher at least 6000 additional *livres*. The STN's director copied the pertinent passages of Girardin's letter intended for Du Peyrou, took his time returning the original to the marquis, and appended a brief note. He invited Girardin to re-open negotiations with the STN. If the entire *Confessions* were included in the transaction, the STN might be willing to go as high as 30 000 *livres* for the package.[98]

Fortunately for the health of the edition, Girardin did not allow his blunder to inspire panic. He addressed one final letter to the STN, on this occasion commiserating politely with the Neuchâtelois and placing responsibility for going with the Genevans upon Du Peyrou.[99] Ostervald attempted one more ploy, indirectly threatening the STG with piracy if the Genevans did not offer him and his associate, the bookseller Joseph Duplain of Lyon, quarter shares in the transaction with Thérèse.[100] An accompanying letter from Duplain to the STG did not even bother with subtlety. The Lyonnais wrote: 'Nous apprenons que vous avés acheté le portefeuille De Rousseau, nous Croyons que Si vous ne voulés pas faire une opération ruineuse, Eviter la

---

95. STN [F.-S. Ostervald] to Girardin, 24 January 1779, *CC*, xliii.56-59.
96. Draft, Girardin to the STN, [13 February 1779], *CC*, xliii.115-16.
97. Girardin to Du Peyrou, 13 February 1779, *CC*, xliii.116-29. Girardin prepared for Du Peyrou's benefit a copy of the letter he had written on 13 February to the STN, and he seemingly blundered into sending the original letter for the STN to Du Peyrou. The copy, along with the private letter intended for Du Peyrou alone, went to the STN.
98. STN [F.-S. Ostervald] to Girardin, [23 February 1779], *CC*, xliii.156-57.
99. Girardin to the STN, 3 March 1779, *CC*, xliii.167-68.
100. Copy prepared by François d'Ivernois, STN to the STG, 13 February 1779, *CC*, xliii.139-40. Interestingly enough, several weeks earlier Du Peyrou had suggested that the STG make an arrangement with the STN, so as to avert future piracies. The idea came to nothing (Du Peyrou to Girardin, 29 December 1778, *CC*, xlii.275-76).

Contrefaçon *inévitable* vous devés vous choisir en France un libraire actif et protegé qui doublera vos espérances Sans compromettre votre mise et vos avances.'[101]

The young entrepreneurs were scandalised, but unfazed. Taking the high road, they informed Girardin that, however much they might be bullied by the STN or Duplain, they never would cheapen the sacred enterprise by converting it into a mere 'affaire de Libraires', and that the marquis 'ne pourra nous blamer D'avoir refusé toute liaison avec pareilles gens'.[102] As matters transpired, true to his word, Ostervald eventually pirated the Geneva edition. Meanwhile, from his perch in Paris, Charles-Joseph Panckoucke heaped scorn upon the STN: 'Vous êtes bien La cause Messieurs que j'ai manqué cette grande et Superbe entreprise. J'en aurai[s] donné jusqu'à 40.mil Livres.'[103] Panckoucke would not be left entirely in the cold. Eventually he obtained exclusive distribution rights to a separate edition of the *Confessions*, Part I, published by the STG for sale in Paris, in a press-run of nearly eight thousand copies.

---

101. Copy prepared by François d'Ivernois, Joseph Duplain to the STG, [February 1779], *CC*, xliii.140.
102. STG to Girardin, [14 February 1779], *CC*, xliii.140.
103. Charles-Joseph Panckoucke to Ostervald, 1 June 1779, *CC*, xliii.311.

4. Rousseau without borders

BETWEEN late 1778 and January 1781 the *trois amis* pursued Rousseau manuscripts intended for the *Collection complète*. Aware that Rousseau had copied parts of the *Confessions* several times, Du Peyrou was chiefly interested in tracking down all versions of the so-called 'mémoires' before rivals of the STG might acquire and attempt to publish their own. Should the worst occur and an unauthorised edition of the *Confessions* appear, Du Peyrou hoped to prepare a case against it. For his part, Girardin insisted upon deciding what could or could not enter the great edition; furthermore, he took for granted his right to alter Rousseau's own texts should the occasion warrant. One consequence of Girardin's editorial imperialism was a fascinating exchange with the owner of an unpublished Rousseau treatise, the 'Considérations sur le gouvernement de Pologne'; and the marquis's efforts at controlling the publication of Rousseau's music engaged him in a dreadful legal struggle with the music's French engraver.

Pursuing the *Confessions*

Because the *Confessions* were emerging as the core of the *Collection complète*, the whereabouts of their manuscripts loomed increasingly important.[1] The *trois amis* were aware of Rousseau's aborted salon readings of his 'mémoires' back in 1770/71. Possibly, they feared, the author had passed manuscripts to acquaintances, and indeed Charles Pinot Duclos possessed one for a time. The *amis* suspected that copies could have been made without Rousseau's knowledge. If an unscrupulous publisher printed a manuscript of the *Confessions* before the *Collection complète* got underway, the *amis*'s project would be gravely compromised.

By the end of 1778 Girardin, Du Peyrou and Moultou confirmed that at least parts of two manuscript copies of the *Confessions* still existed. The first, containing Books I to III and part of Book IV, was in Du Peyrou's hands. Rousseau had prepared this manuscript in England. Suspecting that his enemies were out to destroy it at all costs, he had placed the manuscript, along with other papers, in sealed packages left with J.-F.-M. Cerjat, a friend of Du Peyrou's living in Lincolnshire. Following Rousseau's departure from England in May 1767, Cerjat shipped his packages to Neuchâtel, and Du Peyrou assumed that their contents eventually would find a place in the edition of Rousseau's complete works which he still hoped to undertake.

---

1. The classic work dealing with the various stages of composition is Hermine de Saussure, *Rousseau et les manuscrits des 'Confessions'* (Paris 1958).

Nearly a year passed, however, before the parcels reached him, by which time the affair at Trye had occurred and Rousseau abrogated his publishing agreement with Du Peyrou. No longer considering himself an editor, the chastened disciple was transformed into a mere caretaker of Rousseau's property. Du Peyrou resealed the items he had begun examining back in 1765 and set them aside. He left the packages he had received from Cerjat wrapped as he found them.[2]

In order to prepare his inventory for the *Collection complète*, Du Peyrou in October 1778 began examining the items in his safekeeping. He found a note in Rousseau's hand labelling package 'H' of those sent from England as 'Un Livre in 4°. Contenant les trois premiers Livres de mes Confessions et le commencement du quatriéme.'[3] Shortly thereafter Moultou informed Du Peyrou that he possessed a manuscript of Books I to VI (Part I) of the *Confessions*, and Du Peyrou proposed that Moultou's manuscript be included in the *Collection complète*. Worried about potential piracies, the Neuchâtel disciple then preferred not to wait for the great edition and suggested publishing Moultou's manuscript in the small preliminary collection which he hoped to print for Thérèse's benefit.[4] He would not, however, inform Girardin that Moultou indeed possessed Books I to VI.

Not necessarily warm to Du Peyrou's proposals, Girardin nevertheless refrained from opposing them; but in his ill-fated letter of 13 February 1779, the one mistakenly sent to the STN, he shared his darkest suspicions with Du Peyrou. He wrote that Moultou possessed the entire *Confessions*, including the devastating story of Rousseau's mature years:

M. de M[oultou] dissimule avec nous. Il a de grands egards et des menagemens a conserver pour des personnes qui ont bien des Liaisons avec Le Camp ennemi. J'étois moralement sur qu'il avoit La totalité des papiers secrets et notamment des C[onfessions]. J'en ai maintenant La Certitude Phisique puisqu'elles ont été Lües en entier pendant son dernier Séjour a Paris et il est bien Singulier qu'il voulut nous induire a Croire que La 2ᵉ. partie avoit été brulée par L'auteur lui même.[5]

Girardin remained vague about his alleged physical proof of Moultou's treachery. At the same time the Genevan tried to direct the marquis's scent in a different direction. He informed Girardin that a *Confessions* manuscript was in the hands of an unnamed Paris academician. It turned out, however, that Rousseau had confided no more than *Rousseau juge de Jean-Jacques* to the academician in question, abbé de Condillac.[6] More worrisome to the *trois amis* was Boubers's announcement of April 1779 that to his own edition in-quarto he intended to add Rousseau's 'Mémoires, *ses* Lettres, *son* Ouvrage sur la

2. Du Peyrou to Moultou, 4 November 1778, *CC*, xlii.94.
3. Copy prepared by Du Peyrou's secretary, Jeannin, 'Note Spécifique des papiers de Mr. J:J:R: entre mes mains', 29 October 1778, *CC*, xlii.73.
4. Du Peyrou to Girardin, 27 September 1778, *CC*, xli.300; Du Peyrou to Girardin, 12 November 1778, *CC*, xlii.111-13.
5. Girardin to Du Peyrou, 13 February 1779, *CC*, xliii.120.
6. Moultou to Girardin, [26 August 1778], *CC*, xli.235.

Pologne, & *nombre de Morceaux d'autant plus piquans, qu'ils ne sont connus que d'un très-petit nombre des Amis les plus intimes de l'Auteur'.*[7] This produced near panic among the *trois amis*, until it became evident that what Boubers meant by 'Mémoires' was merely the piracy he intended to make of the STG's edition.

Relying upon his memory and papers at hand, Du Peyrou attempted to reconstruct the itinerary of the mysterious third manuscript. His chief clue was a letter to him from Rousseau, dated 12 January 1769. In it the writer noted that what he had sent Du Peyrou from England could be complemented by materials in the hands of a person he identified as 'la dame a la marmelade de fleur d'orange'.[8] Du Peyrou learned from Thérèse that the 'dame' in question was the abbesse de Gomerfontaine, Anne-Jeanne Du Poujet de Nadaillac. Just prior to his departure from Trye in June 1768 Rousseau had confided papers to Mme de Nadaillac.[9] Did they include a *Confessions* manuscript? Du Peyrou wrote to the abbess and asked her. She replied that she had returned some of Rousseau's papers to the writer in 1770 and enclosed a copy of his request for them.[10] Rousseau's note was tantalising: 'permettez, Madame, que je vous prie de vouloir bien me faire passer par une voye sûre le Cahier de *Confessions* dont vous avez bien voulu être dépositaire et que j'ai besoin de revoir en ce moment'.[11]

Du Peyrou wondered what Rousseau had meant by the term 'Cahier de *Confessions'*. The disciple recalled having brought a sealed parcel to Rousseau during the fateful November 1767 visit to Trye. It belonged to the collection of packages the writer had left with Du Peyrou prior to the flight from Môtiers two years earlier. In December 1778 Du Peyrou suspected that the parcel borne to Trye did indeed contain a very early draft of the *Confessions*, and that Rousseau subsequently deposited this package with Mme de Nadaillac.[12] For Moultou's benefit the Neuchâtel businessman described (mistakenly it would turn out) what he had brought to Trye as 'un 8° relié en veau assés epais'. He asked Moultou whether that accurately described the size and binding of the *Confessions* which the Genevan possessed.[13] There is no record of Moultou's reply.[14] On 29 December 1778, however, Du Peyrou informed Girardin that the copy of the first six Books of the *Confessions* to be used for

7. *Gazette de Leyde* 33 (23 April 1779), p.4, *CC*, xliii.234-35.

8. Rousseau to Du Peyrou, 12 January 1769, *CC*, xxxvii.9.

9. De Saussure, *Rousseau et les manuscrits des 'Confessions'*, p.204-205.

10. Anne-Jeanne Du Poujet de Nadaillac, abbesse de Gomerfontaine, to Du Peyrou, 5 October 1778, *CC*, xxxviii.358-59.

11. Rousseau to Anne-Jeanne Du Poujet de Nadaillac, copy prepared by Mme de Nadaillac for Du Peyrou, 20 July 1770, *CC*, xxxviii.70.

12. Du Peyrou to Moultou, 5 December 1778, *CC*, xlii.191.

13. Du Peyrou to Moultou, 5 December 1778, *CC*, xlii.191. See de Saussure, *Rousseau et les manuscrits des 'Confessions'*, p.361-62, for her comments concerning Du Peyrou's lapses of memory.

14. Moultou's copy, the so-called 'Geneva manuscript' presently located in the bibliothèque publique et universitaire de Genève, ms. fr. 227, is in two volumes. The first, containing Books I to VI, is an in-octavo, 159 pages, and measures 183 × 111 mm. The second volume, containing Books VII to XII, is an in-quarto, 133 pages, and measures approximately 224 × 180-190 mm. The volumes were rebound in the nineteenth century.

the *Collection complète*, which he at last admitted Moultou was holding, was very definitely *not* the same item he had transported to Trye back in 1767.[15]

In pursuing his detective work Du Peyrou proved to be both right and wrong. His delivery to Rousseau at Trye in November 1767 was not the *Confessions* at all, but rather a sealed package of letters and other documentation intended to assist the writer in getting on with Part II of his 'mémoires'.[16] Furthermore, what Rousseau deposited with Mme de Nadaillac six months later included these papers, plus scattered sections of the *Confessions* he had freshly made.[17] Du Peyrou had never actually read any of this material, which Rousseau apparently recovered from Mme de Nadaillac as he prepared the final drafts of his autobiography in 1770 and 1771.[18] Whether the so-called 'Cahier de *Confessions*' still existed in the winter of 1779 is doubtful.[19] Though incorrect about the details, Du Peyrou nevertheless accurately suspected that Rousseau eventually had composed two publishable manuscripts of the *Confessions*, at least, he believed, up to and including Book VI. They were prepared between October 1769 and late 1771, and the Neuchâtel disciple knew that Moultou was holding one of them.[20] But where was the other? Moultou believed it had disappeared in the reputed inferno of papers set by Rousseau just prior to his departure for Ermenonville in May 1778. Du Peyrou, however, was not so certain.

Du Peyrou confided to Girardin that the final words of Moultou's manuscript, written in an ink different from the rest, represented the author's decision to impose silence upon himself following completion of Book VI.[21] Nevertheless, Du Peyrou was unable to conclude the matter to his satisfaction. In what may be construed as a hunch embellished by suspicion, he appeared to be baiting Girardin: 'Si la Suite [of the *Confessions*] n'est pas en vos mains, ni

15. Du Peyrou to Girardin, 29 December 1778, *CC*, xlii.276.

16. De Saussure, *Rousseau et les manuscrits des 'Confessions'*, p.361-62.

17. Mme de Nadaillac did send to Girardin what remained of Rousseau's deposit (draft, Girardin to Mme de Nadaillac, 26 November [1778], *CC*, xlii.158-61).

18. De Saussure, *Rousseau et les manuscrits des 'Confessions'*, p.197-201, 362. Rousseau included Part II in his readings, motivating Mme d'Epinay to request police intervention to silence him (Louise de La Live d'Epinay to Antoine-R. de Sartine, 10 [May 1771], *CC*, xxxviii.228-30; see as well Manuel, *La Police de Paris dévoilée*, i.97-98).

19. Leigh believes that the manuscript of the *Confessions* seized by Girardin when he ransacked Rousseau's writing table after the author's fatal stroke was indeed the *cahier* held in trust by Mme de Nadaillac between 1768 and 1770 (see *note explicative* d, *CC*, xlii.89). On the other hand, Hermine de Saussure offers internal evidence suggesting that the *cahier* contained sketches for the aborted Part III of the *Confessions* (see *Rousseau et les manuscrits des 'Confessions'*, p.196 and note 3, p.204, 247 and 264).

20. Du Peyrou was as yet unaware, however, that the manuscripts included Part II, that is, Books VII to XII.

21. Du Peyrou to Girardin, 29 December 1778, *CC*, xlii.276-77. For the marquis's benefit, Du Peyrou quoted from Moultou's manuscript: 'Telles ont été les erreurs et lés fautes de ma jeunesse. J'en ay narré l'histoire avec une fidelité dont mon Cœur est content. Si dans la Suite j'honorai mon age mur de quelques vertus, je les aurois dites avec la meme franchise, et c'etoit mon dessein. Mais il faut m'arreter ici. Le tems peut lever bien des voiles, Si ma memoire parvient á la posterité, peut ëtre un jour elle aprendra ce que j'avois á dire. Alors on Saura pourquoi je me tais. Fin.'

en celles de l'Abbé de C[ondillac] elle n'existe pas.' Did Du Peyrou suspect that Girardin was not revealing all he knew? To head off the possibility that the marquis might somehow gain access to Part II of the *Confessions* and seek to publish it, Du Peyrou mentioned that he was holding valuable documentation, without which any edition of Part II would be incomplete.[22]

When it became certain that Condillac possessed only *Rousseau juge de Jean-Jacques*, Moultou sought to reassure Girardin that Part II of the *Confessions* no longer existed, that in fact Rousseau had himself destroyed it. Allegedly quoting Rousseau, Moultou cited the author's wish not to emulate his enemies by engaging in a war of slander with them. The difficulty with this theory, Moultou finally had to admit, was that Rousseau had no such scruples concerning the vituperative *Rousseau juge de Jean-Jacques*. Copies of these semi-autobiographical 'Dialogues' were in the hands not only of Condillac, but also of Brooke Boothby, d'Angiviller and himself. Moultou therefore advised Girardin to maintain vigilance in the hunt for Part II of the *Confessions*, a request that the marquis considered wholly disingenuous.[23] At this point Girardin informed Du Peyrou of his certainty that Moultou was hiding the manuscript of Part II from them.[24]

It was in this atmosphere of burgeoning mistrust that the project to publish the *Collection complète* unfolded. Even while agreeing to compose a preface for the edition and underwriting part of the STG's investment, Moultou asked to remain virtually anonymous in the affair.[25] Girardin contemptuously attributed such passivity to the Genevan's desire not to alienate useful social connections who had hated Rousseau.[26] Certainly, suspicion of what the *Confessions* might contain worried many, not the least of whom was Du Peyrou, as he recalled Rousseau's coolness towards him since the disastrous incident at Trye. Therefore the Neuchâtel disciple was not particularly disappointed by the apparent lack of success in finding Part II.[27] Du Peyrou knew that Part I

22. Du Peyrou to Girardin, 29 December 1778, *CC*, xlii.277.
23. Moultou to Girardin, [19 January 1779], *CC*, xliii.47.
24. Girardin to Du Peyrou, 13 February 1779, *CC*, xliii.120-21.
25. Moultou to Girardin, [*c.* 25 March 1779], *CC*, xliii.204-205: 'je veillerai avec plaisir a l'édition de M^r. R. come simple correcteur d'imprimerie, je dois fere cela pour mon ami, & j'aurais voulu fére davantage; mais je ne le puis plus; il est plus Sur pour moi de me tenir à l'écart, la gloire de M^r. R. n'y perdra rien car m^r Du P. vous Secondera, Monsieur, avec le Zéle de l'amitié la plus tendre et la plus éclairée.'
26. Girardin to Du Peyrou, 13 February 1779, *CC*, xliii.120.
27. Du Peyrou to Girardin, 2 February 1779, *CC*, xliii.77-78. Indeed Rousseau's main reference in the *Confessions* to the devoted Du Peyrou, a short paragraph in Book xii, was hardly flattering. Rousseau commented upon Du Peyrou's infirmities, chiefly gout and deafness, as influencing the disciple's cold and phlegmatic character. Then the author concluded that Du Peyrou's wealth was a liability to their relationship: 'J'ai appris à douter qu'un homme jouissant d'une grande fortune quel qu'il puisse être, puisse aimer sincerement mes principes et leur auteur' (*OC*, i.602-603.) Fear of what Rousseau might have written about him in the *Confessions* influenced Diderot's pre-emptive strike in the *Essai sur la vie de Sénèque le philosophe, sur ses écrits, et sur les règnes de Claude et de Néron* (1779), p.120-21. Without mentioning Rousseau, Diderot referred transparently to a certain memoir-writer as an ingrate, coward and atrocious individual, 'un

stopped long before his acquaintanceship with Rousseau. Any detailed or damaging mention of himself was unlikely.

Part II, however, was a different story. If the *Collection complète* was to represent a multi-layered rendering of Rousseau's life and work, Du Peyrou actually would have preferred editing the writer's correspondence, an artlessly formed record, to publishing Rousseau's carefully contrived (and probably damaging) recollections of his sufferings. Once he learned that the STG's draft of a prospectus for the *Collection complète* might be misconstrued as promising both Parts I and II of the *Confessions*, Du Peyrou became extremely agitated.[28] By spring 1779 the Neuchâtel disciple was convinced that the second half of the *Confessions*, even if found, ought to be omitted from the *Collection complète*. The only legitimate way of keeping it out was to appeal to Rousseau's apparent wishes. Du Peyrou therefore converted what was alleged into a certainty. He requested that the STG announce nothing more than the '*6 premiers Livres des Confessions* parce que lés intentions de l'auteur ne permettent pas la publication actuelle des autres Livres'.[29] On the other hand, overwhelmed with a desire for vengeance towards Rousseau's enemies, Girardin wanted to leave the edition of collected works open-ended. Wherever Part II might be, for the time being it could remain in reserve. One day, though not in the present, the marquis believed, the *Confessions* in their entirety would serve as Rousseau's ultimate weapon wielded from the grave.[30]

Chasing down the *Considérations sur le gouvernement de Pologne*

Though Girardin's quest for stray manuscripts of the *Confessions* was limited to allegations of Moultou's perfidy, his pursuit of other unpublished writings proved more aggressive. Among the papers Rousseau had brought to Ermenonville was an eighty-seven-page manuscript in the author's hand. It bore the title: 'Considerations Sur Le gouvernement de Pologne'. Pages 83 to 86 were missing, apparently torn from the manuscript. Girardin read the piece and rhapsodically informed Du Peyrou of what he found:

> On y trouve toutte Le feu de La jeunesse, et L'energie de L'age mur. Il semble que son genie Se fut encor exalté par La Consideration du bien de L'humanité. Cet ouvrage est veritablement sublime, puis qu'a la theorie profonde du Contract social, il reunit La pratique qui pourroit faire La felicité, et perpetuer L'existence d'une nation que cet ouvrage pourroit relever, si elle ètoit encor Capable de Le Comprendre.[31]

---

artificieux scélérat, qui, pour donner quelque vraisemblance à ses injustes & cruelles imputations, se peindroit lui-même de couleurs odieuses' (see *CC*, xlii.177).
28. Prospectus draft for the *Collection complète* with Du Peyrou's annotations, [8 February 1779], *CC*, xliii.96-100.
29. Du Peyrou to the STG, 15 May 1779, *CC*, xliii.277.
30. Girardin to Du Peyrou, 3 February 1779, *CC*, xliii.82.
31. Girardin to Du Peyrou, 4 October 1778, *CC*, xlii.12. See Otto Forst de Battaglia, 'Un peu de lumière sur les *Considérations*', *Annales de la Société Jean-Jacques Rousseau* 17 (1926), p.97-119.

Girardin summarised the fate of the work which, even without his commentary, was fraught with conspiratorial intrigue worthy of the political events surrounding it. At the request of a Lithuanian nobleman, Count Michael Wielhorski, and instigated by the former secretary of the French embassy at St Petersburg, C.-C. Rulhière, Rousseau in April 1772 completed the 'Considérations' which he had begun six months earlier. What had originally inspired them was the anti-Russian uprising of the Polish Confederates, begun in 1769, against the puppet regime of King Stanislas Poniatowski. Following a botched attempt to kidnap Stanislas, which divested the Confederates of whatever French support they might have aspired to, the spirit of the revolt flagged; and Rousseau, author of *Du contrat social*, was offered the opportunity to revive it with an appeal to Polish patriotism. Unknown to him, however, the rulers of Prussia, Russia and the Hapsburg Empire were themselves preparing a lesson in *Realpolitik* for would-be Polish revolutionaries: the First Partition. The approach of this sinister event notwithstanding, Rousseau responded to the patriots with the 'Considérations', which he sent to Wielhorski for private dissemination in manuscript.[32]

Girardin took up the story with the manuscript's arrival at Wielhorski's. According to the marquis, a malevolent servant of Wielhorski's copied it and sent the duplicate to one of Rousseau's antagonists in France, d'Alembert, in Girardin's colourful phrase, 'le plus *grand Géometre de La Secte*'. Within days of receipt d'Alembert's copy was transcribed again. It circulated privately in Paris and most recently a version had been offered for publication to N.-B. Duchesne's widow. According to Girardin, Thérèse was falsely accused of being the source of the alleged Duchesne copy. Rumour had it that she had sold the manuscript for a thousand *écus*. The marquis then parted from his immediate subject to launch a tirade against d'Alembert and other members of the encyclopedists' 'secte', out to ruin the *Collection complète* prior even to its publication, and he urged Du Peyrou to be discreet in future correspondence.[33]

Certain as he was that more than one copy of the 'Considérations' existed in Paris, Girardin hoped to destroy the credibility of them all.[34] Following his revelation to Du Peyrou, he wrote to Wielhorski, reporting the injurious rumour directed at Thérèse, asking the count whether the original manuscript of the 'Considérations' still was in his hands and requesting the identities of other possible possessors of copies.[35] Wielhorski confirmed that he still held the original 'Considérations'. Since Rousseau had been paid nothing for

32. For the historical background of the 'Considérations' see Jean Fabre's introduction in *OC*, iii.ccxvi-cclv.
33. Girardin to Du Peyrou, 4 October 1778, *CC*, xlii.4-8.
34. The previous week Du Peyrou had informed Girardin that aside from correspondence, one of the three manuscripts in Moultou's possession was 'Sur la Pologne, d'environ 200 pages in 8°. The other two were 'Une Oraison funebre du feu Duc d'Orleans pere de celui d'aujourd'-hui' and 'Un fragment de la Continuation d'Emile, ou des Solitaires' (see Du Peyrou to Girardin, 27 September 1778, *CC*, xli.299).
35. Girardin to Count Michael Wielhorski, [end of October 1778], *CC*, xxxix.286-87.

them, Wielhorski offered Thérèse 600 *livres* as compensation.[36] The count then addressed a letter to Thérèse, explaining that at least one copy of the 'Considérations' had floated round Paris during Rousseau's lifetime. In fact the bookseller Le Jay (really Pierre Guy) had possessed it, but police lieutenant Sartine, at Wielhorski's urging, prevented its publication.

Wielhorski added that only he and the Polish aristocrat, prince Adam Czartoryski, initially had seen the 'Considérations', and surely the prince was not guilty of copying them indiscreetly. Wielhorski also noted, however, that one of his young followers in Poland subsequently borrowed the 'Considérations' for an evening and did transcribe them without permission. The count regretted that this manuscript apparently had made its way to France, and he believed it to be the one which veuve Duchesne was preparing for publication. Nevertheless, unwilling either to name his compatriot or yield his autograph copy, Wielhorski ceded what he deemed to be publication rights for the 'Considérations' to Thérèse, along with the offer of 600 *livres*. The count asked that, should she desire to publish the copy in Girardin's hands, it first be examined by a censor from the French Foreign Office.[37]

This reply did not satisfy Girardin in the least and provoked a testy response from the marquis. Speaking for Thérèse, he refused Wielhorski's 600 *livres* and demanded a precise explanation of how the copy of the 'Considérations' had gotten into Le Jay's (Guy's) hands. Even more important, Girardin asked, how had d'Alembert obtained his copy? Girardin accused Wielhorski of withholding valuable information from him. Identifying himself as executor of Rousseau's literary wishes, and 'ne remplissant en cette occasion que Les fonctions que Le sort funeste, et La Confiance de M. Rousseau m'ont imposées', Girardin solicited a complete reckoning.[38]

It took nearly two months for Wielhorski to respond. Insisting upon his veracity, the count recalled being told that d'Alembert's secretary had provided Le Jay (Guy) with the encyclopedist's copy. Wielhorski, however, denied knowing how d'Alembert had acquired it. Two other possibilities of leaks existed, but he doubted whether either of them was the source of d'Alembert's manuscript. Wielhorski admitted to having loaned his own copy to the duc de La Rochefoucauld, and he acknowledged once having a secretary who had copied other items of his without permission. Then Wielhorski addressed the issue of ownership. He reminded Girardin that the 'Considérations' had not simply been confided to him by Rousseau. Rather, they were a gift, and Thérèse had to realise that her claim to them existed only with his personal authorisation.

Facing this assertiveness, Girardin was hardly prepared for the contrite conclusion Wielhorski appended to his letter. The count wrote that it presently would be dangerous for him if an authorised version of the 'Considérations'

36. Wielhorski to Girardin, 29 November 1778, *CC*, xxxix.287-88.
37. Wielhorski to Marie-Thérèse Levasseur, 30 November 1778, *CC*, xxxix.289-90.
38. Girardin to Wielhorski (Girardin's copy), 15 January 1779, *CC*, xxxix.291-92.

were published without some necessary suppressions. Implicit as well was his fear that an unauthorised and uncensored version might somehow get published. He therefore was offering his autograph manuscript to Girardin, along with recommended editorial changes. 'Par ce moyen', Wielhorski concluded, 'vous ferés tomber l'édition faite subrepticement, quand même elle paroitroit, en mettant à la tête de l'édition un avertissement que c'est la seule faite de mon consentement ainsi que sur la copie originale de l'auteur.'[39] The reasoning behind Wielhorski's move was pragmatic. The Polish political situation in 1779 was far different from what it had been in 1771. The First Partition had been completed and, backed by Catherine II's army, the Russian ambassador Saldern was attempting to run what was left of the country. The national resistance now hoped to convert King Stanislas Poniatowski into a legitimate symbol for its patriotic cause, and insulting references to him by the erstwhile ally of the Confederates in a book now eight years old would be both outdated and counterproductive.

Girardin was overjoyed by Wielhorski's offer of the original manuscript, and the prospect of having to censor Rousseau's own words had no adverse effect upon the marquis. As will be seen shortly, amending Rousseau's text in the interests of alleged clarity or genuine expediency was quite consistent with Girardin's editorial strategies. For the moment he was happy to oblige Wielhorski. According to Girardin, therefore, the count and his friends had no cause for alarm. The French marquis would respect all suppressions and changes made by the Lithuanian count. Acquired from the manuscript's owner, Girardin's version of the 'Considérations' was intended to render all other editions counterfeit and to guarantee further legitimacy to Wielhorski's manuscript. Girardin urged the count to ask French foreign minister Vergennes to refuse entry into France of any other edition of the 'Considérations'.[40]

In May 1779 Wielhorski wrote a letter to Vergennes which accompanied his copy of the 'Considérations'. He informed the French foreign minister of the impending publication in Paris of the essay, which, however, was based upon a clandestinely obtained manuscript. Wielhorski noted that the version to be published had been obtained without his approval. Moreover, 'elle peut être infidele dans plusieurs endroits et dans d'autres trop fidele, et qu'enfin elle peut me compromettre'.[41] Wishing to suppress the publication, Wielhorski noted that he intended his autograph manuscript for Girardin's edition alone, making small changes and excisions judged indispensable, and he asked Vergennes to use his police authority over political works to ensure that the 'Considérations' appeared only with the count's adjustments. Since Rousseau had written the essay exclusively for him, Wielhorski claimed the proprietary right to oppose publication of any other version, and he granted Vergennes the

39. Wielhorski to Girardin, 12 March 1779, *CC*, xxxix.293-94.
40. Draft, Girardin to Wielhorski, 31 March 1779, *CC*, xxxix.294-95.
41. Wielhorski to Charles Gravier, comte de Vergennes, [20 May 1779], *CC*, xxxix.296.

privilege of making modifications desired by the French government. Finally Wielhorski enclosed a copy of his own requested alterations.[42]

Vergennes sent Wielhorski's manuscript of the 'Considérations' and the count's requested changes to Girardin, who acknowledged receipt with a remarkable letter to the foreign minister. In it he supported Wielhorski's wish to frustrate all other editions. Girardin urged Vergennes to block publication of any manuscript of the 'Considérations' other than that prepared for the STG's proposed *Collection complète*. The marquis rationalised his position with appeals to Wielhorski's sense of honour and Thérèse's need for subsistance. Girardin also noted that one of Rousseau's works officially prohibited in France, *Emile*, was to be included in the *Collection complète*; he pleaded for the STG's edition of the treatise to be tolerated in the same manner as were much less authoritative versions presently circulating. Failing to mention that two other books condemned by the Parlement of Paris, *Du contrat social* and the *Lettre à Christophe de Beaumont*, also were included in the *Collection complète*, Girardin concluded by requesting special favour for the STG edition and special vigilance against piracies of it. Finally he appealed to Vergennes's concern for bibliographical veracity. The marquis stated that only two versions of the 'Considérations' in Rousseau's hand existed: Wielhorski's and the one which Girardin found among the writer's papers and was sending to Geneva. By protecting them against clandestine productions, Vergennes's action might serve both the French language and the author's intent. In other words, for Girardin a doctored version of Rousseau's own manuscript bore greater legitimacy than copies, however complete and unabridged they might be.[43]

The minister of foreign affairs refused to bite, however. Even prior to receiving Girardin's letter, Vergennes had informed Wielhorski that he had no interest in reading either Rousseau's manuscript or the count's changes. The minister wrote: 'Il m'a paru, Monsieur, que c'etoit le moyen le plus simple pour ne pas me mettre dans le cas de connoitre ce que je n'aurois peut etre pas pû approuver, et pour laisser aux personnes dont c'est le devoir a s'opposer a la publication de cet ecrit, s'il n'est pas de nature à entrer en France.' Sincere or not, Vergennes asked Wielhorski to believe that the French foreign ministry would not concern itself with publication of the 'Considérations', and he clearly stated his wish to remain uninvolved in any matter that had to do with Rousseau, 'un homme aussi célèbre par ses fautes que par ses talens'. Vergennes concluded that 'moins un Ministre se montre dans ce qui

42. The major excisions that Wielhorski requested, and which were honoured in the STG version of the 'Considérations', are the three paragraphs following *notation* (*e*) in the Pléiade edition (*OC*, iii.1039-40). The paragraphs, which were among the pages torn from Girardin's manuscript, allude to the feeble character of King Stanislas Poniatowski and to the disposition of his person by the Confederates, once they liberated Poland from its rapacious neighbours. The STG edition also honoured Wielhorski's request to omit Rousseau's term 'illégale' with reference to the Polish diet of 1768 (*OC*, iii.996). Independently, either Girardin or Du Peyrou excised an uncomplimentary reference to the government of Bern (*OC*, iii.1006 (*e*)).

43. Girardin to Vergennes, [24 June 1779], *CC*, xxxix.299-300.

peut engendrer des querelles litteraires, plus il fait sagement'.[44] Responding to Girardin, Vergennes repeated his desire to remain both neutral and anonymous, adding his pleasure at leaving to administrators of the French Book-trade Office the responsibility for policing publication and distribution of the 'Considérations'.[45]

Armed with Vergennes's hint that he would not pursue very aggressively illegitimate editions of the 'Considérations', Girardin informed Wielhorski that his own ability to persuade the publishers of the *Collection complète* to print a censored version now was compromised.[46] Vergennes might have his reasons for tolerating Rousseau's sarcasms regarding Catherine the Great and Stanislas Poniatowski; at the same time, businessmen in Geneva surely had theirs in wishing to deny precedence to juicier piracies over their own authorised, but excised, edition. As matters transpired, in its published text the STG honoured Wielhorski's wishes and let his expurgations stand.[47] Apparently French book-trade authorities dissuaded veuve Duchesne from publishing her edition after all, for no bibliographical record of it exists. Piracies of the *Collection complète*'s version did appear in 1782, and the following year P.-F. Gosse of The Hague and François Grasset of Lausanne collaborated upon an edition of the 'Considérations'.[48] The first edition to re-insert the sentences missing from all late eighteenth-century versions did not appear until 1801.[49]

Concerning the semi-autobiographical *Rousseau juge de Jean-Jacques*, it probably was Thérèse Levasseur who informed Girardin that d'Angiviller, Condillac and Brooke Boothby possessed different manuscript copies. D'Angiviller and Boothby held incomplete manuscripts, while Condillac had the original autograph. Girardin experienced difficulty obtaining any of the three manuscripts. Condillac maintained that by keeping the 'Dialogues' sealed until the dawn of the new century, he was following Rousseau's instructions to him; Boothby insisted on doing as he pleased with his manuscript. Believing that the 'Dialogues' should remain unpublished, d'Angiviller nevertheless offered

44. Vergennes to Wielhorski, 25 June 1779, *CC*, xxxix.301.

45. Vergennes to Girardin, 2 July 1779, *CC*, xxxix.301-302.

46. Draft, Girardin to Wielhorski, [*c.* 3 July 1779], *CC*, xxxix.302-303.

47. 'Considérations sur le gouvernement de Pologne et sur sa réformation projetée', in *Collection complète des œuvres de J.-J. Rousseau, citoyen de Genève*, 12 vols (Geneva, [STG] [1780-]1782) (hereafter cited as *Collection complète*), i.415-539, in-4°; 24 vols, ii.253-442, in-8°. Wielhorski to Girardin, 20 November 1779, *CC*, xxxix.304-305.

48. Aside from the STN's piracy of the *Collection complète*, a separate edition of Rousseau's essay appeared as the *Considérations sur le gouvernement de Pologne, et sur sa réformation projetée, par J.-J. Rousseau*, in-32° (London 1782), p.1-189, followed by the *Discours sur l'économie politique*, p.191-272. In 1783 the following edition appeared: the *Considérations sur le gouvernement de la Pologne et sur sa réformation projetée et lettres sur la législation de la Corse, dans lesquelles tous les souverains trouveront des choses utiles, par J.-J. Rousseau, citoyen de Genève*, in-12° (The Hague and Lausanne 1783), p.1-173. The volume also included Rousseau's *Jugements* upon abbé de Saint-Pierre's *Projet de la paix perpétuelle* and *Polysynodie*.

49. *Considérations sur le gouvernement de Pologne, et sur sa réformation projetée en avril 1772*, in *Œuvres de J.-J. Rousseau, citoyen de Genève*, 2 vols, in-8° (Paris An ix [1801]), ii.161-278.

to show Girardin what he possessed.[50] But there is no record that he kept his word. Following a period of overly discreet silence and even denial, Moultou released the information that Rousseau had given him yet another autograph copy of the 'Dialogues'.[51] At first the *trois amis* agreed to honour Condillac's interpretation of the author's alleged wishes. Once Boothby published the 'premier dialogue' in 1780, however, they feared that an unscrupulous bookseller might release the entire set of paranoid musings. Therefore Moultou considered it inappropriate to keep his manuscript under wraps.[52] In censored form it would appear in the *Collection complète* as volumes xxi and xxii in-octavo and as volume xi in-quarto.

Rousseau's music

Girardin pursued other manuscripts besides the 'Considérations' and 'Dialogues'. He wrote to Rousseau's Swiss disciple, Madeleine Delessert, requesting the 'Lettres' on botanical subjects which the writer had prepared for her between 1771 and 1774. Du Peyrou would make use of the letters, as well as early drafts of them, in the *Collection complète*.[53] Then there was Rousseau's music. Several weeks after the writer's death, Girardin developed the idea of accompanying the *Collection complète* with a separate edition of Rousseau's compositions, to be engraved in Paris, the anticipated profits going to Thérèse. The marquis wrote to George Simon Harcourt, one of Rousseau's hosts in England during the writer's exile there. Following his customary rhapsody over Rousseau's last days and alluding to his self-imposed burden as disciple-in-chief, Girardin asked Harcourt for assistance in tracking down papers Rousseau might have left in England. He specifically mentioned the score of the opera-ballet, *Les Muses galantes*, composed between 1743 and 1745, which he believed to be held by Phoebe Davenport, granddaughter of Rousseau's English landlord. Girardin added that he was prepared to negotiate with directors of the Opera in Paris over additional scores he hoped to locate, and he intended to open a subscription in France and England for the entire corpus of engraved music.[54]

In the inventory he sent to Du Peyrou of papers Rousseau had left at Ermenonville, Girardin noted six packages of scores. These included the first act and pieces from the second act of the pastoral *Daphnis et Chloé*, composed

---

50. Girardin to Du Peyrou, 4 October 1778, *CC*, xlii.19.
51. Moultou to Girardin, [*c.* 25 March 1779], *CC*, xliii.204. Moultou admitted to possessing the postscript to the 'Dialogues', known as the 'Histoire du précedent écrit'. He probably informed Du Peyrou orally that he was holding the entire manuscript.
52. Boothby's edition is described bibliographically in Dufour, *Recherches*, i.242-43. See as well Brooke Boothby to Marc-Michel Rey, 16 April 1780, *CC*, xliv.199-200.
53. Draft, Girardin to Madeleine-Catherine Delessert, 7 November 1778, *CC*, xlii.101-102. The eight 'Lettres élémentaires sur la botanique à Mme de L***' would appear, in rather butchered form, in the *Collection complète*, vii. 529-88, in-4°; xiv.429-518, in-8° (see *OC*, iv.1149-97).
54. Girardin to George Simon Harcourt, 30 July 1778, *CC*, xli.101-103.

between 1774 and 1776, and airs from *Le Devin du village* that Rousseau had reworked in 1774.[55] In two of the packages Girardin located ninety-four songs which, he judged, would make for a separate subscription.[56] As he presented his plans, Girardin confided to Du Peyrou a fear which would plague him as long as he was involved with Rousseau's literary legacy: that a long-forgotten blood relative might appear and contest Thérèse's claims to revenue deriving from the *Collection complète*. After all, though Rousseau had considered Thérèse as his life-partner, their 'marriage' was hardly constituted according to prescribed forms and might well be challenged.[57] Therefore, Girardin believed, subscriptions to a rapidly produced collection of music, most evidently the ninety-four songs, might at least guarantee Thérèse some income.[58]

What Girardin failed to foresee was that the collection of songs, which he labelled the *Consolations des misères de ma vie*, would embroil him in a nasty civil lawsuit. No Rousseau relative disputed Thérèse's claim to the songs; rather it was their would-be publisher, the Paris music-seller François Le Marchand, who brought Girardin grief. Following Thérèse's acquisition of a royal *privilège* on 26 August 1778, according her the right to publish her husband's music, Le Marchand assumed responsibility for producing and distributing the *Consolations*. As payment for his labour he requested 4 *livres* per subscription. Thérèse (that is, Girardin) agreed to provide advances for engraving the plates, as well as for purchasing paper, ink and miscellaneous items.[59] Shortly thereafter an announcement for the *Consolations* was placed in the *Journal de Paris* and the subscription opened. The collection would be engraved in in-folio format and was promised to subscribers by 1 February 1779. The price per subscription was one *louis d'or* (24 *livres*). Parisians were to arrange their subscriptions directly with Le Marchand. Subscribers in provincial French towns and in London, Vienna, Amsterdam and Brussels were provided with a list of local booksellers who would accept their orders.[60]

Initially matters went well for Girardin. Believing Mme de Nadaillac still to be holding some of Rousseau's music and other items, the marquis requested them from her.[61] An acquaintance of his, Pierre-A. Benoît, invested in the

55. *Dictionnaire de Jean-Jacques Rousseau*, ed. Frédéric-S. Eigeldinger and Raymond Trousson (Paris 1996), p.189-90, 212-13 (articles by Daniel Paquette.) The libretto for the original *Le Devin* is in *OC*, ii.1093-114.

56. The edition published in 1781 (Paris, Esprit and Deroullède de La Chevardière) would contain ninety-six songs, airs and duets. Rousseau composed the music. Friends such as Corancez, the comtesse d'Egmont and Lebègue de Presle supplied the lyrics. See *OC*, i.1686, note 2, ii.1166-73; and *Dictionnaire de Jean-Jacques Rousseau*, p.171-72.

57. On the 'marriage' see Jean Guéhenno, *Jean-Jacques Rousseau*, translated by John and Doreen Weightman, 2 vols (London and New York 1966), ii.227-28.

58. Girardin to Du Peyrou, 4 October 1778, *CC*, xlii.8-10.

59. Copy written by Girardin of the contract between François Le Marchand and Thérèse Levasseur, [7 October 1778], *CC*, xlii.34-35.

60. Original prospectus in Girardin's hand, [*c.* 20 October 1778], *CC*, xlii.47-48, published in the *Journal de Paris* 295 (22 October 1778), p.1182-83.

61. Draft, Girardin to Mme de Nadaillac, [5 November 1778], *CC*, xlii.99-101.

Consolations project and served as intermediary between Girardin and Le Marchand.[62] Plans also were made for Le Marchand to engrave Rousseau's new and revised airs for *Le Devin du village*. In a transaction negotiated by Benoît, Girardin received 6000 *livres* from the directors of the Paris Opera so that they might perform *Le Devin* with the new music. Girardin next conceived of asking Europe's leading composers to complete *Daphnis et Chloé*.[63] Finally the marquis went to work on the *Consolations*, switching around musical passages and, in his fashion, 'improving' upon the versification.[64] Assuming responsibility for publicity, Girardin scolded Olivier de Corancez, editor of the *Journal de Paris*, for prematurely publishing a song to be included in the *Consolations*.[65] The marquis printed up prospectuses for the *Consolations* and asked Du Peyrou to take charge of distributing advertisements in Switzerland.[66] Du Peyrou persuaded the STN to manage subscriptions for the cantons.[67]

Progress towards publishing the *Consolations* ended abruptly on 12 December 1778, when Girardin learned that Le Marchand was bitterly attacking Benoît. The issue apparently stemmed from disagreements over paying the engravers. Moreover, Le Marchand was making little progress with the song cycle, and he was not pursuing potential subscribers aggressively. The seriousness of the dispute was such that, following an unsuccessful attempt at negotiation, Benoît insisted that Thérèse break her contract with Le Marchand, while he would try to recover the plates and subscription payments from the publisher. Benoît then volunteered to assume direct responsibility for engraving the plates and distributing the *Consolations*.[68] Girardin agreed to the revocation of the contract,[69] but the marquis underestimated Le Marchand's intransigence and influence. Meanwhile time was passing and with it any possibility for subscribers to obtain their *Consolations* by the announced publication date of 1 February 1779. Le Marchand refused to yield the plates and appealed to Paris police lieutenant J.-C.-P. Le Noir, who ruled that Thérèse's contract with the publisher was to stand.[70]

Benoît was stunned. He and his associate, François-Joseph de Foulquier, now envisaged a drastic remedy. Girardin would appeal against Le Noir's

62. Girardin to Pierre-Antoine Benoît, 9 November 1778, *CC*, xlii.105-107.

63. Girardin to Du Peyrou, 13 November 1778, *CC*, xlii.121.

64. Draft, Girardin to Benoît, [15 November 1778], *CC*, xlii.129-30.

65. 'Un Abonné' [Girardin?] to the *Journal de Paris*, 24 November 1778, published in the *Journal de Paris* 332 (28 November 1778), p.1336-37, *CC*, xlii.155-56. Corancez rejected Girardin's protest, noting that by printing the song he was giving free publicity to the impending collection.

66. Girardin to Du Peyrou, 4 [November] 1778, *CC*, xlii.86-89.

67. Du Peyrou to Girardin, 12 November 1778, *CC*, xlii.111-13.

68. François-J. de Foulquier and Pierre-A. Benoît to Girardin, [12 December 1778], *CC*, xlii.212-14; letter prepared for Marie-Thérèse Levasseur breaking the contract with Le Marchand, [12 December 1778], *CC*, xlii.215.

69. Girardin to Benoît, 15 December 1778, *CC*, xlii.229-30.

70. Foulquier and Benoît to Girardin, [30 December 1778], *CC*, xlii.280-82; H. Monin, 'Les œuvres posthumes et la musique de J.-J. Rousseau aux "Enfants trouvés" ', *Revue d'histoire littéraire de France* 20 (1915), p.48-55.

decision; Thérèse was to break off contact with Le Marchand, and she was to sell the scores of the *Consolations* to a third party. Whoever purchased them was to renegotiate with a new music publisher, honour all previous subscriptions and re-set a publication date. Girardin and Benoît understood that Le Marchand's plates might prove unrecoverable. At least, however, the unstable publisher would be removed from the picture.[71] Foulquier offered to purchase the *Consolations* from Thérèse, but there is no evidence that he did so.[72]

In appealing Le Noir's decision Girardin intended to argue that Le Marchand had actually been turning down potential subscribers. Du Peyrou theorised that the publisher did so because he wished to prepare an edition of the *Consolations* on his own, or as a piracy in association with François Grasset of Lausanne.[73] Meanwhile, as Girardin's appeal endured delay after delay, the Paris Opera scheduled a performance of *Le Devin du village* with Rousseau's new music. The public was electric over the prospect of the fresh tunes to be incorporated in Rousseau's greatest stage success, and the performance was offered on 20 April 1779. Unfortunately the critical reception proved disappointing. Writing in the *Journal de Paris*, Olivier de Corancez observed that Rousseau's changes were not so dramatic as had been expected, and a lackadaisical performance on the part of the singers marred the presentation. According to Corancez, the audience seemed to prefer the old airs to the new ones.[74] The review provoked an angry rebuttal from the Opera's director, A.-P.-J. de Vismes de Valgay, who defended his singers. De Vismes de Valgay noted that hesitations on the vocalists' part were not due to interpretive insecurities or memory lapses, but rather to 'la quantité prodigieuse de fautes de prosodie qui se trouvent répandues dans la partition, & que l'on ne s'est pas permis de corriger pour ne pas altérer les intentions de l'Auteur'.[75] The Opera soon abandoned the new airs.

Subsequent performances of *Le Devin du village*, on 23 April and 3 May, were advertised as being faithful to the original score and enjoyed a warmer reception than the revised version.[76] Girardin could not resist getting involved in the fray. In a letter to Corancez, published by the *Journal de Paris* on 25 April, the marquis insisted that the initial failure of *Le Devin du village*'s revival was due to misreadings by the performers. Girardin accused the directors of distorting Rousseau's musical objectives. Though Girardin veiled his protest in anonymity, he later confided to Du Peyrou that he was its author – as though his display of exclusive awareness of Rousseau's intent left any doubt![77] Concluding his letter to the *Journal de Paris*, the marquis expressed a hope that the

71. Foulquier and Benoît to Girardin, [30 December 1778], *CC*, xlii.280-82.
72. Foulquier to Girardin, [5 January 1779], *CC*, xliii.7-9.
73. Du Peyrou to Girardin, 9 February 1779, *CC*, xliii.100-101.
74. *Journal de Paris* 110 (20 April 1779), p.440-42, *CC*, xliii.222-24.
75. Anne-P.-J. de Vismes de Valgay to the *Journal de Paris*, 23 April 1779, published in the *Journal de Paris* 114 (24 April 1779), p.459, *CC*, xliii.233.
76. *Remarque*, *CC*, xliii.224.
77. Girardin to Du Peyrou, 27 May 1779, *CC*, xliii.299.

public would not judge the revised *Le Devin* on the basis of a single 'représenta-tion détestable'.[78]

Returning to the music he intended to engrave, Girardin decided to publish the incomplete *Daphnis et Chloé* quickly and as it stood, rather than wait for expert composers to complete it.[79] This strategy relieved Du Peyrou, who was growing increasingly testy over editorial liberties with Rousseau that the marquis was taking. Du Peyrou also was curious about the fate of Girardin's appeal concerning the *Consolations*, which seemed stalled in the creaky machinery of the French judicial system.[80] In the meantime, contrary to Du Peyrou's advice and despite the fiasco at the Opera, Girardin asked Benoît to hire an engraver to score Rousseau's new music for *Le Devin du village*. With the *Consolations* in judicial limbo, by offering songs from Rousseau's most cele-brated opera and the fragments from *Daphnis et Chloé*, Girardin hoped to avert subscriber lawsuits or desertions.[81] Moreover, in Girardin's view the music that Rousseau undertook near the end of his life was to provide evidence that he still could compose with originality and vigour. Such creative acuity therefore would be the most appropriate response to Rousseau's enemies, 'car il n'y a sortes d'indignités et D'impostures que toutte Cette Infernal Clique n'ait debitées et fait Debiter a ce Sujet'.[82]

The fragments from *Daphnis et Chloé* were prepared in August 1779 and appeared near the end of the year. The Paris publisher Jacques Esprit under-took the edition.[83] Controversy accompanied even this seemingly innocuous work. Rousseau originally had persuaded Olivier de Corancez, editor of the *Journal de Paris*, to write the lyrics. For Rousseau the words had little import-ance; Corancez, however, thought otherwise. When Rousseau considered publishing *Daphnis et Chloé* shortly before his death, Corancez offered what he reckoned to be important changes to his original words; and once he learned of the impending publication of the posthumous edition, the journalist-lyricist asked Benoît to place his alterations at the head of the score and respect his desire for anonymity. According to Corancez, Benoît adhered to the latter request, but refused to print the amended lyrics. Corancez protested to Du Peyrou, who probably intervened on his behalf.[84] Eventually Benoît was per-suaded to change his mind, informing Girardin: 'Il est certain que d'après les loix de la Librairie l'auteur des Paroles d'un Poëme a droit d'en empecher la publication s'il le veut et je pense qu'il est prudent d'eviter toute discution a cet

---

78. 'Un Abonné' [Girardin] to the *Journal de Paris*, [21 April 1779], published in the *Journal de Paris* 111 (25 April 1779), p.461-63, *CC*, xliii.224-27.
79. Girardin to Du Peyrou, 7 May 1779, *CC*, xliii.256.
80. Du Peyrou to Girardin, 16 May 1779, *CC*, xliii.281.
81. Girardin to Benoît, 27 May 1779, *CC*, xliii.292.
82. Girardin to Du Peyrou, 3 July 1779, *CC*, xliii.342.
83. *Fragments de Daphnis et Chloé, composé du premier acte, de l'esquisse du prologue et de différents mor-ceaux préparés pour le second acte et le divertissement, paroles de M***, musique de J.-J. Rousseau* (Paris, Jacques Esprit 1779). Richomme engraved the music and Drouët engraved the words. The cost to purchasers of the *Fragments* was 12 *livres*. See the *Dictionnaire de Jean-Jacques Rousseau*, p.189-90.
84. Guillaume Olivier de Corancez to Du Peyrou, [16 October 1779], *CC*, xliv.55-58.

egard.'[85] As might be expected, Girardin did not agree with Benoît and huffily criticised Corancez for addressing his complaint to Du Peyrou and not himself.[86] Having at least the sense not to alienate the editor of the *Journal de Paris* any more than necessary, Girardin reluctantly accepted a compromise. Rousseau's original manuscript stood as written; Corancez's amended lyrics appeared as an annex.[87]

The *Fragments de Daphnis et Chloé* were the first item of Rousseau's posthumous heritage to see light of day.[88] Meanwhile Girardin's lawsuit with Le Marchand over the *Consolations* was getting nowhere. What was worse, Thérèse, potential beneficiary of the publication and sale of the *Consolations*, would blow that project sky-high. Between July 1778 and November 1779 she had served as Girardin's 'guest' at Ermenonville, adopted by the marquis's family at the ostensible wish of her late husband. As time passed Thérèse resented her status and considered herself a hostage, released occasionally to wail on the outer banks of the île des Peupliers while boatloads of the faithful were rowed across the pond to pay homage to Rousseau's tomb. Goaded by Girardin's chief butler, John Bally, on the eve of publication of the *Fragments de Daphnis et Chloé*, Thérèse announced to the marquis that she was forsaking Ermenonville.[89] In Bally's company she fled and the couple rented a cottage in the nearby village of Plessis-Belleville.

Furious, Girardin decided that under no circumstances was Thérèse's name now to be associated with the *Consolations*. The marquis drafted a letter to her which he asked Benoît to approve, indicating that, while the suit with Le Marchand was far from settled, he and Benoît had already spent a considerable sum on paper, copper plates and lawyers. According to the marquis, the amount invested in the *Consolations* exceeded the 3000 *livres* Girardin had advanced to Benoît in Thérèse's name. Of course Girardin failed to mention that the 3000 *livres* were in fact properly Thérèse's: half the sum obtained from the Paris Opera in return for performance rights to the revised *Le Devin du village*. Meanwhile Girardin reminded Thérèse that he already had given her 1804 *livres* collected from English subscribers to the *Consolations*. He proposed that she keep this sum, and he would deliver to her the 3000 unspent *livres* acquired from the Opera's directors. Not a word was said about Le Marchand's and Girardin's lawsuit, but Thérèse was supposed to release any claim she might hope to stake to the scores or to the forthcoming edition of the *Consolations*. Benoît was to take over the venture. If profits derived from the subscription, they were not to go to Thérèse but to Paris's foundling home, the Hôpital des enfants trouvés. This was a particularly cruel gesture, since

85. Benoît to Girardin, [21 October 1779], *CC*, xliv.61.
86. Girardin to Benoît, 22 October 1779, *CC*, xliv.61-62.
87. 'Avis des éditeurs', *Fragments de Daphnis et Chloé* (1779), not paginated. *CC*, xliv.75-76.
88. Exception made for the leaks of Rousseau's 'Mémoire' of February 1777 (*CC*, xl.243-44) and the short preface to the *Confessions* which appeared in separate numbers of the *Journal de Paris* (20 and 30 July 1778).
89. Girardin to Du Peyrou, 3 November 1779, *CC*, xliv.71-72.

the Hôpital had been the dumping ground for Thérèse's abandoned children with Jean-Jacques. Was Girardin not reminding her of her irresponsibility as a mother?[90]

Aware that Thérèse was in no position to challenge his ultimatum and take him to court over ownership of the *Consolations*, Girardin was confident that Rousseau's widow would accept his offer. Fearful himself of an unsuccessful outcome of the lawsuit with Le Marchand, Girardin urged Benoît to keep in reserve the unspent 3000 *livres* as long as possible. The money might yet have to be used to compensate subscribers in case the *Consolations* failed to get off the ground.[91] Thérèse accepted Girardin's conditions.[92] She was entitled to 4804 *livres*, 3000 of which were to be withheld until the financial responsibilities for the *Consolations* were settled.[93]

In January 1780 the *Six nouveaux airs du Devin du village* joined the *Fragments de Daphnis et Chloé* on the market.[94] Neither sold well, even when discounted at the publisher's cost price of 10 *livres* the pair.[95] By May Girardin's year-and-a-half long appeal over the *Consolations* still had not been settled. The *Consolations* were sixteen months overdue and an estimated 1200 subscribers had grown impatient if not downright enraged. On 10 July the French Royal Council itself rendered a ruling. It favoured Girardin and Benoît, finally discharging Le Marchand from engraving and distributing the *Consolations*. Le Marchand was ordered to release the subscriptions he held and give them to Benoît.[96] Benoît then prepared an optimistic new prospectus:

L'Ouvrage qu'on annonce aujourd'hui aura pour titre: *LES CONSOLATIONS DES MISERES DE MA VIE, ou RECUEIL D'AIRS ET ROMANCES, PAR J. J. ROUSSEAU*, gravé sur cuivre, avec le plus grand soin, imprimé sur de beau papier, & orné d'un Frontispice avec le Portrait de l'Auteur; il contiendra dans 200 pages, de format petit *in-folio*, près de cent morceaux différens, dont plusieurs Duos dialogués, ou Scènes de Société, le tout avec accompagnement; & pour la commodité du plus grand nombre des Amateurs, on a fait transposer sur la clef de Sol la partie du Chant des Morceaux qui en ont été susceptibles. Le prix de chaque Exemplaire broché en carton, sera de 24 l. de France, qu'on ne paiera qu'en le recevant.[97]

Benoît refused to promise a publication date, but hoped that distribution of the *Consolations* would not be delayed beyond 1 December 1780. He also worried about the losses he might yet suffer, to the point of requesting that the French

90. Girardin to Benoît, 6 November 1779, *CC*, xliv.77-80.
91. Girardin to Benoît, 26 November 1779, *CC*, xliv.97-99.
92. Marie-Thérèse Levasseur's cession of Rousseau's *Consolations* as drafted by Benoît, [23 December 1779], *CC*, xliv.113-14.
93. Marie-Thérèse Levasseur's formal cession of the *Consolations*, [13 January 1780], *CC*, xliv.124-27.
94. Jacques Esprit had been commissioned to publish the *Six nouveaux airs* (Paris 1779).
95. Benoît to Du Peyrou, 5 May 1780, *CC*, xliv.226-28.
96. Final settlement between Benoît and Le Marchand, [23 December 1780], *CC*, xliv.364-66.
97. New prospectus for the *Consolations* of Rousseau, [early September 1780], *CC*, xliv.322-23. The subscribers' list is located in the archives du Musée de l'assistance publique, Paris, ms. 525.

Keeper of the Seals, Hue de Miromesnil, relinquish his claim to gift copies.[98] But new tensions erupted, now between Benoît and Girardin, over the legal costs of the suit with Le Marchand and the additional expenses of publishing the *Consolations*. In November 1780 Benoît requested 2900 *livres* above and beyond the 3000 *livres* he was holding in trust for Thérèse and the 800 additional *livres* Girardin claimed to have sent him. Even though Benoît apparently considered these new sums as a loan rather than a contribution, Girardin refused to pay.[99] This provoked an angry outburst from Benoît: 'On veut abusé de mon honnetété p[r] me refuser le salaire d'un travail très considerable que j'ai fait parce que je n'ai pas pris les precautions que la mefiance prescrit ordinairement.' Benoît went on to complain about the expenses, bribes and time that the entire *Consolations* affair had cost him.[100] He obtained little satisfaction from Girardin, who himself had incurred significant court costs versus Le Marchand. But Benoît went ahead with the *Consolations* anyway. They appeared early in April 1781, more than two years after the date originally promised. To authenticate their validity, Benoît offered Rousseau's manuscript scores to the French Royal Library.[101]

An embittered Benoît considered the *Consolations* to have been an intolerable burden. He went so far as to try to squeeze multiple subscriptions from members of Louis XVI's court, citing the Hôpital des enfants trouvés as beneficiary.[102] In August 1781, for 2400 *livres*, he ceded the plates of the *Consolations* and unsold copies of various scores to Jean-Pierre Deroullède, a Paris music merchant who had become publisher of the song cycle following the debacle with Le Marchand. Along with 288 plates, Deroullède acquired from Jacques Esprit 621 unsold copies of *Le Devin du village* and *Daphnis et Chloé*, as well as miscellaneous song scores held by Esprit and his correspondants.[103]

The matter concluded in November with Benoît's accounting, conducted for the benefit of the administrators of the Hôpital des enfants trouvés. Self-serving though Benoît's report was, it added several details which filled out the story. First of all, when Le Marchand had finally settled with Benoît in December 1780, the Paris music dealer was virtually bankrupt. He had been victimised by the economic difficulties besetting the book-trade in the capital over the past two years. To ensure the restoration of everything concerning the *Consolations* (copper plates and subscriptions) before Le Marchand's creditors

98. Benoît to [F.-C.-C.-B. Le Camus de Néville, director of the government's Book-trade Office], [early September 1780], *CC*, xliv.323-24.

99. Girardin to Benoît, 24 November 1780, *CC*, xliv.356-57.

100. Draft, Benoît to Girardin, [20 December 1780], *CC*, xliv.363.

101. Certification of placement of Rousseau's music manuscripts into the Bibliothèque du roi, [10 April 1781], published in the *Supplément à la Collection des œuvres de J.-J. Rousseau*, 3 vols (Geneva [STG] 1782), at iii.616, in-4°, *CC*, xlv.16-18. The manuscripts at present are in Paris, BNF, Rés. Vm⁷ 667.

102. Pierre-Dominique Bertholet, dit Campan, to Benoît, 11 April 1781, *CC*, xlv.18-19.

103. Cession by Benoît to J.-P. Deroullède of plates and unsold music of Rousseau, [17 August 1781], *CC*, xlv.37-39.

might seize them, Benoît assumed responsibility for Le Marchand's appeal costs in the suit with Girardin. This at least closed the case. Benoît estimated that sales of only 475 (not the estimated 1200) copies of the *Consolations* had brought him 11 400 *livres*. To this he added the 3000 *livres* which he held for Thérèse (and which she apparently never would receive) and 471 *livres* obtained for *Daphnis et Chloé*. Income therefore came to 14 871 *livres*. Total expenses came to 14 486 *livres*. The administrators of the Paris Foundling Home were therefore entitled to 385 *livres* of profit plus the 2400 *livres* that Deroullède had offered for the plates and remaining scores.[104]

The three topics described above – Du Peyrou's quest for manuscripts of the *Confessions*, Girardin's efforts at obtaining the original text of the *Considérations sur le gouvernement de Pologne* and the publication of Rousseau's music – illustrate the opportunities and frustrations experienced by the editors of the *Collection complète*. Fifteen years following the aborted general edition he had wished to make with Rousseau, Du Peyrou perceived his second chance. Painful interpretations of Rousseau's design haunted his every move. Once Du Peyrou concluded that Moultou's manuscript of the *Confessions*, Part I, was the Master's preferred copy, as close to an 'Ur-text' as he hoped to find, Du Peyrou determined that it had to be published, or else unscrupulous printer-booksellers might get hold of so-called 'mémoires' and falsify Rousseau's intentions. Locating original manuscripts of the *Confessions* became Du Peyrou's passion, though he remained ambivalent about Part II of them, should that exposé of Rousseau's deepest paranoia surface.

In his obsessive way Girardin also hunted down original texts. Convinced that he was Rousseau's truest disciple, the marquis never agonised over what texts to print or how he would print them. For Du Peyrou's benefit Girardin broadcast his suspicions that Part II of the *Confessions* existed – he had no qualms about accusing Moultou of harbouring it – but between 1778 and 1782 he seemingly had his own reasons for not wanting Part II in print. Girardin could afford to wait for the right moment to publish, as long as it was he who directed the course of Rousseau's posthumous revenge. The marquis fought hard to obtain the original manuscript of the *Considérations sur le gouvernement de Pologne*, as well as manuscripts of Rousseau's music. When it came to printing these pieces, he was convinced of his privilege to excise and amend Rousseau's words. Behind Girardin's editorial sleights of hand lay his certainty that he was the Master's spokesman. The purest *rousseauiste* ideology guided him. Yet so absolute was Girardin's conviction as to the rightness of his cause that he easily submitted to utilitarian considerations during his editorial adventures. He assured Wielhorski not to worry, that the *Considérations* would be properly excised and at the same time would retain their authority. To the modern critic such tampering with an author's text is akin to assault. Girardin would have disagreed vigorously. He was certain that he embodied Rousseau's wishes.

---

104. Benoît's account of the *Consolations* affair, [7 November 1781], *CC*, xlv.48-55.

5. Thérèse

The marquis's hostage

GIRARDIN envisioned the *Collection complète* as considerably more than a vehicle for Rousseau's ideas. Beyond any pure literary intention, the marquis sought to vindicate the writer as educator, prophet and martyr. Of course, in pursuit of such redemption Girardin was not alone. By 1778 a wealth of anecdotes concerning Rousseau had been recorded, and as an author he was attaining mythic status.[1] With the *Collection complète* the seigneur of Ermenonville hoped to seize control of competing *rousseauismes* by placing documentary evidence of his hero's struggles beside the two *Discours*, *La Nouvelle Héloïse* and *Emile*. In this way the entire story could be unveiled in narrative layers and its moral significance emphasised.

Girardin, however, was a born puppeteer and his editorial arrogance sometimes moved even Jean-Jacques off centre-stage. The marquis also assigned roles to secondary characters, including Rousseau's widow. Since Thérèse Levasseur was to be the financial beneficiary of the *Collection complète*, Girardin initially wished to create a persona for her worthy of both his generosity and Rousseau's genius. As a living ornament stalking the banks which fronted the île des Peupliers, Thérèse was supposed to be a perpetual mourner, serving the shade of her husband. In the *Confessions* Rousseau's description of her was that of a steadfast servant who, while failing to comprehend the reasons behind the Master's every need, more or less satisfied his physical wishes: a good, dull woman, somewhat extravagant in her tastes, a ready sexual vessel, passively accepting the world because there is no other choice, and standing by her man even at the sacrifice of motherhood itself.[2]

The difficulty with this benign image was that it rubbed against a contrary one. While very few contemporaries, if any, were conversant with Boswell's now suppressed journal entries for 31 January to 12 February 1766, where the young cavalier apparently had detailed thirteen casual sexual encounters with Thérèse while accompanying her to England to be reunited with Rousseau, the woman's contemporary reputation still was very poor.[3] Rousseau's

---

1. The *Mémoires secrets* (attributed to Bachaumont) contained the fullest collection of didactic anecdotes. For an analysis of their content see Raymond Birn, 'Fashioning an icon: Jean-Jacques Rousseau and the *Mémoires secrets*', in *The 'Mémoires secrets' and the culture of publicity in eighteenth-century France*, ed. Jeremy D. Popkin and Bernadette Fort (Oxford 1998), p.93-105. On the cultural sociology of the 'shy star' Leo Braudy writes: 'In his desire to be recognised for what he is himself, Rousseau is the true child of a new world of books and pictures, increased literacy and widely expanded audiences, which burgeon and thrive because they are unhampered by national boundaries and class tastes' (*The Frenzy of renown*, p.376).

2. *OC*, i.353-54, 356-58, 413-16, 561-62.

3. Excerpted from *Boswell on the Grand tour: Italy, Corsica and France*, ed. Frank Brady and F. A. Pottle (New York [1955]), p.293-94; *CC*, xxviii.347-48.

sudden death did little for Thérèse's stature, and rumours of the great man's suicide deeply implicated her.[4] For example, the Russian observer Denis Fonvizine reported the false news that Rousseau had stabbed himself in the heart upon learning of Thérèse's covert sale of the *Confessions* to a Dutch publisher.[5] Shortly thereafter, in a letter to J. J. Bodmer, Johann Heinrich Meister substituted for the suicide story a better substantiated one of an apoplectic stroke. Nevertheless, Thérèse's alleged perfidy remained in central focus. Quoting his son who had just written to him from Paris, Meister noted: ' "On imprime dans ce moment deux Volumes de Manuscrits qui lui avoient été volés à ce qu'on croit par sa femme, la plus mechante Creature qui existe sur la terre" (heritiere de l'esprit de Xantippe) "et qui n'a cessé de le brouiller avec ses meilleurs Amis".'[6]

Still deeply pained by the affair at Trye eleven years earlier, Du Peyrou was himself all too willing to blame Thérèse for sowing Rousseau's mistrust of worthy friends, of which, he wrote, 'Je suis peut être l'exemple le plus singulier de cette verité.'[7] Du Peyrou had readily enough accepted Girardin's idea for the *Collection complète*; from the start, however, the Neuchâtel millionaire considered the income the marquis was seeking for Thérèse to be excessive, and he feared that Girardin was in her clutches.[8] Yet Du Peyrou was more generous towards the widow than were other acquaintances in Rousseau's life. Disgusted by what he interpreted as Thérèse's greed, the writer's physician Lebègue de Presle found her entitled to no compensation whatsoever for the fruit of her late husband's genius.[9]

Because a devoted widow was essential for the legacy he was moulding, Girardin initially challenged the negative image of Thérèse circulating during the summer of 1778. The autopsy performed upon Rousseau's body laid to rest (or so Girardin thought) the suicide story, and the marquis developed his own tale of the philosopher's death. In it Thérèse played an honourable, though necessarily passive, role, and Girardin placed into Rousseau's mouth the request for Thérèse's 'adoption' by himself and the marquise. Without making a saint of

---

4. Tales of Thérèse's alleged responsibility for Rousseau's misery and even her complicity in his death have survived well into the twentieth century. For a survey and full bibliography see Laurent Müller's entry, 'Levasseur, Marie-Thérèse', in the *Dictionnaire de Jean-Jacques Rousseau*, particularly p.542-44.

5. Denis Ivanovitch Fonvizine to his sister, [5 July 1778], translated from the Russian into French in Joseph Suchy, 'Les *Confessions* à la mort de Rousseau, un témoignage sur une "préréception". Deux lettres peu connues de Denis Fonvisine', *Œuvres et critiques* 3 (1978), p.126-27; *CC*, xli.4-6.

6. Johann Heinrich Meister to Johann Jakob Bodmer, 13 July 1778, *CC*, xli.20.

7. Du Peyrou to Moultou, 5 August 1778, *CC*, xli.134.

8. Du Peyrou to Moultou, 26 September 1778, *CC*, xli.295-96.

9. Lebègue de Presle to Girardin, 14 [August 1778], *CC*, xli.171-74. Lebègue estimated Thérèse's annual income as thoroughly sufficient for her needs: 400 *livres* willed to her by Marshal Keith, Rousseau's one-time protector and former governor of Frederick II's territory of Neuchâtel; 300 *livres* from Marc-Michel Rey; and 400 *livres* from veuve Duchesne. He was as yet unaware of the 700 *livres* per annum with which Girardin would provide her from the money found among Rousseau's papers.

Portrait of Pierre-Alexandre Du Peyrou (anonymous)
(*Bibliothèque publique et universitaire, Neuchâtel*)

Thérèse, Girardin nevertheless defended her right to benefit from the *Collection complète*. According to him, such was her husband's wish. The marquis wrote to a disbelieving Lebègue de Presle: 'Notre ami n'a laissé qu'une personne qui Lui fut Chère. Elle a été jusques a sa mort La Compagne de sa vie. J'ai vû, j'ai connû ses dispositions et ses Intentions dernieres ainsi je n'ai plus qu'une seule maniere de faire tout pour luy. C'est de faire tout pour elle.'[10]

To award the *Collection complète* an authoritativeness found nowhere else, Girardin needed Thérèse. Her public statements, while actually composed by the marquis, were essential for the success of the edition. The first of them appeared in Samuel Swinton's *Courrier de l'Europe* on 6 October 1778, and as much defended Thérèse's own conduct as it repudiated rival editions which lacked the widow's sanction. Seeking to tarnish Boubers's lavish in-quarto, which allegedly contained youthful letters and writings by Rousseau never published before, Thérèse noted that:

ni Son mari, ni elle n'ont jamais vendu Le moindre manuscript de Sa Composition depuis Les ouvrages de luy qui sont Imprimés depuis Longues années. Ainsi tout écrit qui ne Sera pas de La propre main de L'auteur, dont L'Editeur refusera de se nommer publiquement, ou qui ne Sera pas présenté a la veuve pour être reconu par elle, et imprimé de Son avœu, ne peut être qu'une falsification, ou une fraude.[11]

Eight months later Thérèse still was issuing public disavowals of any role purportedly played by herself or her famous companion in Boubers's edition.[12]

Mistrusting Thérèse, Du Peyrou wished to release her from active participation in the *Collection complète*. He therefore urged that the *trois amis* and STG offer her a monetary settlement in return for her abandonment of present and future proprietary claims to her husband's corpus. Those claims were surely constructed upon a rickety foundation. After all, Thérèse's 'marriage' to Rousseau in 1768 had been performed according to a rite composed by Rousseau himself, not one authorised by civil or ecclesiastical authority. It therefore was quite possible that any title she claimed to respectable widowhood and legitimate inheritance rights might be challenged.

But who could supplant Thérèse as heir to Rousseau's papers? For his part Du Peyrou doubted whether he still could call himself Rousseau's sole literary executor. Moultou seemed to have inherited that role, while Girardin boasted that he was Rousseau's chosen 'dépositaire'. However the ownership question was to be settled, the *amis* agreed that it was essential to remove Thérèse from

10. Corrected draft, Girardin to Lebègue de Presle, [11 August 1778], *CC*, xli.156.
11. Corrected draft in Girardin's hand, Marie-Thérèse Levasseur to Samuel Swinton, 23 September 1778, published in the *Courrier de l'Europe* 28 (6 October 1778), p.222, *CC*, xli.292-93.
12. Draft prepared by François d'Ivernois, corrected by Girardin and signed by Thérèse, Marie-Thérèse Levasseur to the *Journal de Paris*, [11 May 1779], published in the *Journal de Paris* 136 (16 May 1779), p.545-46, *CC*, xli.292-93; draft prepared by d'Ivernois, corrected by Girardin and signed by Thérèse, Marie-Thérèse Levasseur to the *Gazette de Leyde*, [11 May 1779], published in the *Gazette de Leyde* (11 June 1779), p.4, *CC*, xli.269-71; draft prepared by d'Ivernois, retouched by Moultou[?], corrected by Girardin and signed by Thérèse, Marie-Thérèse Levasseur to the *Courrier de l'Europe*, [11 May 1779], *CC*, xli.268-69.

the picture. Du Peyrou had requested an immediate meeting with Girardin and Moultou in Neuchâtel, both to work out the details of compensation for Thérèse and to draw up the inventory for the edition.[13] He leaned towards an annuity benefit for the widow. Girardin, however, kept delaying the encounter. As early as October 1778 he was experiencing difficulty with Thérèse, who insisted upon a lump sum cash settlement rather than an annuity.[14] For his part, fearing the appearance of rival claimants to the heritage and the inevitable prolonged lawsuits, Girardin was reluctant about turning over to Thérèse a large sum of money before the edition even was completed. Arguments with Thérèse over her settlement made Ermenonville something less than paradise, and the widow Rousseau saw herself not as Girardin's guest but as his prisoner. During 1779 the relationship between Thérèse and her husband's arch-disciple would pass from strained to intolerable, exploding violently in January 1780.

The contracts for the *Collection complète*

While Girardin was working through the details of publishing Rousseau's music, he emerged with an asking price for the *Collection complète*. Announcing that in 1764 the Lyon bookseller Jean-Baptiste Réguillat had offered 19 000 *livres* for a revised corpus, the marquis estimated that fifteen years later 24 000 *livres* would represent a fair payment.[15] After all, the new edition would be adding much previously unpublished correspondence, the *Essai sur l'origine des langues*, the *Considérations sur le gouvernement de Pologne*, *Rêveries du promeneur solitaire* and the *Confessions* (Part I). Though he considered 24 000 *livres* to be too much, Du Peyrou presented Girardin's offer to the STG. He preferred that Thérèse cede her rights to the *trois amis* and not to the young Genevans, whose financial supports were fragile and likely to collapse beneath a legal challenge initiated by potential rivals to the inheritance.[16] Assured a *permission tacite* by Geneva's authorities, the members of the STG probably balked at being relegated to a nearly invisible role, and for the moment at least Du Peyrou deferred to their pride. On 9 December Moultou informed Girardin that the STG had accepted the price of 24 000 *livres*. In return for Rousseau's papers the publishers would offer Thérèse either a lump sum or else lifetime annuity payments representing 9 or 10 per cent of the principal. If Thérèse chose the annuity, Moultou and Du Peyrou would guarantee it.[17]

Thérèse, however, wanted cash on the barrel-head, which made Du Peyrou as unhappy as Girardin. The Neuchâtel disciple incorrectly accused the marquis of colluding with Rousseau's widow to understate her present

13. Du Peyrou to Girardin, 27 September 1778, *CC*, xli.298-302.
14. Du Peyrou to Moultou, 28 October 1778, *CC*, xlii.61-63.
15. Girardin to Du Peyrou, 13 November 1778, *CC*, xlii.117-18. For Réguillat's opening proposal to Rousseau on 8 June 1764 see *CC*, xx.166-68.
16. Du Peyrou to Moultou, 28 November 1778, *CC*, xlii.168-72.
17. Moultou to Girardin, [9 December 1778], *CC*, xlii.206-207.

income. According to Du Peyrou, once the transactions for the *Collection complète* and music were settled, 'Cette femme aura beaucoup plus qu'elle ne merite, tandis que R. a vecu dans une espece d'indigence.'[18] On 19 January 1779 Moultou informed Girardin that the STG was drawing up a contract. The young Genevans offered Thérèse 24 000 *livres* in two instalments, one-third payable in two years and the remainder payable a year after that.[19] She accepted the settlement.

By 26 January 1779 the definitive contract was ready. The STG agreed to produce 'une Edition générale des ouvrages de feu M^r. Jean Jacques Rousseau'. Du Peyrou and Moultou would furnish the STG with manuscripts at their disposal as well as those supplied to them by Girardin. Meanwhile Thérèse would cede to the STG all claims to her husband's works, known or unknown. Exception was made for the music, those works which Rousseau had no intention of publishing during the eighteenth century and those which he or his friends considered unworthy of publication. A list of writings that would comprise the edition followed, including those in the hands of Thérèse [Girardin], Moultou and Du Peyrou. The second part of the contract engaged the STG to pay Thérèse 24 000 *livres* in the two instalments. Once Du Peyrou supplied the STG with the first shipment of corrected manuscripts, Thérèse would begin collecting 5 per cent annual interest on the 24 000 *livres*. Only one format was specified, an illustrated in-quarto. The STG, however, held out the possibility of other volume sizes. The first shipment of books was promised thirty months after Du Peyrou's initial delivery of manuscripts.[20]

A tribute to Thérèse's persistence, the contract of 23-26 January 1779 certainly favoured her interests. Despite Du Peyrou's belief that she was getting more than she deserved, and Girardin's fears that Rousseau's relatives might challenge her inheritance, Thérèse had managed to lock in 24 000 *livres* plus interest, to be paid in full no later than January 1782. Because her status at Ermenonville remained dependent upon Girardin's goodwill, however, Thérèse had no cause for complacency. Girardin could hardly be elated by the prospect of Rousseau's widow acquiring a windfall of more than 24 000 *livres* in three years and then possibly forsaking Ermenonville for good. Thérèse had a vital place in the marquis's construction of the Rousseau legend and he could not afford to lose her. Almost immediately, therefore, Girardin spoke of having Du Peyrou and Moultou revise the contract, allegedly to protect the edition from threats to Thérèse's claim. Besides potential challenges to her legitimate widowhood, other embarrassing questions were possible, not the least of which concerned the whereabouts of the couple's abandoned children. What if one of the children were found alive? If

18. Du Peyrou to Moultou, 16 December 1778, *CC*, xlii.242.
19. Moultou to Girardin, [19 January 1779], *CC*, xliii.48.
20. Contract between Du Peyrou and Moultou on the one hand, and the STG on the other, for the publication of the *Collection complète des œuvres de J.-J. Rousseau, citoyen de Genève*, [23 and 26 January 1779], *CC*, xliii.53-56.

challenges to Thérèse's claim were made following payment of the 24 000 *livres* but prior to publication of the *Collection complète*, everything would be endangered. Girardin could not abide that prospect.[21]

The marquis therefore proposed that one-third or one-half of Thérèse's 24 000 *livres* be held back to pay off Rousseau's blood relatives should they appear to dispute the widow's inheritance.[22] Though increasingly disturbed by the marquis's manoeuvres ('toutes ces finasseries qui ne sont point de mon gout, ne menent qu'à des dif[f]icultés'),[23] Du Peyrou soon allowed his disdain for Thérèse and fears for the edition to overwhelm his sense of contractual honour. On 27 February 1779 Du Peyrou informed Moultou that the notion of holding in reserve two-thirds of Thérèse's inheritance now appealed to him.[24] And in June he reminded Moultou of the main reason for it: 'Mais je pense que vous avés oublié dans les causes de ses [Rousseau's] malheurs, une dés principales, l'ascendant de sa gouvernante sur son esprit, et le caractére de cette femme.'[25]

Meanwhile, at Ermenonville relations between Thérèse and Girardin deteriorated. Controlling the gold left by Rousseau, possibly 14 000 *livres* worth, around 23 March 1779 the marquis drew up a contract to pay Thérèse a derisory annuity of 500 *livres*.[26] A month later he added 200 *livres* to it.[27] Girardin's strategy was clear: it was essential for Thérèse to remain wholly dependent upon him. Therefore any income due her was to be in driblets distributed by himself. Thérèse, however, was not accepting her situation passively and Girardin blamed her unhappiness upon female capriciousness. Writing to Benoît in June the marquis noted with exasperation: 'Je ne desire par mon attachement inviolable pour son mari que de faire tout ce qui peut Lui convenir, mais Le plus grand Malheur c'est qu'elle même ne veut pas

---

21. The matter could have been simplified, or more probably complicated, by a will that Rousseau had drawn up at Môtiers on 29 January 1763. He brought it to England, where it apparently still existed in 1779. Neither Du Peyrou nor Girardin seemed aware of it, however. The will was copied in England in 1784 and the original subsequently disappeared. The copy reads: 'J'institue et nomme mon unique Heritiére et legataire universelle Therese le Vasseur, ma gouvernante: voulant que tout ce qui m'appartient et qui peut se transmettre de quelque nature et en quelque lieu qu'il soit, même mes Livres et Papiers et le produit de mes Ouvrages lui appartiennent comme à moi même; bien fâché de ne pouvoir mieux payer vingt ans de services de soins et d'attachement qu'elle m'a consacrés et durant lesquels elle n'a même reçu de moi aucuns gages. / J'exclus de ma succession tous mes parens en quelque dégré qu'ils soient, et notamment les deux plus proches, savoir Susanne Goncerue [*sic*] née Rousseau, ma Tante, et Gabriel Rousseau mon cousin germain leur légant à chacun cinq sols de légitime, non par mépris ni dérision, mais pour obéir à la Loi du pays où je vis' (see *CC*, xv.355). A rough draft exists today at Neuchâtel's bibliothèque publique et universitaire, ms. R. 284, f.71-73.
22. Girardin to Du Peyrou, 13 February 1779, *CC*, xliii.117.
23. Du Peyrou to Moultou, 13 February 1779, *CC*, xliii.135.
24. Du Peyrou to Moultou, 27 February 1779, *CC*, xliii.157-58.
25. Du Peyrou to Moultou, 5 June 1779, *CC*, xliii.314.
26. Notary's hand, formulation of an annuity paid by Girardin to Marie-Thérèse Levasseur, [23 March 1779], *CC*, xliii.199-201.
27. Hand of a notary's assistant, [22 April 1779], *CC*, xliii.230-32.

Commencer par Le savoir elle même, et qu'elle Change sans cesse D'idée. Tout cela joint a mes propres affaires m'afflige et me tourmente Sans cesse.'[28]

The marquis's complaints smacked of disingenuousness. Though one of the investors in the STG, the Geneva bookseller Gabriel Cramer, had been willing to guarantee the 24 000 *livres* due Thérèse, Girardin, with the accord of Du Peyrou and Moultou, decided to nullify the contract of 23-26 January 1779.[29] The long-delayed meeting of the *trois amis* and members of the STG finally occurred on 18 September at Du Peyrou's palatial town-house in Neuchâtel. As they drew up a new contract defining the edition, the *amis* clouded the issue of who actually owned the manuscripts. Adopting Girardin's strategy, they called themselves trustees and possessors ('dépositaires & possesseurs') of Rousseau's papers. The STG was to pay the *amis* 24 000 *livres* for the manuscripts, and Thérèse was identified merely as the potential beneficiary of the proposed edition. How much she was entitled to for her 'entretien honnête' never was spelled out. Nevertheless, 'agissans de concert' with her, the *amis* ceded to the STG 'tous les morceaux qui doivent composer ledit recueil authentique des Ecrits de Monsieur Rousseau'.[30]

The STG promised the *trois amis* a single payment of 24 000 *livres* plus interest by 1 October 1782.[31] Next, on 21 September, the *trois amis* signed their own convention, granting Thérèse semi-annual payments of 600 *livres*, representing 5 per cent interest on the 24 000 *livres*. The convention failed to say a word about Thérèse's alleged ownership rights. In fact, the question of rightful inheritance seemed to have been dismissed altogether, and the annuity granted to her took on the air of a gift – a pure act of generosity on the part of Rousseau's *amis*. They now agreed to place the principal in trust. Upon Thérèse's death the 24 000 *livres* were to be awarded to the children of Jean-Jacques Rousseau, if any could be found. Lacking this, the principal would be divided among the writer's living relatives.[32]

The revised contract with Thérèse had been Girardin's doing. He concluded that she had to be denied rights to Rousseau's papers, particularly those he had expropriated. Returning to Ermenonville, the marquis informed Du Peyrou that Rousseau's widow approved of the new convention. But his phrase – 'Dieu La maintienne en ces bons Sentimens pour son propre bien et repos' – suggested less than perfect accord.[33] Several days later, in the midst of his agonising lawsuit with Le Marchand, Girardin informed Benoît that there were additional difficulties with Thérèse: 'c'est que La personne qui devroit receuillir Le fruit des soins et des sentiments que nous donnons a La memoire de son mari, est precisement celle qui agit Le plus Contr'elle même. Il seroit

---

28. Girardin to Benoît, [11 June 1779], *CC*, xliii.318.
29. Gabriel Cramer to Marie-Thérèse Levasseur, [8 September 1779], *CC*, xliv.10.
30. 'Traité et Convention', [18 September 1779], *CC*, xliv.22-23.
31. 'Traité et Convention', [18 September 1779], *CC*, xliv.25.
32. Original in the hand of Du Peyrou's private secretary, Jeannin, convention among the *amis de Rousseau*, [21 September 1779], *CC*, xliv.28.
33. Girardin to Du Peyrou, 7 October 1779, *CC*, xliv.44.

aussi impossible de Calmer un torrent Des montagnes que de L'empecher de se tourmenter continuellement elle et Les autres.'[34] Finally, on 22 October, Girardin confided the worst: 'celle qui en receuillera Le fruit S'en montre de jour en jour plus indigne'.[35]

Thérèse's revolt

What was happening at Ermenonville? Thérèse was making no secret that she considered herself to have been cheated by the new contracts signed at Neuchâtel in her name. Six powerful men, along with their lawyers, bankers and accountants, had divested a poor, semi-literate, sixty-year-old laundress of her rightful heritage! Scenes and tears notwithstanding, Thérèse nevertheless had the last laugh. For she no longer was alone. Accompanied by Girardin's Irish butler, John Bally, Rousseau's widow informed Girardin that she was leaving Ermenonville for good. On 3 November the marquis admitted to Du Peyrou that his life had been a hell ever since his return from Switzerland. Thérèse had shown him nothing but ingratitude, and now this was compounded by her announcement that she intended to marry Bally. Ever the seigneur, Girardin could not resist accusing Thérèse of a double spite, first by fleeing and then by depriving him of a useful servant, a fine *valet de chambre*, though probably the only individual who would want her! Girardin claimed to have offered Bally a far more secure future than that which Thérèse proposed, but 'L'idée d'etre maitre chés lui L'a totalement entrainé.' Girardin cited the litany of Thérèse's sins and concluded by noting the stain she now was casting upon her late husband's name.[36]

It is tempting to perceive the vengeance of the weak in Thérèse's flight with Bally to the nearby village of Plessis-Belleville. Certainly her departure deprived Girardin of his chief *rousseauiste* ornament, after the tomb itself. In the years that followed, while Thérèse vainly tried to extract from the STG and its successors the 24 000 *livres* she believed her due, Bally would stand at her side. Nevertheless, because she forsook dignified widowhood for a liaison with a servant, Thérèse saw her reputation among her late husband's disciples reach rock bottom, and the *trois amis* felt vindicated in their shabby treatment of her. Instead of interpreting Thérèse's flight with Bally as a panicked reaction to the convention of 21 September, Du Peyrou self-righteously concluded that it justified withholding future payments from her.[37] He cast abuse upon 'la plus odieuse et la plus vile dés femmes, que j'avois toujours regardée comme l'unique Auteur dés calamités qui ont accompagné la vie infortunée de l'homme le plus fait pour la paix, et le bonheur'. Du Peyrou now considered it perfectly appropriate for Girardin to request suspension of the 1200-*livre*

34. Girardin to Benoît, 15 October 1779, *CC*, xliv.52.
35. Girardin to Benoît, 22 October 1779, *CC*, xliv.62.
36. Girardin to Du Peyrou, 3 November 1779, *CC*, xliv.72.
37. Du Peyrou to Moultou, 24 November 1779, *CC*, xliv.96.

annuity.[38] For his part Girardin agreed that turning the financial screws on Thérèse was the most appropriate way to punish her for her shameful conduct. The marquis urged Benoît to compensate English subscribers to the *Consolations des misères de ma vie* with the 3000 *livres* held in trust for Thérèse, should the project to publish the songs fall through.[39]

In her cottage at Plessis-Belleville Thérèse was not yet finished with Girardin. If her flight with John Bally turned out to be her first shocker, her revelations concerning Girardin's expropriation of her husband's manuscripts were her second. The marquis claimed to have provided Du Peyrou with an inventory of everything Rousseau had allegedly left at Ermenonville.[40] At the Neuchâtel meeting Girardin confirmed what he held and began supplying Du Peyrou with manuscripts. But the euphoria surrounding the Neuchâtel conference dissipated. Girardin's imperiousness and claims to have enjoyed Rousseau's total confidence, despite having known the writer intimately for just several weeks, galled Du Peyrou, whose unwavering devotion over a decade and a half had been rewarded by a chill on Rousseau's part during the writer's last years.

Then there was Girardin's interpretation of the edition. The marquis considered it to represent a supreme act of vengeance against the encyclopedist cabal which had allegedly tormented Rousseau for two decades. Girardin requested Rousseau's papers and letters from their possessors without informing the other two *amis*. He made textual changes in Rousseau's manuscripts that Du Peyrou considered whimsy at best and falsifications at worst. He accused Moultou of disloyalty towards the project. Finally Girardin appeared to possess greater knowledge of the details of Rousseau's life, all the more peculiar owing to the short time-span of the marquis's friendship with the writer. This pretended intimacy on the part of an egocentric aristocrat caused the reticent and introverted Du Peyrou considerable grief; it was Thérèse, however, who brought the pan to boiling point.

On 18 January 1780 Thérèse wrote a letter to Du Peyrou that jolted him profoundly. By now, she said, Girardin had undoubtedly informed the Neuchâtel businessman of her departure from Ermenonville: 'Il étoit tems que j'en Sorte Par toutes les disgraces de toute Sa maison, Et de luy même, tous les Passe droits qu'il m'a fait depuis la mort de mon Mary, Voulant être le mètre de tout.' Thérèse bitterly recounted a confused tale of betrayal and larceny, and she emphasised the need to escape her imprisonment. She informed Du Peyrou that the story of her marriage to Bally was a ruse, intended merely to liberate her from Girardin: 'Ainsy je ne voulois point être en tutelle de luy ny être encloitré a ne point voir mes amis.' Then Thérèse produced her newest revelation. Quitting Ermenonville, she requested from Girardin 'tout ce qu'il avoit encore a moy au Sujet des Papiers qu'il dit les

38. Du Peyrou to Girardin, 16 December 1779, *CC*, xliv.109-10.
39. Girardin to Pierre-Antoine Benoît, 26 November 1779, *CC*, xliv.97-99.
40. Girardin to Du Peyrou, 4 October 1778, *CC*, xlii.4-22.

Confessions et une Partie des dialogues, et Bien autre Papiers qu'il á fait
Copier depuis la mort de mon mary. Il m'a toujours deffendu d'en Parler tant
a vous qu'a M^r. Moultout.'[41]

What did this mean? Everyone knew that Girardin had sequestered Rousseau's papers immediately after the writer's death. According to Thérèse,
Rousseau had warned her of the marquis's deviousness.[42] In two subsequent
letters Thérèse went into detail over the manuscripts taken by Girardin, maintaining that the marquis had not informed Du Peyrou of everything he had
found. Girardin had failed to mention two volumes of letters and, what was
most shocking of all, he had told the *amis* nothing about the complete manuscript of the *Confessions* he had come across. Thérèse wrote that the 'livre de
Confession' in Girardin's hands 'étoit pareille a Ceux qu'il a donné A
Mr. Moüilletout [Moultou]. Mon Mary en avoit gardé l'original encas que
Son Amy m'üt renié'. According to Thérèse, promising to remit manuscripts
and letters to her and then changing his mind, Girardin essentially held her
hostage for them.[43]

Thérèse added that the marquis took over the papers at the very moment
the autopsy upon Rousseau was being performed: 'Il prît les manuscrits
cachetés, marchant sur le bout du pied, il portât le tout dans son Chateau,
ensuitte, il révint chercher le reste avec des domestiques.' Subsequently Girardin unsealed everything and made copies of whatever he wished. Thérèse gave
a detailed physical description of the manuscript of the *Confessions*, 'en petit
formât, entre l'in-8° et le petit in-4°. assé Epais, écrit d'un caractére très
minutté et serré'. According to her, it was Rousseau's final draft, the version
he had given to Moultou being a copy of it, and her husband had apprised
Thérèse of its existence a mere hour before his death. Because Lebègue de
Presle informed her that certain parts of the *Confessions* would be better suppressed, Thérèse suspected that Girardin had read them with the doctor, and
she believed that the marquise de Girardin had seen them too.[44]

Undoubtedly written under Bally's supervision, Thérèse's final letter to Du
Peyrou describing Girardin's perfidy was fraught with melodrama:

Enfin, pour briser la chartre privée, où M. de Girardin m'enterroit vivante, malgré
qu'il possédât, tout ce que mon mari avait laissé, argent, papiers, renseignemens,
nottes, Musique, lettres, que mon sort dependit absolument de sa bonne foi, je sortit

41. In a secretary's hand, Marie-Thérèse Levasseur to Du Peyrou, 18 January 1780, *CC*,
xliv.132-33. A short letter from Thérèse to Girardin, demanding Rousseau's papers, has survived
in the Girardin archives at Chaalis: Marie-Thérèse Levasseur to Girardin, [*c*. 10 November
1779], *CC*, xliv.80-81. The incredible orthography indicates that, unlike several of Thérèse's
letters to Du Peyrou, it was written without prompting from Bally: 'ge nores pas pances que monsieur deu Giradin ores difame la famedeu gan gaque vous diteu que voüs lemes Cete onetomeu
emoi geu vous di quesanespa geu leu dires touteu mavi que sanes pa.'

42. Marie-Thérèse Levasseur to Du Peyrou, 18 January 1780, *CC*, xliv.133.

43. In a secretary's hand, Marie-Thérèse Levasseur to Du Peyrou, 11 February 1780, *CC*,
xliv.153-54.

44. In a secretary's hand and autograph signature, Marie-Thérèse Levasseur to Du Peyrou,
6 March 1780, *CC*, xliv.175-77.

de son Chateau, ou plutôt de ma prison; j'escaladai les barrieres qui m'enfermoient, sous la vigilance des guichetiers, à qui, il avait confié ma garde, moi qui, plus de 30 années, n'ait suby qu'un joug paisible, amical, et le plus doux peut-être qu'une femme vertueuse puis desirer.[45]

Thérèse noted that Girardin was exploiting the very remains of her husband in order to embellish his vulgar theme park: 'Il désiroit posseder dans son parc, les mânes précieuses de mon mari, elles y réposent illégalement, sans formes judiciaires, ce qui rend cette terre célébre, et flatte l'orgueüil de M. de Girardin.'[46] Thérèse informed Du Peyrou that Girardin had tolerated her being assaulted at his table and had withheld pensions due her, including back-payment of the one a conscience-stricken Hume had acquired for Rousseau from King George III of England. She accused Girardin of having prevented her from accompanying him to Neuchâtel, and when a member of the STG, d'Ivernois, was visiting Ermenonville, she was forbidden to speak with him. Thérèse added (erroneously, it would seem) that Girardin also made a copy of the 'Dialogues' from d'Angiviller's manuscript. Finally, in order to expose Girardin's one last lie, that concerning Rousseau's final words, Thérèse related to Du Peyrou what she claimed to be the genuine description of her husband's death:

En mourant, en quittant le terrestre séjour d'Ermenonville, où la fatalité semblait l'avoir poussé, malgré sa répugnance, quels furent ses derniers mots, ils sont ressents, et le seront toute la vie à ma mémoire. J'en frémis. Il m'a dit, après que j'eûs ouvert la fenestre pour lui donner de l'air, s'étant trois fois frappé la poitrine, mourant et regardant le Ciel, y élevant les bras, invôquant pour lui et pour moi les bénédictions de l'Eternel, comme un homme divin qui voïoit les bras de Dieu prêts à le recüeillir, me recommandant à sa toute puissance, comme s'il eût pressentit ce qui arrive, les maux inoüis que veut me faire M. de Girardin. Il m'a dit, ah! Presle, dans quelle Maison m'as tu placé? J'y meure. Et en m'addressant tout ce qu'il pouvoit encore exprimer, ma femme, Girardin a de l'Esprit; il est fin, il aime l'argent; méfiés vous en. Tout fut dit, il cessa d'être, et M. de Girardin était déjà dans la chambre.[47]

Appealing to Du Peyrou's goodwill – 'Je n'ai guére que vous dans le monde pour me soutenir dans mes adversités' – Thérèse pleaded with her husband's old friend to believe her story. 'Si vous avez tant aimez mon mary; ne me refusez point vôtre protection et vôtre Souvenir.' She had, in effect, been deprived of a pair of corpuses: her husband's remains, illicitly embellishing foul Ermenonville, and her husband's manuscripts, stolen from her by the *châtelain* himself.

Thérèse's intervention had important consequences. First of all, because Du Peyrou accepted her account, relations between him and Girardin fell apart and the making of the *Collection complète* was to endure an entirely new set of tensions. Next, in light of communications breakdowns, editorial problems increased and unforeseen delays ensued. For his part, lacking Thérèse,

45. Marie-Thérèse Levasseur to Du Peyrou, 6 March 1780, *CC*, xliv.177.
46. Marie-Thérèse Levasseur to Du Peyrou, 6 March 1780, *CC*, xliv.177.
47. Marie-Thérèse Levasseur to Du Peyrou, 6 March 1780, *CC*, xliv.179.

Girardin had to rescue the Rousseau myth he was building as best he could, remanipulating it and joining efforts to demonise the widow. This led the marquis to delegitimise entirely Thérèse's claims to the legacy, and he would actively pursue alternative petitioners – the missing Rousseau children in particular, and lacking them, other blood relatives. Cousins appeared from distant and exotic places, as far away as Iraq, goaded on by Girardin to demand their share. Furthermore, in Girardin's hands, Part II of the *Confessions* would be ready, if need be, to embellish the heritage. If he would have to pay off Rousseau relatives with it, so be it. Finally, the marquis had to move rapidly to consecrate his hallowed site, to make of Ermenonville a place of pilgrimage, meditation and miracle, the geographical core from which Rousseau's new world was to arise.

III

The *Collection complète des œuvres de J.-J. Rousseau, citoyen de Genève*

6. Competing editorial visions

The sources of conflict

EVEN before Thérèse Levasseur's revelation of Girardin's treachery, conflicting visions and hidden agendas among the three editors threatened the integrity of the great project. From the start Moultou had been a hesitant contributor. Though flattered by Rousseau's hasty award to him of a manuscript copy of the *Confessions* back in May 1778, the worldly ex-pastor wondered what he should do with the unsolicited literary missile. Initially only Moultou's son Pierre knew that he possessed it, and even after Girardin admitted to holding the second manuscript copy, Moultou *père* asked Pierre to harbour the secret of Rousseau's gift.[1]

In his relations with Girardin, Moultou flattered the marquis, but the cagey French aristocrat was not easily taken in. Cherishing his self-image of avantgarde outsider, Girardin chided Moultou over the Genevan's lofty social and political connections, accused him of being weak-willed and repeatedly warned Du Peyrou that their *ami* was not to be trusted.[2] Despite Girardin's insistence that Moultou held much more than Part I, until his break with the marquis in June 1780 Du Peyrou appears not to have suspected anything more than what the former pastor had told him. Once he learned that Moultou indeed did possess a complete copy of the *Confessions*, Du Peyrou offered to keep the knowledge to himself until such time as would be deemed prudent to publish Part II.[3]

It is likely that Moultou's lengthy association with Rousseau was what prevented Du Peyrou from reacting as violently to the Genevan's secret as he did once he learned of Girardin's. For his part Du Peyrou was heartbroken over Rousseau's refusal to consider him to be anything more than an acquaintance during the last eleven years of the writer's life, but the millionaire disciple never openly translated his disappointment into jealousy concerning Moultou's favoured status.[4] On the contrary, Du Peyrou conceded to the Genevan the drafting of the prospectus and authorship of the preface to the *Collection complète*, honours which Moultou accepted reluctantly.[5] In contributing to

---

1. P.-C. Moultou to Pierre Moultou, 17 May 1780, *CC*, xliv.238-39.
2. Draft, Girardin to Moultou, 18 March [1779], *CC*, xliii.195-98; Girardin to Du Peyrou, 13 February 1779, *CC*, xliii.120; Girardin to Du Peyrou, 8 April 1779, *CC*, xliii.216.
3. Du Peyrou to Moultou, 14 June 1780, *CC*, xliv.254-55.
4. Du Peyrou to Moultou, 5 August 1778, *CC*, xli.134: 'si Mr Rousseau avoit conservé pour vous jusques à sa fin, les plus tendres sentimens, les miens pour lui, n'avoient point partagé son changement à mon égard'.
5. Du Peyrou to Moultou, 13 January 1779, *CC*, xliii.30. Moultou eventually composed a preface of a single paragraph, while Du Peyrou wrote the lengthier 'Dédicace aux mânes de Jean-Jaques Rousseau'.

the *Collection complète* Moultou insisted upon anonymity, and he earned Girardin's further contempt by likening himself to no more than an anonymous proofreader for the edition.[6] Fearful of the injury that *Rousseau juge de Jean-Jacques* might do not only to the reputation of the writer but also to his own standing among aristocratic acquaintances, Moultou initially opposed including these paranoid ruminations of the Master's old age in the *Collection complète*.[7] The role Moultou ultimately felt most comfortable with was that of shadow financier, negotiating between the STG and the *trois amis*. Eventually his timidity and ambivalence concerning the edition would irritate even Du Peyrou.[8] To Moultou's dismay, however, in terms of time and money he ended up as an extremely heavy investor in the project.

Du Peyrou's self-designated role in the edition was far more complex than Moultou's. Rejected confidant and patron, discouraged that his own deafness and gout disallowed him the pleasures of normal social intercourse, Du Peyrou considered himself the wronged victim of Rousseau's mistrust during the last decade of the writer's life. The discarded disciple therefore thirsted for redemption and believed that the *Collection complète* would continue and fulfil the mission aborted by Rousseau's flight from Môtiers and the fiasco at Trye. Du Peyrou's hope was that Rousseau's *œuvre* and edited correspondence might form the nucleus of a vast, multilayered autobiography. Supplemented by contributions from friends and enemies alike, the *Collection complète* would make comprehensible to the world that nomadic and misunderstood life, and the work laid aside in 1765 would be at last achieved.[9]

Establishing the central editorial office for the *Collection complète* at his elegant new residence in Neuchâtel, Du Peyrou – shipper, financier and absentee plantation owner in his native Surinam – undertook his own moral crusade to vindicate Rousseau. He would arrange the texts, organise their disposition on the page and fret over line spacing, print size and both ink and paper quality.[10] A need for self-redemption helps explain the liberties Du Peyrou took and the intensity of emotion with which he approached his task. The terrible experiences at Môtiers and Trye haunted him, and he was compelled to show that he had remained worthy of discipleship. Although

6. Moultou to Girardin, [*c.* 25 March 1779], *CC*, xliii.204-205. Moultou informed his friend J.-H. Meister that fear of upsetting authorities in Geneva caused him to lay low (Moultou to Meister, 12 January 1779, *CC*, xliii.26-29).

7. Moultou to Girardin, [*c.* 7 February 1779], *CC*, xliii.91; Moultou to Girardin, [*c.* 25 March 1779], *CC*, xliii.204.

8. Du Peyrou to Moultou, 8 January 1781, *CC*, xlv.1-3.

9. See Robert J. Ellrich, 'The cultural meaning of the anti-Rousseau tradition', *Romance quarterly* 38 (1991), p.311: 'It is hard to think of an instance in which the person of the author has so consistently acted as a catalyst in the reaction to the works'. See as well Julia Simon, *Mass enlightenment* (Albany, N.Y. 1995), p.85.

10. Du Peyrou to Pierre Boin of the STG, 16 January 1779, *CC*, xliii.38-42; Du Peyrou to Girardin, 19 October 1779, *CC*, xliv.58-60.

Rousseau no longer was present to forgive and approve, Du Peyrou might at least find expiation through his lonely editorial labours.[11]

Unlike Du Peyrou, Girardin had no burden of guilt to weigh him down. Although his self-proclaimed rights to discipleship allegedly reached back decades, in May 1778 his acquaintanceship with Rousseau had been barely four years old. Moreover, the origins of the liaison he shared with the writer were contractual, not emotional: around 1774 the marquis had hired Rousseau to copy music for him. Thus for Girardin the knots of perceived interdependence which bound Du Peyrou and, for that matter, Moultou to Rousseau were lacking. Once Rousseau arrived at Ermenonville, however, the relationship between the writer and the marquis changed completely. The former now was to endure the hospitality of the latter. Rousseau had consented to come to Girardin's estate as a last resort. Once there, the little pavilion where the writer resided, his meals, indeed even the family outings and exchanged visits, necessitated expressions of gratitude which Rousseau had always detested. For the final six weeks of his life he leaned upon Girardin for his very survival. Meanwhile, supreme mythmaker that he was, the marquis revelled in the role of courtly seigneur tending to his dependent guest. Following Rousseau's death, Girardin considered it a moral duty to remain in charge: to construct the tomb, approve the pilgrimages, adopt the widow and, above all, supervise the heritage.

Yet there was even more to it. The marquis envisioned himself as not merely a disciple but the veritable incarnation of the Master: a prophet in the wilderness. He therefore completed and 'improved upon' Rousseau's unfinished writings, particularly the *Rêveries du promeneur solitaire*; he never failed to rail against *encyclopédisme*, against 'Le Langage de L'esprit, et Celui du mercenaire Ecrivain [Diderot] auprès de celui de L'homme de Cœur dont la franchise Conduit La plume.'[12] Girardin's mythomania was boundless; his complaints against property tax increases imposed upon him were converted into a moral crusade against the entire *ancien régime*.[13] At first seeming to agree in principle with Du Peyrou over the purpose of the *Collection complète*, Girardin allowed the Neuchâtel businessman a free hand with routine copyediting and proofreading. When it came to hard decisions of suppressing texts, or for that matter of hiding entire manuscripts, Girardin had no qualms about inventing petitions from the grave. As he edited, Du Peyrou genuinely agonised over

11. Du Peyrou to Girardin, 27 June 1779, *CC*, xliii.331: 'Je Souhaitte passionnement de me montrer plus digne de la Confiance de mon pauvre et malheureux ami, que peut être il ne l'a crû lui même, et plus je vois d'acharnement á le calomnier, plus Sa memoire me devient chére et respectable, et redouble mon zele á seconder Sés volontés et jusques á Sés desirs.'
12. Girardin to Du Peyrou, 27 February 1780, *CC*, xliv.163.
13. *Note explicative* c, *CC*, xliv.143; Girardin to Du Peyrou, 27 February 1780, *CC*, xliv.164; Girardin to Benoît, [5 September 1780], *CC*, xliv.327: 'Le jugement de La Cour des aydes ne m'a point ètonné. C'étoit L'Intèret public dont il s'agissoit et jusques aux magistrats semblent aujourd'huy S'accorder à Le sacrifier. Cet évenement m'afflige profondément, parcequ'il montre que La Gangrène a gagné jusqu'au cœur et qu'il ne peut plus y avoir aucune ressource a Espèrer.'

whether he was fulfilling Rousseau's wishes. For his part Girardin had the dead Rousseau assent to the marquis's points of view, as the writer had indeed been forced to do during that late spring and early summer of 1778.[14]

Initially Du Peyrou and Girardin had veiled their differences behind the curtain of epistolary politeness and strained perceptions of common purpose; nevertheless the seeds of disgreement had been planted. As mentioned above, Du Peyrou held packages of manuscripts and letters left by Rousseau during different stages of the writer's itinerant career.[15] No exact inventory had been drawn up of them. In October 1778, however, Du Peyrou made an accounting of what he possessed and sent the list to Girardin.[16] It enumerated a huge, heterogeneous collection of printed items, manuscripts and letters, the nucleus of what was to become the *Collection complète* and the Rousseau archive found today at Neuchâtel's public and university library.[17]

In the letter to Girardin which accompanied his list Du Peyrou stated his concern over potential piracies. To avoid what he considered the most threatening one, he proposed that the *amis* quickly negotiate publication of the *Collection complète* with Boubers of Brussels, who already had printed nine volumes of his beautifully illustrated in-quarto edition.[18] Boubers especially worried Du Peyrou. His volume viii had contained certain of Rousseau's youthful pieces and some letters addressed to Mme de Warens between 1732 and 1739. If Boubers had been so skilful at acquiring these materials, might he not somehow locate a manuscript of the celebrated 'mémoires'? Du Peyrou feared so. For that matter, so did Girardin. Because he believed, however, that Boubers's edition was financed by the encyclopedist 'party' in Paris, the so-called *secte philosophique* which he despised, the marquis refused unequivocally to have anything to do with the Brussels publisher. He therefore vetoed Du Peyrou's proposal of co-operation.[19]

There were other sources of strain: the marquis's false report of Rousseau's finances at the writer's death and his reluctance to release the money to Thérèse; his need to maintain her dependence upon him; his manipulation of potential publishers to secure what Du Peyrou considered an inflated price for the edition; his obsession with potential rival claimants to the heritage and hints at paying them off with part of Rousseau's literary estate; his insistence

14. Girardin came to see himself as virtual co-author of the *Rêveries du promeneur solitaire*, turning into a finished text Rousseau's incomplete manuscript and pencilled jottings on a set of playing cards. The marquis also added a conclusion to the *Rêveries* which Du Peyrou found unacceptable (Girardin to Du Peyrou, 3 February 1779, *CC*, xliii.82; Du Peyrou to Moultou, 28 June 1780, *CC*, xliv.273).

15. Hermine de Saussure has done the best job to date of unravelling the destiny of Rousseau's papers. See her *Etude sur le sort des manuscrits de J.-J. Rousseau* (Neuchâtel 1974).

16. Copy prepared by Girardin's secretary, Jeannin, 'Note Spécifique des papiers de M^r. J:J:R: entre mes mains', [October 1778], *CC*, xlii.69-74.

17. In 1794 Du Peyrou would give the papers to the newly established library.

18. Du Peyrou to Girardin, 29 October 1778, *CC*, xlii.64-69. The bibliographical reference for the Boubers edition is Dufour, *Recherches*, ii.18-19.

19. Girardin to Du Peyrou, 13 February 1779, *CC*, xliii.118, 124.

upon speaking for the writer's ghost as to what should or should not enter the *Collection*. As early as February 1779 an exasperated Du Peyrou wrote to Moultou: 'N'etes vous pas depositaire de la volonté expresse de nôtre pauvre ami, et devés vous alleguer d'autres motifs que cette volonté clairement enoncée, et si Mˢ de G. persiste à vouloir l'emporter sur lés intentions de Rousseau, il n'a qu'à arranger tout seul la besogne. Je ne m'en mele plus et ne livre rien.'[20] Of course Rousseau's wishes were not always crystal clear. Take, for example, *Rousseau juge de Jean-Jacques*. Because it was injurious to so many, Moultou considered the 'Dialogues' to be inappropriate for the edition. On the other hand, invoking the spirit of revenge, Girardin was eager to see them in print. Brooke Boothby's publication of the first 'Dialogue' rendered the issue moot, and the entire *Rousseau juge de Jean-Jacques* found its way into the *Collection complète*.

From disagreement to crisis

The issue of dealing with living individuals unflatteringly treated by Rousseau was a genuine concern for the editors. It necessitated quick decisions. Failure to reach them in time might result in embarrassing pre-emptive attacks upon Rousseau, such as Diderot's in his *Essai sur la vie de Sénèque* (1779) and *Essai sur les règnes de Claude et de Néron* (1782). Others who had played controversial roles in the life of Rousseau (Malesherbes for example) expressed apprehension to one or more of the editors.[21] As the only *ami* whose name actually would appear editorially in the *Collection complète*, Du Peyrou was torn between a desire not to see individuals unjustly slandered and a compulsion to let Rousseau have his say. The Neuchâtel disciple claimed faithfulness to the text: 'je dois être plus Sensible que qui que ce Soit, á ce que le public ne Soit induit á aucune erreur, et á me mettre en etat de justifier et l'employ et la fidelité des piéces qui doivent la composer'.[22]

For his part Girardin made inconsistent distinctions between active editing and 'improving upon' Rousseau's texts. He was eager to have every word of *Rousseau juge de Jean-Jacques* published, yet he accommodated himself readily to Wielhorski's pleas to censor the *Considérations sur le gouvernement de Pologne*. In the latter instance Du Peyrou acquiesced. Largely to assuage Moultou, Du Peyrou also consented to reduce proper names to their initials in Part I of the *Confessions*.[23] But accommodation had its limits. Du Peyrou could not tolerate Moultou's wish to suppress entire paragraphs in the *Confessions* that the ex-pastor feared to be incriminating, and disagreement over some phraseology in the *Rêveries du promeneur solitaire* illustrated to Du Peyrou just how far apart he and Girardin were over proper editing strategies.

20. Du Peyrou to Moultou, 27 February 1779, *CC*, xliii.157.
21. Malesherbes to Moultou, [*c.* June 1780], *CC*, xliv.273-78; Malesherbes to Moultou, 26 July 1780, *CC*, xliv.297-302; draft, Malesherbes to Moultou, [August 1780], *CC*, xliv.309-17.
22. Du Peyrou to Girardin, 27 June 1779, *CC*, xliii.331-32.
23. Du Peyrou to Moultou, 5 June 1779, *CC*, xliii.315.

Pierre-Antoine Benoît, Girardin's partner in the bungled sale of Rousseau's music, disliked a reference to himself in the fourth 'Promenade' of the *Rêveries*. Rousseau was describing a humiliating moment at an al-fresco dinner given by Mme Vacassin, where the hostess's daughter confronted him with the leading question of whether he ever had had any children. The writer lied by responding negatively. Rousseau's account had Benoît present at the meal. Uncomfortable at being mentioned as a passive witness to Rousseau's mortification, Benoît asked Girardin that he be removed from the scene. Responding to the request, the marquis informed Benoît that there would be no problem: 'D'ailleurs comme je suis entierement Le maître et le redacteur de cet ouvrage, il ne sauroit y avoir La moindre difficulté a faire a ce sujet ce qui vous agrée.'[24]

Writing to Du Peyrou, Girardin then improved upon his editorial sleight of hand by recommending a text change different from that which Benoît had requested. Rousseau's words had read: 'Il y a quelque tems que M. Foulquier m'engagea contre mon usage à aller avec ma femme diner en maniére de Pic-nic avec lui et *son* ami Benoit chez la Dame Vacassin restaurantrice.'[25] The marquis proposed to replace the phrase with: 'M. Foulquier et Benoit mes amis [m'engagèrent...]', as though acknowledgment of belonging to Rousseau's inner circle would be sufficient to assuage Benoît's sensitivities.[26] Du Peyrou, however, could not accept Girardin's proposed change. For the editor in Neuchâtel, increasing the number of Rousseau's acquaintances would play havoc with biographical truth: 'Comment faire dire *M: F et B més amis,* á un homme qui Se peint complettement isolé Sur ce globe?' Du Peyrou asked the marquis. He then suggested to Girardin that it would be preferable to suppress Benoît's name entirely and merely write: 'M^{rs}. F. et un de ses amis'.[27] The STG edition restored Rousseau's text, abbreviating the proper names to their initials.[28]

Particularly interesting about this exchange is the fact that Du Peyrou's objection had more to do with his interpretation of the course of Rousseau's life than with the issue of textual fidelity. For Du Peyrou, by the time of Mme Vacassin's dinner Rousseau was the abandoned prophet, and no suggestion of a contrary view was to cloud this perception. Another incident linked to the *Rêveries* further illustrates Du Peyrou's sense of textual veracity. Girardin had written a postface for the *Rêveries* which Du Peyrou considered entirely inappropriate. But how to reject the marquis's contribution without appearing to insult him? The Neuchâtelois appealed to the *auto*-biographical integrity of the *Collection complète*, indicating that works not of Rousseau's hand had to be excluded from the core of the edition. He tried to satisfy Girardin by insisting that the marquis's remarks could be saved for an eventual supplement.[29]

24. Girardin to Benoît, 4 [October 1779], *CC*, xliv.39.
25. *OC*, i.1034, my emphasis.
26. Girardin to Du Peyrou, 7 October 1779, *CC*, xliv.44.
27. Du Peyrou to Girardin, 19 October 1779, *CC*, xliv.58.
28. *Collection complète*, xx.295, in-8°.
29. Du Peyrou to Moultou, 17 April 1780, *CC*, xliv.201.

Because Du Peyrou envisioned the *Collection complète* as the authoritative source for Rousseau's life and work, the disclosure by Thérèse of Girardin's sequestration and suppression of the *Confessions* was particularly appalling. Having vaguely suspected Girardin of concealing items, Du Peyrou now heard Thérèse's direct accusation.[30] For the Neuchâtel disciple Girardin's behaviour was a clumsy attempt to hoard Rousseau's life for himself: the basest treachery. Still, when Du Peyrou first received Thérèse's disclosure, he could barely believe it. For several weeks he kept the matter to himself. Even when mentioning it to Moultou, Du Peyrou was sceptical.[31] But once Thérèse revealed the news of Girardin's seizure of Rousseau's papers, Du Peyrou understood why, after merely brief acquaintance, the marquis had such intimate knowledge of the writer's life.[32]

A grave crisis now confronted Du Peyrou. Challenging Girardin without a plan might explode all the delicate partnerships and destroy the edition. Du Peyrou then would be deprived of his mission and Rousseau of his literary apotheosis. Dangers were real. New sets of pirated or false editions were being announced. They threatened to twist both texts and biographical veracity.[33] Furthermore, what would become of the papers the marquis was holding? Faced with the threat of a lawsuit, would Girardin hide them? Or, what seemed to Du Peyrou the worst of all possibilities, might a court of law force the marquis to give them to Thérèse? Granted her husband's papers, she then would be free to sell them to the highest bidder and Du Peyrou's magnificent project would be lost forever. The Neuchâtel businessman believed that, whatever the costs, he had to get hold of the manuscripts in Girardin's hands. He therefore offered Thérèse his assistance. He would seek to get Girardin to hand the papers over to Thérèse. But she then was to yield them, as well as future claims to anything else, to Du Peyrou and Moultou.[34]

To a letter which condescendingly scolded Thérèse for her general behaviour, Du Peyrou appended a statement for her signature, authorising the passage to him of her husband's manuscripts. Du Peyrou then announced that Moultou's son Pierre would shortly bring the statement to her and that she should unburden herself to the young man.[35] As Pierre Moultou headed

---

30. Du Peyrou to Moultou, 23 December 1778, *CC*, xlii.266.

31. Du Peyrou to Moultou, 10 February 1780, *CC*, xliv.151.

32. Marie-Thérèse Levasseur to Du Peyrou, 11 February 1780, *CC*, xliv.153-54; Marie-Thérèse Levasseur to Du Peyrou, [6 March 1780], *CC*, xliv.174-80; Du Peyrou to Moultou, 8 March 1780, *CC*, xliv.181-85.

33. In the *Gazette de Berne* (26 April 1780), p.4, F. La Combe of Lausanne mentioned that he was receiving subscriptions for 'les œuvres complettes de J.J. Rousseau, 21 vol. petit format; le vol. à 1 L. 10 de France' (see *remarque* i, *CC*, xliv.216). Serving as agent for the STN, on 27 April 1780 Louis-Sébastien Mercier informed F.-S. Ostervald that subscriptions would be opened in Frankfurt for the STN's anticipated piracy (*remarque* iii, *CC*, xliv.217).

34. Du Peyrou wrote to Moultou: 'Je suis, on ne peut plus incertain sur le parti à prendre avec Mr de G. au sujet des manuscrits qu'il s'est aproprié. Je pense qu'avant tout, il faut engager la veuve à nous ceder ses droits, et à nous autoriser à lés reclamer' (Du Peyrou to Moultou, 10 April 1780, *CC*, xliv.193).

35. Du Peyrou to Marie-Thérèse Levasseur, 18 April 1780, *CC*, xliv.204-207.

for Plessis-Belleville to obtain Thérèse's accord, Du Peyrou confronted Girardin by mail. Following some lengthy complaints about his health and state of mind, the Neuchâtel editor at last came to the point and mentioned Thérèse's initial letter, where 'elle Se plaint de la Suppression de plusieurs de sés papiers manuscrits, en particulier dés Confessions, d'un Metastase enrichi de notes marginales, &c. &c., Sur le Sort désquels, vous lui aviés recommandé le Silence le plus résolu vis à vis de M^r. Moultou, et de moi &c. &c'.[36] Although Du Peyrou informed Girardin that he initially had doubted Thérèse's revelations, he added that subsequent letters from her incontrovertibly confirmed them. Du Peyrou expressed dismay over Girardin's seeming lack of confidence in the Neuchâtel businessman's vocation to bring everything pertaining to Rousseau to light, and he requested the restitution to Thérèse of all papers sequestered by Girardin.

Upon receiving Du Peyrou's letter, Girardin rushed back a reply in which self-righteous indignation deflected a half-admission that he indeed was keeping two sealed packages in reserve to compensate Rousseau's abandoned children, should they show up and claim their inheritance. For Du Peyrou's benefit the marquis accused Moultou of hiding his own manuscript of the *Confessions*. Girardin reserved his most vicious condemnation for Thérèse who, he said, had turned Du Peyrou against him:

j'aurois du moins désiré que Les peines Les plus accablantes, qui sont celles de toutte espece que m'a Causées une femme, ou plutot un serpent dont La bonté n'a jamais fait qu'echauffer Le venin, ne se fussent pas enfin étendues jusques a vous; je n'avois malheureusement pas besoin de cette derniere preuve pour savoir que c'est un monstre de méchanceté & hypocrisie, et de fausseté, qui Se feroit tout Le mal possible a elle même pour en pouvoir faire a quelqu'un, et dont L'unique plaisir seroit de brouiller toutte La terre.[37]

However much Du Peyrou might be tempted to agree with Girardin's assessment of Thérèse's responsibility for the disasters in Rousseau's life, on this occasion the Neuchâtel disciple refused to let the marquis carry the day. Du Peyrou denied being manipulated by the widow's tears, defended Moultou's conduct and asked Girardin what he intended to do with his manuscript of the *Confessions*.[38] Girardin's reply was a full admission that he held the manuscript. But he integrated the manner in which he had obtained it into his larger myth of Rousseau's last wishes. According to Girardin, just prior to the writer's fatal stroke Thérèse had received orders from her husband 'de me dire qu'il comptoit assés sur mon amitié pour s'en rapporter a moy comme a un Pere Pour Le soin de touttes ses affaires, et Pour réclamer auprès de tous ses Depositaires, et de me remettre Les Clefs de son secretaire et tous ses papiers'. Opening the late Rousseau's desk drawer in the presence of Thérèse, Girardin

---

36. Du Peyrou to Girardin, 25 April 1780, *CC*, xliv.215.
37. Girardin to Du Peyrou, 30 April [1780], *CC*, xliv.217.
38. Du Peyrou to Girardin, 7 May 1780, *CC*, xliv.228-31.

claimed to have found merely 3800 to 3900 *livres* in gold and two sealed packages.[39]

The marquis recounted that several days later, again with Thérèse as witness and accompanied by Lebègue de Presle, he had unwrapped Rousseau's packages and begun reading the manuscripts. Indeed they included the entire *Confessions*. Girardin informed Du Peyrou that at the start of Part II (Book VII) Rousseau had written unequivocally that his memoirs were not to be published until the deaths of all interested parties. The marquis claimed that his attitude towards the *Confessions* was predicated upon this wish. Moreover, wrote Girardin, Thérèse informed him that Rousseau had given Moultou a second copy of the *Confessions* – 'la totalité' – as well as copies of all the other 'new' writings. As Moultou was in Paris at the time of Rousseau's death, Girardin claimed to have invited the Genevan to Ermenonville, ostensibly to discuss the prospective edition; but he received no reply. Finally, Girardin maintained that Thérèse was the one who had wished to hide the existence of the Ermenonville manuscript of the *Confessions* from the other *amis*. Concerning Du Peyrou's essential question, what he intended to do with the *Confessions* now that they had been uncovered, Girardin threw the issue back at the Neuchâtel disciple: 'Que dois je faire et de Cet ecrit et de La Musique des Muses galantes? Car je vous assure que je voudrois pour beaucoup n'avoir pas une seule Ligne entre Les mains, et surtout rien de commun avec cette funeste femme.'[40]

In a subsequent exchange Du Peyrou accused Girardin of inconsistency, if not disingenuousness. According to Du Peyrou, back in February 1779 the marquis had written that, concerning Rousseau's manuscripts, the only options were either '*tout publier à present, ou tout bruler*'.[41] Now Girardin wanted to suppress part of the corpus and publish the rest. Since the marquis was holding the *Confessions* in trust for Thérèse and since she wished to yield the manuscript to Du Peyrou, the latter advised Girardin to release it.[42] The seigneur of Ermenonville demurred. Changing his story, he now insisted that it was Rousseau who had commissioned him to hold the writer's papers; Thérèse had nothing to do with the matter. As much as he himself might wish to publish everything, Girardin claimed a need to abide by Rousseau's command and withhold Part II of the *Confessions* until after the deaths of the parties mentioned in it: 'Combien je voudrois pouvoir etre delivré du seul reste d'un Dépot qui me peze autant, et qui ne m'attire de touttes parts que Dégouts et chagrins. Neanmoins je pense qu'il me faut bien Le garder puisque j'ai èté chargé des Dernieres Intentions de L'auteur.'[43]

39. Girardin to Du Peyrou, 17 May 1780, *CC*, xliv.236.
40. Girardin to Du Peyrou, 17 May 1780, *CC*, xliv.237.
41. Du Peyrou to Girardin, 1 June 1780, *CC*, xliv.245. Girardin's words had been: 'entre Le parti de tout publier, ou celui de tout bruler dans ce qui compose Sa dèfence et sa vie je ne pense pas qu'il puisse y avoir de milieu' (Girardin to Du Peyrou, 13 February 1779, *CC*, xliii.121).
42. Du Peyrou to Girardin, 1 June 1780, *CC*, xliv.244-46.
43. Girardin to Du Peyrou, 10 June 1780, *CC*, xliv.252.

Du Peyrou suspected that Girardin wished either to publish Part II of the *Confessions* himself or else to use the manuscript to pay off Rousseau relatives who might contest Thérèse's inheritance. Because of Moultou's timidity and aristocratic connections, the marquis was reasonably sure that the Geneva partner never would release *his* version of Part II for publication. Meanwhile, in June 1780 Moultou at last informed Du Peyrou that he indeed did possess Rousseau's entire manuscript. If he considered this to be a second betrayal, Du Peyrou hid his feelings. His first priority was to save the *Collection complète*. Furthermore the Neuchâtel disciple wished to solidify his axis against Girardin. Therefore, while perceiving that he might yet have to sue the marquis in Thérèse's name, Du Peyrou maintained cordial relations with Moultou and agreed to keep the Genevan's secret.[44]

Within a few weeks relations between Du Peyrou and Girardin broke down entirely. The marquis tried to thwart Du Peyrou's possible lawsuit by claiming that it might result in a court-ordered destruction of the *Confessions* manuscript.[45] This argument did not impress the Neuchâtel editor, who by now had received Thérèse's agreement to cede all of her husband's papers to him.[46] Following a curative trip of two months to the hot springs at Le Valais, in September 1780 Du Peyrou addressed a last angry letter to Girardin, which the marquis returned after making a copy for himself. He reminded Girardin that however much the *amis* might scorn Thérèse, she remained sole heir to her husband's property. To defend Thérèse's rights, Du Peyrou hinted at resorting to Louis XVI's justice.[47] Girardin responded with a petulant request for copies of whatever papers Du Peyrou intended to submit to the courts, and correspondence between the pair ceased.[48] Meanwhile the marquis's postface to the *Rêveries du promeneur solitaire*, as well as his other 'improvements' of Rousseau's text, continued to infuriate Du Peyrou. Just prior to the trip to Le Valais, Du Peyrou wrote: 'les corrections verbeuses, lâches, impropres par les expressions font un contraste parfait avec le stile chaud, serré et vigoureux de J.J. O Dieux! que devenoient les manuscrits de cet infortuné entre lés mains d'un pareil homme.'[49]

Influenced by Moultou and others who feared that a lawsuit over the *Confessions* might result in the public disclosure and subsequent piracy of Part II, with the attendant embarrassments for those insulted in the work, Du Peyrou

---

44. Du Peyrou to Moultou, 14 June 1780, *CC*, xliv.254-55.
45. Girardin to Du Peyrou, 27 June 1780, *CC*, xliv.269-70; Girardin to Du Peyrou, 20 July 1780, *CC*, xliv.293-94.
46. Prepared by a secretary, Marie-Thérèse Levasseur to Du Peyrou, [11 July 1780], *CC*, xliv.286.
47. Du Peyrou to Girardin, 5 September 1780, *CC*, xliv.324-26.
48. Girardin to Du Peyrou, 13 September 1780, *CC*, xliv.329-30.
49. Du Peyrou to Moultou, 28 June 1780, *CC*, xliv.272-73. After his disagreement with Thérèse, Girardin wished to edit the *Rêveries* as an act of vengeance directed towards her. As he informed Du Peyrou: 'Je n'ai pas besoin de vous dire que je dois changer maintenant bien des Choses dans la Conclusion, Surtout celles qui concernent cette femme qui depuis s'est montrée tellement indigne de ce nom' (Girardin to Du Peyrou, 5 February 1780, *CC*, xliv.141).

failed to take Girardin to justice.[50] Furthermore, he probably had second thoughts about the unpleasant distractions of courtroom drama with an experienced adversary like the marquis. Therefore Du Peyrou backed down. Girardin kept Thérèse's manuscript until 1794, when, under house arrest during the Revolution, he was persuaded to return it to her.

The prospectus for the *Collection complète*

Between January 1779 and August 1780, the date of the first delivery of the *Collection complète*, Du Peyrou refused to allow the strain of relations with Girardin to deter him from his primary task: converting thousands of manuscript and printed pages at his disposal into a structured moral tale relating Rousseau's exemplary life and work. It ultimately was decided to publish the *Collection complète* in at least two formats. The first delivery was to contain eight volumes in-octavo or four volumes in-quarto. The shipment would comprise *La Nouvelle Héloïse*, the fragment 'Les amours de milord Edouard Bomston', *Emile* and the latter's abbreviated sequel, *Emile et Sophie, ou Les Solitaires*. Because 'Les amours de milord Edouard Bomston' and *Emile et Sophie* were the only genuinely new pieces, the editors and publishers risked incurring the disappointment of subscribers.[51] After all, while remaining an officially prohibited book, *Emile* had been available in France for years.[52] Neither 'Les amours de milord Edouard Bomston' nor *Emile et Sophie* gave purchasers much reason to shell out 24 *livres* for the in-octavo volumes or 40 *livres* for the in-quartos. 'Les amours de milord Bomston' occupied only seventeen pages of the in-quarto and twenty-six of the in-octavo. Slightly more substantial, *Emile et Sophie* occupied sixty-five pages of the in-quarto and fewer than a hundred pages of the in-octavo.[53] As a depressing account of Sophie's infidelity and Emile's loneliness, however, *Les Solitaires* embarrassed even Moultou and Du Peyrou, who wrote in a brief 'Avis des éditeurs': *'Plus le tableau qu'il nous présente*

---

50. Moultou had to respond to contemporaries worried about publication of the entire *Confessions*. As he wrote to Suzanne Necker: 'Je vous remercie de ce que vous me dites des memoires de Rousseau. Soyés Sure que rien de ce qui ne doit pas paraitre ne paraitra' ([22 October 1780], *CC*, xliv.349).

51. As early as May 1779 the Geneva bookseller Jean Gosse predicted that however much the producers of the *Collection complète* might stress the authoritativeness of their edition, a saturated market would greatly reduce customers' orders: 'jusqu'a présent je n'en ai pas encore pu placer aucun, parce que tous ceux qui ont dejà Ses premiers ouvrages ne les veulent pas a double' (Jean Gosse to Henri-Albert Gosse, 12 May 1779, *CC*, xliii.272).

52. For the period between 1762 and 1777 Jo-Ann McEachern lists thirty-six separate French-language editions of *Emile*; for the years between 1762 and 1778 she lists forty-four French-language editions of *La Nouvelle Héloïse* (see McEachern, *Bibliography*, i.769-71 and ii.439-41). See also Moultou's comment to Girardin [*c.* 7 February 1779]: 'Emile S'imprime et Se vend tous les jours à Paris' (*CC*, xliii.91).

53. 'Les amours de milord Edouard Bomston' appeared at iii.513-30 of the in-quarto edition of the *Collection complète*. In the in-octavo it appeared at v.350-76. *Emile et Sophie, ou Les solitaires* appeared at v.449-514 of the in-quarto and x.233-331 of the in-octavo.

est empreint du génie de son sublime Auteur, & plus il est révoltant. Emile *désespéré*, Sophie *avilie! Qui pourroit supporter ces odieuses images!'* [54]

By publishing familiar titles first, the *amis* and STG intended to merge Rousseau's wishes into a conscious marketing strategy.[55] Had they begun the edition with an unpublished and eagerly anticipated work like Part I of the *Confessions*, they thought they would open themselves up to immediate piracy.[56] After all, the risk was small for *contrefacteurs* to publish the one or two volumes in demand, take their profits and ignore the remainder of the STG's edition. Faced then with having to fill out their own sets with titles which had been on the market for years, despite pleas of authoritativeness, the STG would risk subscription cancellations and certain ruin. Therefore the counter-strategy of withholding greatly anticipated pieces for later volumes, the *amis* believed, would force potential pirates to incur the expense of following the publishing rhythm of the *Collection complète*. Faced with such a prospect they might renounce their villainous schemes. The *amis* and STG therefore reserved the *Confessions*, *Rêveries* and correspondence for later volumes because, as everyone anticipated, few pirates were sufficiently patient to craft a meticulous imitation of an entire set in hopes of reaching a certain best-seller in their ninth or tenth volume.

But this design was based upon hope and untested assumptions: first, that no additional manuscripts of a widely desired item such as the *Confessions* would wind up in the hands of pirates; second, that subscribers to the STG's edition were more patient than potential pirates and willing to duplicate their old *Emiles* or *Nouvelles Héloïses* prior to filling out new sets with the heretofore unpublished pieces; and third, that potential pirates would give up rather than wait out the STG to obtain the desired items. As matters transpired, the initial hope was confirmed. Each of the *trois amis* held the only copies of the *Confessions* in existence; no clandestine manuscripts surfaced. The second and third assumptions, however, proved wrong. Subscribers betrayed reluctance about investing in an entire multivolume edition, however much 'authorised', merely to obtain Rousseau's heretofore unpublished titles as part of their sets. Certain pirates patiently awaited the STG's publication of the heart and soul of Du Peyrou's 'total' autobiography – the *Confessions*, 'Dialogues', *Rêveries* and

54. *Collection complète*, v.451, in-4°.
55. Back in 1765 Rousseau had proposed devoting volume ii of the Môtiers edition (in-quarto) to *La Nouvelle Héloïse*. Volume iii and part of volume iv were to have contained *Emile*. Volume i was to have contained Rousseau's political works, including *Du contrat social*. For their *Collection complète* the *amis* and STG followed Rousseau's general pattern, though delivery of volume i was delayed. See Rousseau to Du Peyrou, 24 January 1765, *CC*, xxiii.181-82; Du Peyrou to the STN, [*c.* 20 October 1778], *CC*, xlii.45-46.
56. Admittedly, this contradicted Du Peyrou's earlier marketing strategy back in November 1778, when he had proposed preceding the *Collection complète* with a small edition which contained Rousseau's unpublished work, including the *Confessions*, Part I (see chapter 3, p.73). It is probable that by September 1779 Du Peyrou no longer feared the existence and publication of a pirated manuscript of Rousseau's 'mémoires'. After all, more than a year had passed since the writer's death. During this time no manuscripts of the *Confessions* had surfaced besides Moultou's and his. Of course he shortly would learn about Girardin's.

correspondence – before committing their thievery, while others simply took the chance of reproducing the entire *Collection complète* in inexpensive duodecimo editions.

Its initial marketing strategy in tatters, the STG responded with alternative publishing schemes: its own cost-conscious in-duodecimo, then a second in-duodecimo, posing as a piracy of its own edition! The Genevans printed a slimmed-down edition limited to Rousseau's *œuvres posthumes*; they made *Suppléments* which could be purchased independent of the *Collection complète*; they produced individually obtainable volumes of the *Confessions* and *Rêveries*. But not even the most imaginative marketing tactics deterred the pirates. Every time the STG developed what it believed to be a viable edition, it had to confront imitators.

As soon as the first contracts between the *amis* and STG had been signed back in January 1779, Du Peyrou took charge of editing. He urged the young Genevans to watch their workers closely, conduct regular inventories of sheets and page proofs, and be certain that nothing was smuggled out of the print-shop.[57] Du Peyrou insisted that high quality characters, ink and paper were the best guarantees against unauthorised imitations, and he held out the hope that a beautiful in-quarto would bring honour to the edition. Curiously enough, while fretting about the infamy of pirates, Du Peyrou was himself willing to 'borrow' from other existing editions. He asked Girardin to obtain for him Duchesne's *Œuvres de M. Rousseau de Genève*, in order 'en tirer ce qu'il y aura de bon'; and he wished to peruse Boubers's edition closely: 'Comme les planches de l'Edition de Bruxelles Sont tres belles, on en pourra faire un choix pour les ouvrages deja imprimés, et voir pour les manuscrits, ce qui Sera le plus convenable.'[58] Du Peyrou prepared the first journal announcements,[59] and he asked the STG to begin working on the prospectus, which he wanted printed on the same quality paper as that used for the edition itself.[60]

Sorting through the manuscripts, letters and notes Rousseau had left with Du Peyrou was an enormous task. The editor also had to decipher the hand-written corrections of published work made by Rousseau back in 1764/65, and he tried to determine the fitness of proof sheets that had languished for years. Du Peyrou now lamented that he had not previously examined all the packages in his possession. Reminding Girardin of the trust that Rousseau had bestowed upon him and him alone, even through their years of partial estrangement, Du Peyrou complained:

Je regrette tous les jours de n'avoir pas fait usage plutot de la permission que l'auteur m'avoit donnée d'examiner tous Ses papiers. Je Serois actuellement bien au fait, et

---

57. Du Peyrou to the STG, 23 January 1779, *CC*, xliii.49-52.
58. Du Peyrou to Girardin, 2 February 1779, *CC*, xliii.77.
59. Advertising in the periodical press turned out to be a problem, because journal editors refused to announce the titles of Rousseau's books officially prohibited in their countries. Du Peyrou wrote to Girardin: 'L'avis á inserer dans les papiers n'a pü ëtre accepté par la raison dit on qu'il est deffendü d'annoncer des livres prohibés' (2 February 1779, *CC*, xliii.77).
60. Du Peyrou to the STG, 30 January 1779, *CC*, xliii.73.

j'eusse pü lui demander bien des éclaircissemens que je ne peux plus avoir. J'ay laissé douze ans et plus, les choses dans l'Etat ou elles m'avoient été remises, et cela par un principe de délicatesse dont j'ay aujourd'hui regret.[61]

Nevertheless, Du Peyrou laboured on, except when the pain from his gout attacks laid him low. It must have been a phenomenal experience for him, stimulating and exhausting, as he worked alone in his exquisite surroundings, sifting through manuscripts and printed pages, hearing Rousseau's voice once more in the correspondence, then finally recreating that prophetic life: a disciple's dream.

Too often, however, the unpleasant reality of the present interrupted Du Peyrou's serene explorations of the past. First, there was the breakdown in relations with Girardin. In addition, the Neuchâtel editor felt particularly responsible for the inexperienced young men who directed the STG, and he involved himself in their publishing decisions. Du Peyrou had a connoisseur's vision; therefore his pampered child was the in-quarto. He originally had wanted a lavishly illustrated edition which would overwhelm all rivals, particularly Boubers's volumes, and he was disappointed when time constraints forced the STG to eliminate engravings in favour of a separate album of illustrations.[62] Du Peyrou agreed with Girardin that the in-octavo would represent the 'mass market' edition of the *Collection complète*; here too, however, he emphasised quality, persuading the Geneva entrepreneurs to set only twenty-four lines per page and not the thirty-two which they had originally envisioned.[63] For the Neuchâtel millionaire the in-duodecimo was the least important edition, a cheap production kept in reserve to challenge pirates.[64]

Concerning relations with potential subscribers, Du Peyrou emphasised scrupulousness. He insisted that the prospectus avoid promising what the publishers could not deliver. For example, in a technical though limited sense Rousseau had participated in Duchesne's edition of *Œuvres* of 1764-1769. Therefore, according to Du Peyrou, it would be misleading for the prospectus to state (as the STG desired) that all the editions made in Rousseau's lifetime were done without his knowledge, and he reminded Moultou that their task was not a mere commercial matter but rather a sacred mission: 'La Veuve traitte avec les libraires pour le prix, et nous, nous traittons pour l'honneur de la memoire de Rousseau, et la sureté de sés manuscrits.'[65] For his part, Girardin never ceased envisioning the edition as anything other than an act of posthumous revenge. He requested a special volume dealing with Rousseau's persecutions. Though he agreed to conclude with Part I of the *Confessions* and the *Rêveries*, the marquis stated his wish to leave room in the future for

---

61. Du Peyrou to Girardin, 25 January 1779, *CC*, xliii.61-62.
62. Du Peyrou to the STG, 1 April 1779, *CC*, xliii.209-10.
63. Du Peyrou to the STG, 30 January 1779, *CC*, xliii.72-73.
64. Du Peyrou to Moultou, 20 February 1779, *CC*, xliii.153; circular letter signed by Pierre Boin, STG to STN, 1 May 1779, *CC*, xliii.250-51.
65. Du Peyrou to Moultou, 27 January 1779, *CC*, xliii.71.

additional blockbusters – such as *Rousseau juge de Jean-Jacques* and, of course, Part II of the *Confessions*.[66]

In February 1779 Du Peyrou received a first draft of the prospectus. It stated that most of the general editions appearing in Rousseau's lifetime either were made without the writer's knowledge or else against his will. On the other hand, the edition presently announced by the STG, '*de l'aveu de la veuve & des amis de l'auteur*', should be regarded as though it were offered by Rousseau himself. In fact, the prospectus draft stated, the edition was essentially the same as that prepared by Rousseau back in 1765 and aborted in the wake of the persecution suffered at Môtiers. The draft explained that the same friend who had been entrusted with that edition of Rousseau, and who had become 'dépositaire de tous ses papiers', now was responsible for the updated collection. Following the author's wishes, the work could be considered as 'préparée [...] par M[r]. *Rousseau* lui-même, elle est son ouvrage; ses amis ne sont que les témoins & les garants de la fidélité de l'exécution'. Distinguished artists were to make the engravings, the collection would appear in three deliveries, eight months apart, fifty de luxe editions would be printed as well and purchasers could subscribe either via the leading booksellers of Europe or else directly to the STG.[67] The discount for booksellers proved to be generous, a 25 per cent reduction, plus a free thirteenth set for every dozen ordered.[68]

A list of the works originally intended for the Môtiers edition then followed, accompanied by a note stipulating that, in response to Rousseau's wishes, all the pieces from his youth as well as those not exclusively from his pen would be omitted from the present version. However, a supplement to which one might subscribe separately would contain pieces pertinent to the writer's career. Finally, the STG added a list of '*Ouvrages faits depuis 1764*', which would be included in the Geneva edition, '*suivant l'ordre philosophique des matières*'. These were:

Lettres & Mémoires sur divers sujets. Mss. [...] Lettres à M. le Maréchal Duc de Luxembourg, sur la Suisse en général, & particuliérement sur le Val de Travers, lieu de son domicile. Mss. Lettres sur la Botanique, Mss. [...] Lettres à M. le Président de Mallesherbes, contenant le vrai tableau & les vrais motifs de la conduite de l'auteur. Mss. Lettres à Botafaco sur la Législation de la Corse. Mss. Lettres à ses amis. Mss. Les Rêveries du promeneur solitaire. Mss. [...] Les six Livres de ses confessions, où il rend compte de sa vie jusqu'à l'époque de son établissement à Paris en 17* [69]

Du Peyrou corrected several items in the draft prospectus. Most of his changes were in the interest of accuracy. For example, he wanted the *Dictionnaire de musique*, Rousseau's partial translation of Tasso, the *Oraison funèbre du feu duc d'Orléans* and '*Un ouvrage sur la constitution de la Pologne*' eliminated from

66. Girardin to Du Peyrou, 3 February 1779, *CC*, xliii.82.

67. Printed draft prospectus for the *Collection complète* with Du Peyrou's annotations, [8 February 1779], *CC*, xliii.96-100.

68. Circular letter with Pierre Boin's signature, STG to STN, 1 May 1779, *CC*, xliii.250-51; Jean Gosse to Henri-Albert Gosse, 12 May 1779, *CC*, xliii.272-74.

69. Printed prospectus annotated by Du Peyrou, [8 February 1779], *CC*, xliii.98-99.

the list of writings which were to have appeared back in 1765. He requested that they instead be placed under the list of *'Ouvrages faits depuis 1764'*. Later, because the announcement of Part I of the *Confessions* suggested that Rousseau had written no more than this, Du Peyrou would request a clarification in the prospectus's final draft. What the editor left unchanged in the prospectus was its interpretation of the purpose of the *Collection complète*. The STG informed potential subscribers that its edition meant to make sense of that irreproachable literary life. Though Du Peyrou's perception of his editorial role differed from the relatively passive portrait which the prospectus attributed to him, he remained clearheaded about his task. For a dozen years this most loyal disciple had borne in his heart poignant and painful images of Rousseau. Now that he at last had assembled the courage to read and reread nearly everything, who better than himself could know and understand the misperceived prophet? Surely not the timorous Moultou, surely not the puffed-up Girardin. Through the edition he would share the 'real' Rousseau with the world. This was cultural manipulation in the most noble of causes.

7. Publishing the *Collection complète*

GIRARDIN's concealment of a *Confessions* manuscript and his refusal to yield it up when confronted by Du Peyrou were not the sole impediment to the successful publication of the *Collection complète*. Cheap in-duodecimo piracies of the edition appeared mere weeks after the first shipment of the STG's stately in-octavos and in-quartos. When European booksellers were slow with their payments to the STG and the young entrepreneurs experienced difficulty making good on their own bills, Moultou, the Genevan bookseller Samuel de Tournes and de Tournes's banking connections had to prop up the entire project. To salvage its investment the STG devised ingenious marketing strategies intended to increase sales.

Unfortunately these ploys converted the *Collection complète* into the *affaire de libraires* detested by Du Peyrou. Other issues discouraged Rousseau's most loyal disciple. Du Peyrou had to face the understandable reluctance of Rousseau's correspondents to see their names displayed in the edition. One of them, Malesherbes, invoked his right to censor letters by Rousseau that he deemed offensive or compromising. Du Peyrou knew that such omissions would have a deleterious effect upon his 'total' moral autobiography, but he had to concur. The timid Moultou played censor with the *Confessions*, Part I, but the former pastor's innate caution failed to insulate him from the grave political unrest that struck Geneva in the summer of 1782, while the final volumes of the *Collection complète* were in course of publication. Moultou and one of the STG members, François d'Ivernois, were forced to flee the republic. Mercifully the edition was spared. Its final and supplementary volumes appeared without incident, and it would be up to the market, not censors nor counter-revolutionaries, to decide the edition's ultimate fate.

The first stage: flashback to 1779

Du Peyrou considered it essential to obtain authenticated manuscripts for the *Collection complète*. These included Rousseau's correspondence, but obtaining letters depended upon the goodwill of their recipients, and permissions to publish often were difficult to acquire. For example, Madeleine-Catherine Delessert initially refused to yield up her letters on botany, and Malesherbes censored pieces of Rousseau's correspondence to him.[1] Setbacks like these notwithstanding, Du Peyrou pushed on. Early in March 1779 a revised draft of the prospectus had listed subscription prices of 10 *livres* per volume for the

---

1. Madeleine-Catherine Delessert to Jean-André Deluc, 9 March [1779], *CC*, xliii.178-79; Chrétien-Guillaume de Lamoignon de Malesherbes [to Moultou], [June 1780], *CC*, xliv.273-78.

in-quarto and 3 *livres* per volume for the in-octavo.[2] Disappointed at having to exclude illustrations from the in-quarto, Du Peyrou urged his partners to remain loyal at least to elegant typography, with the magnificent *imprimerie royale* edition of Buffon's works serving as model.[3]

For Girardin and the STG speedy publication was essential. Furthermore, in order for the *Collection complète* to succeed, the *amis* had to outmanoeuvre Boubers and other rivals hunting down Rousseau manuscripts. From Ermenonville Girardin was generous with marketing advice. He urged Du Peyrou to have the STG concentrate upon the in-octavo, that is, the edition which could be published most quickly and with widest distribution potential. In Girardin's view (which proved correct) identical publication deadlines for the in-quarto and in-octavo would produce unacceptable delays.[4] As early as spring 1779 the STG noted that reader interest in Rousseau was peaking, and politely urged Du Peyrou to hurry with his editing.[5] Meanwhile Moultou manoeuvred his way out of writing a lengthy general preface, thereby earning additional contempt from Girardin.[6] Driven to his bed by both gout and stress, Du Peyrou nevertheless resisted overly hasty editing and asserted that only a carefully conceived product could do justice to Rousseau's memory.[7]

However principled and deliberate Du Peyrou was, he underestimated the competition. On 23 and 28 April 1779 Boubers published notices in the *Gazette de Leyde* and *Courrier du Bas-Rhin* for what he called 'les œuvres posthumes' of Rousseau. He claimed to have in press Rousseau's 'Mémoires, *ses* Lettres, *son* Ouvrage sur la Pologne' and rare and piquant items known only to the author's most intimate friends. Boubers reminded readers that he already had made good on nine volumes of his edition, including one volume (the eighth) which *'contient nombre de Pièces, qui n'ont jamais été imprimées'*, and that his set already incorporated thirty illustrations.[8] Aiming his shaft directly at the *amis* and STG, he boasted:

2. Draft of printed prospectus titled 'Recueil des Ecrits de J.J. Rousseau, proposé par Souscription, à Genève, *chez la Société Typographique. In-4° & in-8°*, avec un Portrait de l'Auteur', [early March 1779], *CC*, xliii.171-74.
3. Du Peyrou to Girardin, 1 April 1779, *CC*, xliii.212-13; Georges-Louis Leclerc, comte de Buffon, *Histoire naturelle, générale et particulière*, 15 vols, in-4° (1749-1767).
4. Girardin to Du Peyrou, 8 April 1779, *CC*, xliii.215-16.
5. Copy prepared by Jeannin, Du Peyrou's secretary, and sent to Girardin, STG to Du Peyrou, [*c.* 15 April 1779], *CC*, xliii.218-19.
6. Girardin to Du Peyrou, 27 April 1779, *CC*, xliii.242.
7. Du Peyrou to Girardin, 20 April 1779, *CC*, xliii.220.
8. *Gazette de Leyde* 33 (23 April 1779), p.4, *Courrier du Bas-Rhin* (Cleves) 34 (28 April 1779), p.272, *CC*, xliii.234-35. The retail price for Boubers's edition customarily was 12 *livres* per volume. This was 2 *livres* more than the asking price for the STG's in-quarto. But Boubers's edition contained Moreau's engravings while the Geneva text did not have illustrations: they were to be purchased separately as an album (see announcement in the *Mercure* (31 July 1779), p.336, *remarque*, *CC*, xliii.391). Rousseau's 'œuvres de jeunesse', a major selling point for Boubers's edition, quickly became a victim of piracy. Veuve Duchesne used them to fill out volume x (the *Supplément*, Neuchâtel [Paris] 1779) of the *Œuvres de M. Rousseau* originally undertaken by her late husband. See *note explicative* a, *CC*, xlii. 233-34.

Cette édition, nous osons le dire avec confiance, est la plus exacte & la plus belle, qui ait encore paru. Nous doutons même, qu'on puisse en donner une dans la suite, qui lui soit comparable. La nôtre aura toujours sur toutes les autres un avantage considérable, celui d'avoir été avoué de l'Auteur, qui même avoit bien voulu guider Mr. Moreau, le Jeune, Dessinateur & Graveur du Roi à Paris, pour la composition des Dessins. Le génie de ce célèbre Artiste *s'est confondu, pour ainsi dire, avec celui de l'Auteur.*[9]

What could all of this mean? Did Boubers possess unknown manuscripts of the *Confessions, Considérations sur le gouvernement de Pologne*, other pieces, and Rousseau's correspondence? It shortly became apparent that Boubers's announcement was merely a crude threat to pirate the STG edition of Rousseau's *Œuvres posthumes* as soon as it appeared. Du Peyrou stressed the need to reply publicly to Boubers.[10] In Thérèse's name announcements were placed in the *Journal de Paris* and *Gazette de Leyde*, disavowing Rousseau's role in the Belgian's edition and citing the STG's *Collection complète* as the only authorised one.[11] Boubers tried to counter-attack. He wrote that he had sought Rousseau's participation in his edition; unable to produce the writer's assent, however, Boubers could merely reassert his intention to print 'en entier les *Œuvres posthumes* de feu M. *Rousseau*' – quite naturally, *following* publication of the STG's edition.[12]

Boubers was not the only threat. As early as February 1779 the STN had stated its readiness to pirate the *Collection complète*.[13] To forestall this the STG informed its Swiss rival that its own in-duodecimo would be sold at the rock-bottom price of 2 *livres* per volume.[14] Then the STG offered the STN the cheap edition at the same preferential rates as the in-quarto and in-octavo – that is, with a 25 per cent discount and free thirteenth copy. But the proposal was insufficiently seductive. The STN would indeed publish its piracy in-duodecimo, copied from the STG's more prestigious editions. In fact, shortly after the appearance of the STG's prospectus, the STN drafted one of its own. The Genevans' strategy of not publicising their in-duodecimo played right into the hands of the Neuchâtel pirates, who described their anticipated edition as small in size and price, a service to readers with modest incomes and an honour to Rousseau's memory. The STN announced its edition as genuinely 'portative in 12° [...] sans faire aucun tort aux éditeurs de Genève [...] mais moins dispendieux & plus co[m]mode pour la lecture'. The Neuchâtelois vowed to follow the same publishing rhythm as the Genevans, their first delivery to be ready three months after the STG's.[15]

9. *Gazette de Leyde* 33 (23 April 1779), p.4, *CC*, xliii.234.

10. Du Peyrou to Girardin, 6 May 1779, *CC*, xliii.253.

11. See chapter 5, p.100.

12. *Gazette de Leyde* (6 July 1779), p.4, *Gazette d'Amsterdam* (23 July 1779), p.3-4, *Gazette de Berne, Supplément* (14 August 1779), *CC*, xliii.348-50.

13. STN to STG, copied by the directors of the STG and sent to Girardin, 13 February 1779, *CC*, xliii.139-40.

14. Circular letter signed by Pierre Boin, STG to STN, 1 May 1779, *CC*, xliii.251.

15. Draft prospectus for the STN's edition of Rousseau's collected works in-duodecimo, [June 1779], *remarque* i, *CC*, xliv.145-46. The final draft of the STN's prospectus appeared in the *Journal helvétique* (February 1780), p.103-107.

Meanwhile, mean-spirited little publications concerning Rousseau emerged from Paris. D'Alembert's eulogy of the late milord maréchal Keith, Rousseau's old benefactor, emphasised Jean-Jacques's alleged ingratitude and forced Du Peyrou to spend precious time preparing a response.[16] The Neuchâtel editor even took his ally Moultou to task over the Genevan's preoccupation with the sensitivities of aristocratic acquaintances in the French capital.[17] Thoroughly exhausted and plagued by gout, during the summer of 1779 Du Peyrou had to take time off from editing and recover at the spa at Le Valais. He could barely stand on his feet.

While Du Peyrou wore himself down editing Rousseau's papers, one of the STG partners, François d'Ivernois, was visiting Paris and Versailles. The purpose of d'Ivernois's trip was to persuade French government officials to allow the *Collection complète* entry into the kingdom despite the prohibitions still applicable to several of Rousseau's books. The arguments of the young publisher were successful, though possibly for political reasons *Du contrat social* would be excluded from the initial delivery of August 1780. D'Ivernois selected the bookseller Jacques Esprit as his sales agent for Paris. Esprit, and after December 1782 his widow, turned out to be the STG's best customers, purchasing nearly one-quarter of the in-quartos sold and nearly one-fifth of the in-octavos.[18]

While in Paris d'Ivernois worried that French government officials might feel misled by the prospectus's inaccurate announcement that Rousseau had written only six books of the *Confessions*.[19] In Thérèse's name, therefore, Girardin sent to the *Journal de Paris* a clumsily worded correction, stating that the six books were 'Les seuls qui ont èté remis par une main Inconnue a un des amis de mon mari en paiis etranger auquel il avoit donné lui même La plus grande partie de tous ses manuscrits.'[20] D'Ivernois also launched the STG's French advertising campaign, both by word of mouth and through announcements

---

16. Du Peyrou to Moultou, 28 June 1779, *CC*, xliii.334-37; Du Peyrou to Wilhelm Muzell-Stosch, 9 October 1779, *CC*, xii.287-90. The eulogy in question is *Eloge de milord maréchal par M. d'Alembert* (1779), especially p.69-75. Du Peyrou's published reply to d'Alembert has not been located. In a letter to Moultou (24 November 1779, *CC*, xliv.96) Du Peyrou stated that Rey was distributing 500 copies of his brochure. It was called *Eclaircissemens définitifs, & sans réplique pour la justification de feu J. J. Rousseau, contre les imputations de mm d'Alembert, Muzell Stosch, & consorts*. With Du Peyrou's approval Linguet published the Neuchâtel disciple's correspondence with Muzell-Stosch, d'Alembert's supporter and Keith's former secretary. See *Annales politiques, civiles et littéraires du dix-huitième siècle* 7 (January 1780), p.475-502.

17. Du Peyrou to Moultou, 28 June 1779, *CC*, xliii.334.

18. 'Récapitulation générale de la vente des œuvres de J. J. Rousseau de tous formats et de la manière dont on en a été payé, et la note qui reste dû par divers (1 août 1784)', verified 11 November 1785 (Geneva, Les Délices, archives de la Société Jean-Jacques Rousseau, ms. R. 159, pièce AA).

19. François d'Ivernois to Girardin, [15 June 1779], *CC*, xliii.321-23. Rousseau had read sections of Part II to selected audiences in 1770 and 1771. It was rumoured that his manuscript had made the rounds (Suzanne Necker to Moultou, [14 June 1779], *CC*, xliii.319-20).

20. Draft in Girardin's hand, Marie-Thérèse Levasseur to the *Journal de Paris*, published in the *Journal de Paris* 159 (8 June 1779), p.638, *CC*, xliii.306.

in the press.[21] Finally, he served as the STG's representative to the Paris engraver, Pierre-Philippe Choffard, arranging with Choffard publication of the proposed separate albums of illustrations for both the in-quarto and in-octavo. This proved to be a complicated matter. First of all, Girardin insisted upon playing the role of aesthetic adviser, selecting subjects and moods for Choffard's chief artist, Charles-Nicolas Cochin.[22] Next, at Girardin's urging Choffard tried to revise his contracts with the STG. His main objective was to wrest loans from the Genevans while turning the sale and distribution of the engravings into his own independent enterprise.[23]

As he recovered from his near breakdown during the summer of 1779, Du Peyrou as yet was unaware of Girardin's sequestration of the *Confessions* manuscript that Rousseau had brought to Ermenonville. The marquis presented himself as a model of probity and trustworthiness, flattering his ailing co-editor. Reminding Du Peyrou that enemies lurked everywhere, Girardin urged his fellow *ami* to show them no mercy. He solemnly promised to remit to Du Peyrou everything that Rousseau had left at Ermenonville, as well as those pieces which the marquis had wheedled from others.[24] Girardin's inventory, prepared on 11 July, included the *Considérations sur le gouvernement de Pologne*, *Le Lévite d'Ephraïm*, the *Rêveries du promeneur solitaire*, a sketch of *Emile et Sophie*, 'Les aventures de Mylord Edouard', notes on botany, 'La scene de Pigmalion, [...] Examen Politique et justificatif de La revolution de L'isle de Corse', and notes and correspondence.[25] Girardin promised to bring the pieces to the long delayed meeting of the *amis* in Neuchâtel.[26]

In August the STG informed Girardin that it had uncovered yet another potential piracy, this time emanating from Lyon. 'Non seulement ils veulent nous contrefaire à l'instar de leurs pareils', the Genevans wrote, 'mais ils prétendent encore obtenir l'exclusion de nôtre édition, tandis que leur scandaleux regrattage seroit admis.' Thus one additional reason made crucial the

---

21. D***, de Geneve [François d'Ivernois] to the *Journal de Paris*, 27 May 1779, published in the *Journal de Paris* 150 (30 May 1779), p.602-603, *CC*, xliii.300-301.

22. Draft, Girardin to Charles-Nicolas Cochin, [late May 1779], *CC*, xliii.301-302; signed draft, Girardin to François d'Ivernois, 1 June 1779, *CC*, xliii.307-10.

23. Secretary's copy, sent by Choffard to Girardin, Pierre-Paul Choffard to the STG, [20 July 1779], *CC*, xliii.371-74; Choffard to Girardin, 20 July 1779, *CC*, xliii.374-76; draft, Girardin to the STG, [23 July 1779], *CC*, xliii.377-79; Choffard to Girardin, [29 July 1779], *CC*, xliii.387-88. The final prospectus for the engravings was ready at the end of August. It foresaw albums containing thirty plates designed by Cochin and engraved for the two separate formats, in-quarto and in-octavo. Publication of the engravings was intended to follow the rhythm of the text, appearing in three separate shipments. The subscription price of the engravings in-quarto was set at 45 *livres*, those in-octavo would run at 33 *livres* (third prospectus, [29 August 1779], *CC*, xliii.406-408). The final contract between Choffard and the STG was prepared at the September 1779 meeting of publishers and editors held at Du Peyrou's residence in Neuchâtel ([18 September 1779], *CC*, xliv.22-28).

24. Girardin to Du Peyrou, 3 July 1779, *CC*, xliii.340-43.

25. 'Etat des papiers dans La Cassette/Pour Monsieur Du Peyrou', in Girardin's hand, 11 July 1779, *CC*, xliii.351-52.

26. Girardin to Du Peyrou, 16 July 1779, *CC*, xliii.359-63.

September conference of *amis* and publishers: to plan defensive strategies against 'les Corsaires de la typographie'.[27]

By September Du Peyrou felt restored both physically and emotionally, and he too looked forward to the meeting. The STG informed him that subscriber interest was high and the editor promised to give d'Ivernois sufficient text shortly for a first printing of five or six in-quarto volumes.[28] By 14 September Girardin had arrived in Neuchâtel and informed Benoît that the initial encounter of the *amis* was going exceptionally well.[29] While the main item of business concerned the contractual revisions at Thérèse's expense, other matters also were settled. Choffard won control over publication and sale of the engravings.[30] The definitive list of Rousseau's writings to enter the *Collection complète* was drawn up. Du Peyrou promised the STG the entire text by June 1781 and the publishers pledged to have their edition on the market a year after that. The *amis* and STG approved the quality of paper and identified the mill which would supply it. They reached an accord concerning type and characters. Everyone agreed that both Moultou and Du Peyrou would certify all final proof.[31]

Though none of the documents of the September conference mentioned how piracies would be challenged, it is clear that the in-duodecimo kept in reserve was to be the STG's chief response to cheap clandestine editions. It surely was a necessary one. As the *amis* and STG wound down their meeting, Abraham Bosset-De Luze, one of the directors of the STN, informed his colleague F.-S. Ostervald that Boubers of Brussels now was requesting a half-share in the STN's anticipated piracy of the *Collection complète*. Boubers even offered to supply engravings for the *contrefaçon*, probably reduced-sized versions of what he had been using for his own in-quarto. Flattered though he was by the proposal, Bosset-De Luze nevertheless advised rejecting Boubers's offer, for the simple reason that the STN's planned piracy already was rich in partners.[32] For example, *sociétés typographiques* in Bern and Lausanne were investing in it.

A year earlier Du Peyrou had considered Boubers to be the most likely publisher of the *Collection complète*. Now that the STG was formally engaged, the Belgian became the most fiendish threat of all. Rousseau's faithful disciple felt compelled to attack him head-on. Du Peyrou therefore prepared a new announcement for the public papers, denying Rousseau's alleged compliance with Boubers's edition back in 1774. He accused Boubers of purchasing the young Rousseau's letters to Mme de Warens from a servant of hers following

27. In Bassompierre's hand, STG to Girardin, [5 August 1779], *CC*, xliii.393.

28. Du Peyrou to d'Ivernois, 2 September 1779, *CC*, xliv.1-2.

29. Girardin to Benoît, 14 September 1779, *CC*, xliv.10-12.

30. Copy, second contract between Choffard and the STG for the illustrations to the *Collection complète*, [18 September 1779], *CC*, xliv.20-22.

31. Contract between the *amis de Rousseau* and the STG, [18 September 1779], *CC*, xliv.22-28. Vimal Duchamp's mill in Ambert in the Auvergne would supply paper for the edition.

32. Abraham Bosset-De Luze to Frédéric-Samuel Ostervald, 23 September 1779, *CC*, xliv.29-30.

her death and then betraying Rousseau's wishes by printing them. Du Peyrou challenged Boubers to publish anything new and worthwhile which would not be pirated from the STG's edition.[33] The editor of the *Collection complète* sent a draft of his attack upon Boubers to d'Ivernois, asking the STG partner to place it in the major journals of Europe.[34]

During autumn 1779, however, the optimistic aura of the Neuchâtel conference dissipated. Once Girardin returned to Ermenonville his relations with Thérèse worsened and she made plans to flee; the liberties the marquis was taking with Rousseau's texts drove Du Peyrou to distraction; Girardin revived his accusations against Moultou; and the marquis became disillusioned with the young STG partners, whom he accused of planning to slip poor quality paper into limited edition sets of the in-quarto.[35] Most significant of all, Girardin's major obsession surfaced: that Rousseau heirs would appear, cousins or even one of the abandoned children, to challenge the September contracts and lay claim to the entire heritage.

Girardin therefore felt obliged to locate Rousseau relatives first and pay them off if need be. He would do so with Part II of the *Confessions* or, if it came to that, with the principal behind Thérèse's annuity. The marquis embarked upon a discreet search for the children of Rousseau and entrusted an acquaintance from Nîmes, Henri Laliaud, to direct the quest.[36] Laliaud went to Montmorency to interview the maréchale-duchesse de Luxembourg, but received no leads from her. Before tracking through the registers of the Hôpital des enfants trouvés in Paris, Laliaud needed precise information from Thérèse about the birth of her eldest child.[37] He urged Girardin to question Rousseau's widow. One can easily imagine the poor woman's extreme distress as the marquis added to her misery at Ermenonville by forcing interrogations upon her concerning the most painful events of her life.

Late in October the STG announced a new crisis. Although booksellers throughout Europe were placing orders, their purchases were on consignment and very little liquid capital actually arrived in Geneva. The STG discovered that it was cash-short. Lacking assistance, it might have to withdraw from the project. Worse than that, its own days suddenly seemed numbered. D'Ivernois was showing more interest in Genevan politics than in publishing Rousseau, Bassompierre grew nervous about the enterprise and Boin feared having to go it alone.[38] Anticipating a disaster, Gabriel Cramer withdrew his investment.

33. Prepared in the hand of Du Peyrou's secretary, Jeannin, and sent to François d'Ivernois, [29 September 1779], *CC*, xliv.36-38.
34. Du Peyrou to François d'Ivernois, 29 September 1779, *CC*, xliv.34-35. There is no record that d'Ivernois complied with Du Peyrou's request.
35. Girardin to Du Peyrou, 7 October 1779, *CC*, xliv.44-45.
36. Once Part II of the *Confessions* was released in 1789, Laliaud would be exposed as yet another maligned disciple (see *OC*, i.613).
37. Henri Laliaud to Girardin, 16 October 1779, *CC*, xliv.54-55.
38. Implicated in Geneva's political unrest and civil strife during 1781/82, d'Ivernois would flee to England just as the *Collection complète* appeared. He never returned.

Who would come to the rescue? Du Peyrou's financial situation was not enviable, for the war in America had cut into his overseas income.

Reluctantly Moultou agreed to supply additional financial backing, and he persuaded the Geneva bookseller Samuel de Tournes to replace Cramer. De Tournes also had powerful family banking connections which might help. Moultou then propped up Boin, Bassompierre and d'Ivernois with a corporate body. The five principal investors in the edition – the STG members, Moultou and de Tournes – formed the 'Société Rousseau'. The Société was intended to last until September 1784, and it was noted that the STG itself would dissolve then. STG members accepted responsibility for half the expenses of the edition, Moultou and de Tournes would be held accountable for the other half. Profits were to be distributed in proportion to the investment of each partner.[39]

The agreement establishing the Société Rousseau estimated press-runs for the *Collection complète*. The hope was to publish the edition in 10 900 sets: approximately 4400 sets apiece for the in-octavo and in-duodecimo, 2000 for the standard in-quarto and 100 for the deluxe limited edition in-quarto. The Société Rousseau promised an investment of 1 *sol* per sheet for the in-quarto and in-octavo, and 8 *deniers* per sheet for the in-duodecimo. In order to pay bills falling due, Moultou and de Tournes agreed to advance the STG 32 000 *livres* by 1 January 1780. Should the STG need funds beyond that amount it could borrow from the Geneva banking firm of de Tournes (Samuel's brother Jean-Louis), Lullin and Masbou. With respect to the details of production and subscriptions, the STG was to remain autonomous. Each month it was to supply Samuel de Tournes with an accounting of income and expenses.[40] Though the fact is not mentioned in the contract, de Tournes loaned or rented additional presses to the STG.[41] At this point the STG seems to have contracted with Amable Le Roy of Lyon to make a second edition of its own in-duodecimo.[42] Finally, the Paris press lord Charles-J. Panckoucke infiltrated the Geneva edition after all, making an ill-advised one-seventh investment in the in-quarto and taking a much wiser one-third in a separate printing of the *Confessions*, Part I, and the *Rêveries*. The press-run for the Panckoucke edition came to nearly 8000 copies and was intended chiefly for the Paris market.[43]

39. Contract forming the Société Rousseau, [1 November 1779], *CC*, xliv.63-65.
40. Contract forming the Société Rousseau, [1 November 1779], *CC*, xliv.65-68.
41. Supplementary contract forming the Société Rousseau, [15 February 1780], *CC*, xliv.156-57.
42. See R. A. Leigh, 'The Geneva edition and the *Confessions*', in *Unsolved problems in the bibliography of Jean-Jacques Rousseau*, ed. J. T. A. Leigh (Cambridge 1991), p.121-33.
43. *Remarque* ii, *CC*, xliv.139; second supplement to the contract of 1 November 1779, [1 August 1781], *CC*, xlv.35-36.

The second stage: 1780

The Société Rousseau saved both the STG and the *Collection complète*. Although his gout attacks returned and slowed the progress of work, Du Peyrou was pleased with the first set of the STG's page proofs.[44] By the end of 1779 d'Ivernois could inform Girardin that three volumes in-octavo were in press.[45] But the marquis continued to complain, first about Cochin's portrait of Rousseau for the edition, then about the quality of the paper the STG was using, and finally about the young Genevans in general. Furthermore, Girardin encouraged Du Peyrou to stage an all-out attack upon d'Alembert, who in his eyes now shared prominence with Diderot as Rousseau's greatest nemesis.[46] Then came Thérèse's revelations, leading to the collapse in relations between the marquis and Du Peyrou. In February 1780 Du Peyrou acknowledged receipt of the last manuscripts supplied by the Frenchman. These included Girardin's 'improved' *Rêveries du promeneur solitaire*, but very definitely *not* the *Confessions*.[47] By late summer correspondence between Du Peyrou and Girardin had ceased for good.

Aside from financial difficulties and the erosion of mutual trust, piracies frustrated the success of the *Collection complète*. The activity of the STN is the best documented case. By February 1780 the STN's prospectus was circulating and pirated volumes from Neuchâtel regularly followed the STG edition.[48] Nor was the STN alone. Piracies of the *Collection complète* were prepared in Bern, Lyon, Reims (Cazin), Heidelberg-Leipzig (the Pfaehler brothers), Zweibrücken (Sanson) and Kehl (Société littéraire-typographique).[49] Most were inexpensive, small format editions: in-12°, in-18° or even in-24°; and

---

44. Du Peyrou to Moultou, 6 December 1779, *CC*, xliv.101-103; Du Peyrou to Girardin, 16 December 1779, *CC*, xliv.108-11. Du Peyrou's new bout with ill-health lasted at least two months. On 10 February he announced to Moultou that he was out of his bedclothes and taking small steps (Du Peyrou to Moultou, 10 February 1780, *CC*, xliv.152).

45. D'Ivernois to Girardin, [24 December 1779], *CC*, xliv.121.

46. Girardin to Du Peyrou, 24 December [1779], *CC*, xliv.114-20. Eventually no portrait was engraved expressly for the *Collection complète*. Subscribers selected their own preferred one. In responding to Rousseau's enemies, honours as polemicist-in-chief in 1779 had to go to Rousseau's indefatigable admirer, Marie-Anne Alissan de La Tour, Mme de Franqueville. She composed and published her *Jean-Jacques Rousseau vengé par son amie, ou Morale pratico-philosophico-encyclopédique des coryphées de la secte* (1779).

47. Du Peyrou to Girardin, 20 February 1780, *CC*, xliv.161-62.

48. Reprinted in the *Journal helvétique* (February 1780), p.103-107. The STN prospectus was called the 'RECUEIL des écrits de J.J. ROUSSEAU, *sur la copie de Genève, proposé par Souscription, in-12, de la Grandeur des Théâtres de Moliere, Racine, Crébillon, &c.*' Because the STG advertised only its in-quarto and in-octavo, the STN stretched legitimacy as far as possible by treating its in-duodecimo as an original production. Yet compared to the STG editions, 'elle n'en différera que par la commodité du format & la médiocrité du prix'. Instead of charging 3 *livres* per volume, cost of the STG in-octavo, each of the STN's volumes would be 1 *livre*, 14 *sols* (see *remarque* i, *CC*, xliv.144-45). The piracy notwithstanding, in June 1780 the STG and STN co-invested in a 'petite édition', probably the in-duodecimo commissioned by Le Roy of Lyon (see Jean Ranson to F.-S. Ostervald, 27 June 1780 and *note explicative* a, *CC*, xliv.271-72).

49. STG to STN, 13 January 1780, *CC*, xliv.127: 'on nous assure que la Société Typ. de Berne nous contrefait'. See as well *note explicative* c, *CC*, xliv.128; *remarques* i, ii, iii, *CC*, xliv.216-17. For

they sold for 1 *livre* and a few *sols* per volume, up to 90 per cent less than the STG's in-quarto and two-thirds less than its in-octavo.[50] Judging from remaindered stock catalogued in the Genevans' post-publication inventories, the selection of several formats by the *amis* and STG had been a dreadful miscalculation. The in-quarto proved to be a sales disaster and pirates undercut the in-duodecimo.[51]

Piracies assuredly were worrisome. Nearly as serious was the fear that manuscript owners might prefer to publish Rousseau's papers on their own rather than grant precedence to the STG. For example, despite Girardin's objections, the Englishman Brooke Boothby reproduced the 'Premier Dialogue' of *Rousseau juge de Jean-Jacques* which the author had given him back in April 1776. Boothby's edition appeared in June 1780. In his preface he claimed that by offering the public the misanthropic ruminations of the writer's old age he had fulfilled Rousseau's personal wishes. Girardin, however, considered the publication by Boothby to be discipleship betrayed. Fortunately Boothby's edition was limited to 1000 copies, although three reprintings shortly followed.[52] The Englishman's marketing methods were artisanal and naive. He tried to use Rey's services for sales on the continent and he actually shipped copies to Girardin for distribution in and around Paris.[53] Once he received the books the marquis returned them to Boothby, via the British ambassador in Brussels.[54]

Another blow to the *Collection complète* concerned Rousseau's four long, self-reflective 'Lettres à M. de Malesherbes' of January 1762.[55] To Girardin's

bibliographical descriptions of some of the piracies see Dufour, *Recherches*, ii.27-32, and McEachern, *Bibliography*, i.512-31, 536-57, 572-79, 586-90.

50. For example, in the *Gazette de Berne* (26 April 1780), p.4, the Lausanne bookseller F. La Combe announced that he was receiving subscriptions for the 'œuvres complettes de J.J. Rousseau, 21 vol. petit format; le vol. à 1 L. 10. de France' (see *remarque* i, *CC*, xliv.216). In a letter to Ostervald (18 June 1780), Bosset-De Luze noted the remarks of the bookseller Rigaud of Montpellier, who 'ecrit qu'il est assailli de toutes parts d'offres de Rousseau, et qu'on lui propose la petite 12° de Lyon a 20s le vol' (*note explicative*, *CC*, xliv.266).

51. In May 1784, 901 sets of the *Collection complète* in-quarto ('papier ordinaire') remained in the STG's warehouse, while 1112 sets had been distributed among Europe's booksellers; 639 sets of the in-octavo were in the warehouse, while 3364 sets had been sold (though not paid for); 2199 sets of the in-duodecimo were in stock, while 1886 sets had been distributed. Therefore, the number actually produced was fewer than the 10 900 originally envisioned. It probably did not exceed 10 250 sets, excluding the in-duodecimo made for Amable Le Roy. As late as July 1786, 2230 sets of the *Collection complète* and 1100 sets of *Suppléments* remained in the ex-STG warehouse (see Geneva, Les Délices, archives of the Société Jean-Jacques Rousseau, ms. R. 159, 'Depouillement de tout ce qui a eté delivré pour le compte de la Societé Rousseau, soit en exemplaires complets des œuvres de tous formats, soit en œuvres separées, depuis le commencement de l'entreprise, jusqu'au 1er may 1784 [...]'). See also *remarque* i, *CC*, xlv.260; Samuel de Tournes to Moultou, 12 [July 1786], *CC*, xlv.326.

52. Girardin to Du Peyrou, 27 February 1780, *CC*, xliv.165; *OC*, i.1904-905.

53. Boothby to Rey, 16 April 1780, *CC*, xliv.199-200; Boothby to Girardin, [25 August 1780], *CC*, xliv.317-18.

54. Alleyne Fitzherbert to Girardin, 13 October 1780, *CC*, xliv.344.

55. E. S. Burt, 'The meeting place of autobiography and censorship: Rousseau's *Lettres à Malesherbes*', *Studies in eighteenth-century culture* 17 (1987), p.289-308.

dismay, at the time of Rousseau's death manuscript copies of the letters had been circulating in Paris. They were carefully composed literary works, nothing less than a key source for the *Confessions* themselves. Late in 1779 Jean-Antoine Roucher astounded both friends and enemies of Rousseau by publishing the 'Lettres' as remarks appended to the eleventh canto of his poem *Les Mois*.[56] No one had given Roucher permission to reproduce the letters, least of all Malesherbes. Girardin considered Roucher's behaviour to be rank opportunism, a cheap way of furthering the poet's literary career. As a matter of fact, when Roucher earlier had wished to place the 'Lettres à Malesherbes' into the *Journal de Paris*, it was Girardin himself who intervened to prevent their insertion.[57]

The appendage to Roucher's poem did not much impress the marquis, whose annoyance heightened when he perused, as yet another extended footnote to *Les Mois*, part of his own description of Rousseau's death, the 'Lettre à Sophie'.[58] Roucher's identification of Girardin as author of the 'Lettre à Sophie' provoked the marquis into firing off a protest to the *Journal de Paris*, which was published on 4 May 1780: 'je n'ai jamais rien écrit qui ait été donné, ni fait pour être donné au Public, relativement au récit de la mort de M. J.J. Rousseau'.[59] Despite his demurral it remains uncertain whether Girardin intended the 'Lettre à Sophie' to go unpublished. But he surely did not relish having to read a version edited by the author of *Les Mois*.

Meanwhile Du Peyrou approached the summer of 1780 in poor health. He was particularly despondent over his conflict with Girardin. Nevertheless, the editor maintained both his standards and critical acumen. On 5 June he explained to Moultou his reluctance over publishing a pair of thirty-year-old letters from Rousseau to abbé Raynal. Du Peyrou's reasoning concerned the issue of accuracy. Though he had access to the issue of the *Mercure* in which Raynal once had printed the letters, he lacked the originals. Du Peyrou also worried that the young Genevans possessed little sense of topical balance for the volumes they were publishing. According to the editor they seemed not to comprehend the incongruity of mingling correspondence and literature in the same tome.[60]

56. 'Quatre lettres à M. le président de Malesherbes contenant le vrai tableau de mon caractère et les vrais motifs de toute ma conduite', in Roucher, *Les Mois*, ii.283-307. A sentimentalist who admired Rousseau, Roucher obtained the office of *receveur des gabelles* from Turgot for his circumstantial piece honouring the marriage of the dauphin and Marie-Antoinette, *La France et l'Autriche au temple de l'hymen*. Politics caught up with him in July 1794, when he was guillotined along with André Chénier.
57. Alexis François, 'La correspondance de J.-J. Rousseau dans la querelle littéraire du XVIIIe siècle', *Revue d'histoire littéraire de la France* 33 (1926), p.355-69.
58. *Les Mois*, ii.307-11.
59. Girardin to the *Journal de Paris* 125 (4 May 1780), p.515, *CC*, xliv.221. A letter from Girardin to Roucher stating dismay over the poet's unproven disclosure accompanied the public announcement (*CC*, xliv.222).
60. Du Peyrou to Moultou, 5 June 1780, *CC*, xliv.247. Concerning the letters to Raynal, Du Peyrou relented.

Meanwhile Du Peyrou recognised that Rousseau's correspondence was indispensable for providing structure to the 'total' autobiography he envisioned, especially if Part II of the *Confessions* were not included. He considered the appropriate place for the letters to be in the *Collection complète*'s supplementary volumes.[61] Du Peyrou and Girardin continued to track down correspondence to recipients who, they hoped, might feel flattered to find their names associated with Rousseau. Many concurred; some agreed to release correspondence if they were allowed to remain anonymous; a few were impervious to blandishments. Malesherbes proved to be an exemplary problem. As director of the French government's Book-trade Office between 1750 and 1763 he had been associated intimately with the publication (and suppression) of Rousseau's major works. Rousseau's letters to him were particularly important not merely for their psychological insights but also as gauges of the writer's views on authorship, censorship, the book-trade and literary property.[62] For his part, even though Rousseau was dead and he himself in involuntary retirement, Malesherbes in 1780 remained sensitive about long past relations with the writer. Above all the former director continued to fret about his failure to have prevented the persecutions suffered by Rousseau over *Emile*. Malesherbes feared what Rousseau might say in the *Confessions* about his administrative ineffectiveness and therefore felt obliged to create his own defensive strategies.[63]

A classic editorial conflict seemed to be looming. In order to tell a full story, Du Peyrou needed Rousseau's letters to Malesherbes. So as to accentuate the theme of his hero's martyrdom, Girardin wanted them published as well.[64] For Malesherbes, however, the documentation had quite a different purpose. It was meant to justify the conduct of the former royal official in a relationship that had been difficult and had concluded unsatisfactorily; for, when all was said and done, and especially during the *Emile* affair, the protector had failed his client.[65] Once the *amis* requested his letters from Rousseau, Malesherbes painfully returned to his files. He co-operated to the extent of permitting the editors to see most of Rousseau's correspondence. Publication, however, was a different matter. In several notes written most probably to Moultou between June and August 1780 Malesherbes reinterpreted Rousseau's letters to him.

61. Most of the correspondence would appear in volume xii of the in-quarto and volumes xxiii and xxiv of the in-octavo.

62. See *Rousseau/Malesherbes: correspondance.*

63. Indeed Rousseau was not particularly generous. See, for example, *OC*, i.512, 534 *passim.*

64. Malesherbes did allow Girardin to read Rousseau's letters. Without requesting permission, the marquis had copies made of them. Preceding his secretary's transcriptions Girardin wrote: 'Lettres a M. de Malesherbes / Copiées par moi sur les originaux qu'il m'a confiées; Elles ne doivent pas être imprimées sans sa permission; mais elles peuvent servir a se rendre Compte de ce qui s'est passé au sujet de L'impression de L'Emile à Paris, et prouvent bien que M. Rousseau n'en devoit etre ni responsable ni puni par le parlement de Paris' (*note critique, CC,* xiv.168-69).

65. See Maurice Cranston, *The Noble savage: Jean-Jacques Rousseau 1754-1762* (Chicago 1991), p.349-53.

Examining thirteen of them, sent between November 1760 and January 1771, he informed Moultou that only two or three pieces seemed worthy of publication.[66]

Those acceptable to the former *directeur de la Librairie* included one letter containing Rousseau's views on book production and literary property, positions, Malesherbes noted, which were contradicted by the writer's own behaviour.[67] A second acceptable letter showed Rousseau capable of gentle irony as he poked fun at a censor's request to 'catholicise' *Julie*.[68] A third deemed tolerable was a generous tribute to Marc-Michel Rey.[69] On the other hand, Malesherbes refused to permit publication of a letter in which Rousseau expressed his anxieties over the simultaneous publication of *Emile* in Paris and Holland, just prior to the book's suppression in both places: 'Cette lettre concerne des tracasseries au sujet de l'édition d'*Emile* que je ne peux pas laisser imprimer. Elle m'entraineroit dans des explications que je ne peux ni ne dois donner', wrote the former director.[70] Malesherbes also wished to have his name deleted as recipient of Rousseau's letter expressing second thoughts about publication of the *Lettre à Christophe de Beaumont*: 'Cette lettre sur la réponse à M. l'Archeveque est très agreable et je conçois que les éditeurs veulent l'insérer dans leur édition. C'est à eux de voir si des égards pour M. l'Archeveque doivent les empecher de la publier. Mais quant á moy je ne dois entrer pour rien dans cette publication.'[71]

Since they illustrate competing strategies employed by addressee and editor, a pair of letters which Rousseau sent from Môtiers in the autumn of 1762 and which were brushed off by Malesherbes as comprising nothing interesting for the public are, on the contrary, worthy of notice.[72] The first was Rousseau's request for copies of the four autobiographical 'Lettres à M. de Malesherbes'

---

66. Malesherbes to [Moultou?], [June 1780], *CC*, xliv.273-78.
67. Malesherbes to [Moultou?], [June 1780], *CC*, xliv.273-74; Rousseau to Malesherbes, 5 November 1760, *CC*, vii.297-302. Nevertheless, Du Peyrou failed to publish the letter in the original *Collection complète*. It appeared in his supplementary volume accompanying Part II of the *Confessions* (*Seconde partie des Confessions de J.-J. Rousseau, citoyen de Genève*, édition enrichie d'un nouveau recueil de ses lettres, vol. iii-vii, in-8° and in-12°, Neuchâtel, Fauche-Borel 1790 (hereafter *Seconde partie des Confessions*), v.350-60).
68. Malesherbes to [Moultou?], [June 1780], *CC*, xliv.274; Rousseau to Malesherbes, 19 February 1761, *CC*, viii.137-38, copy prepared for the *Collection complète*. It was published as a 'Lettre a M. De ***', in *Collection complète*, xii.235, in-4°; xxiii.441, in-8°.
69. Malesherbes to [Moultou?], [June 1780], *CC*, xliv.274-75; Rousseau to Malesherbes, 7 May 1762, *CC*, x.232-33. The letter was withheld from the *Collection complète* and published by Pierre Moultou in the so-called *Second supplément* of 1789: 'Lettre à M. de ***', in *Second supplément à la Collection des œuvres de J.-J. Rousseau* (Geneva [Barde and Manget] 1789), xvii.38, in-4°; xxxiii.56-57, in-8°.
70. Malesherbes to [Moultou?], [June 1780], *CC*, xliv.275; Rousseau to Malesherbes, 11 May 1762, *CC*, x.236-38.
71. Malesherbes to [Moultou?], [June 1780], *CC*, xliv.275, copies prepared for Girardin and Du Peyrou respectively; Rousseau to Malesherbes, 6 March 1763, *CC*, xv.259-60; 'Lettre a M. de ***', in *Collection complète*, xii.320, in-4°; xxiv.36-37, in-8°.
72. Malesherbes to [Moultou?], [June 1780], *CC*, xliv.275.

sent to the director in January 1762 and published by Roucher in *Les Mois*.[73] For Girardin or Du Peyrou, what could be more significant than a request for the pieces which would set the tone for the *Confessions* and, by extension, Rousseau's major literary purpose for the remainder of his life? On the other hand, for Malesherbes, the four 'Lettres' were somewhat of an embarrassment. By 1780 he must have harboured regrets at having been the honoured recipient of Rousseau's outpouring, and he was unhappy that lax security measures had permitted their circulation and eventual publication by Roucher. Malesherbes preferred that none of this be recalled and therefore requested his correspondent to suppress Rousseau's letter from Môtiers.

The second letter, acknowledging Rousseau's receipt of what he had solicited from Malesherbes, underscored the writer's state of mind during his early months at Môtiers and illustrated concerns which would haunt him as long as he lived. To cite several examples and their decoding: (1) 'le paquet m'est arrivé tout ouvert et l'envelope entiérement dechirée' (decoded: the despicable cabal is reading my mail); (2) 'Quant à l'intérest que vous ont dit prendre à moi des gens en place qui se sont crus obligés de foudroyer contre moi (je transcris vos termes) je leur en sais peu de gré' (decoded: what do I care if powerful colleagues of yours plot against me? I know you are on my side); (3) 'Quelque jour peut-être, je vous rendrai compte de la suite de mes sentimens, et de l'effet qu'a produit en moi cette dernière épreuve; j'y gagnerai toujours, si elle m'apprend encore à me mieux connoitre [...] grace au ciel ma tâche est faite; je n'aurai plus de souci sur ce point' (decoded: I'll have my revenge; I promise the *Confessions* to the world). Finally, as he learned that the De La Porte–Duchesne edition of the *Œuvres complètes* was under way, Rousseau commented unfavourably upon the quid pro quo arranged by Malesherbes and the maréchale-duchesse de Luxembourg in return for the 6000 *livres* he had gotten for *Emile*: (4) 'Cela est à peine croyable [...]. Ces gens-là me regardent comme déjà mort et se partagent tranquillement mes dépouilles' (decoded: thanks to you, my livelihood, the insurance policy for my old age and Thérèse's, is going up in smoke).[74]

Malesherbes cited personal reasons for wishing to suppress other correspondence: one letter he claimed to be overly flattering; in reality it consoled him for his fall from office in 1763.[75] Another letter offered Malesherbes solace for the recent suicide of his wife, a matter the former *directeur* found better left unspoken.[76] Finally, with respect to two letters dated November 1771, in which the aging Rousseau rejected a proposal by Malesherbes to exchange a difficult living as music copier for a healthier charge as botanist at public

73. Rousseau to Malesherbes, 26 October 1762, *CC*, xiii.249-50.
74. Rousseau to Malesherbes, 7 December 1762, *CC*, xiv.167-69.
75. Rousseau to Malesherbes, 11 November 1764, *CC*, xxii.43-45. Du Peyrou published this letter in the fifth volume of his 1790 supplement to the *Collection complète*, xxviii.272-76.
76. Rousseau to Malesherbes, 17 January 1771, *CC*, xxxviii.167-68. The letter of condolence did not bring glory to Rousseau, who failed to restrain himself from mentioning that Mme de Malesherbes had herself been fooled by the 'cabal' against him.

expense, the one time patron and protector commented: 'Ces deux lettres ne peuvent interesser personne et si elles paroissoient il faudroit expliquer que c'estoit le projet que tant de personnes ont eu de luy faire du bien malgré luy.'[77] In his first letter Rousseau declined Malesherbes's offer because he feared that the post of public botanist would cost him his intellectual freedom.[78] In the second letter Rousseau declined because he feared that his work would be unappreciated by the French, 'qui ont de fausses idées de la botanique et si peu de gout pour l'étude de la nature'.[79]

Rousseau's old protector, therefore, seemed to be dissociating himself from the intimacy he once had shared with the late writer. In part it was fear of what he might one day find in the *Confessions* that lay behind Malesherbes's desire to keep the old relationship muted. By honouring Malesherbes's requests and by not identifying him as the recipient of the letters which they did publish, the editors of the *Collection complète* respected the sensibilities of the former director. Malesherbes, however, did not allow the matter to rest there. Upon receiving the first shipment of the *Collection complète* in advance of general publication and after having read the Boothby edition of *Rousseau juge de Jean-Jacques*, he responded to Moultou's request for a personal assessment of Rousseau.[80] 'Je pense comme vous', Malesherbes wrote, 'que le Dialogue imprimé à Londres manifestera au public que cet homme illustre avoit une manie qui alloit jusqu'à la démence, c'etoit de croire que l'univers entier et chaque homme qu'il connoissoit en particulier n'etoit occupé que du projet de le persecuter.'[81] According to Malesherbes it fortunately was Rousseau's logic and eloquence, not his paranoia, that marked most of his writings. Nevertheless Malesherbes expressed fear that the bile of the 'Premier dialogue', which so exaggerated the wrongs Rousseau considered to have been done to him, would prevail in the second part of the *Confessions* and other unpublished writings. For that reason the former director asked Rousseau's friends and editors to confront the issue of the writer's misguided sense of victimisation. Rather than seek to justify Rousseau's behaviour at all costs, they should warn posterity of it: 'Ses partisans doivent être aussi attachés au vrai que lui, et puisqu'il est vrai qu'il avoit le defaut ou plustôt le malheur dont nous parlons, il faut l'avouer.'[82]

77. Malesherbes to [Moultou?], [June 1780], *CC*, xliv.275-76.
78. Rousseau to Malesherbes, 2 November 1771, *CC*, xxxviii.285.
79. Rousseau to Malesherbes, 11 November [1771], *CC*, xxxviii.289.
80. Malesherbes to Moultou, 26 July 1780, *CC*, xliv.297-302. Moultou had worried that the paranoia embedded in *Rousseau juge de Jean-Jacques* would damage Rousseau's reputation as a moralist. In a letter to Malesherbes he wrote: 'Nous avions aussi cet ouvrage, Monsieur, mais nous n'en voulions publier que des fragments.' He added: 'Les cœurs honêtes & Sensibles déploreront en le lisant, l'effet cruel des persecutions. Elles ne purent corrompre le caractère de Rousseau, il était à l'épreuve de tout, mais Sa raison revoltée contre l'injustice en fut presque altérée' (Moultou to Malesherbes, [12 July 1780], *CC*, xliv.289-90).
81. Malesherbes to Moultou, 26 July 1780, *CC*, xliv.297.
82. Malesherbes to Moultou, 26 July 1780, *CC*, xliv.302.

Several weeks later Malesherbes again rummaged through his papers and came across documentation concerning the publishing history of *La Nouvelle Héloïse*. He shared the information with his correspondent. According to the former director, the most important item concerned his efforts to award Rousseau a French *privilège* for the novel. Had he originally consented to have *La Nouvelle Héloïse* passed on to a Paris publisher (Robin), Rousseau would have been compensated with 6000 *livres*. As Malesherbes told it, Rousseau initially agreed to the proposition. When he believed himself compromised by changes requested by the royal censor Picquet, changes which Malesherbes had considered minimal, the writer backed out. Rousseau then refused to co-operate and *La Nouvelle Héloïse* never was granted an exclusive *privilège* in France. Instead Robin published his censored version without Rousseau's approval. Out of sympathy for the writer, Malesherbes claimed to have obtained the 1000-*livre* honorarium for Rousseau, who accepted the money.[83]

Anticipating publication of Rousseau's own revelations one day, Malesherbes offered his own psychological evaluation of the writer. He insisted upon Rousseau's obsessive self-mortification. Contrary to accusations levelled by Rousseau's more malevolent critics, Malesherbes credited the writer with never acting from bad faith. Rousseau's indignation towards those who wished to draw him out of poverty or persecution was based upon his desire to live that way: 'Il vouloit etre malheureux, il vouloit etre pauvre, et par une suite du même sentiment il a voulu sur la fin de sa vie etre persécuté, et il estoit indigné contre tous ceux qui vouloient le tirer de la pauvreté ou le soustraire à la persécution.'[84] His flight from France over *Emile* had nothing to do with concern for his own safety. Only when told that the maréchale de Luxembourg was being compromised by his presence did he consent to leave. Moreover, Malesherbes divulged that his friendship with Rousseau deepened only when he informed the writer that his services were being offered not as a favour but as a consequence of his bad conscience. But the ex-book-trade administrator's attempts at pulling Rousseau from his misery during the final years in Paris turned the writer against him. According to Malesherbes, had he lived in a time when philosophers were still burned, Rousseau would have made an exemplary hero. But it was his misfortune to exist in the more tolerant eighteenth century. Like don Quixote, the writer had to battle windmills of his own making.[85]

Malesherbes's pathetic, self-pitying Rousseau could not have been more at odds with Girardin's vengeful warrior or, for that matter, with Du Peyrou's ethical preceptor. The disciples publishing the *Collection complète* envisioned the Master's confrontations as titanic moral struggles, which they felt obliged to record. But Malesherbes thoroughly demythologised Rousseau. For the old

83. Malesherbes to Moultou, [August 1780], *CC*, xliv.309-12. There are interesting points of contrast between Malesherbes's somewhat self-serving interpretation and the narrative covered above in chapter 1.
84. Malesherbes to Moultou, [August 1780], *CC*, xliv.311.
85. Malesherbes to Moultou, [August 1780], *CC*, xliv.312-15.

patron, his former client was no hero-martyr but rather a wretched masochist, dreaming of princesses to carry off while choosing to live with 'une paysanne laide et imbecille'. As far as Malesherbes was concerned, Rousseau's greatest pleasure ('sa jouissance la plus delicieuse') was to be universally despised, and his genuine misfortune stemmed from encountering those who refused to comply. As Malesherbes saw it, the supreme irony occurred in 1778, once Rousseau was placed in Ermenonville: 'dans un lieu de delices, dans des especes de Champs Elisées ou rien ne luy manquoit et ou il luy estoit impossible de se dire malheureux et persecuté'. This paradise proved to be the ultimate trap: 'il tomba dans le desespoir, et ce fut sa fin'.[86]

Needless to say, the editors of the *Collection complète* failed to grant Malesherbes a forum for his grim assessment of Rousseau's personality. Once Part II of the *Confessions* appeared in its separate editions of 1789 and 1790, it was Rousseau who had the final word. Meanwhile, draped in the mantle of spurned benefactor, throughout the 1780s Malesherbes continued to envision himself as defender of the weak. He hoped, however, that on these latter occasions Protestants and Jews might be more appreciative of his efforts than writers had been.[87] His self-image of benevolent patron never left him; he proved incapable of interpreting Rousseau's rebuffs as dodges from the ensnarement of clientage.

In June 1780 Du Peyrou learned that Moultou possessed Part II of the *Confessions*. Because Girardin remained his main problem, the Neuchâtel editor agreed to keep this knowledge from the marquis.[88] On 20 July Du Peyrou received Thérèse's cession of her claims to the corpus. Whether this would stand up even in an *ancien régime* courtroom is questionable, for the cession was clumsily backdated to 4 July 1778, two days after Rousseau's death.[89] Du Peyrou again travelled to Le Valais for his health, and the first shipment of the *Collection complète* was distributed to booksellers for their subscribers.[90] Pressures were mounting for the STG to conclude the entire edition as rapidly as possible. Nasty rumours still persisted that, betrayed by Thérèse, Rousseau had committed suicide at Ermenonville.[91] Works unfriendly to Jean-Jacques kept appearing, not merely hurriedly prepared pamphlets, but respectable multivolume editions like J.-B. de La Borde's *Essai sur la musique ancienne et*

---

86. Malesherbes to Moultou, [August 1780], *CC*, xliv.316.

87. Pierre Grosclaude, *Malesherbes. Témoin et interprète de son temps* (Paris 1961), p.355-87, 559-602, 631-49; Raymond Birn, 'Religious toleration and freedom of expression', in *The French idea of freedom: the old regime and the declaration of rights of 1789*, ed. Dale Van Kley (Stanford 1994), p.292-95.

88. Du Peyrou to Moultou, 14 June 1780, *CC*, xliv.255-56.

89. Original, prepared by a secretary, with Thérèse Levasseur's handwritten approval, *CC*, xliv.286. While the cession was backdated to 4 July 1778, the approval was dated 11 July 1780.

90. The complete list of bookseller-purchasers may be found in Geneva's archive of the Société Jean-Jacques Rousseau, Les Délices, ms. R.159: 'Règlement définitif de comptes de les Sociétés Rousseau et typographique [...]', 11 November 1785 and 24 April 1786.

91. Jean Gosse to Henri-Albert Gosse, [13 July 1780], *CC*, xliv.291.

moderne.[92] La Borde took Rousseau to task for musical plagiarisms, paradoxes and errors, and he reiterated Rousseau's alleged ingratitude towards Voltaire. This last revelation particularly offended Du Peyrou. Moreover, La Borde claimed to have seen and read the entire *Confessions.*

Following his break with Du Peyrou, Girardin continued to fear that an unscrupulous publisher would expose Part II of the *Confessions.* With Thérèse gone, the marquis considered the 'mémoires' of Rousseau's mature years as his prize, in fact as his hostage. Should a Rousseau relative appear claiming the legacy, Girardin might always locate a potential publisher, sell Part II and compensate the would-be heir with the money he received. Or else, should events warrant it, the marquis might publish Part II on his own. Girardin therefore was horrified when in July 1780 a bookseller from Namur in the Austrian Netherlands informed him that he was holding '20 Exemplaires de la vie et Memoires de feu Mr. J.J. Rousseau'. The dealer asked Girardin by what means he should send the books to Ermenonville.[93] As matters turned out, Girardin had no cause for panic, for the volumes were not a secret edition of the *Confessions* but only Boothby's incomplete edition of *Rousseau juge de Jean-Jacques.* Still, until he learned the truth, Girardin brooded, and the appearance of Boothby's edition brought him little solace.

As a matter of fact, nothing served more to lower Rousseau's literary stock than did the 'Premier dialogue'. Upon reading Boothby's edition, the duchesse de La Rochefoucauld expressed the horror of aristocratic high society that had once coddled Rousseau; she informed her friend Moultou that she had to take up the *Lettre à d'Alembert* as a panacea: 'J'ai absolument besoin de ce contrepoison pour me guerir de la lecture du premier Dialogue.'[94] Remarking upon the publication of the 'Premier dialogue', Bachaumont's *Mémoires secrets* would parrot the duchesse's view: 'C'est un mauvais service qu'on rend à ce grand homme; c'est le délire d'une imagination noire, d'un philosophe atteint de la fièvre chaude.'[95] Finally, Boswell commented: 'I was roused by his eloquence, but saw with a sound [second] look that he was mad.'[96]

Completing the *Collection complète*: to August 1782

Once he returned to Neuchâtel from Le Valais in mid-September 1780, Du Peyrou found the first shipment of the *Collection complète* awaiting him. He did not at all like what he saw. Rousseau's preface to *Emile* was missing, several pages were printed in duplicate, 'Les amours de milord Bomston' was mislead-

92. 4 vols (1780).

93. Emmanuel Flon to Girardin, [14 July 1780], *CC*, xliv.292.

94. Duchesse Marie-Louise de La Rochefoucauld d'Anville to Moultou, 20 August 1780, *CC*, xliv.308.

95. xv.296 (23 August 1780). Additional accounts appeared in Bachaumont's reports of 9 and 12 September: xv.314-15, 319-22).

96. *Private papers of James Boswell from Malahide castle, in the collection of lt colonel Ralph Heyward Isham,* ed. Geoffrey Scott and F. A. Pottle [Mount Vernon, N.Y. 1928], xiv.123.

ingly labelled a continuation of Part VI of *La Nouvelle Héloïse*, and *Les Solitaires* was incorrectly identified as a continuation of Book v of *Emile*. A sentence in the edition identifying the maréchale de Luxembourg as owner of the 'Milord Bomston' manuscript was both garbled and ungrammatical.[97] In a surly mood, Du Peyrou addressed Moultou: 'Il est d'abord bien demontré que la plus grande négligence a accompagné cette premiere livraison, et ce n'est pas le moyen de s'attirer ni la confiance du public, ni l'ap[p]robation dés amis de l'auteur.'[98] Meanwhile the STN was busily arranging subscriptions for its piracy. From Paris Ostervald's agent Jacques-Pierre Brissot began placing orders.[99]

Then in October 1780 the *Journal encyclopédique* infuriated Du Peyrou by levelling a terrible charge against Rousseau, accusing him of having stolen the musical score of *Le Devin du village* from an obscure Lyon composer named Grenet or Garnier. The editor of the *Journal encyclopédique*, Pierre Rousseau, recalled that in 1750 Grenet [Garnier] had mistakenly sent him a letter asking why the journalist had never acknowledged receipt of the score of *Le Devin*, as yet unknown to the public. In his response, Pierre Rousseau noted, he informed Grenet [Garnier] that he had never received the score, and suspected that the Lyonnais's letter was meant for someone else with a similar name. Once the opera became Jean-Jacques's triumph, Pierre Rousseau claimed to have questioned the accredited composer about the incident; however, he never obtained a satisfactory reply.

In subsequent years the *Journal encyclopédique* turned hostile towards Jean-Jacques. In his review of Boothby's edition of the 'Premier dialogue' in October 1780, Pierre Rousseau revived suspicions that his namesake never had composed *Le Devin du village*, but had stolen it from the obscure Grenet [Garnier].[100] The musician-botanist Louis-Henri Lefébure responded with a spirited defence of Jean-Jacques which was published in the *Journal de Paris*.[101] Two years later, in the first *Supplément* of the *Collection complète*, the STG reproduced the *Journal encyclopédique*'s allegation and Lefébure's reply.[102] Meanwhile the battles between *rousseauisme* and *encyclopédisme* continued unabated. D'Alembert thought that a note appearing in the Boothby edition of the 'Premier dialogue' had charged *him* with musical plagiarism. The encyclopedist wrote a defence of the originality of his *Eléments de musique*, which he

97. The offending sentence read: 'Cette pièce qui paroit pour la première fois, a été copiée sur le manuscrit original & unique de la main de l'Auteur qui appartient, & existe entre les mains de *Mad. la Maréchale de Luxembourg*, qui a bien voulu le confier' (*Collection complète*, iii.513, in-4°; iv.350, in-8°).

98. Du Peyrou to Moultou, 13 September 1780, *CC*, xliv.331.

99. Jacques-Pierre Brissot de Warville to Ostervald, 17 September 1780, *CC*, xliv.339-40; Brissot de Warville to Ostervald, 15 October 1780, *CC*, xliv.345.

100. *Journal encyclopédique* 7 (October 1780), p.289-91. See *note explicative* a, *CC*, ii.340-42; and *remarque*, *CC*, xliv.350.

101. 342 (7 December 1780), p.1394-95, *CC*, xliv.357-62. A brochure defending Rousseau appeared as well: [de Marignan], *Eclaircissements donnés à l'auteur du 'Journal encyclopédique' sur la musique du 'Devin du village'* (1781). See *remarque*, *CC*, xlv.47.

102. *Supplément à la Collection des œuvres de J.-J. Rousseau*, iii.302-309, in-4°; v.450-55, in-8°.

sent to the *Mercure*, all the while sarcastically suggesting that the author of *Rousseau juge de Jean-Jacques* must have been demented: 'L'Auteur, quel qu'il soit (car peut-être est-ce un ennemi de feu M. Rousseau) paroît avoir la tête fort dérangée; tous ceux qui ont lu cette Brochure en conviennent; mais c'est un malheur dont il ne faut que le plaindre, & dont il ne s'agit point ici.'[103]

Displeased though he was with both the distracting controversies and the first volumes of the *Collection complète*, Du Peyrou nevertheless scrupulously continued editing texts and correspondence. He also received the disturbing news that the STG, cash-short again, was withholding Thérèse's annuity payments. Following Thérèse's departure from Ermenonville, Du Peyrou considered himself responsible for the widow's well-being. He therefore suggested that he and Moultou serve as the conduit for the sums due Thérèse, thereby maintaining a common front to ensure her receipt of payment.[104] Meanwhile the STG badgered Du Peyrou for copy, and the latter considered the publisher's demands unreasonable until he could organise and arrange his material into a comprehensive unit. Du Peyrou's opinion of the STG was sinking, and he accused the young entrepreneurs of reducing the noble project to a petty money-making scheme. Moultou's hesitations about assuming an active role in the editing process further exasperated Du Peyrou. He therefore pleaded with the Genevan to spend several months with him in Neuchâtel, so that the pair could work together on moulding the manuscripts and correspondence into the literary shrine which the *amis* had envisaged two years earlier.[105]

Between late January and mid-March 1781 Moultou did lodge with Du Peyrou, and the pair made headway. Moultou brought the manuscript of *Rousseau juge de Jean-Jacques* that Rousseau had handed him along with the *Confessions* back in May 1778. During their work sessions the two *amis* decided to publish all three dialogues of *Rousseau juge de Jean-Jacques* in the *Collection complète*.[106] Much of their labour involved editing (and, at Moultou's insistence, censoring) the second and third 'Dialogues'.[107] In addition it was during their sessions that Du Peyrou and Moultou worked out the contents of supplementary volumes to the *Collection*. These would include so-called minor works of Rousseau's (most pirated from volume viii of Boubers's edition), as well as correspondence and commentaries by defenders and critics of the writer.[108]

103. D'Alembert to the editor of the *Mercure*, 29 September 1780, published in the *Mercure* (14 October 1780), p.85-87, *CC*, xliv.340. For Rousseau's remark in the 'Premier dialogue' see *OC*, i.766.

104. Du Peyrou to Moultou, [18 September 1780], *CC*, xliv.333. See as well Du Peyrou to Moultou, 1 November 1780, *CC*, xliv.352-53.

105. Du Peyrou to Moultou, 8 January 1781, *CC*, xlv.2.

106. The 'Dialogues' would be misleadingly labelled 'la seconde partie des Mémoires'.

107. *Collection complète*, vol. xi, in-4°; vol. xxi-xxii, in-8°. Moultou suppressed thirteen passages and notes in the second and third 'Dialogues' because of their attacks upon individuals or corporate bodies.

108. The prospectus for the *Supplément* appeared in July 1781. It promised two volumes in-quarto and four volumes both in-octavo and in-duodecimo (printed circular entitled 'Avis/ DE LA SOCIETE TYPOGRAPHIQUE DE GENEVE, *sur le* SUPPLEMENT A LA

The prospectus advertised the *Supplément* as absolutely necessary for subscribers to the *Collection*. It eventually formed volumes xiii to xv in-quarto and volumes xxv to xxx in-octavo and in-duodecimo.

Subscribers to the *Collection complète* received their second delivery in April 1781. It included volume i in-quarto (or volumes i and ii in-octavo), that is the political writings missing from the first shipment;[109] the *Lettres* to d'Alembert and Christophe de Beaumont, and the *Lettres écrites de la montagne*; the prize-winning *Discours* of 1750 and Rousseau's responses to its critics; theatre, music and poetry; and selected correspondence.[110] Meanwhile pirates were busy. Veuve Duchesne announced preparations for the *Supplément à la Nouvelle Héloïse* ('Les amours de milord Bomston') and *Supplément à l'Emile, ou De l'éducation (Les Solitaires)*. The STN quickly published its in-duodecimo piracy of the STG's first shipment. It was not alone. From Paris Brissot informed Ostervald that at least nine different piracies of the *Collection complète* were about to inundate France: 'La votre sera goutée, Si vous parvenés à La faire entrer prom[p]tement car elle est Jolie et pas Chere.'[111]

What of Girardin following his break with Du Peyrou? Between July and December 1780 the marquis was preoccupied with his land-tax protest, the publication costs of the *Consolations* and his increasingly strained relations with Benoît. Early in 1781 he sent d'Ivernois a list of those who ought to receive complimentary copies of the *Collection complète*. Among individuals named was a certain Jean-François-Xavier Rousseau. He was the grandson of Noé Rousseau; the latter was the brother of Jean-Jacques's grandfather David. Jean-François-Xavier therefore was the writer's second cousin and Girardin mistakenly took him to be the closest blood relative. An exotic member of the footloose Rousseaus, Jean-François-Xavier, or 'Rousseau le Persan' (1738-1808), was born in Ispahan, where his father had settled in 1708, and he was to die in Aleppo. He had wide trading interests in the Middle East and held diplomatic missions, including that of French consul in al-Basra. Late in 1780 he was in France, seeking investors for a scheme which promised the wealth of the Orient, and apparently met Girardin at Ermenonville or in Paris.[112] Initially the marquis did not find Jean-François-Xavier's investment programmes particularly seductive; however, the pair agreed on one matter: Thérèse never was to see the 24 000 *livres* promised the *amis* by the STG for the *Collection complète*.

Because Girardin always had feared the appearance of a lost cousin and had intended to hold Part II of the *Confessions* in reserve to pay off emerging heirs,

COLLECTION DES ECRITS DE JEAN-JAQUES ROUSSEAU, *qui paroîtra en même tems que la 3e. Livraison'*, [15 July 1781], *CC*, xlv.29-31).

109. Because it stuffed the *Discours sur l'inégalité, Lettre à M. Philopolis, Du contrat social, Discours sur l'économie politique* and *Considérations sur le gouvernement de Pologne* into an oversized first volume in-quarto, the STG was forced to place the remainder of Rousseau's political writings (those revising abbé de Saint-Pierre) into volume xii.

110. Vol. vi-ix, in-4°; vol. xi-xviii, in-8°.

111. Jacques-Pierre Brissot de Warville to Ostervald, 23 April [1781], *CC*, xlv.21.

112. *Remarque, CC*, xlv.24-25.

it was not difficult for him to come to terms over the issue of Thérèse's inheritance, and 'Rousseau le Persan' laid claim to the 24 000 *livres* Thérèse considered to be hers. For the moment Girardin was non-committal and merely offered Jean-François-Xavier a deluxe free copy of the *Collection complète* ('in-4°, grand papier').[113] Isolated from Du Peyrou, Moultou and the publication activities of the STG, however, the marquis increasingly sympathised with the bid of 'Rousseau le Persan'. Yet he had to remain wary in the event that one or more of Jean-Jacques's abandoned children should suddenly surface. Girardin continued his search for them, but results remained inconclusive.[114]

Du Peyrou was correct when he observed that in the STG's exploitation of Rousseau's corpus, commercial considerations were taking precedence over moral ones. On 1 August 1781 the Société Rousseau and STG added a codicil to the contract of November 1779. The Société Rousseau formally acknowledged two-thirds financial responsibility for a separate edition of Part I of the *Confessions* and the *Rêveries* that the STG was preparing for Panckoucke and the Paris market. The Société Rousseau also agreed to publish a second separate edition of the *Confessions*, Part I, and the *Rêveries* on its own, in-octavo, for readers uninterested in securing the entire *Collection complète*.[115] Moreover the STG prepared Rousseau's *Œuvres posthumes*. These simply were in-octavo sets containing the *Confessions*, Part I, the *Rêveries*, *Rousseau juge de Jean-Jacques*, *Considérations sur le gouvernement de Pologne* and other works published for the first time. They were intended for readers who had no desire to purchase the entire *Collection* but wished to acquire writings they did not yet possess.[116] Despite the fact that Moultou was party to these attempts at dismembering the *Collection*, Du Peyrou confided to the Genevan his dismay at what was happening: 'vous le sentés vous même, cette Edition a si peu repondû à nos esperances, qu'elle ne vaut pas de vôtre part le moindre sacrifice'.[117]

Indeed Moultou had already begun to contemplate something new, a successor edition of Rousseau's works, once the STG's projects were completed. Because he foresaw the prospective edition as reasserting the original intentions of the *amis* and possibly including Part II of the *Confessions*, Du Peyrou

113. Girardin to François d'Ivernois, [late February/early March 1781], *CC*, xlv.6. The oriental dress and fiery eyes of 'Rousseau le Persan' reminded observers of Jean-Jacques in his Armenian costume. Corancez noted another similarity: Jean-François-Xavier tended towards paranoia. Both he and his late cousin 'charroient dans leur sang le même principe de maladie' (see Guillaume Olivier de Corancez, *De J.-J. Rousseau, extrait du 'Journal de Paris', des n°s 251, 256, 258, 259, 260 et 261, de l'An VI* (1798), p.45-47).

114. Antoine-Louis Chaumont de La Millière to Girardin, *CC*, xlv.23.

115. Accord between the Société Rousseau and STG to publish the *Confessions*, Part I, [1 August 1781], *CC*, xlv.35-36.

116. *Œuvres posthumes de Jean-Jacques Rousseau, ou Recueil de pièces manuscrites, pour servir de supplément aux éditions publiées pendant sa vie*, 9 vols, in-8° (Geneva 1781-1782). Samuel Fauche pirated this edition so as to complete his own, 12 vols, in-8° (Neuchâtel 1782). See Dufour, *Recherches*, ii.21.

117. Du Peyrou to Moultou, 17 October 1781, *CC*, xlv.44.

was tempted by the idea, 'si elle peut se faire sans nuire aux droits et aux interets de nos entrepreneurs actuels'.[118] The Neuchâtel businessman must have wondered what truly lay behind Moultou's scheme, for the Genevan always had been reluctant about publishing Rousseau's autobiographical writings, and the correspondence, *Rousseau juge de Jean-Jacques* and entire *Confessions* would have to serve as the core of any new edition. In all probability Moultou's change of heart had less to do with salvaging Rousseau's memory than with redeeming a poor investment. Even prior to the third shipment of volumes it was clear that the STG's decision to spend so heavily on the in-quarto had been a marketing mistake, and the enterprise was spinning towards financial disaster.

Du Peyrou's immediate concerns were editorial, however, not monetary. During the sessions at Neuchâtel the previous winter he had argued with Moultou over insertions of Rousseau's correspondence in the concluding volume of the *Collection complète*. The Genevan reacted with his customary timidity, trying to limit most of the letters for publication to those which Rousseau had written to him and to Du Peyrou. But Du Peyrou desired a more comprehensive selection. He asked Moultou to add to the *Collection complète* Rousseau's letters to François-Henri d'Ivernois (father of the STG partner), and he also requested that a key letter, suppressed by Moultou, be reinstated.[119] R. A. Leigh believes that Du Peyrou's choice of correspondence in the edition was arbitrary.[120] I see the matter differently. For the disciple, Rousseau's letters knotted the autobiography together, complementing the essays, fiction and *Confessions*.[121] Du Peyrou had his way. Volume xii of the in-quarto, the last published prior to the *Supplément*, contained 205 letters, all but six from Rousseau. They were addressed to at least ninety different correspondents.

Yet Moultou refused to be outmanoeuvred. In many letters published in the *Collection complète* Rousseau's addressee either would be left unidentified or else would be identified only by an initial. What truly irritated Du Peyrou were Moultou's attempts at censoring sections of Part I of the *Confessions* which the Genevan believed to be compromising. Du Peyrou found such adulteration to be counter-productive. After all, individuals still were alive who had heard from Rousseau's own lips phrases which Moultou intended to suppress. In fact, during his trip to Paris in September 1780 François d'Ivernois had read them aloud to selected friends. Two of them, the duchesse de La Rochefoucauld d'Anville and Suzanne Necker, expressed their dissatisfaction with what they had heard, and Moultou assured Mme Necker that what offended her would never see light of day.[122] But Du Peyrou strongly disagreed. He

118. Du Peyrou to Moultou, 17 October 1781, *CC*, xlv.44.
119. Du Peyrou to Moultou, 20 October 1781, *CC*, xlv.46.
120. *Note explicative* b, *CC*, xliv.45.
121. I explain my position in the following chapter.
122. Duchesse de La Rochefoucauld d'Anville to Moultou, 19 September 1780, *CC*, xliv.335-37; Suzanne Necker to Moultou, [October 1780], *CC*, xliv.347-48; Moultou to Suzanne Necker, [22 October 1780], *CC*, xliv.349-50.

believed that cuts made by Rousseau's *amis* would play into the hands of the writer's enemies, who then might cite the omissions as proof certain of the indecent nature of the work. Writing to Moultou, Du Peyrou noted: 'le retranchement de ces passages fera plus de tort à l'auteur que leur publicité. Le public une fois persuadé que les amis de R. ont fait dés retranchemens, croira tout ce [que] ses ennemis voudront faire entendre des cés suppressio[ns] [m]ais que faire?'[123]

In April 1782, Moultou's attempts at censorship notwithstanding, the STG's independent editions of the *Confessions*, Part I, were published.[124] In fact the volumes intended for Panckoucke appeared three months before subscribers to the *Collection complète* obtained their *Confessions* in the third shipment of the set.[125] Diderot's attack upon Rousseau in the *Essai sur les règnes de Claude et de Néron*,[126] published in March 1782, offered the *Confessions*, Part I, ideal publicity, negative though it was, and Panckoucke's edition of 8000 copies practically sold out. The Versailles bookseller Poinçot pleaded with the STN to get on with its piracy.[127] Ostervald obliged,[128] and so did others. Complaining about the price he had to pay for the STN's *Confessions*, Poinçot informed Ostervald that he already could acquire an edition in Paris for 5 *livres*, less than the price the Neuchâtelois were charging, and he would not have to worry about shipping delays. Behind this edition was the banker-entrepreneur Batilliot, who financed purchase of 7000 of the STG's *Confessions*, and whose younger brother sold yet cheaper editions, in-duodecimo, for 4 and 3 *livres* apiece.[129] Counting veuve Duchesne's recent piracy, Poinçot estimated that in May 1782, 24 000 copies of the *Confessions*, Part I, and the *Rêveries* were available in the French capital.[130] According to Bachaumont, there was no problem with official censorship. The *Confessions* 'se vendent même avec une sorte de tolérance'.[131]

123. Du Peyrou to Moultou, 20 October 1781, *CC*, xlv.46.
124. *Les Confessions de J.-J. Rousseau, suivies des Rêveries du promeneur solitaire*, 2 vols, in-8°.
125. The *Confessions*, Part I, and the *Rêveries du promeneur solitaire* formed volume x of the in-quarto and volumes xix and xx of the in-octavo.
126. i.125-40, 352-56.
127. Poinçot to the STN, 5 March 1782, *CC*, xlv.60-61; Poinçot to the STN, 10 March 1782, *CC*, xlv.69-70.
128. Between 13 April and 18 May 1782 the STN printed 2000 copies of the *Confessions*, Part I, and sold 1200 of them to Poinçot (see *remarque*, *CC*, xlv.78-79). Poinçot complained that the Neuchâtel piracy was costing him nearly as much as the legitimate edition would have done (see Poinçot to the STN, 20 April 1782, *CC*, xlv.79-80). While awaiting his shipment Poinçot ordered 100 copies of the STG's edition, which was expedited by the Geneva bookseller Barthélemy Chirol. Chirol sent the books via Neuchâtel and Lyon, charging 550 *livres* for the copies and shipping expense. Interestingly enough, the intermediary in Neuchâtel was none other than the STN, which also sent Poinçot twenty-five copies of its piracy of the STG's *Œuvres posthumes* (See Barthélemy Chirol to the STN, 10 April 1782, *CC*, xlv.77-78).
129. *Note explicative* a, *CC*, xlv.87-88. On 24 May Poinçot asserted that an in-duodecimo could be obtained in Paris for as little as 50 *sols* (2 1/2 *livres*) (*CC*, xlv.101).
130. Poinçot to the STN, 8 May 1782, *CC*, xlv.86-87.
131. *Mémoires secrets*, xx.242 (10 May 1782).

Initial reaction to the *Confessions*, Part I, followed party lines. On the one hand, comtesse de Boufflers informed King Gustav III of Sweden that the work 'peut etre celle d'un valet de basse cour au dessous meme de cet etat, maussade en tout point, Lunatique et vicieuse de la maniere la plus degoutante'.[132] Of course the comtesse never forgave Rousseau for the quarrel with Hume, holding Jean-Jacques responsible for the Scotsman's premature death, so her biases might be understandable. Affecting a literary aesthetic in keeping with the tastes of his aristocratic subscribers, La Harpe in the *Correspondance littéraire* was only slightly less disapproving. For the manuscript newsmonger the *Confessions* served as yet another example of the 'shock literature' of the time, in keeping with the vulgar trash spewed out by Linguet, Louis-Sébastien Mercier and Rétif de La Bretonne: 'on y voit un orgeuil sans pudeur et sans borne, une arrogance folle, un mépris insolent pour tout ce que le bon sens apprend à respecter, un oubli complet de ce qu'on doit au public et à soi même'.[133] On the other hand, the *Mémoires secrets* attributed to Bachaumont regretted that the published *Confessions* stopped too early, at 1742.[134] While Métra admired the honesty of Rousseau's self-awareness, the journalist criticised, of all things, the author's apparent discretion: 'Il devoit faire connoître ces charlatans de vertu qui ont usurpé le nom de philosophes & même celui de sages, dont il fut la dupe & la victime, & sous l'oppression desquels ont gémi tant d'autres dupes.' Of course it was Moultou who hid the identities of the 'virtuous quacks' behind an initial, yet Métra sensed a holding back, a self-censorship, especially noticeable in the unfinished character of what was published.[135]

It would take a perceptive Scotsman, John Gillies, future royal historiographer, to note the centrality of the *Confessions* in Rousseau's corpus and, by extension, to understand Du Peyrou's purpose in turning them into a key element of the *Collection complète* itself. Writing from Lausanne, possibly to Andrew, son of the London printer William Strahan, Gillies observed:

[The *Confessions*] seem the most interesting & instructive of all the works of that Great writer, who has animated the cold elegance of the French language, with a fire & vigour, of which it had been long deemed uncapable. The Confessions lay hold of you. It is impossible to take them up without reading them from beginning to end. What has rendered them particularly entertaining to me, & must have the same effect on all those who have taken delight in his works, is that the singular, yet authentick history, or rather adventures of his life, related with circumstantial minuteness in his confessions, point out the spring and source of the paradoxical and romantic opinions scattered in other works, particularly Emilius & Heloïse. Their translation would be soon executed, and I think could not fail of being a very successful undertaking.[136]

132. Comtesse Marie-Charlotte de Boufflers-Rouverel to King Gustav III of Sweden, [1 May 1782], *CC*, xlv.83.
133. Jean-François de La Harpe to Andrei Petrovich Shuvalov, [20 May 1782], *CC*, xlv.95-96.
134. xx.242 (10 May 1782).
135. [François Métra], *Correspondance littéraire secrète* (1775-1793), xiii.46-49; *remarque*, *CC*, xlv.88-89.
136. John Gillies to Andrew Strahan[?], [18 May 1782], *CC*, xlv.90-92.

The appearance of Part I of the *Confessions* accelerated the pace of rousseau-mania in the French capital. Suzanne Necker would inform Moultou that democratised public opinion, not academic guardians of taste, now seemed to be defining cultural achievement: 'le grand nombre à présent décide des succès et les gens de lettre[s] suivent la foule qui les suivoit autrefois; Rousseau à donc triomphé par le Stile enchanteur et par Cette profonde Sensibilité empreinte sur toutes ses lignes'.[137]

One particular incident in Paris caused even the dour Du Peyrou to smile.[138] On 21 June the playwright Charles Palissot informed the *Journal de Paris* that he had just paid the price of the fanaticism of taste. During a recent perform-ance at the Théâtre français of his twenty-two-year-old comedy in verse, *Les Philosophes*, an audience riot broke out. Provoking the incident was the cele-brated appearance, in Act III, of his ancient Rousseau-figure, the valet Crispin on all-fours, pulling a head of lettuce from his pocket and reciting the incendiary lines:

> En nous civilisant, nous avons tout perdu,
> La santé, le bonheur, et même le vertu.
> Je me renferme donc dans la vie animale;
> vous voyez ma cuisine, elle est simple & frugale.[139]

Palissot tried to explain to the *Journal* that his satire was not at all directed against Rousseau; and, in truth, hypocritical *philosophes*, most notably Diderot, received far ruder treatment in the piece. Having caused a sensation back in 1760, twenty-two years later Palissot still was suggesting that 'les Charlatans de Philosophie' were behind the most recent tempest.[140] The Théâtre français, however, yielded to public pressure. When *Les Philosophes* was performed a few evenings later, the Crispin scene was deleted and an innocuous *dénouement* written in. Though, initially at least, the changes were applauded, Palissot was disgusted.[141] In its sanitised form the play would have little success.[142]

In Geneva during the summer of 1782 a more serious drama than *Les Philo-sophes* affected public life and bore potential consequences for the *Collection complète*, its publishers and editors. Fourteen years earlier Geneva's burgher political grouping, the Représentants, influenced by Rousseau's political writ-ings, had claimed sovereignty for the legislative General Council which they dominated. On the other hand, the corporate aristocracy, the Négatifs, who spoke for the executive branch of government, the Small Council, had

137. Suzanne Necker to Moultou, [28 August 1782], *CC*, xlv.118.
138. Du Peyrou to Moultou, 13 July 1782, *CC*, xlv.113.
139. Charles Palissot de Montenoy, *Les Philosophes, comédie en trois actes, en vers, représentée pour la première fois par les comédiens français ordinaires du roi, le 2 mai 1760* (1760), p.85.
140. Charles Palissot to the *Journal de Paris*, [21 June 1782], published in the *Journal de Paris* 173 (22 June 1782), p.700-701, *CC*, xlv.107-109.
141. Palissot to the *Journal de Paris*, [26 June 1782], published in the *Journal de Paris* 178 (27 June 1782), p.729, *CC*, xlv.111-12.
142. *Notes explicatives* a and h, *CC*, xlv.109-10.

claimed rights to veto the General Council's decisions and looked to France, Zurich and Bern to enforce their position. Meanwhile the proletarian Natifs, dispossessed politically, expressed their ambitions with noisy street demonstrations. Little was settled. Following the latest *natif* demonstration in 1781, the Représentants admitted to the General Council all adult males with three generations of residence in Geneva. There were no further qualifications based upon property or birth. This increased the General Council by one-quarter, to around 1700 voters, and radicalised politics in the republic.[143]

But the Natifs had not finished. In April 1782 they began taking up arms and the Négatifs appealed to the guarantor powers to stabilise the situation before it got completely out of hand. On 2 July troops from France, Zurich and Bern occupied Geneva. A rump General Council was cowed into accepting pacification. The General Council itself lost deliberative rights. Majority vote to elect its syndics was abandoned, the popular political 'circles' Rousseau had admired were abolished and military exercises forbidden. Most of the Natifs who recently had entered the General Council were now disbarred. Twenty-one Représentants were forced into exile, including the young publisher François d'Ivernois. Others, including Moultou, decided to emigrate. From Neuchâtel on 13 July Du Peyrou wrote to his fellow editor: 'Cette foule de citoyens emigrans leurs foyers, et se refugiant dans une terre etrangere, m'offre le spectacle le plus déchirant; et la crainte d'un avenir encore obscur acheve de me navrer le cœur.'[144]

How would those behind Geneva's counter-revolution of 1782 react to seeing published in their city the works of their most seditious former citizen? Would French foreign minister Vergennes, instigator of the pacification, tolerate the very appearance of the *Collection complète* in the republic, much less its export to France? D'Ivernois did not exactly lessen tensions when he published anonymously a *Tableau historique et politique des révolutions de Genève dans le dix-huitième siècle*, disingenuously dedicated to Louis XVI! In his highly partisan account d'Ivernois linked Rousseau's activity in Geneva to the course of popular political unrest there – from the time of the writer's rejuvenating visit in 1754 to his condemnation, abdication of citizenship and publication of the *Lettres écrites de la montagne* a decade later.[145]

Despite the responsibility awarded Rousseau for Geneva's turmoil, the occupying powers did tolerate the STG's publishing activity, and Vergennes refused to interfere with the import of the *Collection complète*. Exiled to Annemasse, Savoy, in early August 1782 Moultou confirmed that the *Suppléments* were nearly printed, that a shipment of thirty to forty sets of the *Collection complète* would be heading overseas to America and that the STG's account books

---

143. R. R. Palmer, *The Age of the democratic revolution*, 2 vols (Princeton 1959-1964), i.109-39, 358-59.
144. Du Peyrou to Moultou, 13 July 1782, *CC*, xlv.112-13.
145. [François d'Ivernois], *Tableau historique et politique des révolutions de Genève dans le dix-huitième siècle* [...] (1782), chapter 3.

soon would be examined.[146] The edition had surmounted the political crisis. The conclusion to its stormy publishing history was about to be written.

146. Moultou to Samuel de Tournes, [7 August 1782], *CC*, xlv.114-16.

8. What readers found in the *Collection complète*

The distribution of texts

SUBSCRIBERS to the in-quarto edition of the *Collection complète* would unpack a dozen fat volumes. If they desired the *Collection's Supplément*, they would get three more. Those who purchased the in-octavo added twenty-four volumes to their shelves; the *Supplément* in-octavo brought the set to thirty. The books were heavy and the text was distributed unevenly. For example, volume ix of the in-quarto, the *Dictionnaire de musique*, ran to 772 pages; but volume xi, *Rousseau juge de Jean-Jacques*, contained only 466 pages. Readers found the layout of the edition to be pleasant to the eye. Each page of the in-quarto contained only twenty-eight lines of text and approximately ten words per line. Despite Girardin's complaints, the paper was of good quality. Volumes have stood the test of two centuries' wear quite well.

Selection and placement of materials for the *Collection complète* followed several principles simultaneously. First of all, Du Peyrou wished to honour Rousseau's intentions for the aborted edition of 1765.[1] Next, in order to keep potential pirates at bay, the juiciest new pieces were to be saved for later volumes. Unfortunately this latter strategy conflicted with another – the need to indicate quickly to potential subscribers that the *Collection complète* not only was the sole authorised edition in existence but also that containing the largest selection of heretofore unpublished items. Finally, there was Du Peyrou's thematic intention. By juxtaposing Rousseau's polemic and fiction alongside writings on politics, education and music, then adding Part I of the *Confessions*, *Rêveries*, 'Dialogues' and selected correspondence, the chief editor hoped to produce the 'total' moral autobiography. Merging the commodified Rousseau with the genuine one, Du Peyrou hoped to mould a life that would touch and change others.

Du Peyrou considered it imperative for Rousseau's teachings and prophecies to be understood against the backdrop of the writer's sufferings and struggles. By the same token Rousseau's correspondence was intended to ratify the essays and fiction. Balancing the theoretical brilliance of *Du contrat social* would be the practical constitutional lessons for Buttafoco of Corsica or Wielhorski of Poland; the personal testimony of the four 'Lettres à M. de Malesherbes' would complement the epistolary sentimentality of *La Nouvelle Héloïse*; Rousseau's botanical ruminations would exemplify the consolations in nature which the writer had found during the later part of his life; *Emile*, the two *Discours*, the polemical *Lettre à Christophe de Beaumont*, *Lettres écrites de la montagne*, and even the youthful poetry and theatre, might be interpreted as stages in a

1. Rousseau to Du Peyrou, 24 January 1765, *CC*, xxiii.181-82.

story of moral growth. After all, no other writer of the century more appro-priately injected the paradoxes and complexities of his being into his work. The crowning glory of the edition, the *Confessions*, however incomplete for the moment, would recall Rousseau's triumph over the weaknesses of his own nature and the persecutions of society. Therefore, having considered the moment opportune to unseal the packages left in 1765, those subsequently sent or given to him for safekeeping and others obtained since Rousseau's death, Du Peyrou had taken upon himself the enormous responsibility of making sense of Rousseau's journey and fulfilling the author's rite of self-justification.

Moultou's introductory remarks in volume i of the *Collection complète* were barely three dozen lines long. They made their point succinctly, however, noting how Rousseau's correspondence would complement his public writings and thereby spin out the moral message: 'C'est-là, c'est dans ces écrits privés que se peint la beauté de son ame, cette candeur qui la distingue, ce rare désintéressement, cette vive sensibilité, cette bienveillance universelle, cet attachement sincere à ses devoirs[,] à ses principes, cet amour ardent de la vérité[,] de la justice[,] de l'honnêteté, ce zele éclairé, si fertile en moyens de consoler, de soulager les infortunés.'[2] Du Peyrou's 'Dédicace aux mânes de Jean-Jaques Rousseau' continued in the same vein, noting the links between the writings and the life, which together would form the appropriate response to the slander of Rousseau's enemies. Du Peyrou added that the Master's lessons were intended for posterity; therefore discipleship obliged the *amis* to bear the message.[3]

Du Peyrou believed that the verdict of posterity would be based upon *his* image of Rousseau. Therefore he invested the volume with an organisational scheme that was both systematic and incremental. Following Rousseau's own wishes of January 1765 the editor had wanted to begin the *Collection complète* with the least personal and most theoretical of the writings, namely those concerned with political questions: the *Discours sur l'inégalité*, *Du contrat social*, the *Discours sur l'économie politique*, Rousseau's edition and critique of the works of abbé de Saint-Pierre and the writer's translation of the first book of Tacitus's *History*.[4] For marketing reasons, however, the STG also wished to incorporate into the first volume in-quarto two pieces never published before: Rousseau's response to Charles Bonnet's critique of the *Discours sur l'inégalité* (the 'Lettre à M. Philopolis') and the *Considérations sur le gouvernement de Pologne*. So as not to overload the volume, the writings concerning abbé de Saint-Pierre and the

2. 'Avant-propos', in *Collection complète*, i.1-2, in-4°. Volume i was released to bookseller-sub-scribers in August 1780. Unless otherwise noted, all citations from the *Collection complète* will be from the in-quarto edition.
3. In *Collection complète*, i.3-7.
4. In 1765 Rousseau had listed the order for volume i as follows: 'Discours Sur l'inegalité. Dis-cours Sur l'Economie politique. Du Contrat Social. Extrait de la Paix perpétuelle. *Extrait de la Polysinodie. *Jugement Sur la Paix perpetuelle. *Jugement Sur la Polysinodie. *Traduction du prémier Livre de l'Histoire de Tacite [...]. NB. Les articles précédés d'une étoile Sont encore en manuscrit' (Rousseau to Du Peyrou, 24 January 1765, *CC*, xxiii.181). For Du Peyrou's plan thir-teen years later see Du Peyrou to the STN, [*c.* 20 October 1778], *CC*, xlii.45.

Tacitus translation were shelved for later inclusion.[5] Volume i of the in-quarto (volumes i and ii in-octavo) therefore followed much of Rousseau's original plan. But actual shipment was held up until June 1782. The reasons for the delay are not clear. It is tempting to hypothesise that negotiations with authorities over *Du contrat social*, still considered a prohibited book both in Geneva and France, delayed publication.

Du Peyrou next had foreseen placing *La Nouvelle Héloïse* into volume ii of the in-quarto and *Emile*, up to and including the 'Profession de foi du vicaire savoyard', into volume iii. Such an arrangement followed compositional and moral principles, as well as the author's plan of 1765. After all, sentiment and education were to be the cornerstones of Rousseau's new world. Sheer bulk, however, necessitated some modification. The first three parts of *La Nouvelle Héloïse* alone came to more than 500 pages. These were packed into volume ii of the in-quarto. The remainder of the novel, with 'Les amours de milord Bomston' misleadingly appended to Part VI of *La Nouvelle Héloïse*, filled out the 530 pages of volume iii. In the in-octavo edition the novel comprised volumes iii to vi.

Emile, with *Les Solitaires* melded into the treatise's Book v, filled the next two volumes in-quarto (volumes iv and v) and four volumes in-octavo (volumes vii to x). A three-page 'Avis des éditeurs' by Moultou and Du Peyrou admitted perplexity at Sophie's infidelity. The co-editors wished that Rousseau had completed his fragment with a cathartic dénouement. Lacking it, however, the reader was asked to find solace by recalling the youthful rapture once shared by the couple: '*Rappellons leurs transports, leurs délices; rappellons jusqu'à leurs traverses.*' Thus *Emile* was to conclude on a note of romantic longing, which coincided with Rousseau's own late-life melancholia.[6]

Back in 1765 Rousseau and Du Peyrou had wanted to devote most of volume iv to two mature polemical works: the *Lettre à Christophe de Beaumont* and the *Lettres écrites de la montagne*.[7] A generation later, however, the in-quarto version of the *Collection complète* already exceeded five volumes before even reaching the *Lettres*. These pieces therefore would have to wait to introduce volume vi. What should accompany them? Having already dealt with most of Rousseau's politics and his monumental masterpieces, the STG now was faced with the problem of integrating Rousseau's remaining mid-sized works into the *Collection*. To Du Peyrou the *Lettre à d'Alembert* seemed an appropriate choice for inclusion in volume vi. Even though the *Lettre à d'Alembert* had been composed much earlier than either the *Lettre à Christophe de Beaumont* or the *Lettres écrites de la montagne*, back in January 1765 Rousseau had wished to have it follow them, opening a new volume devoted largely to the theatre.[8]

Since the *Lettre à d'Alembert* responded to a specific circumstance, establishment of a theatre in Geneva, it edged away from the theoretical towards the

5. They accompanied the correspondence in volume xii.
6. *Collection complète*, v.450-52.
7. Rousseau to Du Peyrou, 24 January 1765, *CC*, xxiii.181.
8. Rousseau to Du Peyrou, 24 January 1765, *CC*, xxiii.181.

concrete and autobiographical. Therefore, believed the STG and Du Peyrou, like the other polemical *Lettres*, it well might fit into the in-quarto's volume vi. Next, wishing to add an original piece to the volume, the STG inserted Rousseau's ironic response to political objections raised against the *Lettre à d'Alembert* by a group of French barristers, the so-called 'Gens de loi', back in October 1758.[9] As a further contribution to the debate on the theatre, the STG concluded volume vi with 'De l'imitation théâtrale, essai tiré des *Dialogues de Platon*'.[10] Overcome by the increasing complexity of his motives, Du Peyrou subtitled the entire volume vi 'La première partie des *Mélanges*'. In the in-octavo the several *Lettres* formed volumes xi and xii.

Forsaking chronological accuracy, volume vii of the in-quarto moved backwards to the Dijon prize-winning *Discours* of 1750 and the writer's responses to his critics over it.[11] Because Du Peyrou insisted that the *Collection complète* must exclude anything not written by Rousseau himself, critical objections to the *Discours* by others were left for the future *Supplément*.[12] The remainder of volume vii, however, proved to be exactly what it promised, 'la seconde partie des *Mélanges*', in other words a hodgepodge. The need for the STG to display the superiority of the *Collection complète* over its rivals now precluded thematic considerations. For example, the volume contained an essay that Rousseau had written in 1751 on the subject of virtue and honour. The essay originally had been intended for a contest sponsored by the Academy of Corsica but never was submitted, and a pirate edition appeared seventeen years later.[13] Its publication naturally disturbed Rousseau, who thought that the source of the piracy was the manuscript the writer had left with Du Peyrou at Neuchâtel. But the surreptitious edition failed to incorporate the revisions that Rousseau had made at Môtiers; therefore Du Peyrou was certain that the essay had been stolen prior to Rousseau placing his manuscript with him.[14] Finally, another dozen years later, Du Peyrou could assure readers of an authoritative edition. The essay opened volume vii of the in-quarto (volume xiii of the in-octavo).[15]

9. 'Réponse à une lettre anonyme relative à quelques passages de la lettre précédente', *Collection complète*, vi.601-605. Corrected draft, Rousseau to the *Gens de loi*, [15 October 1758], *CC*, v.177-81.

10. *Collection complète*, vi.607-33. Duchesne had published 'De l'imitation théâtrale' in volume v of the *Œuvres de M. Rousseau de Genève* (Neuchâtel 1764-1769), p.1-38.

11. *Collection complète*, vii.27-163.

12. *Supplément à la Collection des œuvres de J.-J. Rousseau*, i.1-242.

13. Initially Elie-Cathérine Fréron had gotten hold of the manuscript and published it in his *Année littéraire* 7 (14 October 1768), p.4-27. Shortly thereafter a Lausanne piracy, falsely attributed to Marc-Michel Rey, appeared: *Discours de M. J.-J. Rousseau de Genève, qui n'a point encore été imprimé, sur cette question: quelle est la vertu la plus nécessaire aux héros, et quels sont les héros, à qui cette vertu a manqué?*, in-8° (Amsterdam, Marc-Michel Rey 1769). Of the Lausanne publication Rousseau informed Rey: 'C'est un vol dont je desirerois extrémement découvrir la source et qui j'en suis très sur, fâche M. Du Peyrou encore plus que moi' (Rousseau to Rey, 31 January 1769, *CC*, xxxvii.35). Rey would publish the *Discours* in his own *Œuvres de J.-J. Rousseau* (Amsterdam 1769), iii.289-306.

14. Du Peyrou to Rey, [6 March 1769], *CC*, xxxvii.63-66.

15. *Collection complète*, vii.5-26, in-4°; xiii.3-31, in-8°.

Two additional pieces appeared for the first time in volume vii of the in-quarto. Rousseau had begun writing one of them, the prose poem 'Le Lévite d'Ephraïm', during his flight from Montmorency to Yverdon in June 1762. He later completed it at Môtiers. Inspired by chapters xix to xxi of the Old Testament's Book of Judges, 'Le Lévite' was a grisly tale of betrayal, murder, and vengeance, reflecting Jean-Jacques's sombre mood when he had composed it.[16] The second piece, the 'Lettres à Sara', has a shadowier provenance. The Swiss literary critic Charly Guyot believed these five passionate love letters to have been written in 1762, after the fashion of an epistolary novel and without biographical significance.[17] Challenging this view, Hermine de Saussure considered the 'Lettres à Sara' to have been composed in 1757, in the heat of Jean-Jacques's affair with Sophie d'Houdetot.[18] In Rousseau's listing of January 1765 'Le Lévite d'Ephraïm' and the 'Lettres à Sara' had been placed side-by-side.[19] No doubt considering both pieces to shed light upon Rousseau's life, Du Peyrou honoured the author's publication wishes. At the same time the placement conformed to the STG's need to attract subscribers by offering 'new' material.[20] Again respecting Rousseau's desires but making no sense thematically, the writer's lyrical fairy tale, *La Reine Fantasque*, followed 'Le Lévite d'Ephraïm' and the 'Lettres à Sara' in volume vii (p.187-98).

In order to prepare readers for the autobiographical materials to come, the STG included an early Rousseau self-portrait in volume vii, his introduction to *Le Persifleur*, the periodical which he and Diderot had considered publishing back in 1748.[21] In the essay Rousseau likened his own fickleness to the atmospheric changes which occur during the calmest of days, a metaphor which would be echoed years later in *Rousseau juge de Jean-Jacques*.[22] Two heretofore unpublished translations followed, the first from Book i of Tacitus's *History* and the second from Seneca's *Apocolokintosis* on the death of Emperor Claudius. The volume concluded with three sets of writings on botany: the *Fragments pour un dictionnaire des termes d'usage en botanique*, the *Lettres élémentaires sur la botanique* that Rousseau had composed for Mme Delessert and her daughter, and his *Lettres à M. de M[alesherbes] sur la formation des herbiers*.[23]

Why include writings on botany in a volume tilting towards the biographical – a volume devoted to the polemics over the first *Discours*, containing a distant harbinger of the *Confessions* and recalling Rousseau's most passionate love affair and deepest professional despair? Rousseau's interest in plants went far into his past, to his time with Mme de Warens, who was a devotee of herbal

16. In the *Confessions* Rousseau wrote of 'Le Lévite d'Ephraïm': 's'il n'est pas le meilleur de mes ouvrages en sera toujours le plus chéri' (*OC*, i.586).

17. *OC*, ii.1947-48.

18. Saussure, *Etude sur le sort des manuscrits de J.-J. Rousseau*, p.60-61.

19. Rousseau to Du Peyrou, 24 January 1765, *CC*, xxiii.182.

20. *Collection complète*, vii.163-200.

21. *Collection complète*, vii.223-34.

22. *OC*, i.795. See Jean Starobinski, *Jean-Jacques Rousseau: transparency and obstruction*, translated by Arthur Goldhammer (Chicago 1988), p.50-53.

23. In what follows I identify anonymous addressees by placing their names within brackets.

medicine. At Môtiers Rousseau had enjoyed his botanical excursions and he began his dictionary of terms there. He continued his collecting on the île Saint-Pierre and at Wootton. Returning to Paris in 1770, over the next half-dozen years Rousseau balanced many mornings spent copying music with afternoons passed outside the city, tracking down plants, cataloguing and pressing them, and preparing herbaria for acquaintances. He corresponded about his discoveries with the duchess of Portland (Margaret Cavendish Bentinck) and with Malesherbes.[24] Most of all he enjoyed writing the elementary letters on botany for the amusement of Mme Delessert and for the instruction of her daughter.[25]

In his plant collecting Rousseau was no scientist, but rather a populariser. Refusing to find anything intellectually useful about botanising, he collected unsystematically. His excursions and cataloguing were therapeutic, largely moral and mnemonic devices meant to seek out inner peace and restore a tranquil past. As Jean Starobinski puts it: 'Plants, symbols of nature's purity, purify Jean-Jacques; it is as though plants possessed the magic power to bestow their innocence on the person contemplating them'; and 'Collecting herbs is an idle occupation, which distracts the mind from its own emptiness and from its persecution. When relived in memory, however, the botanical walk is an island of happiness.'[26] It is likely that Du Peyrou interpreted Rousseau's botanical writings as additional pieces in the autobiographical puzzle.

Compared to volume vii, volumes viii and ix of the in-quarto (xv to xviii of the in-octavo) were models of unity. They moved towards Rousseau's work as versifier, composer and music theorist. The 'Première partie' of volume viii opened with the short play *Narcisse* (1732; revised later) and its preface defending the principles of the Dijon prize-winning *Discours* (p.1-53). Then came the verse-play *L'Engagement téméraire* (1747), published for the first time (p.53-119); the operas *Les Muses galantes* (1745) and *Le Devin du village* (1752) (p.119-80); and the 'scène lyrique' *Pygmalion* (1762) (p.191-201). In his advice to Du Peyrou in January 1765 Rousseau had foreseen publishing all of these pieces in this order for the aborted Môtiers edition.[27] Following some miscellaneous poetry, the 'Seconde partie' of volume viii contained the *Dissertation sur la musique moderne* (1743), the *Essai sur l'origine des langues* (1753?-1761?), published for the first time, and the *Lettre sur la musique française* (1753) (p.233-495). Volume ix of the in-quarto (volumes xvii and xviii of the in-octavo) completed Rousseau's contribution in this vein by incorporating the entire *Dictionnaire de*

24. The letters to Malesherbes on creating herbaria were published in volume vii of the *Collection complète*, p.589-98.

25. The texts of the letters to Mme Delessert used by Du Peyrou derived from autograph manuscript copies. At the request of Mme Delessert, Moultou and Du Peyrou suppressed personal asides. For the unexpurgated texts see *CC*, xxxviii.251-57, 276-80; *CC*, xxxix.49-56, 69-75, 80-91, 138-46, 151-62, 233-39.

26. *Jean-Jacques Rousseau: transparency and obstruction*, p.236-37.

27. Rousseau to Du Peyrou, 24 January 1765, *CC*, xxiii.181-82.

musique. Originally published in 1768, the *Dictionnaire* included revised versions of Rousseau's *Encyclopédie* articles.[28]

Volume x of the in-quarto (volumes xix and xx of the in-octavo) at last contained what subscribers had been anticipating: 'la premiere Partie des *Mémoires* composée des Confessions & des Rêveries du Promeneur Solitaire'.[29] The individual editions made for Panckoucke and Batilliot in Paris, as well as the edition published for the *Œuvres posthumes* and even the STN's piracy, preceded the *Collection complète*'s volumes by several weeks.[30] Therefore the faithful subscribers obtained only the fourth edition of the *Confessions* and of the *Rêveries*. Volume xi of the in-quarto (volumes xxi and xxii of the in-octavo), accompanying shipment of volume x, announced misleadingly on its title page: 'Contenant la seconde Partie des *Mémoires*, ou Rousseau Juge de Jean-Jaques, en trois Dialogues'.

Why would the STG imply that the 'Dialogues' be considered Part II of Rousseau's 'Mémoires'? All three editors knew that this was stretching veracity and all three knew the whereabouts of the as yet unpublished Part II of the *Confessions*. The rapid appearance of successful piracies of Part I may well have caused the STG and editors of the *Collection complète* to deem their edition to be gravely threatened; therefore their mislabelling could have been a panicked marketing device. On the other hand, Moultou and Du Peyrou perhaps convinced themselves that, in terms of auto-justification, the 'Dialogues' indeed were a genuine sequel to the *Confessions*.[31] At any rate the STG let stand Brooke Boothby's 'Avertissement' to his June 1780 edition of the first 'Dialogue', and subscribers to the *Collection complète* were the first to receive *Rousseau juge de Jean-Jacques* in its entirety. Almost in its entirety, that is. Moultou suppressed thirteen passages of notes from the second and third 'Dialogues' and from Rousseau's 'Histoire du précédent écrit' which concluded the volume. He censored whatever he considered to be too violent or insulting to others.[32]

The *Collection complète* as autobiography: personal testimony of 1750-1762

Volume xii of the in-quarto (volumes xxiii and xxiv of the in-octavo) contained Rousseau's correspondence: the threads intended to bind together the texts of the 'total' moral autobiography. The letters printed by Du Peyrou

28. *Dictionnaire de musique, par J.-J. Rousseau*, in-4° (Paris, veuve Duchesne 1767[8]).

29. Title page of vol. x of the *Collection complète*, in-4°.

30. The separate editions appeared by mid-May 1782. The eighth and ninth volumes of the *Œuvres posthumes de Jean-Jacques Rousseau* appeared before 1 June. The STN's edition was printed days after the volumes prepared for Panckoucke.

31. Subsequent editions, including volume i of the Gallimard-Pléiade, maintained the original presentation formula (see *OC*, i.1-656, 657-976).

32. For references to the omissions see Robert Osmont's 'Notes et variantes' to *Rousseau juge de Jean-Jacques* in *OC*, i.1666, 1672, 1688, 1710, 1733, 1745, 1753, 1755 and 1760. On page 446 of volume xi of the in-quarto was printed, 'Fin du second volume des Mémoires'.

included first drafts and author's copies, as well as originals (or copies of originals) sent by recipients. Du Peyrou filled nearly six hundred pages with Rousseau's letters, written over a twenty-two year period, between July 1750 and August 1772. In all there were 197 of them. By including three letters from Voltaire, three from Tressan and one each from Diderot and C.-G. Leroy, Du Peyrou broke his pledge to limit the edition to Rousseau's words; however, the editor deemed these items to be essential for understanding Rousseau's inquiries and replies.[33]

Although Du Peyrou never stated it openly, the correspondence, like the *Rêveries* and *Rousseau juge de Jean-Jacques*, was intended to hold the place for Part II of the *Confessions* until the time arrived for the latter's publication. After all, Part I concluded in 1742, and both Girardin and Moultou were refusing to admit openly that they possessed the manuscripts of Part II. The correspondence therefore would compensate for lacunae, reveal Rousseau at his most artless, and present texts describing events in his life and illustrating the evolution of his personality and thought.[34] Nowhere does it appear that Du Peyrou considered publication of Rousseau's letters to represent a violation of trust. The reading public certainly was accustomed to seeing correspondence in print; newspapers and pamphlets regularly employed the epistolary form, and the use of correspondence to attain novelistic verisimilitude was well established. Rousseau himself had been a master of the letter-essay, and his conflict with Hume had been recorded via printed letters. As far back as 1763 Marc-Michel Rey had published Rousseau's own *Lettres diverses*.[35]

Du Peyrou presented the letters either in accordance with their subject matter or else in rough chronological order. The Neuchâtel disciple tried to live up to his claim as a faithful editor. As with Part I of the *Confessions*, he sometimes protected individuals by hiding a proper name behind an initial. He even displayed reluctance at identifying himself, and occasionally fell victim to unintentional lapses and word omissions. On the other hand, both Ralph Leigh and I have found instances where Du Peyrou, perhaps at the

33. My abbreviation *CC* continues to refer to Leigh's edition of the correspondence. The citation *Collection complète* refers to Du Peyrou's edition. Wherever possible I note the provenance of the letters printed in the *CC* and in the *Collection complète*. Furthermore, whenever the differences between the texts of the *CC* and the *Collection complète* are significant, I make mention of the fact.

34. The artlessness must be taken with a grain of salt, since Rousseau obviously intended certain letters for publication.

35. The literature on the eighteenth-century epistolary novel is enormous and this is no place to review it. Dena Goodman recently has illustrated the growing interest in the printed letter among literary and cultural historians of the Enlightenment. See her article, 'Epistolary property: Michel de Servan and the plight of letters on the eve of the French Revolution', in *Early modern conceptions of property*, ed. John Brewer and Susan Staves (New York and London 1996), p.339-64. Elsewhere see Janet Gurkin Altman, 'The letter-book as a literary institution 1539-1789', *Yale French studies* 71 (1986), p.17-62; and several of the essays in *Ecrire. Publier. Lire. Les correspondances (problématique et économie d'un 'genre littéraire')*, ed. Jean-Louis Bonnat and Mireille Bossis (Nantes 1982). As Goodman points out ('Epistolary property', p.361), debates over epistolary 'artlessness' mostly engage literary critics of the seventeenth century.

request of an addressee, consciously omitted sentences or entire paragraphs from letters. Still, he never believed he was falsifying Rousseau. Most of Du Peyrou's slips, it is safe to say, represent the mistakes of an overworked and at times troubled editor, not the censor of Rousseau's words and ideas.[36]

The initial set of letters, spanning the time between the first *Discours* and disgrace over *Emile*, comprised a wealth of *rousseauviana*, revealing the writer's epistolary views on religion, education, fame, freedom of expression and other matters. For the most part the correspondence as presented by Du Peyrou moved from the theoretical towards the personal, thereby replicating the pattern exhibited by the textual presentation of previous volumes.

The correspondence dealing with Rousseau's religious views commenced with the celebrated letter to Voltaire on providence, subsequently retouched by the author.[37] First published in 1758, it already had been printed at least five times.[38] As a source for the savoyard vicar's profession of faith in *Emile*, the letter was central to an understanding of Rousseau's religious evolution. Du Peyrou published Voltaire's response of 12 September 1756, which wished to avoid any prolonged exchange.[39] He then skipped thirteen years, moving on to Rousseau's letter of 15 January 1769 to 'M***' [Aymon de Franquières], written from Bourgoin. Still unsettled following his return to France from England, Rousseau found consolation in a stoical theism that reaffirmed the 'profession de foi' published seven years earlier. The writer urged his sceptical correspondent to accept worldly evil with the knowledge that life renews itself. He added that the goodness within human hearts is sufficient reason to acknowledge the existence of God, and to deny this goodness is to destroy virtue, the quest for which is life's most worthwhile struggle.[40] Du Peyrou concluded this sampling of Rousseau's religious views with the partial text of a letter to Leonhard Usteri written in July 1763. It was a summary defence of Book IV, chapter 8, of the suppressed *Du contrat social*, illustrating the incompatibility between Christianity and most civil institutions.[41]

---

36. In what follows I shall note Du Peyrou's most glaring sins of omission. At times of course he did not have access to the letter that Rousseau actually sent to a correspondent. Instead he had to edit an early draft or even a text that Rousseau might later have prepared for eventual publication. Leigh's notes in the *CC* meticulously distinguish between the letters actually received by Rousseau's correspondents and variants.

37. Copy prepared by Rousseau in 1764 for the aborted Môtiers edition of his collected works, Rousseau to Voltaire, [18 August 1756], *Collection complète*, xii.91-113; copy prepared in 1756 by Voltaire's secretary Wagnière from the original letter, *CC*, iv.37-71. There are considerable differences between the texts prepared in 1756 and 1764. Rousseau kept retouching his master draft. Leigh's 'Notes critiques' describe the textual differences in some detail (see *CC*, iv.58-64).

38. *CC*, iv.54-57.

39. Signed original, Voltaire to Rousseau, 12 September 1756, *Collection complète*, xii.113-14; *CC*, iv.102-103.

40. Copy mostly in Rousseau's hand and submitted by Girardin to Du Peyrou, Rousseau to [Laurent Aymon de Franquières], 15 January 1769, *Collection complète*, xii.114-34; *CC*, xxxvii.13-27.

41. An incomplete copy prepared for Du Peyrou, Rousseau to Leonhard Usteri, 18 July 1763, *Collection complète*, xii.141-45; signed original, *CC*, xvii.62-67.

Next came letters which touched upon other topics central to Rousseau's thought: childhood education, social engineering, the emptiness of fame and conceptions of authorial freedom. The first letter was addressed to Prince Ludwig-Eugen of Württemberg. It offered maxims on the proper moral upbringing of the prince's little daughter and complemented Rousseau's observations in *Emile* and *La Nouvelle Héloïse*.[42] A letter to Mirabeau *père* underscored Rousseau's hostility towards what he considered the 'legal despotism' of physiocracy. The author of *Du contrat social* took the *ami des hommes* to task for formulaic naiveté: 'vous donnez trop de force à vos calculs, & pas assez aux penchans du cœur humain, & au jeu des passions. Votre système est très-bon pour les gens de l'Utopie, il ne vaut rien pour les enfans d'Adam'.[43] A letter to abbé Raynal, following award of the Dijon Academy's essay prize, expressed the writer's ambivalence towards fame and applauded the enticements of obscurity.[44]

Following another letter to Raynal's *Mercure*, this time decrying the use of copper utensils because of their alleged health dangers,[45] Du Peyrou published one to 'M. P*** à Geneve' [Jean Perdriau]. The subject was the dedication of the *Discours sur l'origine de l'inégalité*. The dedication was stirring up Genevan politics. Some members of the Small Council considered it satirical, others believed that it would ignite social antagonisms. Moreover, the ruling elites of Geneva wondered how they could accept the dedication of a work whose principles opposed their own tenets on government and society. In writing to Perdriau, Rousseau upheld the sincerity of his dedication and defended his failure to request permission from Geneva's Small Council before offering it. He wrote that his strategy was based upon his principles of literary freedom: as an author he should have the autonomy to dedicate the *Discours* as he saw fit, and the members of the Small Council were free to reject it as *they* saw fit. At the heart of the matter was the issue of authorial liberty.[46]

That Rousseau might argue for another writer's freedom of expression, even at his own expense, was next illustrated in letters urging the retention of Palissot in the Academy of Nancy, despite the unpleasant barbs in his play *Le Cercle*. Appealing to the comte de Tressan to intervene with Lorraine's duc Stanislas Leszczynski on behalf of Palissot, Rousseau wrote: 'Mais si tout son crime est d'avoir exposé mes ridicules, c'est le droit du théatre; je ne vois rien en cela de

42. Copy prepared for Du Peyrou, Rousseau to Ludwig-Eugen, prince of Württemberg, 10 November 1763, *Collection complète*, xii.145-59; *CC*, xviii.115-27.
43. Copy probably prepared for Du Peyrou, Rousseau to Victor Riquetti, marquis de Mirabeau, 26 July 1767, *Collection complète*, xii.162; *CC*, xxxiii.238-42.
44. Fragment of a signed copy, Rousseau to abbé Guillaume-Thomas-François Raynal, [25 July 1750], *Collection complète*, xii.165-66; originally published in the *Mercure* (September 1750), p.64-66, *CC*, ii.132-35. There are slight differences between the two texts.
45. Originally published in the *Mercure* (July 1753), p.5-13, Rousseau to abbé Raynal, [June 1753], *Collection complète*, xii.167-71; *CC*, ii.221-27.
46. Copy prepared by Du Peyrou from the original, *Collection complète*, xii.172-79; signed original, Rousseau to [Jean Perdriau], 28 November 1754, *CC*, iii.55-64.

répréhensible pour l'honnête homme, & j'y vois pour l'Auteur le mérite d'avoir su choisir un sujet très-riche.'[47]

Having introduced the correspondence thematically, Du Peyrou now abruptly switched over to a chronological pattern documenting Rousseau's literary and moral pilgrimage. A polite refusal to adhere to a request that he praise Empress Maria Theresa for her cultural embellishment of Vienna preceded the writer's qualified acceptance of Vernes's commission to defend the honour of Geneva in face of d'Alembert's shocking *Encyclopédie* article.[48] This in turn led, a few weeks later, to the letter breaking with Diderot.[49] Prefacing the upcoming *Lettre à d'Alembert*, another letter to Vernes stated Rousseau's disgust with *encyclopédiste* materialism. The writer added, however, that his position did not necessarily place him in accord with Calvinist biblicism:

croirai-je qu'un Scythe ou un Africain, soient moins chers au Pere commun que vous & moi, & pourquoi croirai-je qu'il leur ait ôté plutôt qu'à nous, les ressources pour le connoître? Non, mon digne ami; ce n'est point sur quelques feuilles éparses qu'il faut aller chercher la loi de Dieu, mais dans le cœur de l'homme, où sa main daigna l'écrire.[50]

A subsequent letter to Vernes further underscored Rousseau's faith in divine providence.[51]

Du Peyrou whisked through 1759 and 1760 with very few letters from Rousseau. But illustrative of the writer's reformist social and political vision, as well as his belief in the sanctity of friendship, three stood out. The first, already published in the *Journal de Paris*, chastised Jean-Edme Romilly, son of Rousseau's watchmaker friend Jean, for the young man's intemperate denunciation of the rich.[52] The second letter consoled Etienne de Silhouette, the recently fallen reform-minded French controller general of finances.[53] The third letter was Rousseau's shocked reply to Duchesne upon receiving from the publisher

47. Autograph copy, Rousseau to Louis-Elisabeth de La Vergne, comte de Tressan, [27 December 1755], *Collection complète*, xii.196; *CC*, iii.243-44. The correspondence between Rousseau and Tressan concerning this 'first' Palissot affair had been published in Rousseau's lifetime (see *Lettres diverses de Jean-Jacques Rousseau citoyen de Genève*, Amsterdam 1763, p.197-215).

48. Corrected copy prepared for Du Peyrou, Rousseau to Franz Christof Scheyb, [15 July 1756], *Collection complète*, xii.202-206; printed from the signed original, *CC*, iv.26-29. The differences between the texts are not significant. Copy prepared by Vernes's secretary and sent to Du Peyrou, Rousseau to Jacob Vernes, 18 February 1758, *Collection complète*, xii.206-209; signed original, *CC*, v.32-35. The differences between the original and the copied texts are not significant.

49. Copy prepared for Du Peyrou, Rousseau to Diderot, 2 March 1758, *Collection complète*, xii.213-16; autograph copy, *CC*, v.47-49.

50. Copy prepared by Vernes's secretary for Du Peyrou, Rousseau to Vernes, 25 March 1758, *Collection complète*, xii.217; signed original, *CC*, v.65-66. The differences between the two texts are insignificant.

51. Copy prepared for Du Peyrou by Vernes, Rousseau to Vernes, 25 May 1758, *Collection complète*, xii.218-21; signed original, *CC*, v.82-84.

52. Copy prepared for Du Peyrou, Rousseau to Jean-Edme Romilly, 6 February 1759, *Collection complète*, xii.226-27; originally published in the *Journal de Paris* (17 February 1779), p.191, *CC*, vi.21-22.

53. Copy prepared by Moultou for Du Peyrou, Rousseau to Etienne de Silhouette, 2 December 1759, *Collection complète*, xii.229; autograph copy, *CC*, vi.214-15. The differences between the

the text of Palissot's new satirical comedy, *Les Philosophes*. Rousseau's agitation had nothing to do with Palissot's mockery of him in the comedy. Rather it was the outrageous pastiche of Diderot that provoked the writer's wrath. For Rousseau, a dead friendship remained a sacred memory.[54]

The next block of letters dealt with the responses of Rousseau to readers' commentary upon *La Nouvelle Héloïse*. In a few cases, most notably Rousseau's letter to [d'Alembert], the editors respected the recipient's anonymity.[55] Rousseau mentioned to Vernes that the public's delirious approval of the novel was, by and large, overly indulgent. Nevertheless, he stood prepared to challenge critics. For example, Vernes's disbelief that the atheist Wolmar could ever display moral rectitude provoked the reply: 'vos griefs contre *Wolmar* me prouvent que j'ai mal rempli l'objet du livre, ou que vous ne l'avez pas bien saisi. Cet objet étoit de rapprocher les partis opposés, par une estime réciproque; d'apprendre aux *Philosophes*, qu'on peut croire en Dieu sans être hypocrite, & aux *Croyans*, qu'on peut être incrédule sans être un coquin.' Rousseau chastised Vernes for not reading the novel's conclusion, where, according to the author, Wolmar experienced a religious conversion.[56]

The mission of authorship: 1762-1765

Following publication of the four autobiographical letters to Malesherbes,[57] nearly half of Du Peyrou's selection of correspondence covered the period between Rousseau's flight from France (June 1762) and his departure from Môtiers (September 1765). The materials inserted by Du Peyrou during this period were meant to slake readers' thirst for Rousseau's reaction to the most trying events of his life. In response to the persecutions, the tone of Rousseau's correspondence grew militant and illustrated a growing hostility towards the institutions of the *ancien régime*. Published for the first time was the writer's letter to [Moultou] (faintly disguised as m. de M.) bitterly likening the Paris Parlement's idea of justice on the eve of its condemnation of *Emile* to the Toulouse Parlement's brutal mishandling of the Calas affair: 'Il y a dans tous les Corps des intérêts auxquels la justice est toujours subordonnée, & il n'y a pas plus d'inconvénient à brûler un innocent au Parlement de Paris, qu'à en rouer

two texts are insignificant. Subsequently Rousseau did not forget Silhouette's political courage, and reproduced his letter in full in Part II of the *Confessions* (see *OC*, i.531-32).

54. Autograph copy, Rousseau to Nicolas-B. Duchesne, 21 May 1760, *Collection complète*, xii.231; *CC*, vii.98-103. Prior to publication by Du Peyrou this letter had appeared in print at least once. It had been published without Rousseau's approval during the public outcry immediately following the play's performance.

55. Autograph copy, Rousseau to [d'Alembert], 15 February 1761, *Collection complète*, xii.234; *CC*, viii.104.

56. Copy (with suppressions) prepared for Du Peyrou by Vernes's secretary, Rousseau to Vernes, [24 June 1761], *Collection complète*, xii.238-39; signed original, *CC*, ix.27-28.

57. *Collection complète*, xii.241-65; 4 January 1762, *CC*, x.4-9; 12 January 1762, *CC*, x.24-29; 26 January 1762, *CC*, x.52-58; 28 January 1762, *CC*, x.63-68. All copies prepared by Malesherbes's secretary and sent to Rousseau in November 1762. The originals are lost.

un autre au Parlement de Toulouse.' The same letter expressed the opinion that Rousseau had fulfilled his task and that martyrdom was his reward: 'Ma carriere est finie, il ne me reste plus qu'à la couronner. J'ai rendu gloire à Dieu, j'ai parlé pour le bien des hommes; ô ami! pour une si grande cause, ni toi ni moi ne refuserons jamais de souffrir.'[58]

Twenty years after Geneva's condemnation of *Emile*, the republic's prohibition of *Du contrat social* and its issuance of the warrant for Rousseau's arrest, the native son's words still rang with indignation: 'Quoi! décrété sans être ouï! Et où est le délit? où sont les preuves? Genevois, si telle est Votre liberté, je la trouve peu regrettable.'[59] Yet the victim would bear no malice. Again to [Moultou]: 'Ne cherchez point à parler de moi; mais dans l'occasion dites à nos Magistrats que je les respecterai toujours, même injustes; et à tous nos concitoyens, que je les aimerai toujours, même ingrats.'[60] Rousseau became increasingly preoccupied with the price he had been forced to pay, and his faith in being able to change ways of thinking was wavering. A letter to the Yverdon notable, Gingins de Moiry, first published in 1763 and reprinted by Du Peyrou, recorded the writer's dismay: 'Tous mes malheurs me viennent d'avoir trop bien pensé des hommes. Ils me font sentir combien je m'étois trompé.'[61] These sentiments were echoed in Rousseau's subsequent letter to [Vincenz Tscharner].[62]

Nevertheless, during the Môtiers period Rousseau would gain some respite, at least initially, and he made new friends. Unfortunately many of these friendships ended badly, the consequence of mutual misunderstanding. Probably recalling his own experience, Du Peyrou underscored the poignancy of those broken relationships by publishing Rousseau's hopeful first letters to the one-time friends. First there was George Keith, 'milord maréchal', the Scots governor of Frederick the Great's territory of Neuchâtel. Rousseau would consider Keith a protector and surrogate father until the latter wearied of the author's growing paranoia and ceased corresponding. The breakdown in relations deeply saddened Rousseau. By spring 1779 Keith was dead and d'Alembert was casting doubts publicly upon the sincerity of Rousseau's gratitude

---

58. Copy prepared for Du Peyrou, Rousseau to [Moultou], 7 June 1762, *Collection complète*, xii.270-71; signed original, *CC*, xi.36-37. Two inconsequential sentences were suppressed in the *Collection complète*.

59. Signed original, Rousseau to [Moultou], 22 June 1762, *Collection complète*, xii.273; *CC*, xi.126.

60. Signed original, Rousseau to [Moultou], 24 June 1762, *Collection complète*, xii.276; *CC*, xi.147.

61. Copy sent by Henri Laliaud to Du Peyrou, Rousseau to Victor de Gingins, seigneur de Moiry, [21 July 1762], *Collection complète*, xii.277; signed original, *CC*, xii.71; previously published in the *Lettres diverses de Jean-Jacques Rousseau citoyen de Genève*, p.213-15. Leigh considers the letter published by Du Peyrou to be an unfaithful rendering. There seem to be two significant mistranscriptions – for example, 'reprocher' for 'rougir' and 'je n'ai perdu par mes malheurs' for 'que perdu par mes malheurs'.

62. Draft, Rousseau to [Vincenz Bernhard Tscharner], 27 July 1762, *Collection complète*, xii.280-81; signed original, *CC*, xii.110-12. Leigh notes significant differences between the two letters.

towards 'milord maréchal'.[63] Moreover, allied to d'Alembert, Keith's former secretary, Wilhelm Muzell-Stosch, refused to send Du Peyrou copies of Rousseau's letters to the Scots aristocrat. So the editor had to certify Rousseau's feelings towards Keith with scraps, for the most part drafts of letters that Rousseau had managed to save. Du Peyrou possessed and published the initial one of July 1762, in which Rousseau introduced himself to Keith and humbly requested asylum on Neuchâtel's soil.[64]

Another actor in the Môtiers drama was the village pastor F.-C. de Montmollin, who first had welcomed Rousseau warmly but then became the writer's nemesis. Eventually Montmollin would question Rousseau's religious sincerity, and his hostile sermons provoked Môtiers's villagers into abusing the writer. To challenge all of this hostility Du Peyrou reproduced Rousseau's moving declaration of Christian faith addressed to Montmollin in August 1762.[65] Finally, there was David Hume. In mid-February 1763 Rousseau had sent a polite response to Hume's invitation of the previous July suggesting that the persecuted writer seek asylum in England. Once their relations broke down, Hume published Rousseau's letter as part of his own dossier of self-justification and Rousseau's alleged treachery, the *Concise and genuine account of the dispute between Mr Hume and Mr Rousseau*. By 1782 the tragedy of their misunderstanding was part of European cultural history, welcomed by Rousseau's enemies but regretted by his disciples. By reprinting Rousseau's gracious first letter to Hume, Du Peyrou was poignantly reminding readers of what might have been.[66]

Du Peyrou next published a selection of Rousseau's social and literary observations, which included the writer's letters to the maréchal-duc de Luxembourg analysing the Swiss national character and describing his new surroundings;[67] to [Niklaus] K[irchberger] offering advice for a lasting marriage;[68] and to [the marquise de Verdelin] contrasting the writer's contempt for the Sorbonne's condemnation of *Emile* with his respect for that of the archbishop of Paris.[69] Following these observations were a pair of letters of crucial

---

63. D'Alembert, *Eloge de milord maréchal par M. d'Alembert*, p.69-75; *CC*, xliii.238-41.

64. Signed and corrected first draft, Rousseau to George Keith, count-marshal of Scotland, [10/11 July 1762], *Collection complète*, xii. 279; *CC*, xii.4-6. Addressing Keith two-and-a-half years later, Rousseau would express his desperation: 'Vous êtes mon seul protecteur, le seul homme à qui j'aye de véritables obligations, le seul ami sur lequel je compte, le dernier auquel je me sois attaché, et auquel il n'en succédera jamais d'autres' (corrected copy, Rousseau to George Keith, 8 December 1764, *Collection complète*, xii.435; *CC*, xxii.183-85).

65. Signed original, Rousseau to Frédéric-Guillaume de Montmollin, 24 August 1762, *Collection complète*, xii.281-83; *CC*, xii.245-48.

66. Signed original, Rousseau to Hume, 19 February 1763, *Collection complète*, xii.313-15; Hume, *Exposé succinct*, p.2-5; *CC*, xv.198-200.

67. Autograph copies, Rousseau to the maréchal-duc de Luxembourg, 20 January 1763, 28 January 1763, *Collection complète*, xii.283-313; *CC*, xv.48-69, 111-30.

68. Du Peyrou's transcription of original draft, Rousseau to [Niklaus Kirchberger], 17 March 1763, *Collection complète*, xii.321-24; original draft, *CC*, xv.285-88.

69. Autograph copy subsequently annotated by Rousseau, Rousseau to [Marie-Madeleine de Brémond d'Ars, marquise de Verdelin], 27 March 1763, *Collection complète*, xii.328-31; copied from

biographical importance: Rousseau's abdication of Genevan citizenship and his dramatic explanation of the act to Marc Chappuis.[70] The disappointment with Geneva marked a crucial evolution in Rousseau's self-fashioning. Instead of serving contemporaries or the erstwhile *patrie*, he would place his bets on the future. As he wrote to Chappuis, 'Je ne dois pas seulement compte de moi aux Genevois, je le dois encore à moi-même, au public dont j'ai le malheur d'être connu, & à la postérité de qui je serai peut-être.'[71]

It is clear that, his political misfortunes notwithstanding, at Môtiers Rousseau was perceiving himself as a moral sage. He indeed was sought out by individuals desiring grand statements of advice or private assistance in times of crisis. For example, a young aristocrat, [Joseph Durey de Morsan], had just received a *lettre de cachet* delivered at his father's behest. [Durey] asked Rousseau to intervene in hopes of getting it rescinded. This prompted a letter from the writer to [the elder Durey] on behalf of the unfortunate, debt-ridden son.[72] Nevertheless, Rousseau was not always taken in by requests of the young. When M.L.P.L.E.D.W. [Prince Ludwig-Eugen of Württemburg] asked the author if *Emile* should serve as an open forum for advice in rearing his child, Rousseau responded sardonically: 'Votre Altesse Sérénissime aura pu voir dans le livre qu'elle daigne citer, que je n'ai jamais su comment il faut élever les Princes; et la clameur publique me persuade que je ne sais comment il faut élever personne.'[73] To an aristocratic young abbé, [Alexandre de Carondelet], who agonised over his inherited class prejudices, loss of religious faith and patriotic ardour, and who addressed the writer as 'père', Rousseau answered caustically that the best advice he could offer was to urge Carondelet to mind his own mother.[74] Though Rousseau might have hoped to end the matter there and then, the insistent nobleman thought otherwise and seized the opening. An eight-letter exchange followed, punctuated by Rousseau's

signed original around 1840, *CC*, xv.335-38. The differences between the two manuscripts are slight.

70. Autograph copy prepared by Rousseau for Moultou, Rousseau to Jacob Favre, [12 May 1763], *Collection complète*, xii.347-48; signed original, *CC*, xvi.164-67. The abdication was first published in the *Gazette de France* 43 (30 May 1763), p.201. As for the letter to Chappuis (26 May 1763), see copy prepared for Du Peyrou in *Collection complète*, xii.348-52; second copy prepared towards the end of the eighteenth century, *CC*, xvi.245-50. While Leigh considers the text he published to be closest to the original letter (apparently now lost), the version published by Du Peyrou was based partially upon a copy prepared by Rousseau for Moultou in 1764 (and also lost). Leigh refers to it as a hybrid text.

71. *Collection complète*, xii.349.

72. Signed first draft, Rousseau to [Durey d'Harnoncourt], 11 September 1763, *Collection complète*, xii.354-55; *CC*, xvii.242-44. The letter apparently had little effect. In his 'notes explicatives' Leigh relates a gruesome family history of alleged embezzlement, murder and incest.

73. Autograph copy, Rousseau to [Prince Ludwig-Eugen of Württemburg], [29 September 1763], *Collection complète*, xii.356; *CC*, xvii.286-87. The writer would later change his mind and counsel the prince.

74. Signed original, Rousseau to [Alexandre-Louis-Benoît de Carandolet], 29 September 1763, *Collection complète*, xii.358; *CC*, xviii.162-63.

exasperation at having to reply to Carondelet's increasingly lengthy and self-absorbed pleas for life formulas.[75]

Du Peyrou never published the justly celebrated letters from 'Henriette' to Rousseau, but he did incorporate the latter's two responses. Rousseau's first one failed to recognise his correspondent's intelligence and the sincerity of her anguished feelings of isolation.[76] His second letter noted the maturity of her sentiments but regretted his inability to ease her pain. Rousseau perceived that 'Henriette''s sense of uselessness was more poignant than Carondelet's, and he urged her to find harmony within herself. Of course, flattered by pleas for authorial advice, Rousseau's own social needs were more than fulfilled and he could easily distribute platitudes such as: 'je sens mieux, de jour en jour, qu'on ne peut être heureux sur la terre, qu'à proportion qu'on s'éloigne des choses, & qu'on se rapproche de soi'. But his concluding remarks that he might be more useful once he located 'Henriette''s first letter, 'noyée dans des tas de papiers', nullified even his paternal good wishes. Poor 'Henriette' probably saw in Rousseau another overly busy man turning her away, an impression confirmed a year later when she unsuccessfully tried to reopen the correspondence, and in 1770 when she failed to obtain an audience with the Master.[77]

Doubtless Du Peyrou did not consider Rousseau's letters to 'Henriette' as dismissive. On the contrary, the editor revelled in the writer's benevolence towards young women, as when Rousseau congratulated 'mademoiselle G' [Isabelle d'Ivernois] for her upcoming marriage and supplied her with his trademark gift, a ribbon sewn by his own hand for the bride's hair.[78] Balancing private images of tender solicitude were public ones revealing the courageous and embattled writer, prepared to dive into the progressive political struggles of his time. Du Peyrou therefore printed Rousseau's four letters to Captain Mathieu Buttafoco of Corsica, which responded to the patriotic request for a model constitution for the island following its latest revolt against its Genoan colonial masters.[79]

75. Signed original, Rousseau to [Alexandre-Louis-Benoît de Carandolet], 6 January 1764, *Collection complète*, xii.360; *CC*, xix.12-14. Du Peyrou published Rousseau's responses of 4 March 1764 and 11 November 1764: copy prepared by Du Peyrou, *Collection complète*, xii.361-65; signed original, *CC*, xix.197-202; copy prepared by Du Peyrou, *Collection complète*, xii.365-68; signed original, *CC*, xxii.40-43.

76. Copy prepared by Du Peyrou, Rousseau to ['Henriette'], 7 May 1764, *Collection complète*, xii.382-88; draft, *CC*, xx.18-24.

77. First draft, Rousseau to ['Henriette'], 4 November 1764, *Collection complète*, xii.389-92; *CC*, xxii.8-11. See as well 'Henriette' to Rousseau, [December 1764-February 1765], *CC*, xxiii.295-300. For the dénouement see 'Henriette' to Rousseau, [28 March 1765], *CC*, xxiv.321-22; 'Henriette' to Rousseau, [18 December 1765], *CC*, xxviii.67-68; Rousseau to 'Henriette', 25 October 1770, *CC*, xxxviii.124-25.

78. Draft, Rousseau to [Isabelle d'Ivernois], 15 May 1764, *Collection complète*, xii.393-94; older copy prepared from original, *CC*, xx.61-63.

79. Copies prepared by Buttafoco and sent to Du Peyrou, corrected by Du Peyrou's secretary, Jeannin, to conform with drafts at Du Peyrou's disposal, Rousseau to Mathieu Buttafoco, 22 September 1764, 15 October 1764, 24 March 1765, 26 May 1765, *Collection complète*, xii.413-27; *CC*, xxi.173-76, 258-61; *CC*, xxiv.299-301; *CC*, xxv.337-39. See Leigh's 'notes critiques', xxi.260.

Though unaware that Buttafoco was playing a double game, using Rousseau to gain credibility with the Corsican leader Pasquale Paoli while at the same time harbouring hopes for an eventual French occupation of the island, the writer was flattered and excited by the prospect of contributing to the revolutionary cause of a mountain people whom he considered untainted by refinements of wealth and luxury.[80] He wrote to Buttafoco: 'Il est superflu, Monsieur, de chercher à exciter mon zele pour l'entreprise que vous me proposez. La seule idée m'éleve l'ame & me transporte.'[81] Initially Rousseau feared that he lacked the physical strength for such an undertaking and declared that his poor health precluded the possibility of a trip to Corsica. Though he had predicted great things from the islanders in *Du contrat social* (Book II, chapter 10),[82] on 22 September 1764 Rousseau wondered whether their recent revolution would hold. He expressed his misgivings to Buttafoco: 'Mais, Monsieur, l'indépendance de votre pays n'est point assurée, tant qu'aucune Puissance ne la reconnoît.'[83] Despite his own fears of French intentions for Corsica, Rousseau nevertheless asked Buttafoco to send him a good map of the island, as well as detailed geographical, demographic, social and historical information.[84]

When Rousseau next wrote to Buttafoco in March 1765, however, everything had changed. In the first place the French had transported garrisons to the five major Corsican towns. Then there was Rousseau's increasingly untenable situation at Môtiers. The writer once more felt the heat of persecution and was in a state of panic. No longer was it a question of writing a constitution for Corsica, but rather of seeking asylum there.[85] Two months later, however, Rousseau felt more secure about remaining in Môtiers, believing that Frederick the Great and 'milord maréchal' would protect him. Physically and emotionally drained, however, he claimed to be in no state to write the complex political document that the Corsicans merited. Moreover, he desired no more trouble with the local authorities. He therefore offered to defer his plans. Rousseau did take his incomplete draft of the 'constitution' to England, but the French purchase and occupation of Corsica in 1769 rendered any further work superfluous.[86] In his last letter to Buttafoco, Rousseau nonetheless promised to retain fond memories of the islanders: 'Peuple brave et

80. Ernestine Dedeck-Héry's study, *J.-J. Rousseau et le projet de constitution pour la Corse* (Philadelphia 1932), reveals the political manoeuvring behind Buttafoco's request, of which Rousseau was unaware. In August 1764, shortly before Buttafoco's first inquiry of the writer, French foreign minister Choiseul signed an accord with Genoa at Compiègne, whereby France would station garrisons in Corsica's five leading towns. This was the prelude to the eventual French purchase of the island from Genoa. Buttafoco did not take very seriously the idealised democratic principles of Rousseau, although General Paoli did.
81. *Collection complète*, xii.413-14.
82. *OC*, iii.391.
83. *Collection complète*, xii.415.
84. *Collection complète*, xii.419.
85. *Collection complète*, xii.420-23.
86. While he was at Trye Rousseau had Thérèse give his draft of the 'constitution' to Mme de Nadaillac, who passed it on to Du Peyrou in 1778. No doubt the latter did not care to risk

hospitalier! Non, je n'oublierai jamais un moment de ma vie que vos cœurs, vos bras, vos foyers m'ont été ouverts à l'instant qu'il ne me restoit presqu'aucun autre asyle en Europe.'[87]

Du Peyrou's inclusion of the letters to Buttafoco was intended to convey to readers Rousseau's sense of the political mission of authorship. But expressing such a public voice bore perils. After June 1762 printers of Rousseau's books in several countries faced at least the possibility of arrest.[88] Furthermore, enemies or the merely irresponsible might borrow and misuse Rousseau's name either to gain publicity for their cause or else to injure his. Already a literary forger had installed, above a falsified Rousseau signature, the supposed 'rénonciation à la Société Civile, & ses derniers adieux aux Hommes' in a pirated edition of *Du contrat social*.[89] Another forger attributed to Rousseau a pamphlet addressed to the archbishop of Auch, denouncing the Jesuits and by implication the archbishop's pro-Jesuit stance. The genuine author, probably P.-F. de La Croix, a barrister in the Parlement of Toulouse, closely imitated the style of the *Lettre à Christophe de Beaumont* and provoked a public disavowal from Rousseau which Duchesne published in 1764. In order to remind readers that Rousseau's perception of conspiracies against him had some merit, Du Peyrou saw fit to reprint the disclaimer nearly twenty years later.[90]

Further reminders of the sacred mission were enshrined in Rousseau's appreciation and encouragement of young writers. Du Peyrou tried to publicise them. In May 1764 the twenty-four-year-old Chamfort had sent Rousseau a copy of his one-act play, *La Jeune Indienne*, recently performed at the Théâtre-Français. Six weeks later the celebrated author generously acknowledged the work of the unknown one, while nevertheless remaining self-consciously didactic and self-promoting: 'L'effet le plus sûr de mes maximes qui est de m'attirer la haine des méchans et l'affection de gens de bien, & qui se marque autant par mes malheurs que par mes succès, m'apprend par l'approbation dont vous honorez mes écrits, ce qu'on doit attendre des vôtres.'[91]

---

alienating foreign minister Vergennes by publishing it. The 'constitution' first appeared in the Streckeisen-Moultou edition, *J.-J. Rousseau, œuvres et correspondance inédites* (Paris 1861), p.59-127.

87. *Collection complète*, xii.424.

88. Jean-Baptiste Réguillat of Lyon would be arrested in January 1767 for having published, in his mother's name, *Du contrat social*. See *note explicative* b, *CC*, xii.226.

89. *Du contrat social, ou Principes du droit politique, par J.-J. Rousseau, citoyen de Genève*, édition sans cartons, à laquelle on a ajouté une lettre de l'auteur au seul ami qui lui reste dans le monde, in-12° (Amsterdam, [falsely attributed to] Marc-Michel Rey 1762), p.207-16. For the text of this apocryphal letter see *CC*, xii.301-306.

90. Signed original, Rousseau to N.-B. Duchesne, 27 May 1764, *Collection complète*, xii.398-400; *CC*, xx.101-105. Originally published as *Lettre de M. Rousseau de Genève, à M**** (Paris, Duchesne 1764). The pamphlet falsely attributed to Rousseau was *Jean-Jacques Rousseau, citoyen de Genève, à Jean-François de Montillet, archevêque et seigneur d'Auch, primat de la Gaule Novempopulanie, et du royaume de Navarre, conseiller du roi en tous ses conseils* (1764). In *La France littéraire* and *Les Supercheries littéraires dévoilées*, J.-M. Quérard attributed the 'rénonciation à la société civile' to La Croix as well. See *note explicative* a, *CC*, xii.150-51.

91. Copy, Rousseau to Sébastien-Roch Nicolas, 'Chamfort', 24 June 1764, *Collection complète*, xii.400-401; *CC*, xx.210-11.

Du Peyrou considered it important to make readers aware of Rousseau's opinion of well-known contemporaries. These judgements clarified the line-ups in the Enlightenment's cultural wars. Certainly the captain of the opposing side was Voltaire, in Rousseau's eyes an unquestioned abuser of literary genius. In a letter to [Du Peyrou], who had sent him a copy of the *Dictionnaire philosophique*, Rousseau responded: 'Il est agréable à lire; il y regne une bonne morale [...]. Mais ce même Auteur est presque toujours de mauvaise foi dans les extraits de l'Ecriture; il raisonne souvent fort mal, & l'air de ridicule et de mépris qu'il jette Sur des sentimens respectés des hommes, réjaillissant sur les hommes mêmes, me paroît un outrage fait à la société.' Interestingly enough, as he edited Rousseau's comments, Du Peyrou excluded the damaging phrase that Voltaire's outrages in the *Dictionnaire philosophique* might be 'punissable devant les Tribunaux humains'. After all, for Rousseau, great spokesman of freedom of expression, to suggest that a veil of censorship be drawn over Voltaire was, to say the least, compromising. As for authors who honourably fulfilled their calling, Rousseau placed the comte de Buffon in the first rank. Again addressing [Du Peyrou], he lauded the naturalist: 'Ses écrits m'instruiront et me plairont toute ma vie [...]. C'est la plus belle plume de son siecle; je ne doute point que ce ne soit là le jugement de la postérité.'[92]

Du Peyrou was not averse to having Rousseau advertise the *Collection complète* from the grave. The devoted editor therefore published the author's letter to Duclos where he first called Duchesne's 'Neuchâtel' edition of his *œuvres* 'incomplet, et qui pis est très fautive', and then added: 'J'ai toujours le projet de faire enfin moi-même un recueil de mes écrits, dans lequel je pourrai faire entrer quelques chiffons qui sont encore en manuscrits.' As for the 'mémoires de ma vie' still awaited by Duclos, Rousseau responded: 'ils sont très-difficiles à faire sans compromettre personne; pour y songer il faut plus de tranquillité qu'on ne m'en laisse, & que je n'en aurai probablement jamais; si je vis toutefois, je n'y renonce pas; vous avez toute ma confiance, mais vous sentez qu'il y a des choses qui ne se disent pas de si loin'.[93]

Twenty-five years later the devoted Du Peyrou therefore was reminding readers that the STG's edition indeed fulfilled Rousseau's wishes of December 1764. Thinly protected by anonymity, Du Peyrou included in the *Collection complète* the writer's letters to him of December 1764 to January 1765 outlining the original project,[94] and another letter to 'milord maréchal' requesting permission to get on with it.[95] As he recalled the short-circuited edition of 1765, Du Peyrou informed readers that Rousseau's forthright conception of

92. Signed original, Rousseau to [Du Peyrou], 4 November 1764, *Collection complète*, xii.429-30; *CC*, xxii.5.

93. Draft copy, Rousseau to Charles Pinot Duclos, 2 December 1764, *Collection complète*, xii.433; *CC*, xxii.147-49.

94. Signed originals, Rousseau to [Du Peyrou], 13 December 1764, 24 January 1765, *Collection complète*, xii.437-40, 443-45; *CC*, xxii.226-28; *CC*, xxiii.179-83.

95. Fair copy, Rousseau to Keith, 11 February 1765, *Collection complète*, xii.454-56; *CC*, xxiii.347-48.

authorship was precisely what had caused the original project to be abandoned. From Holland to Switzerland the bitter truths of the *Lettres écrites de la montagne* had infuriated *ancien régime* governments. In France as late as 1782 *Du contrat social* and *Emile* remained prohibited books. So as to remind the world that he was editing no ordinary author, Du Peyrou printed Rousseau's letter to him of 7 February 1765, announcing the suppression of the *Lettres écrites de la montagne* in Geneva and The Hague. For Rousseau the struggle for freedom of expression was one of life or death, and there was no doubt that Voltaire was on the side of repression:

Monsieur, j'ai par-tout des amis puissans, illustres, & qui, j'en suis très-sûr, m'aiment de tout leur cœur; mais ce sont tous gens droits, bons, doux, pacifiques, qui dédaignent toute voie oblique. Au contraire, mes ennemis sont ardens, adroits, intrigans, rusés, infatigables pour nuire, et qui manœuvrent toujours sous terre, comme les taupes. Vous sentez que la partie n'est pas égale. L'Inquisiteur [Voltaire] est l'homme le plus actif que la terre ait produit, il gouverne en quelque façon toute l'Europe.[96]

The remaining letters from Môtiers published by Du Peyrou exposed the emotional swings that Rousseau had endured during the six months preceding his flight of September 1765. During his struggle with pastor Montmollin and the Neuchâtel clergy he became depressed over what he considered to be the disastrous personal cost of his corpus. He wrote to [Moultou]: 'Je ne regarde aucun de mes livres sans frémir; & tout ce que je desire au monde, est un coin de terre où je puisse mourir en paix, sans toucher ni papier ni plume.'[97] He betrayed confusion about the proper course to take. On the one hand, he wished to remain in Môtiers so as to confound his enemies there; on the other, he felt that residing in their midst would besmirch his international reputation.[98] On 9 March 1765 Rousseau promised Montmollin that he would publish nothing about religion while he lived in Môtiers.[99] Two weeks later he informed Samuel Meuron, public prosecutor for Neuchâtel, that he was prepared to depart.[100] Ultimately Rousseau decided to stay as long as he could without compromising his beliefs.[101] He challenged the right of the Môtiers consistory to define the contents of his faith and remained on tense

---

96. Signed original, Rousseau to [Du Peyrou], 7 February 1765, *Collection complète*, xii.452; *CC*, xxiii.310-12.

97. Signed original, Rousseau to [Moultou], 9 March 1765, *Collection complète*, xii.461; *CC*, xxiv.180-82. Besides respecting Moultou's anonymity, Du Peyrou suppressed sections of this letter, particularly Rousseau's mistaken identification of Jacob Vernes as author of the hostile *Sentiment des citoyens*. Voltaire was the genuine author.

98. Signed original, Rousseau to [Du Peyrou], 14 March 1765, *Collection complète*, xii.466; *CC*, xxiv.216-17. Du Peyrou suppressed several sentences in this letter.

99. Draft, Rousseau to Frédéric-Guillaume de Montmollin, [10 March 1765], *Collection complète*, xii.464; signed original, *CC*, xxiv.187-88. There are slight differences between the texts published by Du Peyrou and by Leigh. Du Peyrou's text first appeared in his *Lettre à M. *** relative à M. J.-J. Rousseau* (1765), p.6-7.

100. First draft, Rousseau to Samuel Meuron, 23 March 1765, *Collection complète*, xii.463-64; copy of signed original, *CC*, xxiv.283-85.

101. Partial fair copy, Rousseau to Keith, 6 April 1765, *Collection complète*, xii.475-77; *CC*, xxv.52-55.

terms with most inhabitants of the village, all the while believing that Neuchâtel's government and its sovereign, Frederick the Great, would protect him.[102]

Du Peyrou reprinted Rousseau's long letter to him of 8 August 1765, declaring open warfare upon Pastor Montmollin.[103] This was prelude to the villagers' stoning of the writer's cottage on the night of 6-7 September and his
subsequent flight. The next letters to appear in the *Collection* were from Rousseau's first place of exile, the île Saint-Pierre, under the jurisdiction of the
canton of Bern. As Rousseau soon informed Du Peyrou, however, the
Bernese Government was commanding him to leave and he had decided to
seek asylum in England, 'où j'aurois dû d'abord aller'.[104] Three days later,
however, in what was to become a much copied letter long before Du Peyrou
published it, Rousseau informed Emmanuel von Graffenried, a sympathetic
member of Bern's ruling council, that he would accept permanent house
arrest on Bernese soil if the cantonal authorities would permit him to stay:

J'y vivrai à mes dépens, & je donnerai sureté de n'être jamais à leur charge; je me
soumets à n'avoir ni papier, ni plume, ni aucune communication au-dehors, si ce n'est
pour l'absolue nécessité, & par le canal de ceux qui seront chargés de moi; seulement
qu'on me laisse avec l'usage de quelques livres, la liberté de me promener quelquefois
dans un jardin, & je suis content.[105]

Unsurprisingly, the request for such living martyrdom was denied.

Crisis and dénouement: 1765-1772

Whether or not Rousseau's offer of voluntary incarceration was merely tactical, it was a Staffordshire manor and not a Bernese prison that eventually provided the writer with his shelter. Du Peyrou traced Rousseau's path to English
exile. Stopping in Strasbourg, Rousseau accepted Hume's fateful offer of
asylum.[106] Next he went to Paris, where he informed François d'Ivernois that
he would refuse to appear incognito: 'Je ne me suis jamais caché, & je ne veux
pas commencer.'[107] At last he crossed the Channel. Following a short stay in

102. Autograph copy, Rousseau to the consistory of Môtiers, 29 March 1765, *Collection
complète*, xii.470-72; signed original, *CC*, xxiv.326-28.
103. Signed original, with notes added by Rousseau and Du Peyrou, Rousseau to [Du
Peyrou], 8 August 1765, *Collection complète*, xii.482-507; *CC*, xxvi.155-77; initially published in
Du Peyrou's documentary defence of Rousseau, the *Seconde lettre relative à M. J.-J. Rousseau, adressée à milord comte de Wemyss* [...] [1765], p.111-62.
104. Signed original, Rousseau to [Du Peyrou], 17 October 1765, *Collection complète*, xii.507;
CC, xxvii.132.
105. Autograph copy, Rousseau to Emmanuel von Graffenried, 20 October 1765, *Collection
complète*, xii.509; signed original, *CC*, xxvii.147-51; originally published in the *Journal encyclopédique* 8 (1 December 1765), p.131-33.
106. Signed originals, Rousseau to [Du Peyrou], 5 November 1765, 10 November 1765, *Collection complète*, xii.517-19 (with suppressions); *CC*, xxvii.225-27, 246-47; originally published in
Hume, *Exposé succinct*, p.7-8. Signed original, Rousseau to Hume, 4 December 1765, *CC*,
xxviii.17-18.
107. Signed original, Rousseau to François-Henri d'Ivernois, 18 December 1765, *Collection
complète*, xii.520 (with suppressions); *CC*, xxviii.65-66.

London, by late January 1766 he found himself in the village of Chiswick, outside the capital, hoping to voyage to Wales if need be, and escape the urban din.[108] The offer of Richard Davenport brought Rousseau to Wootton. His first impressions there were positive. He expressed his appreciation to Hume, who was performing so many services on his behalf: 'Faire un homme heureux c'est mériter de l'être.' Cut off from social life by the barrier of the English language, Rousseau desperately needed one uncompromisingly intense friendship. He identified Hume as its object. Though reciprocity on the part of the phlegmatic Scotsman was impossible, Rousseau remained undeterred: 'aimez-moi pour moi qui vous dois tant; pour vous-même; aimez-moi pour le bien que vous m'avez fait. Je sens tout le prix de votre sincere amitié; je la desire ardemment; j'y veux répondre par toute la mienne, & je sens dans mon cœur de quoi vous convaincre un jour qu'elle n'est pas non plus sans quelque prix.'[109]

Hume was constitutionally disinclined to share Rousseau's love. The English stay then turned sour when the *St James's chronicle* (1-3 April 1766) published Horace Walpole's letter to Rousseau, falsely signed Frederick II of Prussia, which treated the writer with contempt but at the same time invited him to Berlin. Du Peyrou did not reproduce the forgery, which had infuriated Rousseau, but he did publish Rousseau's letters of protest at its appearance in print to the editor of the *Chronicle* and to Count Strafford.[110] This was but the beginning of a year of great anguish. On 19 April Rousseau again wrote to Strafford. He exploded over what he perceived to be slights, insults and secret plots proliferating against him in England: 'Mylord, les malheureux sont malheureux par-tout. En France on les décrete; en Suisse on les lapide; en Angleterre on les déshonore: c'est leur vendre cher l'hospitalité.'[111] Rousseau suspected that Hume, on good terms with the *encyclopédistes* of Paris and patricians of Geneva, surely had something to do with the suspected plots. So he decided to break with the Scotsman (23 June 1766): 'Adieu, Monsieur, je vous souhaite le plus vrai bonheur; mais comme nous ne devons plus rien avoir à nous dire, voici la derniere lettre que vous recevrez de moi.'[112] Nevertheless, once Hume requested a further explanation, Rousseau responded with his lengthy accusation of treachery.[113]

108. Signed original, Rousseau to François-Henri d'Ivernois, 29 January 1766, *Collection complète*, xii.522 (with suppressions); *CC*, xxviii.236-38.

109. Signed original, Rousseau to Hume, 22 March 1766, *Collection complète*, xii.523; *CC*, xxix.49-50; Hume, *Exposé succinct*, p.17-19.

110. Draft, Rousseau to Henry Baldwin, editor of the *St James's chronicle*, *Collection complète*, xii.527; *CC*, xxix.96-97; *St James's chronicle* (8-10 April 1766), p.4. Draft, Rousseau to William Wentworth, Count Strafford, [7 April 1766], *Collection complète*, xii.526; *CC*, xxix.98-99.

111. Autograph copy, Rousseau to [William Wentworth, Count Strafford], 19 April 1766, *Collection complète*, xii.528-30; *CC*, xxix.123-25.

112. Du Peyrou forsook copying the original, which Hume already had printed in his self-justification of 1766, the *Exposé succinct*. Instead he used Rousseau's early draft which excluded the blanket accusation: 'Vous vous êtes mal caché, je vous connois' (*Collection complète*, xii.536; signed original, *CC*, xxix.274-76).

113. Draft, Rousseau to Hume, 10 July 1766, *Collection complète*, xii.537-67; Hume printed the received text in his *Exposé succinct*, p.46-110; signed original, *CC*, xxx.29-54.

Rousseau's editor next reproduced eighteen letters composed by the writer in England between 20 July 1766 and 13 May 1767. Several of them illustrated Rousseau's two major occupations during that time: his quest for psychological relief by collecting plants and herbs and his search for emotional release by composing his autobiography. In the first draft of a letter to Keith, where Du Peyrou took the liberty to edit out some phrases, Rousseau wrote that his botanising had become 'une passion d'enfant, ou plutôt [...] un radotage inutile & vain'. Yet how he enjoyed it! As for the *Confessions*, Rousseau already was convinced of the absolute uniqueness of his undertaking. He wrote to Keith the words which would find their echo in the opening sentence of the 'mémoires': 'Je ferai ce que nul homme n'a fait avant moi, & ce que vraisemblablement nul autre ne fera dans la suite. Je dirai tout, le bien, le mal, tout enfin; je me sens une ame qui se peut montrer.'[114]

In his last letters from England reproduced by Du Peyrou, Rousseau was clearly unravelling. He betrayed violent anger and lamentable self-pity. He informed the publisher Pierre Guy, one-time associate of the now dead Duchesne, that Hume simply was a pawn in the *encyclopédiste* plot hatched in Paris.[115] More poignant was Rousseau's reaction to Keith's weariness at having to respond to the author's paranoia. Above all Rousseau feared that 'milord maréchal' might take the side of his Scots compatriot Hume.[116] Fed up with Rousseau's complaints, Keith decided to break off the correspondence altogether. This shattered Rousseau, who responded: 'Serois-je dans votre disgrace? Ah! dans tous les malheurs qui m'accablent, voilà le seul que je ne saurois supporter.'[117] Pathetically Rousseau tried to change Keith's mind,[118] but to no avail.

With all the distress, Rousseau's last months in England nevertheless marked a period of new beginnings. Du Peyrou noted one of them. On 31 January 1767 the writer wrote to Mirabeau *père*, Victor Riquetti, welcoming the invitation of asylum offered by the *ami des hommes* but doubting whether the time was opportune to chance a return to French soil. Rousseau also confided

---

114. Draft (with suppressions), Rousseau to Keith, 20 July 1766, *Collection complète*, xii.568; same draft, *CC*, xxx.124-27. The three paragraphs suppressed by Du Peyrou concerned the request of the republican Rousseau that 'milord maréchal' use his influence with Frederick the Great to obtain titles of nobility for François-Louis d'Escherny and François-Henri d'Ivernois.

115. Incomplete copy prepared for Du Peyrou around 1780, Rousseau to Pierre Guy, 2 August 1766, *Collection complète*, xii.569-72. The *London chronicle* (4-6 September 1766), p.236, and *Lloyd's evening post* (5-8 September 1766), p.263, published an English translation of excerpts from this letter. In his *Œuvres complètes de J.-J. Rousseau* (Paris 1823-1826), i.220-22, V.-D. de Musset-Pathay published the remainder of the letter. Du Peyrou's incomplete draft and Musset-Pathay's concluding sections are published in *CC*, xxx.196-200.

116. Draft, Rousseau to Keith, 7 September 1766, *Collection complète*, xii.574-75. For example: 'Seroit-il possible que les terribles clameurs de M. Hume eussent fait impression sur vous, & m'eussent, au milieu de tant de malheurs, ôté la seule consolation qui me restoit sur la terre?' (*CC*, xxx.332-33).

117. Draft, Rousseau to Keith, 11 December 1766, *Collection complète*, xii.583; *CC*, xxxi.254-55.

118. Drafts, Rousseau to Keith, 8 February 1767, [19 March 1767], *Collection complète*, xii.592, 595-96; *CC*, xxxii.119-20, 224-25.

to Mirabeau the pleasure he had found wandering through the English countryside in purposeless fashion. Rousseau regretfully rejected Mirabeau's generous offer to rescue him from his so-called useless existence, concluding rather disingenuously: 'Puisse le public m'oublier comme je l'oublie! S'il ne veut pas m'oublier, peu m'importe: qu'il m'admire ou qu'il me déchire, tout cela m'est indifférent [...]. Je suis tout entier où je suis, & point où sont ceux qui me persécutent.'[119] Another letter to Guy, however, betrayed Rousseau's loneliness and melancholia: 'O mon cher Monsieur Guy, faut-il donc mourir dans ces contrées éloignées, sans revoir jamais la face d'un ami sûr, dans le sein duquel je puisse épancher mon cœur?'[120]

During his stay in England Rousseau found solace by responding to requests for personal advice. A precious minority still considered him a sage. On the one hand, he might brush off a pretentious critique of his work (in Latin) by a middle-aged English surgeon, Edmund Jessop;[121] on the other, when his correspondent was a young, titled noblewoman who addressed him as 'l'Oracle de la vertu sur Terre', he still could be seduced. Carolina-Frederica von Salm-Grumbach, countess von Wartensleben, informed him of an acquaintance, like herself a German disciple, who was abandoning wife and child to pursue a goal of overturning the hidebound government of his minuscule principality. The author of *Du contrat social* responded by stating his general opposition to politically inspired violence: 'Pour moi je vous déclare que je ne voudrois pour rien au monde avoir trempé dans la conspiration la plus légitime [...] le sang d'un seul homme est d'un plus grand prix que la liberté de tout le genre-humain.' Concluding that in pursuit of their sacred causes the great revolutionaries of history saw no need to abandon their families, Rousseau informed the countess that perhaps her compatriot simply was unbalanced. More likely, the writer concluded cynically, he was seeking an excuse to be rid of his wife.[122]

The remaining two dozen letters in Du Peyrou's edition covered Rousseau's return to France, beginning with his arrival at Calais on 22 May 1767 and concluding five years later. For Du Peyrou this clearly was a period of dénouement, Rousseau's correspondence yielding up moods of melancholic resignation punctuated by hopes that the virtuous minority would eventually justify his life and work.[123] When it looked as though the Genevan bourgeois revolu-

119. Possibly the signed original, now disappeared, Rousseau to Victor Riquetti, marquis de Mirabeau, 31 January 1767, *Collection complète*, xii.588; signed corrected draft, *CC*, xxxii.81-86.

120. Copy prepared for Du Peyrou by Henri Laliaud (contains additions and suppressions), Rousseau to Pierre Guy, 7 February 1767, *Collection complète*, xii.592; signed original, *CC*, xxxii.113-16.

121. Copy prepared for Du Peyrou, Rousseau to [Dr Edmund Jessop], 13 May 1767, *Collection complète*, xii.600-601; signed original, *CC*, xxxiii.55-57.

122. Autograph copy, Rousseau to [Caroline von Salm-Grumbach, countess von Wartensleben], 27 September 1766, *Collection complète*, xii.578-82; *CC*, xxx.384-88. Leigh wonders whether Rousseau actually sent his letter to the countess (see *note explicative*, *CC*, xxx.388).

123. Autograph copy, Rousseau to [Marie-Madeleine de Brémond d'Ars, marquise de Verdelin], 11 September 1767, *Collection complète*, xii.602-604; *CC*, xxxiv.92-95.

tion of 1768 against the canton's patriciate might turn violent, Rousseau coun-selled passivity and even exile to the rebels.[124] In quest of redemption follow-ing the revolution's success, Rousseau informed François-Henri d'Ivernois that if the reformed Small Council lifted its ban against him, he would welcome the decision; however, no one should harbour hopes that he ever would reside in his birthplace again.[125] Botanising still brought him pleasure, yet self-pity often was in command. In February 1770 Rousseau angrily repri-manded the playwright-actor Buirette de Dormont de Belloy for suggesting that Belloy's fate paralleled his own: 'Vous m'avez ressemblé, dites-vous, par le malheur [...]. Etes-vous seul en terre étrangere, isolé, séquestré, trompé, trahi, diffamé par tout ce qui vous environne, enlacé de trames horribles dont vous sentiez l'effet, sans pouvoir parvenir à les connoître, à les démêler?'[126]

True, Rousseau still possessed sufficient detachment to offer sardonic literary advice to the likes of Belloy, moral counsel on rearing an aristocratic brat to the tutor, abbé Jean Maydieu,[127] and platitudinous 'nourriture à votre âme' for the nubile young comtesse Louise-Rose de Berthier, whose palpitat-ing anxiety attacks over what she perceived to be her inner emptiness inspired seven separate responses from the ageing visionary.[128] The fire still was there, the paranoia as well. The last of the letters reproduced by Du Peyrou was addressed to the marquise de Mesmes, a one-time privileged witness to Rous-seau's salon readings from the *Confessions* before they were stopped by the French police.[129] On 14 August 1772 the writer regretfully turned down a social invitation from the marquise, stating his intention to withdraw from such occasions. He pleaded serenity: 'La conduite de mes contemporains à mon égard ne permet à ma raison de leur accorder aucune estime. La haine n'entra jamais dans mon cœur. Le mépris est encore un sentiment trop tour-mentant. Je ne les estime donc, ni ne les hais, ni ne les méprise. Ils sont nuls à mes yeux, ce sont pour moi des habitans de la lune.'[130]

---

124. Signed original, Rousseau to François-Henri d'Ivernois, 29 January 1768, *Collection complète*, xii.606-607 (omitting the third paragraph); *CC*, xxxv.62-65.

125. Signed original, Rousseau to François-Henri d'Ivernois, 24 March 1768, *Collection complète*, xii.609-12 (omitting a paragraph referring to the alleged conspiracies directed at him); *CC*, xxxv.220-22.

126. Rousseau to Buirette de Dormont de Belloy, 19 February 1770, *Collection complète*, xii.626; *CC*, xxxvii.241-45. P.-L. Buirette de Dormont de Belloy, *Œuvres complètes* (1778), iii.407-11.

127. Copies prepared for Du Peyrou, Rousseau to [abbé Jean Maydieu], 9 February 1770, [28 February 1770], 14 March 1770, *Collection complète*, xii.635-48; signed originals, *CC*, xxxvii.231-36, 308-11, 331-36.

128. Copies prepared for Du Peyrou, Rousseau to [Louise-Rose Rabaud de La Chaussade, comtesse de Berthier], 28 October 1769, 7 December 1769, 17 January 1770, 2 February 1770, 16 March 1770, 7 July 1770, 13 July 1770, *Collection complète*, xii.649-63; signed originals, *CC*, xxxvii.163-65, 205-209, 220-21, 341-43, xxxviii.56-58, 61-62; Du Peyrou's copy, *CC*, xxxvii.182-84.

129. *OC*, i.656, 1611-12.

130. Corrected draft, Rousseau to Anne-Marie Feydeau de Brou, marquise de Mesmes, 14 August 1772, *Collection complète*, xii.673-74; copy from signed original, *CC*, xxxix.96-100.

The first *Supplément à la Collection des œuvres de J.-J. Rousseau*

Du Peyrou's choice of Rousseau's last letters tried to make a case for the author's alleged serenity while facing the prospect of martyrdom. But the assertions of inner peace were not particularly convincing. More credible was Rousseau's self-promotion as an eighteenth-century Diogenes, vainly seeking out unbiased interlocutors who might debate with him without rancour: 'J'ai porté par-tout ma lanterne inutilement, je n'ai point trouvé d'homme ni d'ame humaine. J'ai vu avec dédain la grossiere fausseté de ceux qui vouloient m'abuser par des caresses si mal-adroites & si peu dictées par la bienveillance & l'estime, qu'elles cachoient même & assez mal une secrete animosité.'[131] Aware that thus far the *Collection complète* lacked interlocutors, Du Peyrou added three supplementary volumes in-quarto (six in-octavo) to supply a voice to Rousseau's antagonists.

Published collectively for the first time were the responses to the *Discours* on the arts and sciences by Joseph Gautier, abbé Le Roi, Claude-Nicolas Le Cat, Stanislas Leszczynski/Father Joseph Menoux, Charles Borde and the anonymous critic falsely identified as the Dijon essay contest judge who had denied Rousseau his vote. (Du Peyrou also published the Academy's disavowal of this latter piece.)[132] The reader was invited to return to volume vii of the edition in-quarto (volumes xiii and xiv of the in-octavo) in order to follow Rousseau's reaction to his critics. Du Peyrou next turned to the debate surrounding *Emile*. Since the treatise still was technically prohibited in Geneva, Holland, France and elsewhere, to draw too much attention to it even two decades after the scandal of 1762 bore some risk. The *Supplément*, therefore, limited its excerpts to the condemnations by the Parlement and archbishop of Paris. Readers could draw their own conclusions.[133]

Reversing his chronological order, Du Peyrou next published what he considered the fundamental documents in the debate surrounding the *Lettre à d'Alembert*. He included the original *Encyclopédie* article 'Genève', the protest against the piece by the city's aggrieved pastors and the rebuttal by d'Alembert of Rousseau's essay.[134] Next, by publishing the short verse plays, *La Découverte du nouveau monde* (1740-1741?) and the incomplete *Iphis* (1737-1740?), scattered poetry and sixteen letters from the author to Mme de Warens (1732-1753), Du Peyrou moved yet further backwards in time. These early

---

131. Rousseau to Anne-Marie Feydeau de Brou, marquise de Mesmes, 14 August 1772, *Collection complète*, xii.672.

132. *Supplément à la Collection des œuvres de J.-J. Rousseau*, hereafter referred to as *Collection complète*, vol. xiii-xv, here at xiii.1-241. Gautier's rebuttal first was published in the *Mercure* (October 1751), p.9-41; Claude-Nicolas Le Cat's first appeared as a pamphlet of 132 pages in-8°: *Réfutation du discours du citoyen de Genève* (1751); King Stanislas/Father Menoux's *Réponse au discours qui a remporté le prix de l'académie de Dijon* initially appeared as a pamphlet of 34 pages in-8° (1751); and Borde's was first published in the *Mercure* (December 1751).

133. *Collection complète*, xiii.248-73.

134. *Collection complète*, xiii.274-343. The original edition of d'Alembert's *Lettre de M. d'Alembert à M. J.-J. Rousseau* [...] was published in a volume of 156 pages in-8° (1759).

writings already had been collected and printed. Boubers published them in volume viii of his edition (1776), and they were pirated shortly thereafter by François Grasset and veuve Duchesne.[135] Du Peyrou gave full credit to Boubers for having first acquired the pieces, a far more gracious gesture than the Brussels publisher's announcement that his impending piracy of *Rousseau juge de Jean-Jacques* was nothing less than the *Confessions*.[136]

Du Peyrou considered Rousseau's letters to Mme de Warens as documentation for Part I of the *Confessions* and *Rêveries*. Yet more important, they related a persistent theme in Rousseau's life, the writer's evolution from dependence to autonomy. The first letter (misdated as 29 June 1732 by Boubers) reveals Rousseau's youthful desire to spend several years in Chambéry at the feet of 'maman', relishing her company while teaching music on the side.[137] Two years later, writing from Grenoble and just a few days prior to his sexual adventure with Mme de Larnage, Rousseau argues for unrestrained expression of noble emotions, while suspecting unfaithfulness on the part of his mistress. Above all he worries about Mme de Warens's poor correspondence habits.[138]

Following his own dalliance with Mme de Larnage on the road to Montpellier, another letter to Mme de Warens (23 October 1737) betrays Rousseau's feelings of guilt over his recent amatory escapade: 'Que voulez-vous, Mme, que je vous dise; quand j'agis, je crois faire les plus belles choses du monde, & puis il se trouve au bout que ce ne sont que sottises; je les reconnois parfaitement bien moi-même. Il faudra tâcher de se roidir contre sa bêtise à l'avenir, et faire plus d'attention sur sa conduite.'[139] Suspecting that Mme de Warens herself has won the attention of a rival, Rousseau tries to ignite her jealousy, crudely suggesting that he will be seeing Mme de Larnage again. Of course 'maman' would have the final say and Rousseau already assumes what it is. On 14 December he reiterates his anxiety: 'Ah! ma chere maman, n'êtes vous donc plus ma chere maman? Ai-je vécu quelques mois de trop?'[140] Once he returns to Chambéry the following February, Rousseau will find Wintzenried in his place.

Nevertheless, Rousseau's letters to Mme de Warens describe an emergence to selfhood. In 1739 he was a pitiful weak link in his mistress's various *ménages à*

135. Grasset's edition read: *Supplément aux œuvres de J.-J. Rousseau, citoyen de Genève, pour servir de suite de toutes les éditions*, in-8° (Amsterdam and Lausanne 1779). Veuve Duchesne's was added as volume x (Neuchâtel [Paris] 1779) of the *Œuvres de M. Rousseau* originally undertaken by her husband back in 1764.

136. *Collection complète*, xiii.347.

137. Rousseau to Françoise-Louise-Eléonore de La Tour, baronne de Warens, [29 June 1732?], *Collection complète*, xiii.441-43; *Collection complète des œuvres de J.-J. Rousseau* [Brussels, Boubers], hereafter *Œuvres* (Boubers), viii.357-58; *CC*, i.16-19. See *OC*, i.208-209, 1329-30.

138. Rousseau to Mme de Warens, 13 September 1737, *Collection complète*, xiii.445; *Œuvres* (Boubers), viii.359-61; *CC*, i.48-51. Rousseau, *Confessions*, in *OC*, i.249-52.

139. Rousseau to Mme de Warens, 23 October 1737, *Collection complète*, xiii.448; *Œuvres* (Boubers), viii.362-67; *CC*, i.53-58.

140. Signed original, Rousseau to Mme de Warens, 4 December 1737, *Collection complète*, xiii.456; *Œuvres* (Boubers), viii. 368-69; *CC*, i.63-65.

trois, lastly sharing the household with Wintzenried and driven to distraction by jealousy.[141] Four years later, however, he is on his own. Freed from Mme de Warens, he proudly relays to her the progress of his several careers. October 1743 finds him a man-about-town in Venice, loosely assuming the title of secretary to the French ambassador Montaigu.[142] Sixteen months later, his diplomatic career over, he is in Paris taking up with Thérèse and entering the musical wars of the French capital. Distanced physically and emotionally from Chambéry, he dispassionately describes to his ex-mistress the public festivities surrounding the marriage of the French dauphin to Princess María Teresa of Spain.[143]

In January 1749 Rousseau announces another career breakthrough to 'maman'. He has been invited to contribute articles on music to the *Encyclopédie*.[144] Finally, in 1753, the celebrity of the first *Discours* behind him, Rousseau reveals how adept he has become at manipulating his public image. Concerning Mme de Warens the tables have turned. She now is the dependent one, and the up-and-coming moralist-composer sends her a bank draft for 240 *livres*. Rousseau then adds nonchalantly that he will snub the royal performance of *Le Devin du village* at the château of Bellevue, though Mme de Pompadour herself will be playing Colin: 'Comme tout cela sera exécuté par des seigneurs et dames de la cour, je m'attends à être chanté faux et estropié; ainsi je n'irai point [...]. Avec toute cette gloire, je continue à vivre de mon métier de copiste qui me rend independant, & qui me rend heureux si mon bonheur pouvoit se faire sans le vôtre & sans la santé.'[145]

Du Peyrou next published a set of letters dated a generation later. The object of Rousseau's correspondence again was an aristocratic woman, though one far more highly placed than Mme de Warens. The underlying theme remained the writer's emergence from submission to dominion. In Rousseau's letters to Margaret Cavendish Bentinck, duchess of Portland, the central passion was scientific, not erotic. Nevertheless, the language of the letters betrayed Rousseau's supplication, apprehensiveness and, eventually, the need to wrest himself free from a perceived female grasp.

141. Rousseau to Mme de Warens, 18 March 1739, *Collection complète*, xiii.456-57; *Œuvres* (Boubers), viii.370-71; *CC*, i.98-99.

142. Signed original, Rousseau to Mme de Warens, 5 October 1743, *Collection complète*, xiii.461-62; *Œuvres* (Boubers), viii.368-69; *CC*, i.198-200. The question of Rousseau's correct title while working for Montaigu would stir up a new controversy with Voltaire in 1766. For Rousseau's explanation in the *Confessions* see *OC*, i.298.

143. Signed original, Rousseau to Mme de Warens, 25-29 February 1745, *Collection complète*, xiii.462-65; *Œuvres* (Boubers), viii.377-79, 389-90; *CC*, ii.73-79.

144. Rousseau to Mme de Warens, 27 January 1749, *Collection complète*, xiii.470-75; *Œuvres* (Boubers), viii.382-83; *CC*, ii.112-15. Concerning Rousseau's references to his contributions to the *Encyclopédie* in the *Confessions* see *OC*, i.347-48.

145. Rousseau to Mme de Warens, 13 February 1753, *Collection complète*, xiii.472-73; *Œuvres* (Boubers), viii.384-85; *CC*, ii.212-13. For the reference in the *Confessions* see *OC*, i.386-87. Finally, supplementing his *Supplément*, Du Peyrou reprinted three additional undated letters from Rousseau to Mme de Warens, *Collection complète*, xiii.473-79. Leigh has dated them as 5 March 1739 (*CC*, i.90-93), *c*. 15 November 1745 (*CC*, ii.90-92) and 24-26 July 1737 (*CC*, i.44-48).

During his time with Mme de Warens Rousseau had shown interest in botany.[146] At Môtiers he envisioned random plant collecting as psychological therapy.[147] Later, while in England, Rousseau began communicating with the duchess of Portland, another amateur who shared his botanical enthusiasm. Du Peyrou acquired transcripts of fifteen letters written by Rousseau to the duchess, and the faithful disciple published them in the *Supplément*. The first letter is dated October 1766. Rousseau plays the role of apprentice receiving lessons from a great lady, and he strikes a subservient pose. Well entrenched as a composer and musical theorist and Europe's most controversial author, he flirts with the duchess, expressing a need to 'belong' to her. He writes: 'vous savez assortir les fossiles, les minéraux, les coquillages, cultiver les plantes, apprivoiser les oiseaux: et que n'apprivoiseriez-vous pas? Je connois un animal un peu sauvage qui vivroit avec grand plaisir dans votre ménagerie, en attendant l'honneur d'être admis un jour en momie dans vôtre cabinet.'[148]

Rousseau played novice to the duchess's alleged expertise, lamenting his deficiencies in botanical nomenclature and his lack of an elementary textbook from which he could learn about the plants of England. As patroness, the duchess then provided him with a copy of John Ray's *Synopsis methodica stirpium britannicarum* (1690), which he found useful. He could not resist informing her of a moral purpose lurking behind his observations of nature: 'Je veux oublier les hommes & leurs injustices. Je veux m'attendrir chaque jour sur les merveilles de celui qui les fit pour être bons, et dont ils ont si indignement dégradé l'ouvrage. Les végétaux dans nos bois et dans nos montagnes sont encore tels qu'ils sortirent originairement de ses mains, & c'est-là que j'aime à étudier la nature.'[149] From Staffordshire Rousseau sent the duchess specimens for identification, all the while apologising for his ignorance and lack of scientific instrumentation.[150]

Once he returned to France and assumed the pseudonym 'Renou', Rousseau again took up his correspondence with the duchess. His self-perception of apprentice was now transformed into that of attendant. Such deference emanating from the self-styled paragon of autonomy flattered the duchess. Rousseau supplied her with continental specimens, identifying them as best he could. Since the duchess had assumed the responsibility of informing Rousseau about Marshal Keith, the 'father' who had abandoned him, the writer could not resist inserting dollops of self-pity into his letters: 'Mais je le suis [plus encore] de Mylord Mareschal, mon ami, mon protecteur, mon pére qui m'a totalement oublié.' He signed off: 'Votre très humble et très obéissant

146. *Confessions*, in *OC*, i.180.
147. *Rêveries*, in *OC*, i.1060-73.
148. Copy prepared for Du Peyrou, Rousseau to Margaret Cavendish Harley Bentinck, duchess of Portland, 20 October 1766, *Collection complète*, xiii.506; signed original, *CC*, xxxi.40-42.
149. Copy prepared for Du Peyrou, Rousseau to the duchess of Portland, 12 February 1767, *Collection complète*, xiii.512-13; signed original, *CC*, xxxii.133-37.
150. Copy prepared for Du Peyrou, Rousseau to the duchess of Portland, 28 February 1767, *Collection complète*, xiii.516; signed original, *CC*, xxxii.187.

serviteur et Herboriste'.[151] Once permanently distanced from the duchess, however, Rousseau again changed the rules of the game. Subsequently he would assume the role of equal, good-naturedly debating with her over the identities of plants about whose nomenclature they disagreed. This represented the third stage in his evolution.[152]

By 1768 the liaison between Rousseau and the duchess of Portland would enter a fourth stage: dénouement. A letter which Rousseau sent her from Lyon lacked the playful tone of previous correspondence, and he regretted that his darkening moods prevented him from satisfying her commissions: 'J'espére être à l'avenir moins malheureux, et pouvoir porter avec plus de succès un titre dont je me glorifie.'[153] The following year, writing from Bourgoin, Rousseau apologised for his meagre harvest and bitterly blamed it upon 'les honnêtes gens [...] en y versant le poison de leurs viles ames'.[154] What followed now was a period of silence lasting more than two years. It was broken in April 1772 with Rousseau's acknowledgment of a gift that the duchess had sent him, a copy of William Mason's poem, *The English garden*.[155] That summer, however, Rousseau again regretted his inability to locate plants which the duchess requested.[156] Following a letter of 11 July 1776 the exchange abruptly ended. The duchess apparently had sent Rousseau some exotic specimens, which he would not accept. He responded curtly, formally addressing the duchess in the third person and bearing her some sarcasm: 'Si la magnificence en est digne d'elle, elle n'est proportionnée ni à ma situation ni à mes besoins.' Rousseau added that he had ceased herborising and had gotten rid of all of his botany books. He wished to return to the duchess another gift of hers, Rumphius's *Herbarium amboinense*; however, he would consider keeping the book simply as a souvenir of their previous exchanges. Clearly Rousseau wished to break off. No 'très obéissant serviteur et Herboriste' terminated his final letter. He asked 'madame la Duchesse' to accept his profound respect and signed off: 'JJRousseau'.[157]

In its evolution from supplicant to attendant to expert, culminating with a break based largely upon fears of dependence, Rousseau's correspondence with the duchess of Portland paralleled his letters to Mme de Warens a generation earlier. In each instance Rousseau initially flattered his correspondent

151. Copy prepared for Du Peyrou, Rousseau to the duchess of Portland, 12 September 1767, *Collection complète*, xiii.519; signed original, *CC*, xxxiv.96.

152. Copy prepared for Du Peyrou, Rousseau to the duchess of Portland, January 1768, *Collection complète*, xiii.522-23; signed original, *CC*, xxxv.9-10.

153. Copy prepared for Du Peyrou, Rousseau to the duchess of Portland, 2 July 1768, *Collection complète*, xiii.524; signed original, *CC*, xxxvi.3-5.

154. Copy prepared for Du Peyrou, Rousseau to the duchess of Portland, 21 December 1769, *Collection complète*, xiii.528; signed original, *CC*, xxxvii.189-93.

155. Copy prepared for Du Peyrou, Rousseau to the duchess of Portland, 17 April 1772, *Collection complète*, xiii.530-31; signed original, *CC*, xxxix.41-43.

156. Copy prepared for Du Peyrou, Rousseau to the duchess of Portland, 19 July 1772, *Collection complète*, xiii.533-35; signed original, *CC*, xxxix.92-93.

157. Copy prepared for Du Peyrou, Rousseau to the duchess of Portland, 11 July 1776, *Collection complète*, xiii.536-37; signed original, *CC*, xl.77-78.

into believing that intimacy defined their relationship. He 'belonged' to one and the other. Of course too much intimacy also might have disastrous consequences, as his relationships with Keith and Hume proved. Nevertheless, all his life Rousseau craved close companionship with intelligent aristocratic women, and the duchess of Portland simply was last in a line beginning with 'maman' and including, most notably, Sophie d'Houdetot. Rousseau rejoiced in controlling the content and pace of the relationship. Should he tire of it, it was finished. Subsequently Du Peyrou invited readers to decode Rousseau's strategies, the affairs becoming part of the public record.

Du Peyrou next published eight letters (17 December 1769 to 7 January 1773) from Rousseau to another devoted amateur botanist, the Lyonnais jurist Marc-Antoine Claret de La Tourette. These letters rarely parted from the business of plant collecting. Though Rousseau initially referred to himself as 'un ecolier radoteur', tracking down plants for distraction and amusement, he informed Claret de La Tourette that he also was projecting a classification scheme which would improve upon those of Tournefort and Linnaeus.[158] Rousseau confided to his correspondent that simple curiosity for botany was the purest and most innocent of pleasures. Yet even with Claret de La Tourette, Rousseau's obsession with the 'conspiracy' never lay far from the surface. He affected lack of interest in 'ce que disent, publient, impriment, inventent, assurent, & prouvent à ce qu'ils prétendent, mes contemporains, de l'être imaginaire et fantastique auquel il leur a plû de donner mon nom'.[159] Alas by this time, January 1772, the devils within were seizing control and Rousseau's therapeutic botanising was about to end. A year later he informed Claret de La Tourette that, except for 'des petits herbiers en miniature' which he was compiling for a few acquaintances, he had lost taste for his excursions. He wrote that he also was about to renounce virtually all correspondence.[160]

Du Peyrou did not wish to terminate the first volume of the *Supplément* on such a negative note. He therefore went back again in time, adding 'Fragmens de divers Ouvrages & Lettres de J. J. Rousseau, écrits pendant son Séjour en Savoie'. These were the so-called de Saussure manuscripts, largely drafts of letters left by Rousseau with Mme de Warens when he had gone to Paris in 1742. When he purchased the de Warens collection for his edition of Rousseau's works, Boubers failed to acquire these papers. Instead the Geneva

158. Signed original, Rousseau to Marc-Antoine-Louis Claret de La Tourette, 27 January 1770, *Collection complète*, xiii.542-45; *CC*, xxxvii.211-14. The germ of Rousseau's scheme was set forth in the letters he addressed to Mme Delessert.

159. Signed original, Rousseau to Claret de La Tourette, 25 January 1772, *Collection complète*, xiii.562; *CC*, xxxix.20-24. Interestingly enough, Claret de La Tourette asked Rousseau whether the latter had been reading from his 'mémoires' to selected groups and whether indeed the autobiography was finished. In his response Rousseau ignored these questions, and Du Peyrou refrained from publishing Claret's side of the correspondence. See Claret de La Tourette to Rousseau, 14 January 1772, *CC*, xxxix.8-10.

160. Signed original, Rousseau to Claret de La Tourette, 7 January 1773, *Collection complète*, xiii.562-64; *CC*, xxxix.128-30.

professor, Horace-Bénédict de Saussure, obtained and subsequently loaned them to Du Peyrou for the *Supplément*.

The collection included letters Rousseau had written to his father between 1731 and 1735 which were illuminating when set beside the self-fashioning of the *Confessions*. One letter, for example, was a desperate plea for reconciliation, very likely the consequence of Isaac Rousseau's negative response to his son's conversion to catholicism.[161] The tone contrasts with Rousseau's suggestion in the *Confessions* that Isaac had tolerated his conversion.[162] In a second letter Rousseau pleads with his father to recognise Mme de Warens.[163] And a third letter pours out the story of Rousseau's infatuation for his mistress. He wishes to study at her side for the remainder of his life, providing her with 'tous les Services qui seront en mon pouvoir'.[164]

Among the remaining letters, one offered insight into yet another infatuation and contrasted with a description of it in the *Confessions*. The letter was written to an unnamed young woman and revealed Rousseau's passionate and unrequited love for her.[165] Was the addressee Suzanne Serre of Lyon, later described in the *Confessions* as chaste, naive and sharing Rousseau's ardour? In the *Confessions* Rousseau claims to have broken off a relationship with the honest Suzanne, owing to their mutual poverty, and insists that he persuaded her to marry a well-to-do young merchant from her home town.[166] Yet the 'Suzanne' of Rousseau's letter comes across as wilful, sexually experienced and apparently not much interested in Jean-Jacques. From what we know of her, the genuine Suzanne better fit the description in Rousseau's letter. She eventually married her merchant, but only after he had become the father of her child.[167] Du Peyrou concluded the first volume (in-quarto) of his *Supplément* with Charles Bonnet's 'Lettre de Philopolis'. This hostile response to the *Discours sur l'inégalité* originally had appeared in the *Mercure* for October 1755. Once more the reader was asked to thumb backwards in the *Collection*, this time to volume i, to locate Rousseau's reaction to his critic.[168]

In contrast to the complicated structure of the *Supplément*'s first volume, the second was a model of unity. One-fifth of it contained texts by Rousseau published for the first time: the *Projet pour l'éducation de M. de Sainte-Marie* (1740), written during the year he served as tutor for the Mably boys; the

---

161. Autograph copy, Rousseau to Isaac Rousseau, [May-June 1731], *Collection complète*, xiii.576-79; *CC*, i.12-15.

162. *OC*, i.144-45.

163. Draft, Rousseau to Isaac Rousseau, [spring 1735], *Collection complète*, xiii.565-67; *CC*, i.24-26.

164. Draft, Rousseau to Isaac Rousseau, [late autumn 1735], *Collection complète*, xiii.569-75; *CC*, i.29-34.

165. Corrected draft, Rousseau to [Suzanne Serre?], [1739], *Collection complète*, xiii.592-95; *CC*, i.103-106; *OC*, i.281-82, 1375-76.

166. *OC*, i.281-82, 1375. Note that in 1782, when the *Supplément* appeared, Book VII of the *Confessions* had not yet been published.

167. Maurice Cranston, *Jean-Jacques: the early life and work of Jean-Jacques Rousseau 1712-1754* (Chicago 1982), p.151-52.

168. *Collection complète*, xiii.607-11; *CC*, iii.151-56.

Oraison funèbre for the duc d'Orléans, which had been commissioned by abbé d'Arty in 1752 but never used; the prose play *Les Prisonniers de guerre* (1743?); and letters to Vincent-Louis Dutens (1767). Du Peyrou also published Rousseau's marginal notes to Helvétius's *De l'esprit* and two letters by Helvétius commenting upon Rousseau's critical reaction, all of which Dutens had recently printed.[169] The remaining four-fifths of the volume contained previously published texts. These were broadsides written both by Rousseau and his enemies and supporters, dealing with the persecution at Môtiers and the controversy with Hume.[170] Once more the reader was reminded that the *complots* of the venerable class of pastors in Neuchâtel and of the encyclopedists of Paris were genuine, not figments of a disturbed imagination.

Except for reprinting in full Charles Borde's second *Discours sur les avantages des sciences et des arts* (1752) and Father Castel's *L'Homme moral opposé à l'homme physique, ou Réfutation du Discours sur l'origine de l'inégalité* (1756), Du Peyrou devoted volume iii of the *Supplément* largely to posthumous assessments of Rousseau. They ranged from purely anecdotal reports to strident defences of the corpus and the life. A flattering *Lettre sur J.-J. Rousseau*, par M. ***, originally published late in 1779 and addressed to 'M. d'Es[cherny]', opened the series.[171] Ultimately attributed to the chevalier de Bruny, the *Lettre* explained away the paradoxes of Rousseau's life and writings and insisted upon the author's uncompromising candour. According to the *Lettre*, *Emile* was Rousseau's masterpiece and also his most dangerous work. Because its intent was to mould a new generation, the treatise gave rise to uncompromising enemies who saw it threatening the very foundations of civilisation. The *Lettre* could not resist contrasting Rousseau's fate with Voltaire's. While the one was universally condemned during his lifetime, the other enjoyed adulation from all sides. Nevertheless, according to the *Lettre*, posterity would recognise Rousseau as the superior moralist whose signature was the recognition and expression of universal duties.

The *Lettre sur J.-J. Rousseau* noted how accusations of insincerity, paradox and false pride had dogged Rousseau all his life. The most incriminating of all, according to Du Peyrou, was the *Journal encyclopédique*'s suggestion that

169. *Lettres à M. D[e] B[ure] sur la réfutation du livre De l'esprit d'Helvétius, par J.-J. Rousseau* (1779). Rousseau had intended to publish a refutation of *De l'esprit*, but the persecution endured by Helvétius over his book caused him to change his mind.

170. The most important texts were: [Voltaire], *Sentiment des citoyens*; [Du Peyrou], *Recueil des pièces relatives à la persécution suscitée à Motiers-Travers contre M. J.-J. Rousseau*, containing the so-called 'Lettre de Goa'; *Réfutation du libelle précédent par m. le professeur de Montmollin, pasteur des eglises de Motiers-Travers & Boveresse*; [Du Peyrou], *Lettre à M. *** relative à J.-J. Rousseau, Seconde lettre relative à M. J.-J. Rousseau, adressée à milord comte de Wemyss*; [Du Peyrou], *Troisième lettre relative à M. J.-J. Rousseau*; [Hume], *Exposé succinct de la contestation qui s'est élevée entre M. Hume et M. Rousseau, avec les pièces justificatives*; *Déclaration adressée par M. d'Alembert aux éditeurs*; *Justification de J.-J. Rousseau dans la contestation qui lui est survenue avec M. Hume*; *Observations sur l'Exposé succinct*; [Bergerat], *Plaidoyer pour et contre J.-J. Rousseau et le docteur David Hume*; [Voltaire], *Le Docteur Pansophe, ou Lettres de monsieur de Voltaire*.

171. *Collection complète*, xv.253-302.

Rousseau had stolen the music for *Le Devin du village*.[172] Pierre Rousseau, editor of the *Journal encyclopédique*, had been unable to produce incontrovertible evidence of his namesake's alleged thievery. Nevertheless, in response to the suspicions raised, Du Peyrou felt obliged to clear Jean-Jacques's name.[173] Therefore he reprinted the *Journal encyclopédique*'s incriminating article,[174] as well as L.-F. Lefébure's letter to the *Journal de Paris* repudiating the allegations.[175] Lefébure made the point of challenging Pierre Rousseau's contrast between earlier (1750) and revised (1775) versions of *Le Devin*. The first version, wrote Lefébure, had been composed 'dans une obscurité paisible', the second 'dans les chagrins d'une gloire persécutée'. By no means was the more recent version of the opera inferior to the earlier one. Each was the product of Rousseau's self-conscious state of mind. Indulging his creative powers in 1750, Rousseau was out to charm listeners with a new art form in a new genre. Twenty-five years later he was celebrated. But according to Lefébure, persecution was the price of fame. The dolorous transformation of the revised *Devin* simply was an object lesson in maturation. Like so many others, the editor of the *Journal encyclopédique* failed to comprehend this.

Du Peyrou next reprinted pieces by Rousseau's most indefatigable correspondent and defender, Marie-Anne Alissan de La Tour de Franqueville (1730-1789). In the *Correspondance complète* Leigh has located 103 letters written by her to Rousseau between October 1761 and November 1776. Nearly three-quarters of them were composed during the first four years of the pair's epistolary acquaintance. Rousseau often found Mme de La Tour de Franqueville exasperating, but until 1772 he kept answering. Leigh's edition records fifty-six of his responses. There is little doubt that the lady was thoroughly infatuated with Rousseau. From the Hume affair on, she published defence after defence of the writer and his cause. Walpole, Voltaire, Diderot, d'Alembert, Naigeon and others were subjected to her wrath. With her co-operation Du Peyrou reprinted her essays and letters to journal editors, many composed under various pseudonyms. If the *Collection complète*, most especially its *Supplément*, harboured the sources of *rousseauisme*, it was Mme de La Tour de Franqueville who reminded readers of the cult's essential element: emphasis upon the prophet's ability to overcome his own passivity

172. See above, chapter 7, p.147. *Journal encyclopédique* 8, part 3 (1765), p.39-40; 7, part 2 (1780), p.284-301.
173. Leigh suggests that Pierre Rousseau's memory might have misled him. In 1750 Rousseau had sketched out in Lyon his verse play *La Découverte du nouveau monde*, and he had shown the text to the Lyonnais musician François David. Did David possibly turn out a musical score which he sent to Jean-Jacques but which mistakenly arrived at Pierre's? What is certain, the *Journal encyclopédique* after 1763 was hostile to Rousseau. The remarks in 1780 were incorporated in a very negative review of Boothby's edition of the first dialogue of *Rousseau juge de Jean-Jacques*, and Pierre Rousseau seized the moment to launch a complete fusillade (see *note explicative* a, *CC*, ii.340-42). In *remarques*, *CC*, xliv.361, Leigh reviews an accusation of plagiarism on Rousseau's part in the *Revue musicale suisse* 4 (July-August 1972), p.210-11: W. Eisenmann, 'Wer komponierte den *Devin du village*?'
174. *Collection complète*, xv.302-306.
175. *Journal de Paris* 342 (7 December 1780), p.1394-95; *Collection complète*, xv.306-309.

and society's persecution, with the resultant reconstitution of both his life and message as an ongoing moral process. Certainly enemies would try to subvert it. But with religious passion the uncompromising and dedicated would battle to maintain its integrity. As Mme de La Tour de Franqueville fervently wrote, responding to Diderot's and Naigeon's strike at the anticipated *Confessions*: 'je n'ai rien à leur abandonner; & je dois défendre tout ce qu'ils attaquent, la beauté de son ame, la pureté de ses intentions, & l'intégrité de sa vie [...] puisque mon coupable silence me rendroit complice de la plus exécrable noirceur que la méchanceté philosophique se soit jamais permise.'[176]

For more than three years Du Peyrou was responsible for reclaiming Rousseau for the *Collection complète*. His content included nearly the author's entire corpus, a significant selection of largely unpublished correspondence and the judgements of Rousseau's critics. Such a wealth of material caused the editor's argumentative thread to become, at times, both knotted and ragged; for the most benevolently inclined reader might detect self-pity, vindictiveness and paranoia lurking behind the great moralist's noblest passages. There were plenty of other hidden ironies as well.[177] When all was said and done, Du Peyrou probably failed to produce the well-integrated 'total' moral autobiography he had intended. Instead he left readers with multi-layered impressions of Rousseau – certainly more complete and exhaustive than anything that had appeared previously. It was the raw stuff of autobiography, from which readers were invited to reconstruct the genuine writer.

176. Mme D.L.M. [Mme de La Tour de Franqueville] to Louis-M.-S. Fréron, editor of the *Année littéraire*, [15 March 1779], *Collection complète*, xv.401-13; originally published in [La Tour de Franqueville], *Jean-Jacques Rousseau vengé par son amie*, p.37-51; *CC*, xliii.185. Among the items by Mme de La Tour de Franqueville which Du Peyrou included in the *Supplément* (volume xv of the *Collection complète*) were: *La Vertu vengée par l'amitié*; *Lettre à l'auteur de la justification de J.-J. Rousseau dans la contestation qui lui est survenue avec M. Hume*; *Réflexions sur ce qui s'est passé au sujet de la rupture de J.-J. Rousseau et de M. Hume*; *Errata de l'Essai sur la musique ancienne et moderne, ou Lettre à l'auteur de ces essais par madame****. Recall the veiled attack by Diderot in the *Essai sur la vie de Sénèque*, p.120-21; and the explicit one by Naigeon, *Essai* [...], p.267-72.

177. Perhaps the most significant was that slave-maintained plantations of Surinam were what provided Du Peyrou with adequate income and leisure to turn into print the words of the century's most celebrated proponent of individual autonomy.

9. Europe's booksellers and the fate of the *Collection complète*

By August 1782 the STG had published the *Collection complète*. It was an ambitious undertaking. The three formats, in-quarto, in-octavo and in-duodecimo, had a combined press-run of 10 241 sets. The supplementary volumes would appear in 1783 in a press-run of 5717 sets.[1] Sets of the *Œuvres posthumes* were prepared for readers who merely desired to fill out their collections.[2] Individual editions containing Part I of the *Confessions* and the *Rêveries du promeneur solitaire* also were printed.[3]

Originally foreseen as a lavish production garnished with original engravings, the in-quarto and its supplement were reduced to a serviceable, non-illustrated fifteen-volume set. The in-octavo and in-duodecimo, each totalling thirty volumes, were considered the most marketable sets.[4] In 1783 the sometime partner in the STG, Jean-François Bassompierre, made the additional 'petit in-12' for the bookseller Amable Le Roy of Lyon. This, in effect, was a piracy of the STG's own edition.[5]

The records of the STG reveal an aggressive and wide-ranging sales strategy that confirmed Rousseau's powerful hold upon pre-revolutionary European readers. In order to entice would-be purchasers, the editors of the *Collection complète* stressed the authoritativeness of their texts. The STG also made a point of emphasising which editions appeared for the first time in the *Collection*: the *Considérations sur le gouvernement de Pologne*; the *Confessions*, Part I; the *Rêveries du promeneur solitaire*; *Rousseau juge de Jean-Jacques*; correspondence; and minor works.[6] Unfortunately the young entrepreneurs who formed the STG overspent their budget.[7] When François d'Ivernois had to flee Geneva for

---

1. Geneva, Les Délices, archives of the Société Jean-Jacques Rousseau, ms. R. 159, 'Dépouillement de tout [...]', Part C, Compte des impressions.

2. See the 'Notices bibliographiques' in *OC*, i.1893-94. The press-run of volumes i to iii of the *Œuvres posthumes* came to 2415 sets; the run for volumes iv to ix came to 883 sets.

3. See the 'Notices bibliographiques' in *OC*, i.1893-94. The 'large character' edition of the *Confessions* and the *Rêveries* (2 vols, in-8°) was published in a press-run of 7972 sets.

4. The combined press-run for all of the smaller format editions turned out to be 8088 sets.

5. Leigh, 'The Geneva edition and the *Confessions*', p.121-33. See as well *note explicative* a, *CC*, xlv.132. In May 1783 Bassompierre offered to sell sets of the 'petit in-12' *Supplément* and the in-octavo *Œuvres posthumes* to the STN (see printed circular letter from Jean-François Bassompierre to the STN, [17] May 1783, *CC*, xlv.149-50). In July Bassompierre acknowledged the STN's order for 200 sets of the 'petit in-12' *Supplément* (1 July 1783, *CC*, xlv.152).

6. Printed prospectus: 'RECUEIL DES ECRITS DE J.J. ROUSSEAU, PROPOSE PAR SOUSCRIPTION, A GENEVE, *chez la Société typographique*. in-4° & in-8°, avec un portrait de l'Auteur', [March 1779], *CC*, xliii.171-73.

7. Geneva, Les Délices, archives of the Société Jean-Jacques Rousseau, ms. R. 159, pièce E. By February 1783 reimbursed travel expenses for the STG exceeded 21 310 *livres*.

political reasons his partners J.-F. Bassompierre and Pierre Boin experienced difficulty paying shopworkers and suppliers of paper, ink and other materials. Nor could they return sums advanced to the STG by investors like Moultou and the veteran bookseller Samuel de Tournes.[8] Because Geneva's civil strife of 1782 forced Moultou into exile, it was left to Boin and de Tournes to liquidate the STG. The publisher's debts were assumed by de Tournes and Moultou, who themselves had to be propped up by the Geneva bankers Gabriel Lullin, Jean-Jacques Masbou and de Tournes's brother, Jean-Louis. Victimised by poor management practices and by piracies of the *Collection complète*, the STG virtually collapsed in April 1783.[9] Pirates cut prices and their cheap copycat editions removed whatever aura Du Peyrou's original one had enjoyed.[10] Then, on the eve of the French Revolution, a rival edition sensitive to rapidly changing political conditions sought to replace the *Collection complète* as the one of record.[11] Finally, faced with a downturn in the economy of the European book-trade, retailers from St Petersburg to Cambridge reneged on their payments to the STG and its creditors.[12]

Marketing the *Collection complète*

One hundred and forty European booksellers ordered sets of the *Collection complète*. The STG was highly flexible in promoting its offerings, even breaking up the nine-volume *Œuvres posthumes* into separate subsets of three and six volumes. As might be expected, France was the major market, with Jacques Esprit of Paris ordering more than twelve per cent (262 sets) of the press-run of the in-quarto and nearly one-fifth (765 sets) of the press-run of the

8. In November 1782 de Tournes had replaced d'Ivernois in the STG. It was clear that the days of the publishing house were numbered (*remarque* v, 21 November 1782, *CC*, xlv.122).

9. Resumé of the dissolution of the STG, 21 April 1783, *note explicative* b, *CC*, xlv.147.

10. Though Walter Benjamin considers the desacralisation of artistic works to be a consequence of mechanical reproductions of them, the loss of a printed original's 'aura' as a consequence of piracies is just as evident. See Benjamin, 'The work of art in the age of mechanical reproduction', in *Illuminations*, ed. Hannah Arendt, translated by Harry Zohn (New York 1969), p.217-51. The so-called 'revolutionary' edition of Rousseau's collected works followed an organisational scheme different from Du Peyrou's.

11. It was advertised as the *Œuvres complètes de J.-J. Rousseau, nouvelle édition, classée par ordre de matières, et ornée de quatre-vingt-dix gravures*. Published by Poinçot in Paris between 1788 and 1793, it attained 38 volumes both in-octavo and in-quarto. The prospectus was attributed to Gabriel Brizard. The initial collaborators to the edition were Louis-Sébastien Mercier (who wrote the Introduction) and Pierre-P.-F. Le Tourneur (who died just as the edition got under way). The engravings did not reach the ninety foreseen in the prospectus. Sixty-eight of them contained modifications of those in Boubers's edition and thirteen were engraved expressly for Poinçot. After November 1792, once each volume appeared its publisher ceremonially presented the appropriate copy to the appropriate revolutionary assembly (see Bonnet, 'L.-S. Mercier et les *Œuvres complètes* de Jean-Jacques Rousseau', p.111-24).

12. Geneva, Les Délices, archives de la Société Jean-Jacques Rousseau, ms. R. 159, Pièce AA, 'Recapitulation generale de la vente des œuvres de J.-J. Rousseau de tous formats et de la maniere dont on en a été payé, et la note de ce qui reste dû par divers au 1 août 1784. Verifié & approuvé a Geneve le 11 novembre 1785.'

in-octavo. Esprit also purchased 259 sets of the in-duodecimo, while his heirs bought 344 sets of *Suppléments* and 140 sets of *Œuvres posthumes*. Esprit died in 1782, just as the third shipment of the *Collection complète* was being delivered. Serving as middlemen for the Paris market, Esprit's heirs proved to be decent risks. By August 1784 they had made good on bills worth 86 530 *livres*, 97 per cent of Esprit's purchase.[13]

Unfortunately the Esprit heirs proved to be the exception. All too common were the non-payers. For example, by August 1784 (and confirmed more than a year later), Mossy of Marseille still owed 41 per cent on his 10 195-*livre* purchase (158 *Collections complètes*, 128 *Suppléments* and 26 *Œuvres posthumes*). Late in December 1784 Moultou travelled to Marseille to chase Mossy down. The bookseller failed to keep an arranged appointment, and Moultou made ten trips to Mossy's shop without finding his elusive debtor. When Mossy could hide no longer, he offered Moultou an i.o.u. which would fall due so far in the future that the creditor considered it worthless. In reporting his mission Moultou reverted to understatement: 'Mr. Favre dit que Mossy est solide, mais qu'il paye avec peine.'[14] Brun of Nantes owed the STG 44 per cent on his 21 724-*livre* purchase (247 *Collections complètes*, 208 *Suppléments* and 263 *Œuvres posthumes*). Parisot of Angers owed 63 per cent on his 7668-*livre* purchase and Mailly of Dijon owed 64 per cent on his 4572-*livre* purchase. Smaller booksellers were yet more remiss: Capel of Dijon owed 65 per cent on his 3939-*livre* purchase; Chabon of Dole owed 66 per cent on his 1288-*livre* purchase; Gerlache of Metz owed 86 per cent on his 1972-*livre* purchase; Le Roi of Caen owed 98 per cent on his 1140-*livre* purchase; and Jacquemart of Sedan owed 99 per cent on his 1422-*livre* purchase.[15]

The figures were not more reassuring for distant clients. Beyond France and Switzerland the two most important purchasers of the *Collection complète* and its subsidiary volumes were Fabre of St Petersburg and Plomteux of Liège. While by August 1784 the former still owed nearly 20 per cent on his orders worth 11 393 *livres*, the latter owed more than 70 per cent on his orders worth 20 326 *livres*.[16] As was the case with French and Swiss bookdealers, the small ones were the least likely to pay. Philibert of Copenhagen owed 44 per cent on his order worth 1552 *livres*, while his compatriot Steinmann owed 98 per cent on his 982-*livre* order. German booksellers seemed to be the worst risks of all. Schmid of Hannover owed 77 per cent; Himburg of Berlin owed 93 per cent. By August 1784 neither Heinsius of Leipzig nor Flörken of Danzig had paid a

13. 'Recapitulation generale', f.1.

14. Pierre Moultou reporting his father's trip to Samuel de Tournes, [6 January 1785], *CC*, xlv.282-83. Paul-Claude Moultou to Samuel de Tournes, [26 January 1785], *CC*, xlv.286.

15. 'Recapitulation generale', f.5, 11, 10, 6, 3, 2, 13. Esprit's heirs owed 3256 *livres*. Mossy owed 4180 *livres*. Brun owed 9480 *livres*. Parisot owed 4869 *livres*. Mailly owed 2929 *livres*. Capel owed 2547 *livres*. Chabon owed 848 *livres*. Gerlache owed 1701 *livres*. Le Roi owed 1080 *livres*. Jacquemart owed 1404 *livres*.

16. 'Recapitulation generale', f.6, 7. Fabre owed 2162 *livres*. Plomteux owed 14 607 *livres*.

sou for their orders.[17] In all, the STG had distributed 440 000 *livres* worth of books. Nearly 12 per cent of this sum was written off as gifts, free copies and discounts. By August 1784 sixty-seven of the 140 European booksellers who had purchased the *Collection complète* and its accompanying sets still owed nearly 85 000 *livres*.[18] Moultou and de Tournes called in sets not yet paid for, with little hope of reselling them.

It is instructive to compare the commercial fate of the STG's edition of Rousseau with an even more ambitious venture, Beaumarchais's collection of Voltaire's works and correspondence, undertaken in the disused fortress of Kehl in 1779 and completed there a decade later. The archive for Beaumarchais's Société typographique et littéraire de Kehl replicates the STG's post-mortem: handwringing over misinvestments and unsold editions, as well as ingenious and desperate efforts to be rid of sets at severe discounts. In 1791, as he presented a copy of the Kehl Voltaire to the French nation, Beaumarchais would claim a deficit of a million *livres*. At the playwright's death inventory taken eight years later, unpaid bookseller invoices totalled 97 757 *livres*. During the period of publication Beaumarchais had coped with the megalomania of an incompetent agent-in-charge, had endured censorship problems with the margrave of Baden who controlled Kehl, and had suffered condemnations by episcopal and royal censorship authorities in France. Like Du Peyrou and the STG, he had encountered piracies and responded to them with ever cheaper editions. The Kehl Voltaire was published in approximately 8400 sets, each containing 70 volumes in-octavo or 92 volumes in-duodecimo. Subscribers – overwhelmingly booksellers – purchased no more than 2500 sets. Many of the rest were remaindered at deep discounts. From his printshop in Kehl Beaumarchais tried to cover losses with piracies of various publications. Ironically enough, among his efforts was an in-duodecimo *contrefaçon* of the STG's *Collection complète des œuvres de J.-J. Rousseau*![19]

At the moment when Beaumarchais undertook his monumental edition of Voltaire, the desperation of the chief investors in the STG's Rousseau had become evident. By November 1783 Bassompierre and Boin were reduced to discounting their books drastically. Among their customers was their most bitter rival, the STN.[20] Bassompierre was particularly interested in selling to the STN unsold copies of the 'petit in-12' he had prepared for Amable Le Roy. Because this edition was actually Bassompierre's own piracy of the STG's legitimate in-duodecimo, the publishing house's co-liquidator undercut himself by engaging in exactly the sort of confused business practice that had brought down the STG in the first place.[21]

17. 'Recapitulation generale', f.9, 14, 4, 4, 5, 4. Philibert owed 682 *livres*. Steinmann owed 961 *livres*. Schmid owed 309 *livres*. Himburg owed 732 *livres*. Heinsius owed 108 *livres*. Flörken owed 990 *livres*.
18. 'Recapitulation generale', f.16.
19. Muir, 'The Kehl edition of Voltaire', p.85-100; Barber, 'The financial history of the Kehl Voltaire', p.152-70; Morton, 'Beaumarchais et le prospectus de l'édition de Kehl', p.133-47.
20. The STG to the STN, 21 April 1783, *CC*, xlv.145-46.
21. Jean-François Bassompierre to the STN, 19 November 1783, *CC*, xlv.238-39.

When it appeared that hundreds of sets of legitimate *Collections complètes* would not find customers, it was Moultou who offered a novel means of disposing of them. He suggested sending to bookseller-purchasers of the edition the false report that a single unnamed middleman was about to buy 1600 unsold sets at a very deep discount. Such a strategy, Moultou thought, would frighten the booksellers into believing that the phantom purchaser was likely to place his sets on the market at a drastically lower price than they were asking. Faced with the unacceptable choices of being stuck with their sets or else releasing them at a loss, the booksellers (so Moultou surmised) would be receptive to his offer that they band together and buy the 1600 warehoused sets.[22] Perhaps concerned over the damage that Moultou's scheme might do to his reputation, de Tournes rejected it as 'plus ingénieux que practicable'.[23]

Fortunately, in March 1784 it looked as though Moultou would be rescued from additional schemes. A genuine purchaser of the STG's overstock had been found. He was the Lyon bookseller Jean-Marie Barret. Barret offered Boin 102 810 *livres* for the sets still warehoused in Geneva. These included 4162 sets of the *Collection complète*, 1330 sets of *Suppléments*, 230 sets of *Œuvres posthumes* and 80 sets of the large-character *Confessions*. Barret agreed to pay in annual instalments of 11 000 to 12 000 *livres* until 1793 and Boin agreed to relinquish all rights to 'les œuvres de Jean Jaques Rousseau'.[24] Compared with what the STG had requested for the *Collection complète* three years earlier, the prices per set to be paid by Barret were discounted by 50 per cent for the in-quarto, 45 per cent for the in-octavo and 60 per cent for the in-duodecimo.[25] Boin accepted the offer.

Moultou testily mentioned to de Tournes that he had not been informed of Boin's sale to Barret. Nor did he like the nine-year terms granted to the Lyonnais.[26] Nevertheless, as a consequence of the failure by European booksellers to pay for their Rousseaus, Boin and de Tournes at least would be salvaging some income. And none too soon. Moultou was astounded when de Tournes informed him that expenses incurred in publishing the *Collection complète* had reached nearly 267 000 *livres*. 'N'y a t il point la l'erreur', the disbelieving Moultou asked.[27] But there was no miscalculation. In the name of the STG, Lullin and his banking partners were compensating the publishers' creditors; and both Moultou and Samuel de Tournes were responsible to the bankers. Should Barret's investment fall through, Moultou and de Tournes might anticipate a loss of at least 80 000 *livres*.[28]

22. Paul-Claude Moultou to Samuel de Tournes, 30 November 1783, *CC*, xlv.243-44.

23. *Note explicative* f, *CC*, xlv.246.

24. Cession by Pierre Boin to Jean-Marie Barret of the unsold sets of the Geneva edition, 27 May 1784, *CC*, xlv.256-59. The stock to be released included 992 *Collections complètes* in-quarto, 770 in-octavo and 2400 in-duodecimo.

25. *Note explicative* b, *CC*, xlv.259-60.

26. Paul-Claude Moultou to Samuel de Tournes, 5 June 1784, *CC*, xlv.261.

27. Paul-Claude Moultou to Samuel de Tournes, 1 July 1784, *CC*, xlv.265.

28. It was small consolation for Moultou and de Tournes to realise that they themselves had advanced a considerable percentage of the 267 000-*livre* debt assumed by Lullin & Company.

Deeply worried about the indebtedness he shared with de Tournes, Moultou again tried to emerge from their predicament by means of an inventive, if not particularly honest, ploy.[29] In September 1784 he notified de Tournes that he possessed a fresh dossier of Rousseau's letters. In light of the intense European-wide interest in the writer's life, Moultou proposed a partnership with de Tournes to publish the correspondence. He foresaw a single volume in-quarto or two volumes in-octavo and would deal only with booksellers who already had paid for their *Collections complètes*. Moreover, Moultou surmised that Barret would be likely to want a shipment of the proposed edition to complement the sets he was purchasing. Moultou tried to tempt de Tournes by concluding: 'Si je voulais doñer ces lettres manuscrites a des libraires que je Sais, j'en pourrais tirer grand parti: Mais nous avons perdu ensemble, Monsieur, je veux donc S'il est possible que nous nous indemniserions ensemble.'[30]

The difficulty with Moultou's scheme derived from the fact that he was not the owner of the Rousseau correspondence to which he referred, and he therefore had no right to publish it. He was not even its guardian. Most of the letters originated from the collections in Du Peyrou's safekeeping. Some time after 1779 Du Peyrou had loaned the original letters or copies of them to Moultou, who promptly had them transcribed. It was these texts that he wished to publish. Happily for Moultou's relationship with Du Peyrou, nothing immediate came of the Genevan's scheme. In 1789, however, following Moultou's death, his son Pierre did indeed publish the Rousseau letters, as well as Part II of the *Confessions*. Pierre reasoned that he simply was trying to recover that part of his inheritance which had disappeared thanks to his father's disastrous backing of the STG. Unimpressed, Du Peyrou became incensed by what he considered to be an unfaithful edition. In 1790 he would respond with his own version of the *Confessions*, Part II, as well as a selection of Rousseau's letters in his possession.[31]

Back in 1785 Moultou *père* still was tracking down booksellers who failed to pay for the sets they had ordered. He insisted that those meeting their obligations should send their payment directly to his bankers, Lullin & Company. In other words Bassompierre and Boin were not to get their hands on any more funds.[32] In June Moultou visited Rigaud of Montpellier, a crypto-Protestant suspected of dealing in illicit books, who apparently never had responded to pleas for the 1279 *livres* he owed. Once confronted by Moultou, Rigaud blamed a former partner for communication breakdowns with his Swiss creditors. Then he complained that his sets of the *Collection complète* were unsellable because they were defective, missing pages. This line of argument impressed Moultou, who informed de Tournes that Rigaud 'est un

29. Paul-Claude Moultou to Samuel de Tournes, [11 September 1784], *CC*, xlv.276.
30. Paul-Claude Moultou to Samuel de Tournes, [11 September 1784], *CC*, xlv.277-78.
31. See below, chapter 10.
32. Cited by Pierre Moultou to Samuel de Tournes, [6 January 1785], *CC*, xlv.282-83.

honête home fort a Son aise'.[33] Nonetheless, no record shows that Rigaud ever made good on his obligation.

But Rigaud was small change. The indebtedness of the Paris banker Batilliot the elder was far more serious. Batilliot had underwritten bookseller purchases of 7000 copies of the STG's separate edition of the *Confessions*, Part I, and the *Rêveries*. Unfortunately in 1783 Batilliot himself became victimised by his debtors' bankruptcies and was short of cash. Statements of his account two years later showed that he still owed 12 396 *livres* for the STG's books, and he finally went bankrupt. Serving as a collection agency for Moultou and de Tournes, the Paris press lord Charles-Joseph Panckoucke estimated that the Swiss creditors might recover no better than 50 per cent of Batilliot's debt. Even this proved to be wishful thinking. Furthermore, Panckoucke himself was 1585 *livres* in arrears.[34]

As long as Barret paid them regularly, Moultou and de Tournes were able to chip away at their indebtedness to Lullin and his partners. But in June 1786 Barret died. As bills poured in, the bookseller's widow found it difficult to meet her late husband's obligations and Moultou worried whether payments would continue.[35] Several weeks later de Tournes reminded Moultou of the books still remaining in the Geneva warehouse: 2230 sets of the *Collection complète* (1500 in-duodecimo, 600 in-quarto and 130 in-octavo) and 1100 sets of the *Supplément* (700 in-quarto and 400 in-octavo).[36] Next, on 16 July de Tournes and Moultou prepared a balance sheet of their investment.

Thanks largely to Barret's payments of 1784 and 1785 the indebtedness of the two partners to Lullin & Company had been reduced considerably. But Moultou and de Tournes also had assumed the STG's responsibility for setting aside 24 000 additional *livres* as payment for Rousseau's manuscripts and papers used in the edition. This amount was what the Neuchâtel convention of September 1779 originally had reserved for the *amis de Rousseau* and was ultimately intended for Rousseau's children, should any appear and make a sufficiently legitimate claim.[37] Moultou and de Tournes invested this sum and used the annual interest accruing from it, 1200 *livres*, to compensate Thérèse Levasseur. But as their indebtedness to Lullin & Company mounted, the pair worried lest one day a legitimate heir might sue for the principal. On the one hand, they believed that Thérèse's small pension was sufficient for her needs. On the other, they shunted aside the demands of Rousseau's closest blood relatives, his three cousins. Everyone now dreaded the thought that one or more of Rousseau's five allegedly abandoned children

33. Paul-Claude Moultou to Samuel de Tournes, [29 June 1785], *CC*, xlv.289.

34. Geneva, Les Délices, archives of the Société Jean-Jacques Rousseau, ms. R. 159, 'Règlement définitif de comptes entre les Sociétés Rousseau et typographiques', *remarque* iii, 11 November 1785 and 24 April 1786, summarised in *CC*, xlv.296-97. Even Moultou failed to pay the STG the 2290 *livres* owed for private purchases made by him of sets of the *Collection complète*.

35. Paul-Claude Moultou to Samuel de Tournes, [7 July 1786], *CC*, xlv.323-24.

36. De Tournes to Paul-Claude Moultou, 12 [July 1786], *CC*, xlv.326.

37. Convention among the *amis de Rousseau*, [21 September 1779], *CC*, xliv.28-29.

might yet appear and stake a claim. Barret's two payments notwithstanding, by late summer 1786 the bookseller's widow still owed Moultou and de Tournes 78 810 *livres* in long-term notes. The bottom line was clear. If veuve Barret could make good on her late husband's investment, Moultou and de Tournes might yet turn a profit. Should she renege, their losses could reach nearly 50 000 *livres*.[38]

When in November de Tournes told Moultou that veuve Barret was experiencing difficulties compensating other creditors, it became evident that she would not meet her commitments. At the least de Tournes was determined to get to the head of the line of her creditors. He hinted at his own probable bankruptcy.[39] But it was the ever industrious Moultou who emerged with a more dignified resolution. Rather than join veuve Barret's creditors in squeezing her dry, he proposed an accommodation. The widow apparently had been able to sell 18 000 *livres* worth of *Collections complètes* she had received in 1784 and 1785 and was requesting four years' grace to pay this sum to Moultou and de Tournes. Moultou was willing to grant the stay on condition that she make good on 12 000 *livres* worth of additional books which already had been sent to her and were piled high in the back rooms of her shop. Once she paid them the grand total of 30 000 *livres*, Moultou and de Tournes believed that they could transfer most, if not all, of the sum to Lullin and his partners. The delay of four years also would buy time for the disposition of the *Collections complètes* and *Suppléments* transmitted to de Tournes's warehouse, where they were gathering dust. Moultou even had a potential customer for these volumes: the Geneva printer-bookseller Jean-Paul Barde. Ever the optimist, Moultou was convinced that twenty retailers might yet be found to relieve both Barde and veuve Barret of their books.[40]

Uncovering Part II of the *Confessions*

As he grasped at straws Moultou was fully aware that he possessed the goldmine that still might rescue his investment: the manuscript for Part II of the *Confessions*. But as a faithful disciple committed to transmitting to posterity an image of Rousseau the unsullied moralist, could Moultou in good conscience print this last piece of the corpus? Certainly Part II of the *Confessions* would complete the 'total' moral autobiography foreseen by Du Peyrou. Unfortunately this last piece had been composed in the deep shadows of persecution and paranoiacally took after enemies real and imagined. The negative critical reception of *Rousseau juge de Jean-Jacques* still remained fresh in Moultou's mind, and the disciple was well informed about Rousseau's own reluctance to make the *Confessions*, Part II, public as long as individuals mentioned in

---

38. Mutual engagement between Samuel de Tournes and Paul-Claude Moultou, [16 July 1786], *CC*, xlv.335-38.
39. Samuel de Tournes to Paul-Claude Moultou, 7 November 1786, *CC*, xlv.342-44.
40. Paul-Claude Moultou to Samuel de Tournes, [10 November 1786], *CC*, xlv.344-46.

them still were alive.[41] True, by 1786 Voltaire, d'Alembert, Diderot and Mme d'Epinay were gone. But others – Sophie d'Houdetot, Saint-Lambert, Malesherbes, the maréchale-duchesse de Luxembourg, Grimm and Holbach – remained active. Should Rousseau's rancour-laden opinions of them appear in print, vilified parties might well protest vigorously to French censorship officials or the police. Furthermore, possessing his own manuscript copy of the *Confessions*, the litigious Girardin could always cause trouble. Who knew what the capricious marquis would do? On the one hand, he considered Part II of the *Confessions* a sacred text; on the other, he was willing to use it as a last-ditch ransom due claimants to the heritage.[42]

Public curiosity about the whereabouts of Part II of the *Confessions* remained rife. For example, at the court of Louis XVI the prince and princesse de Beauvau-Craon surmised correctly that Moultou was sheltering a manuscript. The Beauvaus asked Suzanne Necker to persuade him to release it for their perusal. She acceded to their request, and in trying to throw her off the track Moultou, faithful vassal of French high society though he was, assumed a strained republican pose. He wrote to Mme Necker: 'Je coñais, Madame, tout le despotisme des grands, je sais que rien ne fléchit leurs volontés altiéres, qu'il faut que le Ciel S'abaisse pour leur complaire, que les morts Sortent de leurs tombeaux pour réveler les Secrets qu'ils veulent Savoir, et délier les Serments qui les génent.'[43] Moultou tempered his indignation by adding that the Beauvaus were undoubtedly spared the haughtiness of their class. Nevertheless, the former pastor lied by stating that he would have to deny the Beauvaus a reading of the manuscript simply because he did not possess it. Instead he broadly hinted that Du Peyrou might have a copy.

Truth be told, by January 1786 Du Peyrou did own one. Part I of Moultou's manuscript had been his working source for the STG's editions of Books I to VI of the *Confessions*. Some time in 1784 Moultou loaned Du Peyrou Part II, and the Neuchâtel businessman had it copied. Without expressly informing Suzanne Necker that Du Peyrou possessed Part II, Moultou hinted that the Neuchâtel disciple would be unlikely to release whatever he was holding. The reason, Moultou wrote, was simple. As one could surmise from the *Rêveries* and *Rousseau juge de Jean-Jacques*, Rousseau's last years were plagued by 'cette humeur noire et melancholique qui le consumait depuis Si longtems. Cette maladie cruelle, le Seul héritage qu'il eut reçu de Ses péres, dénaturait tous les objets à Ses yeux, & versait Sur les actions les plus iñocentes, les plus estimables, qui Se rapportaient à lui, le poison de Sa Sombre manie.' Moultou suggested that Rousseau's followers were obliged to protect the writer's heroic image for posterity, even at the price of silencing him: 'Si ces confessions existent, il est plus que probable que les amis de Rousseau

41. *Confessions*, Part II, Book VIII, in *OC*, i.400.
42. In a letter to Moultou dated 29 November 1783 Du Peyrou hinted that Girardin might yet be amenable to publishing Part II of the *Confessions* in collaboration with the erstwhile *amis* (*CC*, xlv.241-42).
43. Paul-Claude Moultou to Suzanne Necker, [23 January 1786], *CC*, xlv.304.

doivent les cacher.' Sending them through the mails risked security. Even if the *Confessions* manuscript arrived safely at the Beauvaus', who could control 'une légére négligence, l'infidélité d'un Secrétaire, la curiosité d'une feme, pardonnés, Madame, quand il S'agit de la réputation d'un ami dont le nom doit vivre?'[44]

Two months later, however, Moultou admitted the truth to Mme Necker. He wrote that he indeed was holding Rousseau's own handwritten copy of Part II of the *Confessions*. Moultou had based his previous denial, he added, upon fears that his correspondence might be opened. Moreover, 'il est possible que [Rousseau] ait confié a quelque autre le même manuscrit, et Si ce proprietaire autre que moi le fesait imprimer, le Soupçon ne tomberait que Sur moi'. Moultou now was willing to let the Beauvaus see the manuscript. But it had to appear that Du Peyrou (not he himself) had provided it: 'il faut que la Princesse elle-même croie que c'est de lui que j'ai obtenu [...]. Il faudrait de plus que persoñe ne Sçut qu'on a vu ce Manuscrit par moi.' Finally Moultou informed Suzanne Necker of his worry that Rousseau's references to Sophie d'Houdetot as mistress of the marquis de Saint-Lambert might compromise the intimate friendship between Saint-Lambert and the prince de Beauvau. Trusting François Vernes to hand-deliver his views to Mme Necker, Moultou signed off with instructions to her: 'Je vous demande en grace de bruler ma lettre.'[45]

Moultou's characteristic timidity amused Suzanne Necker. She saw no reason to destroy his letter and responded that Rousseau's revelations of liaisons lasting a quarter-century would embarrass no one at the French court: 'la vieillesse qui enlaidit tout semble être ici le fard du vice; un attachement déshonnête consacré par le tems prend peu à peu une sorte de dignité'.[46] At last comprehending the potential difficulties for Moultou provoked by their request, the Beauvaus withdrew it. According to Mme Necker, Moultou's secret would remain safe. He breathed a sigh of relief.

But rumours circulating that he indeed possessed Part II of the *Confessions* no doubt caused Moultou to rethink his reluctance about publishing it. He also was fearful that Girardin might change his mind about keeping the Ermenonville copy unpublished. If the marquis decided to release the manuscript he was holding, Moultou's would lose considerable worth. Shortly before his admission to Mme Necker the Genevan received a cryptically worded letter from Du Peyrou which responded to a suggestion Moultou had recently made. It apparently had to do with printing the Genevan's manuscript, emphasising that it was the only one revised by Rousseau himself and handed over to his disciple. If the manuscript were published with appropriate publicity it might reduce Girardin's to first-draft status. Should the marquis protest Moultou and Du Peyrou promised to reveal the unsavoury manner in which Girardin's

44. Paul-Claude Moultou to Suzanne Necker, [23 January 1786], *CC*, xlv.304-305.
45. Paul-Claude Moultou to Suzanne Necker, [20 March 1786], *CC*, xlv.308.
46. Suzanne Necker to Paul-Claude Moultou, [3 May 1786], *CC*, xlv.313.

manuscript 'est tombé entre les mains de son possesseur actuel, et comment le dépositaire du second choisi par l'auteur lui-même a acquis la connaissance de l'existence du premier'.[47] Half a dozen years following their rupture Du Peyrou remained unwilling to show Girardin any mercy. He wrote that he and Moultou were to act 'de façon à ne compromettre M. de G. qu'autant qu'il se compromettrait lui-même en publiant son manuscrit. J'ai parmi mes papiers des lettres de la veuve [Thérèse] qui me rend compte de cette affaire, et d'autres lettres de M. de G. qui avoue la possession du manuscrit. Ce sont des pièces de réserve à conserver.'[48]

Moultou's sudden death in June 1787 aborted the potential collaboration with Du Peyrou to publish Part II of the *Confessions*. Meanwhile it had become clear that veuve Barret would never make good even on a fraction of her debt. De Tournes's situation therefore became more unenviable than ever. He was responsible to Lullin & Company for the STG's unpaid bills, he was guarantor of the sum the STG was to have paid for the Rousseau manuscripts and he was supplier of Thérèse's 1200-*livre* annual pension.[49] Furthermore, a month prior to Moultou's death de Tournes learned that the 24 000 *livres* put aside for the Rousseau manuscripts had been misinvested and the principal now was reduced to 15 520 *livres*. This new disaster placed Thérèse's pension in jeopardy. Moreover, goaded by Girardin, Rousseau's cousins were demanding the entire 24 000 *livres* and threatening a lawsuit. The financial ruin that de Tournes had feigned in 1784 now seemed a distinct possibility.[50]

De Tournes obtained a temporary respite when the Lyon bookseller Joseph-S. Grabit made an offer for sets of the *Collection complète* that veuve Barret had defaulted upon. Grabit, however, proposed only a fraction of what the widow still owed, and the expiration of his terms stretched out even beyond hers, to 1797. Unfortunately, by this latter date the revolutionary cataclysm would sweep Grabit from business. Meanwhile, once de Tournes and Pierre Moultou did manage to abandon their burden and the accounts were closed on the *Collection complète* in June 1797, the old Genevan bookseller found it nearly impossible to determine what, beyond emotional costs, the financial losses of the great edition had come to. He thought that he had left 23 000 *livres* worth of debts and bills unpaid.[51]

---

47. Du Peyrou to Paul-Claude Moultou, [14 March 1787], *CC*, xlv.374.
48. Du Peyrou to Paul-Claude Moultou, [14 March 1787], *CC*, xlv.374.
49. Eventually the Moultou heirs would have to shoulder some of this burden. Shortly before his death Moultou made an accounting of his resources. He estimated his worth at 556 000 *livres*, his advances to the STG at 16 000 *livres* and his debts at 43 400 *livres* (Geneva, archives of the Société Jean-Jacques Rousseau, ms. R. 160, f.145). See as well *note explicative* a, *CC*, xlv.402.
50. Paul-Claude Moultou to Samuel de Tournes, [11 March 1787], *CC*, xlv.368-69.
51. Definitive ruling terminating the Société Rousseau, [1 June 1797], *CC*, xlix.69-78.

Thérèse, her inheritance and the Rousseau cousins

The 24 000 *livres* which the STG had promised for Rousseau's manuscripts back in September 1779 were a source of pain that would plague the *Collection complète*'s investors for nearly twenty years.[52] Thérèse Levasseur insisted that she was the appropriate beneficiary, but the *amis de Rousseau* believed that she would poorly use such a large infusion of income. In its place she therefore was offered 600 *livres* every six months.[53] Girardin had pressed for this paltry settlement, all the while insisting it was a gift and not an annuity, because he worried that one of Rousseau's abandoned children would appear and demand the entire 24 000 *livres*. When no direct descendant showed up, the marquis became seduced by the argument that Rousseau's closest blood relations, the writer's three cousins, were entitled to share the sum.

During his lifetime Rousseau had wished to protect Thérèse from losing her inheritance. On one occasion, at Montmorency in March 1758, he had signed a 'Reconnoissance et obligation', leaving his household items to her. At the time Rousseau also recognised an indebtedness to Thérèse of 1950 *livres*, his interpretation of adequate payment for thirteen years of domestic and sexual service.[54] Five years later, at Môtiers, Rousseau wrote his will, naming Thérèse sole heir and specifically excluding all blood relations from inheriting his property.[55] The document disappeared, however, as did at least one additional copy composed by Rousseau at Wootton. The transcript of a later copy survives today, though Girardin, Moultou and Du Peyrou probably were unaware of its existence.

Setting up housekeeping with Bally at Plessis-Belleville, at first blush Thérèse's financial situation appeared far from desperate. Until Rey's death she received from the Amsterdam bookseller an annual 300-*livre* pension. This was augmented by approximately 700 *livres* per year supplied by Girardin, 400 *livres* per year from Marshal Keith's estate and the 1200 *livres* promised her by the STG.[56] Thérèse also was chasing down arrears on King George III's English pension for Rousseau, which the writer never had

52. Contract between the *amis de Rousseau* and the STG, paragraph 7, [18 September 1779], *CC*, xliv.25.
53. Convention among the *amis de Rousseau*, [21 September 1779], *CC*, xliv.28: '1°. Que les interets annuels de la Somme de Vingt quatre mille Livres de France, obtenue de la Société Typographique de Geneve, seront appliqués à l'entretien de Dame Marie-Therese le Vasseur, Veuve de Monsieur Jean Jaques Rousseau & lui seront comptés de six mois en six mois, contre son reçu, en quelque lieu que soit son Domicile. 2°. Qu'à l'époque fixée au premier Octobre mil sept cent quatrevingt deux pour le payement de la dite Somme de vingt quatre mille Livres par la Société Typographique, ce Capital sera placé surement et convenablement au gré de nous Soussignés, pour le dit Capital être conservé dans son entier, et revenir après la mort de la dite Dame Marie Therese Le Vasseur Veuve Jean Jaques Rousseau aux Enfans du dit Sieur Jean Jaques Rousseau, s'il s'en présentoit aucuns, et à défaut d'iceux, pour être reparti aux Parens et Héritiers naturels du sus dit Sieur Jean-Jaques Rousseau suivant l'exigence du cas.'
54. 'Reconnoissance et obligation', 8 March 1758, *OC*, i.1221-23.
55. 'Testament de Jean Jaques Rousseau citoyen de Geneve', *OC*, i.1224-25.
56. The allowance Girardin gave Thérèse was deducted from Rousseau's cash fund that the marquis had found at the writer's death.

collected, and she accepted royalties from the Paris Opera for the revised *Devin du village*.[57] She still anticipated obtaining 3000 *livres* from the Girardin–Benoît edition of Rousseau's songs, and the marquis was holding in trust for her the gold he had found inside Rousseau's writing desk on 2 July 1778. Unfortunately Thérèse never had been much of a money manager and Bally proved to be a further drain. Appointing himself Thérèse's financial adviser, he urged her to lay claim to the entire 24 000 *livres* which the STG had offered the *amis de Rousseau* for Rousseau's papers.[58]

Submerged by bills and experiencing great difficulty in obtaining payment from booksellers for the *Collection complète*, Boin and Bassompierre were unable, even if willing, to acknowledge Thérèse's demands. In fact the young publishers found it impossible to pay her the semi-annual 600 *livres*. Though they tried to maintain appearances, by 1783 their STG was in ruins and Moultou and de Tournes had reluctantly assumed financial responsibility for Thérèse. Meanwhile Girardin had met 'Rousseau le Persan' and became captivated by a personality even more *rocambolesque* than his own. Between offers urging Girardin to invest in bizarre financial schemes, this Rousseau garbed in middle-eastern robes convinced the marquis of the justice of his claims to the heritage of his illustrious cousin, most specifically to a piece of the 24 000 *livres* paid for the writer's manuscripts. Once she learned from Girardin of the existence of 'Rousseau le Persan', Thérèse protested vigorously to the STG: 'pourquoi ça iroit-il à un cousin que je ne connois ni d'Eve ni d'Adam [...]. Je demande que mon bien, non pas celui des autres. Personne n'a autorité sur mon bien: il est à moi et non à d'autres.'[59]

Girardin knew that Thérèse was addressing requests for the 24 000 *livres* to Geneva and he had no wish to support her claims. According to the terms of the convention of 21 September 1779, the entire principal belonged to the *amis*; they might dispose of the money as they saw fit. The marquis informed the STG that Thérèse was entitled to nothing more than the interest on the principal as long as she lived (1200 *livres* per annum).[60] Out of touch with Du Peyrou and Moultou for more than a year, Girardin apparently was unaware that the STG itself was collapsing. But in order to frustrate Thérèse's claim and, conversely, protect that of 'Rousseau le Persan', the marquis reestablished communication with Du Peyrou. He proposed that the 24 000 *livres* be invested in Paris, that the interest continue to be awarded to Thérèse and that the principal be divided among Rousseau's 'heritiers naturels' upon her death.[61]

57. Ralph A. Leigh, 'Rousseau's English pension', in *Studies in 18th-century French literature presented to Robert Niklaus* (Exeter 1975), p.120-21.
58. Marie-Thérèse Levasseur to the STG, 29 August 1783, *CC*, xlv.229-33.
59. Marie-Thérèse Levasseur to the STG, 29 August 1783, *CC*, xlv.229.
60. Girardin to the STG, 1 October 1783, *CC*, xlv.235.
61. Du Peyrou to Paul-Claude Moultou, 29 November 1783, *CC*, xlv.241-42.

Bearing a grudge towards Thérèse that he would carry to the grave, Du Peyrou concurred with Girardin's proposal. Moultou went along as well.[62] By now Moultou and de Tournes had assumed the STG's responsibility for the 24 000 *livres*. Lullin & Company agreed to stand up for the sum if need be. The money was duly invested, though Girardin mistakenly still considered it to be the STG's. In February 1784 he again warned Boin and Bassompierre never to dream of compensating Thérèse with anything more than 5 per cent semi-annual interest. Girardin even opposed converting the interest on the sum into a guaranteed annuity for her.[63]

In short, Girardin wanted to avoid any hint that Thérèse held an inheritance right. In his view the 1200 *livres* per year constituted a gift from the *amis* and nothing more. Faced with such intransigence, Rousseau's widow sought professional help. In mid-March 1784 the Paris notary Simon Levebure wrote to Boin: 'Mad^e. La veuve de Jean Jacques Rousseau, Créanciere de votre societé Typographique, d'une somme de 24,000₶, vient de me charger de sa procuration pour Recevoir Cette somme ainsi que les Interêts.' Levebure requested the name of Boin's banker in Paris so that Thérèse could lay hands on the funds.[64]

Boin replied that the *amis de Rousseau*, not Thérèse, had sold Rousseau's papers to the STG: 'ils ont traité avec nous pour la cession des ouvrages de m. Rousseau, dont ils etoient les depositaires, & non point la veuve, ils l'ont fait conformement aux desirs du defunt dont ils connoissoient les volontés, et non point en vertu d'aucun pouvoir ou procuration de sa veuve.'[65] According to Boin, it was in response to a request of the *amis de Rousseau* that the STG had agreed to pay Thérèse 600 *livres* every six months. Recently, Boin admitted, he had expressed willingness to convert the sum into guaranteed lifetime annuity payments. The *amis* [that is, Girardin], however, refused to allow him to do so. Boin conceded that, owing to the failure of the *Collection complète* project, he would be hard pressed to pay anyone 24 000 *livres*. Still, because he wished to maintain the fiction that the STG was solvent, he neglected to tell Levebure that Moultou and de Tournes now were the ones supplying Thérèse's income.[66]

In June Levebure requested from Boin all documentation pertaining to the sale of Rousseau's manuscripts.[67] Boin refused to comply, maintaining that Thérèse had no rights to the documents. Nor, Boin repeated, did she have rights to any part of the 24 000 *livres* paid for Rousseau's papers. Boin repeated his willingness to convert Thérèse's semi-annual interest payment into an

---

62. Paul-Claude Moultou to Samuel de Tournes, 4 January 1784, *CC*, xlv.247-49.

63. Girardin to Pierre Boin, François d'Ivernois and Jean-François Bassompierre, 13 February 1784, *CC*, xlv.251.

64. Simon Levebure to Boin, [12 March 1784], *CC*, xlv.252.

65. Boin to Levebure, 23 March 1784, *CC*, xlv.254-55.

66. Boin to Levebure, 23 March 1784, *CC*, xlv.254-55.

67. Levebure to Boin, 8 June 1784, *CC*, xlv.262.

annuity, but added that he could accomplish it only with express instructions from the *amis* of Rousseau.[68]

During the summer of 1784 Boin still hoped that a guaranteed life annuity would satisfy Thérèse and rid him of her claims. At length Du Peyrou lifted whatever objection he might once have had to the annuity, noting that it would be to Thérèse's benefit to accept an established sum in lieu of fluctuating interest payments on the 24 000 *livres*, especially if the principal were in danger of disappearing.[69] Moultou also was willing to settle with Thérèse, even though he and de Tournes would be the true source of the annuity.[70] After all, Moultou was as eager as Boin to avoid a lawsuit with Rousseau's widow, which probably would uncover the silent-partner role he shared with de Tournes. As expected, however, Girardin adamantly opposed renegotiating Thérèse's terms. In Girardin's view a blood relative, not Rousseau's concubine, was the writer's genuine heir. For the marquis that individual was 'Rousseau le Persan'.[71]

On the following day Thérèse herself addressed a moving and pathetic letter to Boin. Referring to the 24 000 *livres*, she restated her claim to compensation for her late husband's manuscripts: 'C'est mon Bien, j'en veut jouir, je Suis Lasse de tous vos discours et vos defaite.' Thérèse added the threat: 'cy Vous ne voulés Point agir honnêtement avec moy de me rendre m'a dite Somme qui m'appartient, J'ay des amis Puissans qui me le feront rendre, Comme m'appartenant legitimement.'[72] Of course it all was a desperate bluff. Thérèse had no powerful friends – not yet, at least; and it was questionable whether she could prove in a court of law that she indeed was the legitimate widow of Jean-Jacques Rousseau. The ceremony at the Auberge de la Fontaine d'Or in Bourgoin on 29 August 1768 had been choreographed and performed by Rousseau himself. No priest, no municipal or state authority had participated. The mayor of Bourgoin, M. de Champagneux, had attended the event, it was true, but merely in tribute to his celebrated resident.[73]

Boin replied to Thérèse that he owed her nothing and urged her to renounce all pretensions. Furthermore, he suggested that she had no widow's rights that would be recognised in a courtroom: 'Si vous venés nous faire un procés nous somes prets a y repondre mais je doute que vous aiés des titres qui vous autorisent a nous attaquer.' Boin repeated that the STG had contracted with the *amis de Rousseau*, legitimate guardians of the writer's manuscripts. They alone might authorise any shift in arrangements with her. By persisting with her

68. Boin to Levebure, 25 June 1784, *CC*, xlv.263-64.
69. Du Peyrou to Boin, [8 August 1784], *CC*, xlv.269-70.
70. Paul-Claude Moultou to Samuel de Tournes, [*c.* 13 August 1784], *CC*, xlv.270-71.
71. Girardin to Pierre Boin, 25 August 1784, *CC*, xlv.271-72.
72. Original in another's hand [John Bally's?], signed by Thérèse, Marie-Thérèse Levasseur to Pierre Boin, 26 August 1784, *CC*, xlv.272.
73. Champagneux's account is given in L. F[ochier], *Séjour de J.-J. Rousseau à Bourgoin, notice par L. Fxxx* (1860), p.30-47. See Recollection of Luc-Antoine Donin de Champagneux, *CC*, xxxvi.231-39.

claim, Boin suggested, Thérèse risked losing everything, most notably the 600 *livres* she had been collecting every six months.[74]

On 10 January 1785 Thérèse complained to Boin that she had not yet received the money due her for the past half year. Once more she accused Girardin of having stolen Rousseau's papers, citing her husband's alleged deathbed request of her: 'Prenné tous les manuscrits ils Sont a vous et que je vous laisse un morceau de Pain aprés m'a mort.' Thérèse resented Girardin's claim that semi-literacy had reduced her to ward status in his household: 'Monsieur De Gerardin n'est Point mon tuteur, aussy Bien que les autres je Suis majeure et aviés droits d'un bien qui m'appartient.'[75] A week later Thérèse angrily berated Girardin himself, accusing the marquis of withholding documentation of her marriage from Simon Levebure: 'Je Suis L'Epouse de déffunt J. Jeacques Rousseau, qui ne S'effassera jamais de ma vie, je Suis L'Epouse de J. Jeacques Rousseau, tout Comme vous Epoux de Madame De Gerardin.' Thérèse next offered a further indictment: 'Depuis la mort de mon mary m'avé vous assé tracassé, m'avé vous assé fait de Peine, vous dite que vous avé aimé mon Pauvre Mary, non Monsieur vous ne L'avé jamais aimé [...] je ne Peu Pas Comprendre que Monsieur Le marquis de Gerardin une homme de Sa sorte Puis faire autant de Peine a la veuve de J. Jeacques Rousseau.' Bitterly, Thérèse threw the ward–guardian relationship in Girardin's face, in fact reversing it. 'J'allois vous dire que je veux être vôtre tutrice, J'ay des amis Puissans, qu'ils ne me rejettent point, Et qui voyent Claire Et nette mon bien qui m'es dub.'[76]

When Boin and Girardin held firm in refusing to recognise her claim to the entire Rousseau inheritance, Thérèse Levasseur resigned herself to collecting her 600 *livres* every six months. She had no doubts about her moral title to the principal, yet she had to admit to a small chance of winning her case. She certainly remained hostile. In May 1785 she exploded when Boin informed her that anonymous parties (de Tournes and Moultou) were paying her allowance. She maintained that she would deal only with Boin.[77] She continued to appeal to principles of abstract justice, but to no avail.[78]

Though Thérèse was unaware of it at the time, her claims to the inheritance were being formally challenged. In May 1786 Jean-François Rousseau, son of Jean-Jacques's cousin Théodore, wrote to his uncle Jean in London. After reading his nephew's letter, Jean Rousseau quoted directly from it in a memorandum he addressed to the Genevan banker Jean-Louis de Tournes: ' "Un objet interessant, m'engage à vous écrire, Mon cher Oncle [...] nous Sommes

74. Pierre Boin to Marie-Thérèse Levasseur, 10 September 1784, *CC*, xlv.274-75.

75. Original, in John Bally's hand[?] and signed by Thérèse, Marie-Thérèse Levasseur to Pierre Boin, 10 January 1785, *CC*, xlv.283-84.

76. Original, in Bally's hand[?] and signed by Thérèse, Marie-Thérèse Levasseur to Girardin, 17 January 1785, *CC*, xlv.284-85.

77. Original, in Bally's hand[?] and signed by Thérèse, Marie-Thérèse Levasseur to Pierre Boin, 30 May 1785, *CC*, xlv.287-89.

78. Original, in Bally's hand[?] and signed by Thérèse, Marie-Thérèse Levasseur to Pierre Boin, 10 June 1786, *CC*, xlv.320-21.

héritiers de 24.000 (je suppose livres Tournois), Capital de la vente des manu-scrits de Jean-Jacques aux libraires de Genêve [...] et il Sera à partager entre vous, le Consul de Bassora ['Rousseau le Persan'] & mon papa, tous trois Cousins du Philosophe au même degré." ' Why were the Rousseau cousins activating their claim at this time? Jean-François made the reason clear. Girardin was instigating him. The marquis had met with young Jean-François and urged him to persuade his father, uncle and cousin to seek out the 24 000 *livres* immediately, rather than wait for Thérèse's death. From London Jean Rousseau wasted no time. Banker brother of Samuel de Tournes, Jean-Louis was a partner in Lullin & Company, underwriters of the 24 000 *livres*. Jean Rousseau demanded his one-third share.[79]

Jean-Louis de Tournes responded that in his opinion, as well as Samuel's, no claimant to Rousseau's inheritance could touch any part of the 24 000 *livres* as long as Thérèse remained alive. Once she died it was up to the *amis de Rousseau* to decide what to do with the principal. For the Rousseaus to call themselves heirs to the 24 000 *livres* was therefore inappropriate: 'vous êtes sans doute les heritiers de feu J.J. Rousseau, vous le savés mieux que moi, mais vous ne pouvés pas vous regarder comme les heritiers d'une Somme qui ne lui a jamais appartenu & qu'il n'a jamais ni connu ni prévu.'[80] This indeed was an unfavourable reading, perhaps even a misreading, of the convention of 21 September 1779. But banker de Tournes's intention was clear. No doubt with the connivance of Moultou and Samuel de Tournes, Lullin & Company had no objection to the 24 000 *livres* simply fading away. Both the bankers and suc-cessors to the STG were as uninterested in seeing the Rousseau cousins collect the entire principal as they were in seeing it fall into the hands of Thérèse Levasseur.

The ever opportunistic Moultou now emerged with an alternative plan. He proposed to Samuel de Tournes that in return for promising the Rousseaus the entire 24 000 *livres* sometime in the future, the luckless successors to the STG might persuade Jean-Jacques's cousins to assume the obligations of the bank-rupt publishing house. The cousins might then be the ones to chase after the STG's debtors and pay its creditors. Furthermore, since the Lyon bookseller Jean-Marie Barret had just died and his widow was in financial trouble, the Rousseaus might be asked to take over the promissory notes for copies of the *Collection complète* from veuve Barret. Admittedly Moultou's scheme was yet another of his very long shots. In return for 24 000 *livres* that they felt entitled to in the first place, the Rousseaus were being asked to salvage the debris of a failed investment. They also were asked to pay Thérèse her 1200 *livres* annually as long as she lived. If the Rousseaus concurred, Moultou and de Tournes would lose most of what they had invested in the *Collection complète*, but at least they would be free of both the STG's debts and Thérèse. Moultou

---

79. Jean Rousseau to Jean-Louis de Tournes, quoting Jean-François Rousseau [16 May 1786], *CC*, xlv.313-16.
80. Jean-Louis de Tournes to Jean Rousseau, [7 June 1786], *CC*, xlv.319.

believed that the Rousseaus' greed might blind them to the accompanying risks: 'Ces Rousseau me paraissent avoir grande envie d'argent, on pourrait par conséquent traiter avantageusement avec eux. Quand on èvaluerait à douze mille livres la rente à faire à la veuve & qu'on leur doñerait le surplus en billiets de Baret, nous ferions je crois une boñe affaire.'[81]

A week later Samuel de Tournes offered a more realistic alternative to Moultou's proposal by informing Théodore Rousseau of his own willingness to keep paying Thérèse her 1200 *livres* annually. But should he take on this responsibility, de Tournes wrote, a deduction would have to be made to the 24 000 *livres* due the cousins.[82] De Tournes's strategy was predicated upon his doubt whether the Rousseaus had any desire to burden themselves with the remains of the STG's investment. What they simply wanted was their inheritance claim, paid as quickly as possible. Glossing over the STG's financial problems, de Tournes offered to pay Thérèse's pension for ten years or as long as she lived. He asked Moultou to guarantee the Rousseaus 12 000 *livres* – half of the original 24 000. Should the Rousseau cousins agree to deal, at least no one needed to worry about a new lawsuit. De Tournes hoped that Girardin would be satisfied and he believed that Du Peyrou would remain neutral.[83]

At first Théodore Rousseau rejected de Tournes's offer and offered a counterproposal to Moultou. Based upon Moultou's initial scheme, it nevertheless abandoned a pair of crucial terms. The Rousseau cousins would not take over the STG's accounts. Nor were they interested in purchasing the unsold sets of the *Collection complète*. Théodore invited the *amis de Rousseau* to identify the Rousseaus as eventual beneficiaries of the entire 24 000 *livres*, and the cousins would accept responsibility for paying Thérèse her 1200 *livres* per annum. Thus the convention of 21 September 1779 would not have to be rewritten and everyone would be satisfied – everyone except de Tournes and Moultou that is, for they still would be held liable for the Rousseaus' claim to the 24 000 *livres* and would remain responsible for the STG's obligations.[84] Faced with Théodore's refusal to succeed the STG, Moultou dropped his elaborate scheme of drawing the Rousseaus into the defunct publisher's indebtedness. Instead he adopted de Tournes's strategy of trying to get the Rousseaus out of the picture as inexpensively as possible. He suggested that the pair coddle and flatter Girardin, convincing the marquis that an annuity for Thérèse was a small price to pay after all. Meanwhile Moultou and de Tournes agreed to stall for time and try to whittle payment to the cousins to an absolute minimum.[85]

Moultou and de Tournes had no alternative. During the autumn and winter of 1786/87 it became clear that veuve Barret would not make good on her purchase of the remaindered *Collections complètes*. Moultou and de Tournes were

81. Paul-Claude Moultou to Samuel de Tournes, [7 July 1786], *CC*, xlv.324.
82. Samuel de Tournes to Théodore Rousseau, 13 July 1786, *CC*, xlv.329-31.
83. Samuel de Tournes to Paul-Claude Moultou, 15 July 1786, *CC*, xlv.334-35.
84. Théodore Rousseau to Paul-Claude Moultou, 15 July 1786, *CC*, xlv.331-33.
85. Paul-Claude Moultou to Samuel de Tournes, [18 July 1786], *CC*, xlv.338-39.

back where they had started, facing huge losses, while Thérèse adamantly complained of having been cheated of her inheritance.[86] De Tournes tried reviving his plan to offer the Rousseau cousins half of the 24 000 *livres* for the writer's papers, with the remainder reserved as an annuity for Thérèse. Moultou was less pleased with this scheme and angrily stated that the Rousseaus were getting an undeserved gift.[87] Théodore Rousseau, however, still insisted upon the entire 24 000 *livres*. As a matter of fact de Tournes suspected Théodore of plotting to exclude even cousins Jean and 'Rousseau le Persan' from the inheritance. He believed that Théodore's true goal was to pass all 24 000 *livres* on to his son, Jean-François. It was a plausible suspicion. After all, Théodore was close at hand in Geneva, while fellow claimants were far away, one in London and the other in Al-Basra.[88]

After some hesitation Du Peyrou agreed to the recomposition of the convention of 21 September 1779.[89] Girardin's acceptance, however, was another matter. At first the seigneur of Ermenonville did not even answer de Tournes's letters. Finally, on 18 April 1787, the marquis wrote that he was unalterably opposed to rewriting the convention and splitting the inheritance in half. With self-righteous hypocrisy Girardin blustered: 'Je n'ai jamais eu, et ne puis avoir d'autre Intention que celle de La justice qui consiste après La veuve qui jouit actuellement du revenu Sa vie durant, de Conserver Le Capital intact aux heritiers Legitimes auxquels il devra passer Suivant Leur ordre de Proximité.'[90] Three weeks later de Tournes sent Moultou the lamentable news that the 24 000 *livres* set aside had been reduced by more than one-third. It was unclear whether the loss of 9000 *livres* had been due to honest misinvestment or illicit siphoning; nevertheless, it was gone.[91] Then came the worst blow of all. On 10 May Pierre Moultou wrote that his father was gravely ill.[92] Four weeks later Paul-Claude Moultou, whose friendship with Rousseau had outlasted anyone else's save Thérèse's, was dead.

Meanwhile Thérèse's financial difficulties accelerated and she addressed increasingly desperate letters to Boin. On 20 June she wrote to him: 'Il faut toûjours M[r]. que j'aye la main a la plume, Pour vous demander ce qui m'appartient [...] vous avé fait vôtre fortune avec les écrits de déffunt mon mary [...]. Je feré voir les Ecrits qui Sont Bien faits a mon nom, Et non aux tiers que vous me marquée toûjours, Et non aux amis de déffunt mon mary.'[93] Once more Thérèse insisted upon her rights to the 24 000 *livres*, denouncing even a

---

86. Original, in Bally's hand[?] and signed by Thérèse, Marie-Thérèse Levasseur to Pierre Boin, 28 November 1786, *CC*, xlv.346-47. On page 4 of Thérèse's letter de Tournes subsequently noted a reply which he dated 12 January 1787. He also noted payment to Thérèse of 600 *livres*.
87. Paul-Claude Moultou to Samuel de Tournes, [11 March 1787], *CC*, xlv.368-69.
88. Samuel de Tournes to Du Peyrou, 2 February 1787, *CC*, xlv.356-63.
89. Du Peyrou to Samuel de Tournes, 17 February 1787, *CC*, xlv.363-66.
90. Girardin to Samuel de Tournes, 18 April 1787, *CC*, xlv.378-79.
91. Samuel de Tournes to Paul-Claude Moultou, 8 May 1787, *CC*, xlv.380.
92. Pierre Moultou to Samuel de Tournes, [10 May 1787], *CC*, xlv.381.
93. Original, in Bally's hand[?] and signed by Thérèse, Marie-Thérèse Levasseur to Pierre Boin, 20 June 1787, *CC*, xlv.386-87.

guaranteed 1200-*livre* annuity settlement. Falling further into debt, Thérèse borrowed 1100 *livres* from Le Plessis-Belleville's baker-innkeeper and was hauled into the court of Châtelet for non-payment of 2000 *livres* due the village grocer. Her meagre property was seized, and as her self-designated guardian, Girardin was summoned to the Châtelet to testify on her behalf.[94] To prevent worse from befalling Thérèse, Girardin reluctantly assumed responsibility for several of her debts, deducting payments for them from the tiny allowance he had been granting her ever since Rousseau's death.[95]

94. 13 December 1787, *CC*, xlv.389-91; [16 April 1788], *CC*, xlv.393-94; [22 April 1787], *CC*, xlv.395; [May 1788], *CC*, xlv.396-97.
95. [May 1788], *CC*, xlv.396-97; copy, [4 October 1788], *CC*, xlv.405-409; Jean-D.-C. Duval to Girardin, [1 January 1789], *CC*, xlvi.1; Marie-Thérèse Levasseur to Girardin, [18 January 1789], *CC*, xlvi.2-3.

10. Publishing Part II of the *Confessions*

Five years of pamphlets

IN his account of the sources of *rousseauisme*, historian Roger Barny reviews the evolution of three appreciative phases during the writer's lifetime. The first was inspired by the eloquence, stylistic energy and argumentative vigour of the early *Discours* and the *Lettre sur la musique française*; the apparent paradoxes of Rousseau's arguments left interpreters puzzled, however, and he was taken to be a kind of sophistic genius. The second phase, following publication of *La Nouvelle Héloïse* and *Emile*, turned Rousseau into the prophet of moral regeneration, leading his readers along the path of virtue. The condemnations of *Emile* and *Du contrat social*, followed by Rousseau's well-publicised exile at Môtiers, offered the writer an opportunity to test his stoic moral code against the tribulations of a persecuted life. In this he achieved some success, avowing never to have retracted a word and becoming a living martyr for his ideas. Faced with the intolerance of governments and churches alike, Rousseau kept his integrity intact. Unfortunately his triumph proved to be premature, and during the late 1760s the public quarrel with David Hume gave rise to a third phase. Rousseau was accused of duplicity towards Hume, and his role as apostle of virtue was badly tarnished. New polemics and satires attacked him, friends deserted, and in pursuit of self-justification he turned to autobiography.[1]

The present study notes that Rousseau was unable to engineer his vindication during his lifetime. Holding him back was a tentativeness about putting the *Confessions* and his explanatory letters into print. Forces beyond his power inhibited him yet further. He received stern warnings about expressing opinions even orally, as was illustrated by the police response to his public readings from the *Confessions* in 1770 and 1771. No authorised edition of all his works appeared while he lived, and by 1778 the writer had simply handed over published and unpublished manuscripts to followers such as Du Peyrou and Moultou. Seizing the papers Rousseau had brought to Ermenonville, it was Girardin who first determined that the ultimate task of discipleship lay in justifying the life via the *Collection complète*. The purpose of the edition evolved as nothing less than codification of Rousseau's reputation via a 'total' moral autobiography, and Du Peyrou eventually was saddled with major responsibility for that sacred challenge. Unfortunately none of the *amis de Rousseau* was able to foresee the compromises and recriminations that publication of the corpus

---

1. Roger Barny, *Prélude idéologique de la Révolution française. Le rousseauisme avant 1789* (Paris 1985), p.14-16. Barny credits the British literary critic Samuel S. B. Taylor with originating the typology (see Taylor, 'Rousseau's contemporary reputation in France', *SVEC* 27 (1963), p.1545-74.

would entail. Bringing to term the *Collection complète* proved to be far more complicated than the disciples ever had dreamed it would be. By 1789, the year the world changed, the task still remained unfinished. Part II of the *Confessions* and an important body of Rousseau's correspondence composed during his mature years had not yet known the transition from manuscript to the printed page.

Incomplete as the Geneva edition might have seemed to its editors, at its core lay invaluable autobiographical materials. The most significant were Part I of the *Confessions*, the *Rêveries du promeneur solitaire*, *Rousseau juge de Jean-Jacques* and selected correspondence. Yet Moultou, Girardin and Du Peyrou wondered whether Rousseau's revelations, observations and accusations had fulfilled the original moral objective. By withholding Part II of the *Confessions* and additional letters, the *Collection complète*'s editors themselves displayed ambivalence towards Rousseau's strategies of auto-justification. The Geneva edition inspired new attacks by those intent upon exposing further contradictions between the writer's stern moral code and tumultuous life story. For some observers Rousseau's embarrassing self-revelations served as roadblocks to his quest for vindication.

D'Alembert and Diderot had launched their annoying pre-emptive strikes against Rousseau because they feared publication of Part II of the *Confessions*.[2] In defence of her hero, Marie-Anne Alissan de La Tour de Franqueville took the lead in responding to the personal attacks by Rousseau's one-time companions.[3] By the mid-1780s other essayists and pamphleteers had digested the autobiographical sections of the *Collection complète* and were showing how the details therein not merely influenced the evolution of *rousseauisme* but also reflected the very cultural tone of pre-revolutionary France. Among the most important pieces in this vein was one composed by a former counsellor and public prosecutor of the Parlement of Grenoble, Antoine J.-M. Servan. Servan was a judicial liberal very much in the mould of Rousseau's one-time protector, Malesherbes. Inactive in the courtroom after 1772, he nevertheless expended considerable literary energy defending individual privacy, advocating extension of civil liberties and denouncing arbitrary decisions masked as royal justice.[4] In 1784 Servan's *Réflexions sur les 'Confessions'* took up issues

2. D'Alembert, *Eloge de milord maréchal*; Diderot, *Essai sur la vie de Sénèque* and *Essai sur les règnes de Claude et de Néron*.

3. *Jean-Jacques Rousseau vengé par son amie* and *La Vertu vengée par l'amitié*. Du Peyrou published *La Vertu vengée* in the *Supplément* to the *Collection complète*: xv.309-32, in-4°. In all probability Mme de Franqueville was unaware of Louise-Florence d'Epinay's autobiographical novel in manuscript, the *Histoire de Mme de Montbrillant*, modern edition by Georges Roth, 3 vols (Paris 1951), revised with Melchior Grimm's assistance. The work's most unattractive character, René, was a thinly disguised Rousseau.

4. Motivated by Beccaria's *Crimes and punishments* as well as *Du contrat social*, Servan's magnum opus, the *Discours sur l'administration de la justice criminelle* (1767), had called for punishments dispensed according to fixed laws expressing the will of society (see Sarah Maza, *Private lives and public affairs: the 'causes célèbres' of prerevolutionary France*, Berkeley and Los Angeles 1993, p.238). In 1772 his unsuccessful defence of the comte de Suze, who had tried to invalidate payments to

which had deeply interested Rousseau himself: intellectual property rights, the boundaries of press freedom and the question of authorship's moral responsibility.[5]

Servan had become highly sceptical about the beneficial uses of print. The medium, he observed, attributes authoritativeness to the fantasies of writers. What is worse, once etched in print, libellous commentary is irreversible: 'Quand une fois la presse a incorporé l'erreur au papier, en vain on verseroit des larmes de sang pour l'effacer; si vous l'anéantissez dans un exemplaire, elle va revivre en deux mille autres. Elle est eternelle.'[6] In Servan's view, public opinion imparted to Rousseau an extraordinary amount of influence, and the ex-jurist considered Part I of the *Confessions*, the *Rêveries* and Rousseau's letters as revealing damaging prejudices disguised as irrefutable facts. For Servan, Rousseau was master composer of the harmful stereotype.[7]

Servan suspected that whatever still remained in manuscript was even more damaging than the *Confessions*, Part I, and the *Rêveries*. The one-time *avocat-général* therefore asked Rousseau's editors to announce that Part II of the *Confessions* never existed or else had been destroyed. Once this was accomplished, whatever might appear as Rousseau's alleged autobiography would be exposed as false.[8] In Servan's view the strategy of the editors of Part I not to identify those individuals most violently attacked by Rousseau, but rather to label them with their initials, had provided insufficient protection.[9] Public guessing-games over identities were turning the innocent into suspects. Servan believed that whoever would be denounced or satirised in print ought to be forewarned and granted pre-publication censorship privileges; and in the *Réflexions* he notes the public humiliation of those who lacked them.[10] For

an actress-mistress, led to Servan's retirement from the bar and stimulated his career as reformist-pamphleteer. See Goodman, 'Epistolary property', p.339-64.

5. *Réflexions sur les 'Confessions' de J.-J. Rousseau, sur le caractère et le génie de cet écrivain, sur les causes et l'étendue de son influence sur l'opinion publique, enfin sur quelques principes de ses ouvrages, insérées dans le 'Journal encyclopédique' de l'année 1783* (1783). There also were editions ascribed to Lausanne and Hamburg. In her recent article, 'Epistolary property', Dena Goodman applies Jürgen Habermas's public/private sphere theories to her analysis of Servan's practical concerns regarding violations of epistolary property. Critical tastes vary, but I consider Goodman's article to be strained when she forces Servan to accommodate Habermas. On the other hand, when she shows how Servan's arguments connected with the crisis in French royal politics during the 1780s, Goodman is quite convincing. In 1784 Servan published a vigorous attack upon the state practice of mail interception, the *Commentaire sur un passage du livre de M. Necker, ou Eclaircissements demandés à messieurs les commis des postes, préposés à décacheter les lettres.*

6. *Réflexions*, p.5-6.

7. *Réflexions*, p.11-12.

8. *Réflexions*, p.12-13.

9. Of course, Servan was unaware of those sections of Part I which Du Peyrou had omitted altogether – for example, Rousseau's homosexual encounter with the Moor during the writer's conversion exercises at Turin (*OC*, i.66-69).

10. In his 'Mémoire sur la liberté de la presse' (1789), Malesherbes proposed an alternative to this idea. An author who submitted his work to a censor and passed muster ought to be exempt from judicial pursuit. On the other hand, an author who trusted his own self-censorship might be sued by the offended party for seditious libel. See [Malesherbes], *Mémoires sur la librairie; mémoire sur la liberté de la presse*, p.301-26.

example, in the seventh 'Promenade' of the *Rêveries* Rousseau accused the
Grenoble lawyer Gaspard Bovier of having knowingly permitted the writer
to taste noxious berries while the pair were walking in the country. When
another stroller warned Rousseau of his potentially fatal predilection, the
writer questioned Bovier about his silence. Bovier, so Rousseau informs us,
lamely stated deference to the great man as his reason; he was fearful of challenging his celebrated companion in any way. As he related the incident,
Rousseau not only mocked Bovier but also let fly a regional slur, poking fun
at the lawyer's 'humilité Dauphinoise'.[11] Servan maintains that neither Bovier
nor, for that matter, the inhabitants of Dauphiné can now eradicate the
insult.[12]

Clearly Servan believed that Rousseau's description of the Bovier incident
never should have appeared in print. But he finds it paling beside the slanderous portrait of Mme de Warens in Part I of the *Confessions*. Servan considers
Rousseau to have stripped of her honour the mistress of his young manhood.
Though she no longer is alive to suffer humiliation, her relatives and surviving
friends must bear the brunt. By violating tombs, Servan writes, Rousseau
infects the living. Women in Mme de Warens's situation may find themselves
compromised, and Servan cites the example of two acquaintances who fear
being identified as latter-day versions of Rousseau's abandoned mistress.[13]
For Servan, Rousseau's tactics of disclosure are dangerously contagious.
Inspired by the author of the *Confessions*, other would-be autobiographers
may well publish their own wild revelations, labelling them 'repentance' literature. But all that the sensationalist 'tell-all' authors will accomplish is the
demolition of reputations, the staining of morals and injury to their neighbours. For Servan, the *Confessions* are bound to give birth to at least twenty
examples of libellous slander.[14]

Servan next moved from the *Confessions* and the *Rêveries* to that allegedly
artless form of autobiographical revelation in the *Collection complète*: the correspondence selected by Du Peyrou for insertion in the edition. Likening the
publication of letters to an epidemic, Servan wishes to protect their authors
from irresponsible use of private musings. He considers the public's desire to
eavesdrop upon the mail of others as a sick passion; the more monstrous the
epistolary anecdote, the more ravenous the appetite for additional scandal.
Servan regards publication of Rousseau's letters, even with their recipients'
approval, to be a subversion of trust; for, in his view, a private letter must be
the common property of both addressee and author. Publishing it without the
express permission of each party is betrayal. Servan extends his theory of
literary property to posthumous works. He unalterably opposes their publi-

11. *OC*, i.1072-73; Servan, *Réflexions*, p.34-35: 'C'est ainsi que le nom de M. Bovier se trouve
gravé en deux lignes comme sur le marbre & sur l'airain.'
12. Bovier did finally respond, in 1802, with his own recollections of Rousseau. See his *Journal
du séjour à Grenoble de Jean-Jacques Rousseau, sous le nom de Renou*, ed. R. Schlitz (Grenoble 1964).
13. *Réflexions*, p.11-12.
14. *Réflexions*, p.51-55.

cation. For him, printing anything without the express consent of its author is the same as theft, with the public serving as accomplice. Authors must protect themselves and be guaranteed the final word: 'C'est que tout écrit, tant qu'il n'a point été communiqué librement par l'auteur même, doit être aux yeux des autres comme s'il n'étoit pas.'[15]

Servan sensed in France the disappearance of traditional controls which had maintained the kingdom's cultural equilibrium. At one time what he calls 'l'opinion publique' was harnessed by monarchical institutions. Most recently, however, it had broken loose from its moorings. Citing an alleged right to free expression, authors indifferent to commonly held values commit libel; and the *Confessions* are the *exemplum primum* of this abuse of the printed word. Servan appeals to the law to reverse the slide into chaos: 'La liberté de l'imprimerie doit être, le plus qu'il est possible, étendue à l'égard des choses & reserrée à l'égard des personnes.'[16]

In his concluding remarks Servan offers a summary evaluation of Rousseau. Echoing Malesherbes, the jurist considers his subject to have been a very clever writer plagued by evolving dementia. The letter to Hume, Part I of the *Confessions*, the *Rêveries*, and especially the 'Dialogues', betray paranoia. For Servan, Rousseau's moral loftiness was cover for his vanity; inevitably he would reduce to scorn those whose esteem he initially desired. Servan finds that Rousseau would have avoided the Paris Parlement's condemnation of his person had he suppressed his name from the title page of *Emile*. But pride inhibited him from adopting anonymity and it was madness, very definitely not courage, that eventually guided his career. Servan's judgement is harsh, and he asks his readers to contrast Rousseau's reaction to persecution with Fontenelle's or Voltaire's. Enduring as much distress as the Genevan, the Frenchmen maintained authentically stoic visions. Never did they knowingly turn on their benefactors. When all is said and done, Servan finds that posterity will not vindicate Rousseau. It will draw up dossiers against him and his enemies alike. Still, the writer was neither a hypocrite nor a Socrates. He was a man of genius; yet his was a drunken kind of genius, rendering him at once amiable, tender and horrifyingly quarrelsome.[17]

The barrister François Chas vigorously rebutted Servan's evaluation of Rousseau. Like Servan, Chas condemns what he perceives to be a floodtide of libellous writings in France of the 1780s; but he cannot blame Rousseau for having inspired them. The age is decadent, of that there is no doubt. Yet for Chas, what more appropriately symbolised the moral rot of the previous generation than its persecution of the century's most honourable writer? Phony progressives had allied with arbitrary governments to condemn Rousseau. Their alleged provocation was Rousseau's success in persuading readers

15. *Réflexions*, p.72.
16. *Réflexions*, p.83.
17. *Réflexions*, p.85-97.

that he was humanity's legislator. Facing the corruption of his accusers, Rousseau understandably adopted the course of misanthropy.[18]

Chas responds directly to Servan's accusations concerning Rousseau's treatment of the Bovier incident and Mme de Warens's sexual morals. Chas writes that Rousseau's account of Bovier's blind deference was ironic, not malicious. Since Bovier has not complained of literary mistreatment, why should Servan? The case of Mme de Warens is more complicated. Rousseau describes her as having taken on lovers with consummate ease, occasionally several at one time. But Chas refuses to interpret this as the writer's betrayal of the lady's honour. On the contrary, Chas considers the pages devoted to her in Part I of the *Confessions* as respectful to a fault. Mme de Warens was no courtesan. She was, in Rousseau's view, a socially reponsible individual, hoping to change men's character, rendering them both amiable and happy. Unlike current-day *mondaines*, she did not sell her favours. Rather she distributed them liberally.[19]

But Mme de Warens also was a married woman. Did Rousseau sanction adultery? Chas thinks not. By taking men she truly loved, Mme de Warens did not outrage nature.[20] By desiring her loves to be happy she fulfilled Rousseau's feminine ideal, and Chas invokes the women of Paris to take her lead. According to the barrister, Rousseau used broad brush strokes to paint the virtues and weaknesses of Mme de Warens. With a straight face, Chas identifies her as a benefactress of the masculine gender.[21]

Chas concludes by finding the good Servan to be the dupe of Rousseau's enemies: a light that went out too soon. Nearly twenty years earlier, Servan's discourse on criminal justice correctly indicted a corrupt system. Now he seems co-opted by what he once had condemned. How then can Servan, whose literary ambitions have sapped his strength, appreciate Rousseau, 'un homme doux, bienfaisant, pauvre, malade & sans crédit'?[22] Against the allegations of Rousseau's madness, Chas invites readers to return to the corpus, which he interprets with the disciple's myopia. Destroying prejudice and advocating universal justice, *Emile* may one day serve as humanity's moral code. *Du contrat social* envisions *le peuple* as the basis for sovereignty. The *Lettres écrites de la montagne* are models of patriotism. The *Confessions* and the *Rêveries* are infused with sincerity. The 'Dialogues' recall the persecutions. Chas sees no evolving insanity in Rousseau's work, but rather a maturation that concludes with serene resignation. As for the most unforgivable event in Rousseau's life, the abandonment of his children to Paris's Hôpital des enfants trouvés, Chas repeats the oft-cited excuse that Rousseau had little choice. It either was the foundling home or exposure to indigence and corruption. Rousseau's solution was blessedly republican. Ignorant of the circumstances

18. François Chas, *J.-J. Rousseau justifié, ou Réponse à M. Servan, ancien avocat-général au parlement de Grenoble* (1783), p.1-11, 62.
19. *J.-J. Rousseau justifié*, p.44, 75-85.
20. *J.-J. Rousseau justifié*, p.91.
21. *J.-J. Rousseau justifié*, p.86-150.
22. *J.-J. Rousseau justifié*, p.240.

of their birth and learning honourable trades, the children probably have become useful citizens.

Between 1783 and 1789 the debate over *rousseauisme* was largely a dispute over the writer's 'total' autobiography. While enemies pointed out the conflict between Rousseau's moral vision and the bizarre revelations in the *Collection complète*, friends sought ways of reconciling the apparent contradictions. Authors resorted to ingenious narrative methods, such as having a fictional-ised Rousseau address accusers in the first person or else rise from the grave to moralise in dialogue.[23] One pamphlet, the *Discours sur les 'Confessions' de Jean-Jacques Rousseau* (1784), by a jurist from Nîmes, Alexandre Delon, was particularly prescient in identifying the *Confessions* as Rousseau's triumph over himself. Rousseau the writer prevailed over Jean-Jacques the habitual thief, premeditated liar and unfaithful friend. Self-discipline, study and reflec-tion became the signs of his victory. For Delon, therefore, the *Confessions* illus-trate humanisation and growth; by exposing all, Rousseau composes an exemplary moral tale. Furthermore, the *Confessions* allow him to control the transmission of his image to posterity.[24]

The autobiographical explications of *rousseauisme* climaxed in 1788/89. First the young Germaine de Staël published her *Lettres sur les ouvrages et le caractère de J.-J. Rousseau*, accusing Thérèse Levasseur of having provoked the writer's paranoia, and reviving the suicide thesis.[25] Several months later comte Antoine-J. de Barruel-Beauvert's *Vie de J.-J. Rousseau* repeated Mme de Staël's assertions while interspersing commentaries, digressions and anecdotes amidst paraphrases of Part I of the *Confessions* and the *Rêveries du promeneur solitaire*.[26] To be sure, Barruel-Beauvert's 'biography' was really hagiography. Yet the count believed that the limitations of his work stemmed not from his worship of Rousseau but from his inability to obtain all available sources per-taining to his subject's life. He particularly complained about not having access to Part II of the *Confessions* and openly suspected that Du Peyrou had been concealing the manuscript of it for years. Barruel-Beauvert therefore urged Rousseau's chief editor to complete his task and get the entire *Confessions* into print: 'Vous savez combien le public impartial brûle de l'obtenir.'[27] Du Peyrou responded coyly, neither denying nor admitting possession of Part II's manuscript.[28] Frustrated, Barruel-Beauvert inserted his letter and Du Peyrou's reply into his *Vie*, thereby tricking the Neuchâtel disciple into scold-ing him publicly for having released private correspondence.[29]

23. [Claire-Marie Mazarelli, marquise de La Vieuville de Saint-Chamond], *Jean-Jacques à M. S... sur des réflexions contre ses derniers écrits* (1784); [Philippe Desriaux], *L'Ombre de J.-J. Rousseau, comédie en deux actes et en prose, par M. L**** (1787).

24. See *remarque* ii, *CC*, xlv.150-51.

25. (1788; Geneva 1979). See as well George A. Underwood, 'Rousseauism in two early works of Mme de Staël', *Modern philology* 13 (1915), p.417-32.

26. *Vie de J.-J. Rousseau, précédée de quelques lettres relatives au même sujet* (1789).

27. *Vie de J.-J. Rousseau*, p.126-27.

28. Barruel-Beauvert, *Vie de J.-J. Rousseau*, p.130-33.

29. *Mercure* 47 (21 November 1789), p.63-68.

Pierre Moultou's edition of the *Confessions*, Part II

Ever since 1784 Du Peyrou had been aware of the existence of three complete copies of the *Confessions*: Girardin's, Moultou's and his own manuscript transcribed from Moultou's.[30] A few individuals knew about the Moultou and Girardin manuscripts. More common was the suspicion that Du Peyrou, sole identified editor of the *Collection complète*, was harbouring his; and Barruel-Beauvert was not the only one pressuring Rousseau's Neuchâtel disciple to release it. In his introduction to the *Œuvres complètes de J.-J. Rousseau* undertaken in 1788, Louis-Sébastien Mercier claimed to speak for public opinion in demanding the liberation of the remainder of the *Confessions*. Mercier asked rhetorically whether the contemptible fears of a few individuals wishing to veil their iniquities ought to deprive the public of such an instructive work. According to Mercier, most of the false demi-gods exposed by Rousseau were dead anyway; and by rights, the precious document belonged to the entire present generation of readers.[31]

Mercier was taking aim at Du Peyrou, who had long wrestled with the issue of public access to Part II. It would have been tempting for Du Peyrou to sell it to a publisher and thereby salvage something for surviving investors in the disastrous STG undertaking. In 1787 Du Peyrou had certainly considered publishing Part II.[32] Ultimately, however, he concluded that Rousseau's wishes ought to prevail over all other factors. But was it truly possible to honour those wishes? Consider the fate of *Rousseau juge de Jean-Jacques*. Abbé de Condillac had insisted upon the author's desire to keep it out of print until 1801. Yet Brooke Boothby published the 'premier dialogue' anyhow. Then, fearful that an unauthorised editor might release the remainder, the *trois amis* had been persuaded to print the entire *Rousseau juge de Jean-Jacques*, albeit with cuts, labelling it misleadingly 'la seconde Partie des *Mémoires*'.[33]

Du Peyrou did not relish a repetition of the incident over the 'Dialogues', whose publication had injured, not benefited, Rousseau's reputation. Moreover, in the text of Part II which he had copied, Du Peyrou could read Rousseau's own words: 'Mes confessions ne sont point faites pour paroitre de mon vivant ni de celui des personnes interessées. Si j'étois le maitre de ma destinée et de celle de cet écrit il ne verroit le jour que longtems après ma mort et la leur.'[34] Addressing what he believed to be Rousseau's intentions and apprehensive about a possible negative public reaction to Part II, Du Peyrou placed his manuscript under lock and key. But he worried that Girardin might yet print the text seized at Ermenonville.

30. Moultou's copy, in Rousseau's hand, presently is in Geneva's bibliothèque publique et universitaire: ms.fr. 227. Du Peyrou's copy is in Neuchâtel's bibliothèque publique et universitaire: ms. R. 17. Girardin's manuscript is in the library of the French National Assembly, Paris, Palais-Bourbon, Cote 1456-57.
31. *Œuvres complètes de J.-J. Rousseau*, i.23-26.
32. See above, chapter 9, p.201-202.
33. Volume xi of the *Collection complète* in-quarto.
34. *OC*, i.400.

As far as Girardin was concerned, Du Peyrou could rest easily. The marquis's proprietary instincts prevailed over all else, and by 1789 Girardin had no wish to share his manuscript with the world. Ever since 2 July 1778 a pair of relics had become fused with his own being: Rousseau's corpse now in the tomb created on the île des Peupliers and the writer's handwritten autobiography stored in the marquis's study. For Girardin to release either was tantamount to a loss of self, a diminishment of intolerable proportions.

But what of the other *Confessions* manuscript composed in Rousseau's own hand, the one housed in Geneva? Even as he lost a fortune with the *Collection complète*, for several years Paul-Claude Moultou had been unwilling to disobey Rousseau's alleged wishes. In 1787 he seemed to be changing his mind, but his death cut short any collaborative publication of the *Confessions*, Part II, with Du Peyrou. Two years later Du Peyrou was fairly confident that Moultou's son Pierre would respect his father's original stance of silence. Therefore the three known manuscripts appeared to be relatively secure. But were others floating around? Early in June 1789 Du Peyrou's friend Isabelle de Charrière related the rumour that Louis-Sébastien Mercier was about to use his new edition of Rousseau's *Œuvres complètes* as a springboard for Part II of the *Confessions*. According to her, Du Peyrou recently had served as Mercier's host in Neuchâtel. While working in Du Peyrou's study, the French journalist purportedly came across the manuscript of Part II and copied it. Mme de Charrière mentioned that a heartsick Du Peyrou was himself the source of the suspicion. Du Peyrou believed that Mercier's self-righteous introduction to the newly undertaken *Œuvres complètes* was intended as a preface to the stolen continuation of Rousseau's autobiography.[35]

Du Peyrou, however, was mistaken. It was not until 1793 that the volumes of the Mercier–Poinçot edition containing the *Confessions* were published.[36] Furthermore, by that time Part II had become common currency. Its original publication derived from a thoroughly unexpected source. On 6 October 1789 the Neuchâtel bookseller Abram-Louis Fauche received a circular letter from his Genevan colleagues Jean-Paul Barde and Gaspard-Joël Manget. Claiming that they were not the publisher in question, but rather represented him, Barde and Manget broadcast the imminent appearance, in-quarto and in-octavo, of a *Second supplément* to the STG's collected works of Rousseau.[37] A week later, in an announcement sent to the *Journal de Lausanne*, Barde and Manget reported that the supplement would serve as volumes xvi and xvii of the original in-quarto of the *Collection complète*, and as volumes xxxi, xxxii and

---

35. Isabelle de Charrière to Jean-Pierre de Chambrier d'Oleyres, 7 June 1789, in Isabelle de Charrière, *Œuvres complètes*, ed. J.-D. Candaux, C. P. Courtney *et al.* (Amsterdam 1981), iii.140; *CC*, xlvi.38-39.

36. Volumes xxiv-xxvi of the *Œuvres complètes de J.-J. Rousseau*. In 1789 Poinçot would publish Parts I and II of the *Confessions* in individual volumes, based upon the STG and Barde–Manget editions.

37. Circular letter by Jean-Paul Barde and Gaspard-Joël Manget to Abram-Louis Fauche, 6 October 1789, *CC*, xlvi.68-69.

xxxiii of the original in-octavo. An in-duodecimo also was promised. The new volumes were announced as containing the remainder of Rousseau's *Confessions* and a previously unpublished selection of the writer's letters.[38]

In several important respects Barde and Manget were misleading their correspondents. First of all, the edition they had announced was not another's, but their very own. Next, by veiling their responsibility for it, the Genevans were seeking to blend their new volumes into the STG's original set. As best they could, Barde and Manget imitated the paper, format and typography of the *Collection complète* of 1782. They left no trace of their own identity on the title page. In reality no connection whatsoever existed between their so-called *Second supplément* and the original *Collection complète*, and the Barde–Manget announcement took the STG's original editor, Du Peyrou, by surprise. The volumes of the *Second supplément* went on sale immediately. On 22 October 1789 the STN arranged a commercial exchange with Barde and Manget, and nine days later the books were available simultaneously in Geneva and at Claude-François Maradan's shop in Paris's rue Saint-André-des-Arts.[39]

As soon as he learned of the impending appearance of the *Second supplément*, Du Peyrou reacted angrily. In a letter to the *Mercure* he absolved himself of any role in the edition. Conveniently forgetting his own preliminary negotiations with Paul-Claude Moultou back in 1787, cut short by Moultou's death, Du Peyrou maintained that publication of Part II of the *Confessions* represented a clear violation of Rousseau's wishes. The disciple confessed to having seen Part II. He even admitted that he had copied it, though with the consent of the manuscript's owner, 'M*** de Genève, que la mort nous a trop tôt enlevé'. Du Peyrou insisted, however, that his copy was intended exclusively for his private study. Never had he intended to print it. Du Peyrou then noted the existence of the third manuscript of the *Confessions*, 'trouvé, à la mort de l'Auteur, dans son Bureau, enveloppé & cacheté'. According to Du Peyrou, with the connivance of Thérèse, 'M. le marquis de G***' had seized the package containing the manuscript, then tore it open and hid its contents from the other *amis de Rousseau*. Du Peyrou also took Mercier to task for rearranging Rousseau's writings in Poinçot's new edition of *Œuvres complètes*, and he lashed out at Barruel-Beauvert for perpetuating the myth of Rousseau's suicide. But the core of his anger was preserved for Girardin. Rousseau's

---

38. Barde and Manget to the *Journal de Lausanne*, 14 October 1789, published in the *Journal de Lausanne* 42 (17 October 1789), p.174; *CC*, xlvi.73. The announced price of the in-quarto volumes was 20 *livres*, the in-octavo volumes were to be sold for 12 *livres*, and the 'grand in-12' for 7 *livres*, 10 *sols*. By the time Barde and Manget inserted their announcement in the *Mercure* (21 November 1789), they had reduced the price of the in-octavo to 10 *livres* and the 'grand in-12' to 6 *livres*. They also were preparing volumes to be incorporated into the Kehl and Cazin editions. A large-print, four-volume, in-octavo edition of the *Confessions*, Parts I and II, was also being prepared. It was priced at 15 *livres*. Part II alone was available in two volumes for 8 *livres*.

39. STN to Barde, Manget & Company, [22 October 1789], *CC*, xlvi.75; *notes explicatives* a[5] and a[8], *CC*, xlvi.70-71.

most faithful disciple suspected incorrectly that the marquis had shredded his last scrap of honour by publishing Part II of the *Confessions*.[40]

Once the *Second supplément* appeared and he had time to peruse it, Du Peyrou shifted his suspicion. He noted that the newly published volumes contained not only Part II of the *Confessions* but also copies of Rousseau's correspondence which Du Peyrou himself previously had loaned to Moultou for the *Collection complète*. The letters had not been used in the STG's edition and it was unlikely that Girardin had gained access to them. Therefore, a new potential culprit emerged: Moultou's son Pierre, who possessed manuscripts of both the *Confessions* and the letters. On 11 November 1789 Du Peyrou icily wrote to Pierre Moultou, requesting return of the Rousseau correspondence which he had loaned to Pierre's father.[41] Du Peyrou then directed another notice to the *Mercure*, denying complicity in the publication of the letters.[42] In a postscript (which the *Mercure* never printed) Du Peyrou noted that he had just begun comparing the Barde–Manget edition with his own manuscript of the *Confessions*, Part II. He did not like what he had found: 'je suis pourtant déjà obligé de changer de langage, & de déclarer qu'il y a plus que des inexactitudes dans cette édition; qu'on s'y est permis, non seulement de corriger le style de Rousseau, ce qui n'est que ridicule; mais encore de supprimer certains passages, & même d'en falsifier d'autres, ce qui est plus que ridicule.' Du Peyrou concluded that such infidelities left him no other recourse than to return to his long-abandoned editing chores. He intended to re-establish Rousseau's text faithfully and publish it in a rival edition. Indeed, to oversee manufacture he already had engaged the Neuchâtel firm directed by Louis Fauche-Borel.[43]

Du Peyrou's edition of the *Confessions*, Part II

As early as 17 November 1789 Du Peyrou had decided upon his edition, and his dear friend Isabelle de Charrière would assist him.[44] Angered by Du Peyrou's allegations in the *Mercure* and fearful that readers would prefer the ripe fruit of Rousseau's old editor to their hastily plucked sample, Barde and Manget addressed a defensive protest to the Neuchâtel disciple. They denied knowledge of Rousseau's alleged intention to delay publication of Part II of the *Confessions* until the new century and they insisted that they had purchased

40. Du Peyrou to the *Mercure*, [27 October 1789], published in the *Mercure* 47 (21 November 1789), p.63-68, *CC*, xlvi.76-79.
41. Leigh believes that the letters published by Pierre Moultou were not identical with those that Du Peyrou had loaned to Paul-Claude (see *note explicative* a, *CC*, lxvi.86).
42. Du Peyrou to the *Mercure*, 19 November 1789, published in the *Mercure* (5 December 1789), p.16-17, *CC*, xlvi.89-90.
43. *Note explicative* c, *CC*, xlvi.90-91. Du Peyrou's comments would appear in Fauche-Borel's prospectus announcing the edition.
44. On the relations between Du Peyrou and Isabelle de Charrière see Philippe Gobet, 'Madame de Charrière et Jean-Jacques Rousseau', *Annales de la Société Jean-Jacques Rousseau* 1 (1905), p.67-93; Raymond Trousson, 'Isabelle de Charrière et Jean-Jacques Rousseau', *Bulletin de l'Académie royale de langue et littérature françaises* 63 (1985), p.5-57.

the manuscript in good faith. They virtually admitted to being its publishers. Yet at the same time they refused to divulge the name of the manuscript's owner and demanded that Du Peyrou issue a public apology for his previous assertions and accusations.[45] Du Peyrou replied condescendingly that his complaints were not directed at Barde and Manget. In his opinion the Genevans were merely pursuing a promising business opportunity. His grievance was with the supplier of their manuscript, the source of an edition which was 'tronquée & même falsifiée dans quelques passages'. Du Peyrou concluded wrongly: 'Vous n'avés imprimé que sur une Copie & une Copie fautive.'[46]

Even with its suppressions and emendations, the Barde–Manget edition poorly served Rousseau's contemporary reputation. A lengthy review in the *Mercure* cheered the moral vision which had given birth to *Emile, La Nouvelle Héloïse* and *Du contrat social*. On the other hand, the reviewer beheld in the *Confessions* a storehouse of vindictiveness provoked by Rousseau's persecutions. For the *Mercure* the memoirs merely 'donnent la clef des bizarreries de son caractère, de sa mélancolie, & de son amour pour la retraite'.[47] For its part, the *Journal de Paris* appreciated Rousseau's description of his love for Mme de [Houdetot]: 'comparable aux lettres les plus brûlantes de la nouvelle Héloïse'. But the journalist also found in the *Confessions* confirmation of Rousseau's late-life instability: 'On avoit pardonné à *Pascal* de voir un précipice toujours ouvert à ses côtés; on ne pardonne pas à *Jean-Jacques* de croire l'univers entier conjuré contre lui.'[48]

An anonymous letter, perhaps written by Gabriel Cramer, urged Du Peyrou not to become mired in another edition of 'ces maudites Confessions qui n'auroient jamais dû voir le jour'. The correspondent urged Du Peyrou to forsake his unabridged edition, which would contain 'les lâches et grossieres insultes dans toute leur integrité [...]. Ce trafic, ou le Soupçon même de ce trafic est indigne de vous, et je vous conjure d'y renoncer, car je prévois que Sans dèfiance à cet égard comme les gens de vôtre trempe le Sont toujours, vous Serez accablé dans cette lutte, où je ne vois rien à gagner pour vous.'[49]

But Du Peyrou failed to heed the advice. He pushed on with his edition, contributing to a prospectus that further infuriated Barde and Manget.[50] The Genevans responded with an announcement published in both the *Journal de Lausanne* and *Mercure*, declaring the legitimacy of their edition. It certainly was not based upon a faulty copy, they wrote, but rather upon 'le *manuscrit original de la main même de Rousseau*'. By way of contrast, Barde and Manget declared, Du Peyrou's anticipated edition was a piracy

45. Jean-Paul Barde and Gaspard-Joël Manget to Du Peyrou, [28 November 1789], *CC*, xlvi.92-93.
46. Du Peyrou to Jean-Paul Barde and Gaspard-Joël Manget, 2 December 1789, in [Du Peyrou], *Pièces relatives à la publication de la suite des 'Confessions' de J.-J. Rousseau* (1790), p.5-6; *CC*, xlvi.104-105.
47. *Mercure* (28 November 1789), p.78-88.
48. *Journal de Paris* (29 November 1789), *Supplément* to no. 333, p.1552-54.
49. G[abriel] C[ramer](?) to Du Peyrou, 4 December 1789, *CC*, xlvi.106-107.
50. Barde and Manget to Du Peyrou, [5 December 1789], *CC*, xlvi.110-11.

('contrefaçon'), copied from the original. Finally the Genevans promised purchasers of their *Confessions* an appendix of all the materials which they had excised for reasons of delicacy.[51]

Having remained silent up to this point Pierre Moultou now joined the offensive of Barde and Manget. In an unsigned letter to Du Peyrou he justified his right to publish Part II of the *Confessions*. Pierre wrote that Rousseau had named Paul-Claude Moultou as executor of the writer's posthumous works, and he was his father's legitimate heir. Pierre added that he had been present when Rousseau gave the entire *Confessions* manuscript to 'Mr. M*'. Furthermore, he insisted that the author had issued no orders about withholding Part II from publication. Next, Pierre attacked Du Peyrou where he knew it would hurt worst. He indicated that the Neuchâtel millionaire had lacked Rousseau's trust and cited Rousseau's lukewarm opinion of Du Peyrou in Part II (Book xii) of the *Confessions*.[52]

This last observation was particularly painful, for it must have reminded Du Peyrou of the incident at Trye in 1767 and his delirious accusation of attempted murder on Rousseau's part. But Pierre did not stop there. He accused Du Peyrou of wishing to make a large profit by publishing Part II in unexpurgated form: 'empruntant le masque de la vérité, & trahissant la confiance d'un ami, [il] veut immoler sur la tombe de Rousseau une foule de victimes'.[53] Of course this allegation smacked of hypocrisy. Du Peyrou's desire to offer Rousseau's autobiography in all of its integrity was based upon a sense of moral obligation, and the Neuchâtel disciple refused to accept a *sou* from Fauche-Borel. By way of contrast, Pierre Moultou played censor to Rousseau because he had no wish to see celebrities embarrassed. Furthermore, he had sold his manuscript to Barde and Manget for a considerable sum.

While Du Peyrou prepared both Part II of the *Confessions* and a set of correspondence, Pierre Moultou pursued ways of protecting his own edition. He admitted to François Coindet, one-time Geneva disciple of Rousseau, that he was behind the Barde–Manget volumes. Then he falsely claimed to have published them hurriedly because he wanted to head off Du Peyrou's slanderous edition. In this manner Pierre ostentatiously assumed the role of protector of reputations, particularly those of Coindet, Mme d'Epinay and Grimm. He supplied Coindet with a copy of his accusatory letter to Du Peyrou and

51. 'Déclaration finale du libraire de Genève', [5 December 1789], *Journal de Lausanne* 50 (12 December 1789), p.204-205; *Mercure* (26 December 1789), p.152-53; *CC*, xlvi.112-13. Censorship authorities in Geneva ensured that the appendix never appeared.

52. *OC*, i.602-603.

53. [Pierre Moultou] to Du Peyrou, [*c.* 6 December 1789], published by Barde and Manget in their *Pièces relatives à la publication de la suite des 'Confessions' de J.-J. Rousseau*, p.9-12; *CC*, xlvi.118. See as well *note explicative* e, *CC*, xlvi.119. During the early nineteenth century Pierre Moultou separated pieces of Rousseau's manuscripts in his possession and placed them on the market with attestations of authenticity. By way of contrast, Du Peyrou willed all the Rousseau manuscripts in his possession to the newly established public library of Neuchâtel.

urged him to place it in the *Mercure*.[54] Coindet, however, was unwilling or unable to do this.[55]

While Barde and Manget justified their edition in a collection of *Pièces relatives a la publication de la suite des 'Confessions' de J.-J. Rousseau*, the *Journal de Lausanne* printed Du Peyrou's reasons for preparing his own. He noted that Rousseau always had insisted upon the integrity of his published work and could not abide having it tampered with. Recognising that an unexpurgated *Confessions*, Part II, would have embarrassed individuals during their lifetimes, Rousseau had made it clear that the story of his mature years should await publication until after the deaths of those mentioned in it. Du Peyrou claimed that both he and Paul-Claude Moultou had honoured Rousseau's wishes. But the appearance of the corrupted Barde–Manget edition was contrary to the will of its author and those he had selected to preserve his manuscripts. The misnamed *Second supplément* was motivated by nothing more than a desire for profits. Because a fraudulent text presently was masquerading as the legitimate edition, Du Peyrou believed that he had to disobey one of Rousseau's wishes in order to honour the other. The pledge to maintain silence no longer held, and the authorised Part II of the *Confessions* would appear shortly. Du Peyrou vowed that he was not selling the manuscript, but rather offering it gratis to its publisher.[56]

In preparing the *Confessions*, Part II, Du Peyrou had to confront some unique editorial problems. What particularly angered him was Pierre Moultou's faithlessness regarding Rousseau's authorial intent. For Du Peyrou an omitted adjective or dropped name now smacked of treachery, and he interpreted his own role as a mission to recover the purity of Rousseau's text. On the other hand, critical readers of the Barde–Manget edition did not necessarily notice Pierre Moultou's omissions; and even the replacement of proper names with initials was tolerated as a gesture respecting an offended subject's sensibilities. What customarily dismayed readers were Rousseau's crude and seemingly irresponsible attacks upon his contemporaries – in other words, those precise words and phrases that Du Peyrou felt obliged to restore.[57]

54. Pierre Moultou to François Coindet, [7 December 1789], *CC*, xlvi.119-20.

55. Once he would read in the Fauche-Borel edition remarks about him by Rousseau that Pierre Moultou had suppressed and Du Peyrou let stand, Coindet may have regretted his lack of co-operation. Rousseau had written: 'J'avois un jeune Génevois appellé Coindet, bon garçon ce me sembloit, soigneux, officieux, zélé, mais ignorant, confiant, gourmand, avantageux' (*OC*, i.506). Rousseau's mention of Coindet as 'hardi' slipped into the Barde–Manget edition. For this Moultou apologised profusely, blaming the insertion upon the stupidity of a shop foreman (see *CC*, xlvi.120).

56. [14 December 1789], published in the *Journal de Lausanne* 52 (26 December 1789), p.212-13, *CC*, xlvi.133-34.

57. For example, on 2 December the *Journal de Paris* printed a defence of the late baron d'Holbach by J.-A.-J. Cérutti, who interpreted the attack upon Holbach by Rousseau in the *Confessions* 'd'une manière d'autant plus cruelle qu'elle semble plus naive & plus simple' (*Journal de Paris* 336, *Supplément* (2 December 1789), p.1567-68; Jean-Antoine-Joachim Cérutti to the *Journal de Paris*, [late November 1789], *CC*, xlvi.99-101).

Not even the Barde–Manget volumes, however, could escape offending readers. The Genevan pastor Jacob Vernes was first to complain. Vernes's frustration with Rousseau went back a quarter-century. In 1764 a scurrilous pamphlet attacking Rousseau's patriotism and religious beliefs had appeared in Geneva under the title *Sentiment des citoyens*. Rousseau was certain that Vernes had composed the pamphlet, even after the pastor's public denial of authorship. Indications should have pointed Rousseau to Voltaire as the genuine author, but Rousseau insisted upon repeating his accusation of Vernes in Part II, Book xii, of the *Confessions*.[58] Pierre Moultou retained the charge in his edition, though he cleverly hid Vernes's name behind the initial 'V'. The pastor was genuinely shaken at seeing Rousseau's accusation resurface, and he wished to clear up the matter. Aware that Du Peyrou was preparing his edition, Vernes requested that a note be affixed to the offending passage, retracting 'l'odieuse imputation qu'il m'a faite de l'infame libelle'. Vernes also asked Du Peyrou for permission to read a memoir by Rousseau explaining why the writer had suspected him of authoring the *Sentiment* in the first place.[59] Du Peyrou had intended to insert this memoir in his edition.

How could Du Peyrou satisfy poor Vernes while remaining true to the purpose of his 'total' moral autobiography? Sensitive to Vernes's plight, François d'Ivernois, the sometime partner in the STG, proposed a bizarre solution. For Du Peyrou's benefit he imagined a scene whereby a resuscitated Rousseau discovered the injustice of his original accusation. Recognising that Part II of the *Confessions* could not be tampered with, d'Ivernois's Rousseau would recommend that Du Peyrou insert a corrective note clearing Vernes of responsibility for the *Sentiment*. As for the essay which Rousseau had prepared to justify his incorrect accusation, according to d'Ivernois, the apostle of Virtue and Truth would have cried out: 'Brulez Brulez cet odieux mémoire.'[60] Unfortunately, for Du Peyrou to destroy Rousseau's text, even a wrongheaded one, was inconceivable. It meant eliminating a piece of his subject's life story. The indefatigable editor insisted upon publishing the memoir. But he did offer some satisfaction to the aggrieved Vernes. First, Du Peyrou added his own note citing incontrovertible evidence of Voltaire's authorship of the *Sentiment*. Next, Du Peyrou awarded Vernes space in his edition to respond directly to Rousseau. The pastor took full advantage of the opportunity, composing 134 corrective notes.[61]

During the first four months of 1790 Isabelle de Charrière and Du Peyrou collaborated upon their edition of the *Confessions*, Part II. They also sifted

58. *OC*, i.634: 'Je reste intérieurement persuadé, convaincu, comme de ma propre existence, qu'il [Vernes] est l'auteur du libelle.'
59. Jacob Vernes to Du Peyrou, [16 December 1789], *CC*, xlvi.137-38.
60. François d'Ivernois to Du Peyrou, 13 December 1789, *CC*, xlvi.129.
61. 'Declaration de J. J. Rousseau, relative à M. le Pasteur Vernes, Accompagnée des notes responsives fournies par ce dernier', *Seconde partie des Confessions de J. J. Rousseau, Citoyen de Genève* (Neuchâtel 1790), v.5-85 [*Suite de la Collection des Œuvres de J. J. Rousseau, Citoyen de Genève*, xxvii.5-85].

through the correspondence, both previously published and unpublished, to complement the *Confessions* and document that exemplary life. Their selection of letters would be purposeful, thereby differing from Pierre Moultou's hodge-podge. Mme de Charrière went yet further. In January she wrote a detailed pamphlet, the *Eclaircissements relatifs à la publication des 'Confessions' de Rousseau*, noting both the author's request that Part II not appear until the new century and Du Peyrou's heretofore loyal compliance with his wishes. According to Mme de Charrière, when he had learned of the impending publication of the continuation of the *Confessions* in October 1789, Du Peyrou was profoundly shocked. But, she added, the faithful disciple ought not have been so surprised, for during the past six months a sea change in public discourse had occurred in French-speaking Europe. As the censorship institutions of the *ancien régime* crumbled, the quest for *sincérité* – that is, transparency or openness – had overwhelmed traditions of secrecy and deception in the entire communi-cations network: 'Mais en 1789 on est en possession d'être sincere pour les grands princes, pour les ministres les plus estimés, & *de leur vivant*, & *avec le public*. Cette *possession* ne semble-t-elle pas donner *le droit* d'être sincere avec tout le monde? Tant de voiles ont été arrachés qu'on ne sent plus qu'il en faille respecter aucun.'[62]

According to Mme de Charrière, therefore, the public's passion for candour and exposure surely led one to expect a long-suppressed manuscript of Rous-seau's to see light of day. Nevertheless, in his rush not to offend useful or socially prominent persons, Pierre Moultou had but partially dropped the veil, and behind his manipulation of the new freedom lay acute economic motives. Mme de Charrière accused Moultou of having asked a very high price for his manuscript. Since selective editing and the profit motive stained Moultou's *Confessions*, Mme de Charrière urged the young editor to make amends. She proposed two solutions. First Moultou should apologise to Du Peyrou; next he should return the money he had received from Barde and Manget.[63]

Moultou did neither, and after 7 January 1790 all communication between him and Du Peyrou ceased.[64] Du Peyrou and Isabelle de Charrière diligently prepared their edition. Rousseau's dedicated disciple wrote a 'Discours préli-minaire' for it, re-establishing his role as trustee of the Master's manuscripts and ever faithful executor of Rousseau's publishing strategies. Du Peyrou con-trasted his activity with that of Pierre Moultou and did not mask his lifelong contempt for Thérèse Levasseur.[65] Mme de Charrière listed a sample of the

---

62. *Eclaircissements relatifs à la publication des 'Confessions' de Rousseau*, in Charrière, *Œuvres com-plètes*, x.189.

63. *Eclaircissements relatifs à la publication des 'Confessions' de Rousseau*, p.191-93.

64. Du Peyrou to Pierre Moultou, [7 January 1790], *CC*, xlvi.165. The last letter contained the Neuchâtel editor's formal notice that he was sending Pierre a portrait of Rousseau that had belonged to Paul-Claude Moultou.

65. *Seconde partie des Confessions*, iii.i-xxiii [*Suite de la Collection des Œuvres de J. J. Rousseau, Citoyen de Genève*, xxv.i-xxiii].

errors made and liberties taken by Pierre Moultou, Barde and Manget for the Geneva edition of the *Confessions*.[66] In the name of Fauche-Borel she also appended a note of appreciation to Du Peyrou.[67]

On 12 June 1790 the *Gazette de Berne* announced publication of the *Seconde partie des Confessions de J.-J. Rousseau, citoyen de Genève, édition enrichie d'un nouveau recueil de ses lettres*. Du Peyrou's edition appeared in five volumes, beginning with volume iii and concluding with volume vii, so as to emphasise continuity with the two volumes that had contained the STG's *Confessions*, Part I, back in 1782. Purchasers had the choice of an in-octavo or in-duodecimo. Taking advantage of its wide-ranging commercial contacts, the STN distributed Fauche-Borel's books throughout Switzerland and France. On 25 June the *Moniteur* published a brief review, finding Du Peyrou's editing to be superior to anything else in existence. Apart from their excellent typography and apparent fidelity to Rousseau's intent, the volumes were praised for containing supplementary texts and previously unpublished letters, which, according to the *Moniteur*, enriched the reader's comprehension of the *Confessions* themselves.[68] On 29 June the *Journal de Paris* favourably contrasted the Neuchâtel edition with that of Geneva; on 23 August the *Moniteur* did the same.[69] By this time Fauche-Borel had published his edition in as many additional combinations as was possible: as a 'continuation' of the STG's *Collection complète* in-octavo and in-duodecimo, excluding the first *Supplément* (volumes xxv to xxix); as a continuation of the separate 'large character' edition of the *Confessions*, Part I; and even as complements to the piracies made by Beaumarchais in Kehl and Cazin in Reims. Recalling the failure of the STG's in-quarto, Fauche-Borel rejected that costly format.

Augmented by the selection of correspondence and marketed in various ways, the Du Peyrou–de Charrière *Seconde partie des Confessions* enjoyed a successful sales run. The new editorial team was not inhibited from republishing previously printed letters written by Rousseau. Nor did Du Peyrou and Mme de Charrière feel a need to censor. The 367 letters they published illuminated five periods in Rousseau's life and underscored his psychological state in each of them: (1) the years spent pursuing his vocation and the initial triumphs; (2) the emotional uproar of the *Nouvelle Héloïse*–l'Ermitage period; (3) the incredibly creative time at Montmorency, marking the composition and publication of *Emile* and *Du contrat social*; (4) the years at Môtiers, incorporating the formation of disciples and involvement with Genevan politics; (5) the anguished period in England, when Rousseau grew frantic over alleged conspiracies and composed the *Confessions*; (6) and finally the declining years back in France, punctuated by Rousseau's failure to supervise an authorised general edition of his corpus.

66. She cited ten specific examples of editorial mishandling (see Charrière, *Œuvres complètes*, x.179-80).
67. Charrière, *Œuvres complètes*, x.181.
68. *Moniteur* 176 (25 June 1790): *Réimpression*, iv.707.
69. *Journal de Paris* 180 (29 June 1790), p.729; *Moniteur* 5 (23 August 1790): *Réimpression*, v.458.

The letters published by Du Peyrou and Mme de Charrière formed a complementary narrative to Part II of the *Confessions* and announced that the great edition had been completed. The 'total' moral autobiography was finished. Yet at the very moment the *Seconde partie des Confessions* was being published, the ground rules for Rousseau's mission were shifting. By 1790 the exemplary life in print no longer was sole source of the message. Another Rousseau was emerging. Pamphlets appeared portraying him as the prophet of a regenerated France. Autobiography (the story of private virtue) was transmuting into political theory (the need for public virtue), and *Du contrat social* eventually would replace the *Confessions* as the Master's dominant text.[70] Assuredly Part II of the *Confessions* had prepared the way for the transformation. As Carol Blum puts it, 'The publication [of Part II] seemed to have accentuated feelings of empathy with Rousseau as a "man of virtue" who had reordered the system of values in France somehow through his own person.'[71] Nevertheless, as politics radicalised, the *ancien régime*'s most celebrated literary martyr metamorphosed into father of the Revolution.[72]

70. James Bennett Swenson's recent book *On Jean-Jacques Rousseau considered as one of the first authors of the Revolution* (Stanford 2001) discusses the emergence of *Du contrat social* as Rousseau's primary text after 1789. According to Swenson, the literary or sentimental writings (primarily *La Nouvelle Héloïse* and *Emile*) formed a unity prior to the French Revolution; after the convocation of the Estates General, 'the already established familiarity with Rousseau the sentimental novelist and theorist of education [...] must have provided a strong motivation for many deputies to turn to the same author's treatise on politics' (p.192-93). Hereafter divergent political groups laid claim to *Du contrat social*, and their readings (or misreadings) of the text regarding representative centralism and direct democracy thereby assured its revolutionary influence. For an elaboration of the manner in which the cult of Rousseau's virtue was manipulated by radical Jacobins, particularly Robespierre and Saint-Just after 1791, see Blum, *Rousseau and the republic of virtue*.
71. *Rousseau and the republic of virtue*, p.144.
72. See, for example, François-Jean-Philibert Aubert de Vitry's *Jean-Jacques Rousseau à l'Assemblée nationale* (1789); G.-F. Berthier's *Observations sur le Contrat social de J.-J. Rousseau* (1789); Achille Isnard's *Observations sur le principe qui a produit les révolutions de France, de Genève et d'Amérique dans le dix-huitième siècle* (1789) and the anonymous *Jean-Jacques, ou Le réveil-matin des représentants de la nation française* (1789). A detailed account of the incarnations of Rousseau in the Revolution is beyond the scope of this study. There is no shortage of interpretations. Half a century ago, for example, Gordon McNeil discussed how the political winds of the Revolution affected the writer's fortunes in 'The cult of Rousseau and the French Revolution', *Journal of the history of ideas* 6 (1945), p.197-212. Joan McDonald's *Rousseau and the French Revolution* (London 1965) was unabashedly revisionist, discovering in the Revolution the continuity of the Rousseau moral myth at the expense of genuine political ideas, at least up to 1791. Most recently Roger Barny has buried readers in an avalanche of Marxist erudition deriving from his five-volume *thèse de doctorat*. Sections have been published as *Rousseau dans la Révolution. Le personnage de Jean-Jacques et les débuts du culte révolutionnaire (1789-1791)*, *SVEC* 246 (1986), and *L'Eclatement révolutionnaire du rousseauisme* (Paris 1988).

11. From print to the Panthéon

Thérèse's revenge

WHILE the French Revolution redefined Rousseau as a harbinger of political regeneration, it reconstituted Thérèse Levasseur as an icon of the people. Considered by supporters and enemies alike as a mischievous shrew responsible for the great man's emotional turmoil, she had traditionally played a negative role in Rousseau's story.[1] Early in 1789 Barruel-Beauvert called Thérèse a vicious peasant and snake in the grass.[2] Germaine de Staël had gone yet further, reviving the perverted mother theme and asserting that Thérèse's sexual passion for the servant John Bally had driven Rousseau to suicide.[3] Though Girardin and Moultou's son Pierre challenged Mme de Staël's thesis, neither had any interest in rehabilitating Thérèse.[4] They continued to be served by the image of a villainous Xantippe. By the end of the year, however, Thérèse found a defender in Du Peyrou's collaborator and Mme de Staël's literary rival, Isabelle de Charrière.[5]

Composed as a first-person confession, Mme de Charrière's *Plainte et défense de Thérèse Levasseur* anticipated the remarkable transformation of Rousseau's servant-companion during the French Revolution. In the *Plainte et défense* Thérèse speaks with authority. She recognises that the class prejudices of Barruel-Beauvert and Mme de Staël make it impossible for them to comprehend Rousseau's egalitarian social vision. Mme de Charrière accuses romantic aristocrats of wanting Jean-Jacques's companion to have been 'une héroïne, un grand esprit, une belle ame, à la maniere de celles qu'on fabrique dans les livres'. Rousseau, however, had accepted Thérèse as she was, and so she had remained: 'une pauvre fille qui ne savoit ni lire, ni écrire, ni voir l'heure sur un cadran'.[6] Eternal victim, Thérèse had borne chains in Rousseau's name while he lived. Now that he was dead she suffered from the persecution of his disciples.

---

1. For a brief summary of the literary hostility towards Thérèse from Voltaire to Mme de Staël see Raymond Trousson's article, 'Isabelle de Charrière et Jean-Jacques Rousseau', p.1, 17-18.

2. *Vie de J.-J. Rousseau*, p.115-16.

3. *Lettres sur les ouvrages et le caractère de J.-J. Rousseau*, p.98, 117.

4. Sophie de Girardin, comtesse de Vassy, to Anne-L.-G. Necker, baronne de Staël-Holstein, [March 1789], *CC*, lxvi.16-17; draft, Pierre Moultou to baronne de Staël-Holstein, [late March/early April 1789], *CC*, lxvi.26-27.

5. The most recent studies of this fascinating Dutch-born novelist and feminist, who would pass half her life in the neighbourhood of Neuchâtel, are C. P. Courtney, *Isabelle de Charrière (Belle de Zuylen): a biography* (Oxford 1993) and Raymond Trousson, *Isabelle de Charrière* (Paris 1994). Her *Œuvres complètes*, noted above, have been published in 10 volumes.

6. *Plainte et défense de Thérèse Levasseur*, in Charrière, *Œuvres complètes*, x.173.

Mme de Charrière notes the absurdity of the suicide thesis. Rousseau never would have considered Thérèse's alleged affair with John Bally, 'un homme de la plus basse classe', as sufficient reason for taking his own life. Du Peyrou's friend and collaborator asks Germaine de Staël: is it customary for a sixty-six-year-old philosopher to be so consumed with jealousy that he would kill himself? She concludes by having Thérèse observe that snobbery deprives the baroness of genuine discipleship and comprehension: 'Selon vous, [Rousseau] se seroit donc mieux consolé si j'eusse aimé un prince. Lui! Jean-Jacques! Allez, madame, vous ne l'avez pas lu, si vous ignorez combien non-seulement les classes lui étoient indifférentes.' The *Plainte et défense* sardonically observes that Mme de Staël has plenty to learn from the semi-literate ex-laundress. But hope is not lost. Thérèse informs the precocious aristocrat: 'Vous êtes jeune, madame; votre esprit peut mûrir, vous pouvez vous défaire de préjugés qui aussi bien ne sont plus à la mode; vous pouvez devenir à la fois plus raisonnable & meilleure.'[7]

Du Peyrou assisted Isabelle de Charrière in publishing her pamphlet. In May 1790, however, she complained to Benjamin Constant that the *Plainte et défense* no longer could be found in Paris, and she wondered whether Mme de Staël's supporters had been seizing copies for consignment to the flames.[8] Notwithstanding Mme de Charrière's pessimism, rehabilitation of Rousseau's widow was striking a chord in revolutionary France. Upon the recommendation of a new advocate for Thérèse, the process-server Antoine-Claude Chariot, on 20 September the Théâtre de la nation (formerly the Comédie-Française) announced an upcoming performance of Corneille's *Le Cid* and Rousseau's *Pygmalion*, the proceeds of which would be given to 'Mme la veuve de Jean Jacques *Rousseau*'.[9] Recalling that back in 1775 Rousseau had not formally approved the Comédie-Française's presentation of *Pygmalion*, but rather had yielded the half-hour *scène lyrique* to the actors, Thérèse first hesitated about accepting the honorarium.[10] But she quickly reconsidered. Once *Pygmalion* was revived successfully, she benefited from the opening night gate receipts of 6048 *livres*.[11]

It was logical for 'progressive' aristocratic disciples like Girardin, Barruel-Beauvert and Germaine de Staël to retain the traditional image of Rousseau the anguished romantic, victimised by institutions like the Parlement of Paris, cliques like the encyclopedists and unfaithful companions like Thérèse.

7. Charrière, *Plainte et défense de Thérèse Levasseur*, p.174-75.
8. Isabelle de Charrière to Benjamin Constant, 29 May [1790], *CC*, xlvi.230-31.
9. Antoine-Claude Chariot to the administrators of the Théâtre de la nation, [11 July 1790], *CC*, xlvi.230-31. See as well *note explicative* a, *CC*, xlvi.245. After several delays the performance took place on 9 October 1790.
10. Marie-Thérèse Levasseur to the administrators of the Théâtre de la nation, 20 September 1790, *CC*, xlvi.244-46; first inserted in the *Journal de Paris, Supplément* (7 October 1790), between p.1142 and 1143. Leigh discusses the controversy surrounding the original performance of 30 October 1775 in *remarque* i, *CC*, xl.28-31.
11. Marie-Thérèse Levasseur to the administrators of the Théâtre de la nation, [11 October 1790], *CC*, xlvi.255-56.

Significantly enough, while converting Rousseau into the virile prophet of political revolution, a more radical segment of opinion than the liberal *noblesse* also had little use for Thérèse. For example, the widely read newspaper, the *Révolutions de Paris*, repeated the canard that she had married an ex-servant of Girardin's. She allegedly had forfeited her title of Rousseau's widow 'en passant du lit du défenseur de la liberté et de la dignité de l'homme dans le lit d'un esclave'. As for the administrators of the Théâtre de la nation, the *Révolutions de Paris* accused these offspring of the 'comédiens du roi, pâture des gentilshommes de la chambre, instrumens de plaisir hors de la loi et au-dessus de la loi' of offering Thérèse mere baksheesh: 'les comédiens, plus charlatans que bienfaiteurs, ne cherchant qu'à humilier les gens de lettres, viennent faire la charité au sublime auteur du Contrat Social, livre sur lequel repose la félicité de la France'![12]

Thérèse understood that she could do nothing to alter the horrific opinion of her held by aristocratic disciples. By attaching herself to Rousseau's fate, however, she might gain the sympathy of revolutionary politicians. Thérèse therefore insisted upon having shared the persecutions endured by Rousseau under the tyranny of the *ancien régime*. In May 1790 she appealed to H.-G. Riquetti, comte de Mirabeau, for financial assistance. Mirabeau, whose estranged father had once offered Rousseau asylum, responded that Thérèse should address her request to the National Assembly itself. He noted: 'La Veuve de Jean Jacques a des droits puissans a la Reconnoissance des amis de la liberté.'[13]

In this instance Thérèse's plea went unheeded, so she requested assistance from a bizarrely different source: Russia's empress, Catherine II. Goaded into doing so by a collector of Rousseau memorabilia, the Russian diplomat Piotr Dubrowski, Thérèse reminded Catherine of the empress's longstanding reputation as a patron of letters.[14] She appended her customary plea to the petition: 'seule, abandonnée, calomniée même, comme [Rousseau] le fut durant sa vie, je sens toute ma détresse'.[15] The tsarina never replied. After all, with revolution having erupted in France and unrest lapping at her western frontier, Catherine could easily distinguish between a harmless *écrivain de métier* like Diderot, whom she once had befriended, and Rousseau, author of the seditious *Du contrat social* and *Considérations sur le gouvernement de Pologne*.

In November Thérèse turned again to the National Assembly. This time her plea brought results. Marie-Ange d'Eymar, a repentant aristocratic deputy, had assumed official responsibility for enshrining Rousseau's memory. D'Eymar recalled the writer's search for vindication expressed in the *Lettre à Christophe de Beaumont*: 's'il existoit en Europe un seul gouvernement vraiment

---

12. *Révolutions de Paris* 65 (2-9 October 1790), p.655-57; *remarque* iii, *CC*, xlvi.254-55.
13. Honoré-Gabriel Riquetti, comte Mirabeau, to Marie-Thérèse Levasseur, [13 May 1790], *CC*, xlvi.199.
14. *Notes explicatives*, *CC*, xlvi.259-60.
15. Marie-Thérèse Levasseur to Tsarina Catherine II of Russia, [10 October 1790], *CC*, xlvi.249.

éclairé, un gouvernement dont les vues fussent vraiment utiles et saines, il eût rendu des honneurs publics à l'Auteur d'Emile, il lui eût élevé des statues'.[16] D'Eymar printed a motion requesting that a statue of Rousseau be erected and placed in the meeting hall of the Assembly itself.[17] Though the vote on d'Eymar's original petition was postponed, Thérèse pursued the opportunity to link her own fate to it. Saddled with debts, bereft of her inheritance and victimised by Girardin and his ilk, the septuagenarian ex-laundress attempted to shed the slander of Barruel-Beauvert and Mme de Staël and seek redemption as a woman-of-the-people.[18]

In December d'Eymar again tried to get the National Assembly to commission an official statue of Rousseau. Meanwhile the (still) Girondin deputy Bertrand Barère became convinced that the revolutionary government could spare a yearly pension of 600 *livres* for Thérèse.[19] Barère's speech to the National Assembly recommending Thérèse's pension was an especially instructive lesson in historical rehabilitation. Noting Thérèse's indigence, he reminded his fellow deputies that the calumny which had dogged Rousseau all his life now chased his widow. Possessing an attestation from the village priest of Le Plessis-Belleville, Barère claimed to hold incontrovertible evidence that Thérèse never had remarried.[20] Barère next cited a letter which Rousseau had written in 1763 to Charles Pinot Duclos, recently published for the first time in Du Peyrou's edition of Part II of the *Confessions*. Believing himself at the time to be near death, Rousseau had considered Thérèse his consolation and requested those who loved him to transfer their sentiments to her: 'c'est un cœur tout semblable au mien'.[21] The deputies were moved. In response to Barère's request of 600 *livres* for Thérèse several murmured: 'Ce n'est pas asséz!' D'Eymar seized the opportunity. He amended Barère's motion, doubling the petition's pension to 1200 *livres* and appending to it his request for Rousseau's statue. The motion passed unanimously.[22]

16. *OC*, iv.1003; cited by d'Eymar in his address to the National Assembly of 21 December 1790, *Moniteur* (23 December 1790): *Réimpression*, vi.696-97; [21 December 1790], *CC*, xlvi.265.

17. *Motion relative à J.-J. Rousseau, par A. M. Eymar, député de Forcalquier, à l'Assemblée nationale, Paris, le 29 novembre 1790* (1790). See Annie Jourdan, 'Le culte de Rousseau sous la Révolution: la statue et la panthéonisation du citoyen de Genève', *SVEC* 324 (1994), p.57-77.

18. Thérèse was well aware of her need to assert her role as co-martyr. In October 1790 Piotr Dubrowsky asked her to recapitulate her version of Rousseau's final minutes. She had her husband die in her arms, all the while specifically noting the absence of Girardin from the scene. In her report a new set of final words emerged from Rousseau's lips, predicting Thérèse's future without him: 'Mon sort va finir, vous allez me survivre, mais ce sera pour continuer de souffrir. Vous ne serez ni épargnée ni ménagée. Craignez tout de l'injustice des hommes. Un jour je l'espére, ce Dieu infiniment bon, et devant lequel je vais paraître, permettra que la vérité soit connüe, et nous serons plaints' (Marie-Thérèse Levasseur to Piotr Dubrowsky, 20 October 1790, *CC*, xlvi.257).

19. *Moniteur* (23 December 1790): *Réimpression*, vi.696-97; [21 December 1790], *CC*, xlvi.263-64.

20. Attestation of Pierre Madin, in *Recueil des pièces relatives à la motion faite à l'Assemblée nationale, au sujet de J.-J. Rousseau et de sa veuve* (1791), p.25; [31 October 1790], *CC*, xlvi.260.

21. *Seconde Partie des Confessions*, vi.175-77. See as well *CC*, xvii.116-17.

22. *Moniteur* (23 December 1790): *Réimpression*, vi.696-97; [21 December 1790], *CC*, xlvi.263-64.

Popular opinion did not accede completely to the emotions of the deputies. For example, the *Révolutions de Paris* made the prescient observation that, no advocate of representative government, Rousseau would have sneered at the thought of his statue gracing the halls of the National Assembly. Nor was the newspaper particularly pleased with Thérèse's behaviour, particularly her acceptance of the Théâtre de la nation's gate receipts of which, it claimed, the author of the *Lettre à d'Alembert* would probably have disapproved.[23] Nevertheless, Thérèse sent the National Assembly a gracious note of appreciation, all the while making certain to hitch her fate to that of her late companion:

J'ai assez vécu, Messieurs, pour voir la mémoire de mon époux vengée et honnorée par la nation Françoise. Victime moi même de la Calomnie, elle n'a cessé de me poursuivre, par la Seule raison que mon Sort avoit été liée à celui de Rousseau. Le decret que vous avez rendu, et la Sanction que Sa Majesté lui a accordée, imposent aujourd'huy Silence à nos enemis: je vois le peuple François que mon mari aimoit, heureux et triomphant de la révolution qui S'est opérée Sous mes yeux dans Son gouvernement.[24]

As his widow became a ward of regenerated France, Rousseau himself was transformed into a political prophet and civic hero. In June 1790 the sculptor Jean-Antoine Houdon had given a bust of the writer to the National Assembly, to be placed near those he had made of Washington and Franklin, and Chariot ceremoniously laid a copy of *Du contrat social* beside it.[25] The following year a public competition was announced for the statue so desired by d'Eymar.[26] The street where the writer had spent his final years in Paris was redesignated 'rue J.-J. Rousseau'.[27] Towns from the Pyrenees to Ermenonville adopted his name.[28] Claude Poinçot dedicated his new edition of Rousseau's collected works to the National Assembly itself, placing volumes as they appeared on the speaker's rostrum.[29] Geneva expressed its contrition. Reinforced by the return of the political exiles of 1782, the Council of Two Hundred demanded abrogation of the condemnations of *Emile* and *Du contrat*

23. *Révolutions de Paris* 6 (1-8 January 1791), p.698-700.
24. *Recueil des pièces relatives à la motion faite à l'Assemblée nationale*, p.25-26; Marie-Thérèse Levasseur to [A.-B.-J. d'André], [3 January 1791], *CC*, xlvi.278.
25. Antoine-Claude Chariot to Bertrand Barère, 21 June 1790, *CC*, xlvi.221-22.
26. Joseph-Marie Vien to Charles-Claude Flahut, comte de La Billarderie d'Angiviller [18 April 1791], *CC*, xlvi.308.
27. *Remarque* vi, *CC*, xlvi.313.
28. Raymond Trousson, *Jean-Jacques Rousseau*, vol. ii *Le Deuil éclatant du bonheur* (Paris 1989), p.471.
29. Claude Poinçot to the National Assembly, [14 April 1791], *CC*, xlvi.303-304. Poinçot tried to market his edition as one sensitive to the needs of an age of revolution and therefore superseding the STG's *Collection complète*. As early as 1788, when Poinçot undertook his edition, he advertised its affordability and easily transportable format. Poinçot's *Œuvres complètes de J.-J. Rousseau, nouvelle édition, classée par ordre de matières, et ornée de quatre-vingt-dix gravures* eventually reached 38 volumes, in-octavo or in-quarto, with a volume of coloured plates 'pour servir à l'intelligence des Lettres sur la Botanique'. The set's volume of Rousseau's music comprised mostly the *Consolations des misères de ma vie*. Thirty of the engravings for the volumes were based upon those by Moreau the younger for Boubers's edition and thirteen more were made expressly for Poinçot.

social, sanctioned the erection of a statue of Rousseau at public expense and issued a declaration that the republic's constitutional base rested upon the principle of equality. The still aristocratic Small Council tempered this revolutionary enthusiasm, claiming that it was powerless to annul previous executive decisions of a legitimate government; but based upon the technicality that Rousseau never had defended himself back in 1762, the long-standing charges against him would be dropped.[30]

Thérèse Levasseur now sought to manipulate the rapidly changing climate and secure two objectives: vengeance over Girardin for having confiscated her husband's papers and acquisition of what she considered her rightful inheritance, the 24 000 *livres* offered by the long-defunct STG for the manuscripts of its edition. The Revolution was closing in on Girardin. On 21 June 1791 J.-P. Marat published in *L'Ami du peuple* an anonymous exposé of anti-Jacobin reactionaries, one of whom was identified as Ducloseaux [Descloseaux] père, 'spoliateur de concert avec le Sr. Girardin des œuvres posthumes de J.J. Rousseau, montant à plus de 30 000 *livres* dont ils ont fait tort à sa veuve'.[31] Girardin protested his innocence that very day, shamelessly announcing his benevolence towards Thérèse:

moi qui n'ai jamais rien fait que suivant les dernières intentions de son mari, et de concert avec elle; et qui ne suis parvenu qu'à force de soins, de peines, de voyages, de dépenses et même de chagrins, à rassembler et à mettre en ordre pour l'édition générale ses différens ouvrages épars dans l'Europe, et à composer à sa veuve un revenu fort au-dessus de ce qu'elle pouvait naturellement attendre.[32]

Girardin advertised his contributions towards the unfortunate, his faith in the people and his indifference regarding slander. And he signed off: 'René Gerardin, membre du club des Cordeliers et des Jacobins'.

Though Marat apologised to Girardin, the difficulties of the repentant marquis were just beginning. In August the National Assembly proposed the transfer of Rousseau's remains from Ermenonville to the unfinished abbey church of Sainte-Geneviève, newly consecrated as the Panthéon to house the remains of France's civic saints. There Rousseau at last might be reconciled with his one-time nemesis Voltaire.[33] Girardin, however, adamantly refused to participate in what he considered an invasion of his property rights. Furthermore, Girardin noted, moving Rousseau violated the writer's desires: 'Dans ces circonstances, Je crois que l'on ne peut sans violer La Loy naturelle, La Loy civile, La Loy Religieuse, et le Droit des Gens, contrevenir aux dernieres volontés d'un Homme, et d'un Etranger, Relativement au Lieu qu'il a marqué lui même pour Le Repos de ses Mânes.'[34] Assembly deputies debated

---

30. *Remarque* ii, *CC*, xlvi.280.

31. Anonymous to Jean-Paul Marat, [*c.* 5 June 1791], *L'Ami du peuple* 494 (19 June 1791), p.3-6; *CC*, xlvi.321.

32. Girardin to Marat, 21 June 1791, *L'Ami du peuple* 510 (4 July 1791), p.4-6; *CC*, xlvi.327-28.

33. *Pétition à l'Assemblée nationale, contenant demande de la translation des cendres de J.-J. Rousseau au Panthéon français*, second sitting of 27 August 1791, *CC*, xlvi.353-74.

34. Girardin to Théodore Vernier, president of the Constituent Assembly, 29 August 1791, *CC*, xlvi.374.

the matter and eventually concurred with Girardin's position. Radicals, including Marat, stood with him for different reasons. They considered pantheonisation to represent the sort of frozen and distant enshrinement that would suffocate Rousseau's ideas.[35] On the other hand, to her confidant Chariot an irritated Thérèse protested against Rousseau's resting place on the île des Peupliers: 'Je suis vraiment outrée de l'imposture et du peu de pudeur de M. Girardin. Quoi, il ose affirmer que les dernieres intentions de mon mari aient été d'être enterré à Ermenonville?'[36]

There matters stood until mid-1793. By this time, of course, the Revolution had entered its radical phase and it was politically wise for Girardin to temper his pugnaciousness.[37] Despite Girardin's alleged Jacobin convictions, the former marquis's pre-revolutionary pedigree now served him poorly. On 31 August 1793 the mayor of Ermenonville visited the Girardins' manor and requested declarations of civic virtue from the couple. Dissatisfied with their response, he placed them under house arrest. The five Girardin children were arrested as well, and Amable-Ours-Séraphin, the little Emile who had served as Rousseau's companion at Ermenonville, died soon after, perhaps in captivity. Six weeks following his incarceration, a beleaguered Girardin received an orthographically challenged letter from Thérèse requesting a copy of the convention of 21 September 1779. Still after her 24 000 *livres*, she noted bitterly: 'Rien me Surprends plus, de votre part, que vous vouliez que Les petits Cousins de Mon Mary puisse Eriter d'un Bien que Mon Mary a travaillier a la Seure de Son front pour Sa veuve. Sa n'est point un Bien de patrie Moine C'est un Bien qui appartient a Moy Même.' Thérèse claimed to have received assurances from Geneva that her inheritance rights were legitimate and she promised to take her case to the National Convention, 'ou je suis Connue et respectée'.[38]

No record exists of Girardin's reply to Thérèse. On 23 October, however, he wrote to the president of the Paris Jacobin Club, Maribon-Montaut, and agreed to have Rousseau disinterred. He had little choice. The *Journal de la montagne* had recorded rumblings in the Jacobin Club, with an anonymous patriot noting that 'un grand homme est encore dans les mains d'un scélérat. Rousseau [c]et ami de l'humanité, est encore au pouvoir de Girardin'.[39] Club members passed a motion to petition the Convention to transfer Rousseau's remains, now considered 'une propriété nationale', to the Panthéon. Depres-

35. *L'Ami du peuple* 543 (2 September 1791). See D. Higgin[s], 'Rousseau and the Pantheon: the background and implications of the ceremony of 20 vendémiaire Year III', *Modern language review* 50 (1955), p.274-75.

36. Marie-Thérèse Levasseur to Antoine-Claude Chariot, 21 September 1791, *CC*, xlvi.390.

37. As early as 1790 Girardin's self-promotion at the expense of Rousseau faced public criticism. Vandals defaced Ermenonville and the popular play *Les Derniers moments de J.-J. Rousseau* was attacked for granting the marquis a role in the writer's deathbed scene.

38. Possibly in Bally's hand, Marie-Thérèse Levasseur to Girardin, [12 October 1793], *CC*, xlvii.176-77.

39. *Journal de la montagne* 140 ('29ᵉ jour de 1ᵉʳ mois an IIᵐᵉ') [20 October 1793], p.1017; *note explicative* b, *CC*, xlvii.180.

sed over having to yield his precious trophy to the nation, Girardin at least desired a say as to how Rousseau would hereafter be displayed: 'Je demanderois seulement que pour se Conformer aux dernieres volontés de Cet ami de la nature et de la vérité, son monument fut transferé en face des Champs Elisées, dans une Isle de la Seine, qui serait planté de peupliers.' Failing to recognise the self-irony, Girardin appended one additional request, that 'par un baptême républicain', he himself be renamed Emile![40]

The *seigneur* of Ermenonville obtained neither of his wishes. For her part Thérèse encouraged the transfer of Rousseau's remains to the cool vault of the Panthéon. Her role in the politicised republic clearly was effacing Girardin's. Thérèse accompanied Jacobins from Paris's Franciade section who brought the petition for the displacement directly to the Convention. On 14 April 1794 the petition was accepted.[41] But the tumultuous political events of spring and summer 1794 delayed action, and it was not until 15 September, more than six weeks following the fall of Robespierre, that Joseph Lakanal, speaking for the Committee for Public Instruction, revived the matter of Rousseau's disinterment. Lakanal was responding to wishes in the Convention to stage Rousseau's pantheonisation as the Thermidorians' first political festival, discrediting Robespierre, Jacobin radicalism and the Republic of Virtue. The ceremony Lakanal had in mind would celebrate reconciliation, placing emphasis upon poplar trees, village music, white-robed virgins, botanists, busy artisans, singing farmers and nursing mothers. After negotiating a date that would follow the pantheonisation of Marat, a momentary sop intended to neutralise old-style Jacobins, Convention deputies agreed upon Rousseau's reburial for the second *décadi* of vendémiaire Year III, that is the week of 11 October 1794.[42] To prepare for the event, public lectures on Rousseau's works were delivered throughout France. Plays, poems and songs were hurriedly written in his honour.[43]

Still under guard at Ermenonville, Girardin was aware of the political decisions being made in Paris.[44] Despite the dangers surrounding him, the ex-marquis took the high moral road. He wrote to the Convention's Committee for Public Instruction, reiterating Rousseau's alleged last wishes to lie within nature's breast, beneath the light of heaven. Girardin noted that in fulfilling Rousseau's desires, he had brought fifteen years of persecution upon himself. But he now was reconciled to political realities. The French republic alone could protect 'le monument du précurseur de la Liberté', and he offered the state not merely the corpse but the entire sarcophagus. Girardin recommended that J.-P. Lesueur, sculptor of the monument he had commissioned

40. Copy, Girardin to Louis-M.-B. Maribon-Montaut, [2 brumaire An II/23 October 1793], *CC*, xlvii.177-82.

41. *Moniteur* (27 germinal An II/16 April 1794): *Réimpression*, xx.216-17.

42. [Joseph Lakanal], *Rapport sur J.-J. Rousseau, fait au nom du Comité d'instruction publique, par Lakanal, dans la séance du 29 fructidor* [...] [1794]; [15 September 1794], *CC*, xlviii.12-25.

43. Higgin[s], 'Rousseau and the Pantheon', p.276.

44. Though the Committee for Public Instruction was delegated to file a report justifying the disinterment, divided opinion among committee members prevented its preparation.

at Ermenonville back in 1780, be appointed to supervise its transfer to the Panthéon.[45]

The fate of the corpus

As the republic prepared to take possession of Rousseau's bones, pieces of the written corpus also found their way into the state's domain. On 20 April 1794 an unidentified member of the Committee for Public Instruction observed that the recently guillotined member of the Committee of Public Safety, Hérault de Séchelles, had possessed autograph manuscripts of both *Emile* and *La Nouvelle Héloïse*. The manuscripts were recovered and deposited into the library of the Committee for Public Instruction.[46] Then, immediately following the fall of Robespierre, Germain Poirier of the Committee on the Arts deposited with the Committee for Public Instruction another trove of papers: six manuscript volumes of *La Nouvelle Héloïse* in Rousseau's hand (the maréchale de Luxembourg's copy, left behind by the comtesse de Boufflers when she emigrated);[47] forty-two letters also in Rousseau's hand, mostly addressed to the maréchale de Luxembourg;[48] and a carton entitled 'Sur J.J. Rousseau' containing five folders recovered from the papers of the recently guillotined Malesherbes.[49] Malesherbes's folders contained the following: letters to him from Rousseau and drafts of replies; items relating to *La Nouvelle Héloïse*, *Du contrat social* and *Emile*; an historical sketch about Rousseau; letters from the comtesse de Boufflers, David Hume, Buttafoco, Olivier de Corancez, Girardin and others; pieces concerning the editions of Rousseau's works; and printed copies of *Pygmalion* and the first *Discours*.[50]

But these contributions were far from all; the most dramatic pronouncement was yet to come. On 26 September 1794, two weeks prior to the disinterment of Rousseau, Thérèse Levasseur appeared once again before the National Convention. She bore a large, sealed envelope containing papers and she addressed the deputies:

Citoyens représentants, J.-J. Rousseau, mon époux, m'a donné, une heure avant sa mort, deux manuscrits avec une inscription qui annonce que son intention est que le sceau apposé sur l'enveloppe ne soit rompu qu'en 1801. Je prie la Convention nationale de confier à son archiviste ce dépôt sacré; elle pèsera dans sa sagesse s'il convient ou

---

45. Copy, Girardin to the Committee for Public Instruction, 28 floréal An II [17 May 1794], *CC*, xlvii.247-48.
46. The *Emile* manuscript, in reality an early draft, now is located in the library of the National Assembly at the Palais-Bourbon (ms. 1427-29), while the *Nouvelle Héloïse* manuscript has been split up and is in several locations (see *OC*, ii.1964-65).
47. Paris, library of the National Assembly, Palais-Bourbon, ms.1433-38.
48. Paris, library of the National Assembly, Palais-Bourbon, ms. P.7074.
49. Malesherbes was executed on 22 April 1794.
50. Signed inventory of Rousseau manuscripts deposited with the Committee for Public Instruction, [10 thermidor An II/28 July 1794], *CC*, xlviii.1-2. Part of Malesherbes's papers were restored to his heirs and part were deposited in the Bibliothèque nationale.

non de prendre des mesures pour que cet ouvrage, que je crois le fruit de longs travaux, voie le jour avant l'époque fixée par l'auteur du *Contrat social*.[51]

The Convention's presiding officer, André Dumont, could hardly contain his excitement. Barely two months following the fall of Robespierre, in the wake of France's madness and terror, was Thérèse transporting from the grave new political lessons for the future that Rousseau had presciently prepared? Some deputies demanded that she open the envelope. But others insisted that Rousseau's wishes be honoured and that his message await the dawn of the new century. Representing those desirous of being informed right away of the contents of Thérèse's envelope, Barère spoke up: 'la révolution a tellement accéléré le progrès des lumières que nous sommes plus avancés que si nous étions en 1900; il ne peut donc y avoir de difficultés sur l'ouverture du paquet'. To win both Thérèse's assent and Convention support, Barère noted the widow's pitiful pension. He insisted that the proceeds from publishing the manuscripts she bore ought to belong to her alone. Thérèse obviously concurred, and further debate revealed that for some time Girardin had possessed the items now in her hands. The deputies urged Dumont to remove them from their envelope so that members of the Committee for Public Instruction might examine them. The Committee then was asked to report its findings to the full Convention as soon as possible.[52]

On the next day, speaking for the Committee for Public Instruction, Lakanal informed the Convention of the fruit of his hasty researches. He could not hide his disappointment: 'Le dépôt ne renferme que le manuscrit des Confessions du philosophe genevois.' Lakanal tried to put a gloss on the matter by noting that the personalities mentioned in Thérèse's manuscript actually were cited by name, not hidden behind initials, and that some variants and ideas in Thérèse's manuscript 'ne sont pas sans intérêt'. Because the request to keep the envelope sealed until 1801 was written in a hand other than Rousseau's, Lakanal saw no need for withholding the manuscript from circulation. He added the observation that it undoubtedly was a late draft, and therefore closer to the writer's genuine intent than the STG, Pierre Moultou and Du Peyrou editions. Lakanal concluded that Thérèse's manuscript should certainly be consulted once a new edition of the *Confessions* was prepared. But the Committee for Public Instruction had to conclude that, on its own merits, the newly recovered manuscript did not warrant immediate publication.[53]

Thus the thrill of autobiography's moral message, which had fascinated the previous generation, had virtually no impact upon the politicians of thermidor. Thérèse's manuscript, of course, was the same one that Girardin had seized among Rousseau's papers back on 2 July 1778; and the instructions not

51. *Moniteur* (8 vendémiaire An iii/29 September 1794): *Réimpression*, xxii.79-80; [5 vendémiaire An iii/26 September 1794], *CC*, xlviii.33.

52. *Moniteur* (8 vendémiaire An iii/29 September 1794): *Réimpression*, xxii.79-80; [5 vendémiaire An iii/26 September 1794], *CC*, xlviii.33.

53. *Moniteur, Supplément* (8 vendémiaire An iii/29 September 1794): *Réimpression*, xxii.83; Lakanal's report, [27 September 1794], *CC*, xlviii.38-39.

to open until 1801 had been written by the erstwhile marquis himself after he broke the original seal and had read the contents. He then resealed the envelope. By the new century, Girardin had hoped, potential claimants to Rousseau's heritage no longer would need to be bought off and the manuscript could be released for publication. What Girardin had not foreseen was the publication of the *Confessions*, Part II, first by Pierre Moultou and then by Du Peyrou. Subsequently, of course, revolutionary events caught up with the marquis; moreover, by 1794, the *Confessions* lost their aura.

It is unclear just when Girardin had yielded his envelope to Thérèse; it probably was quite recently. Incarcerated at Ermenonville, Girardin bitterly came to realise that Thérèse now was a political personality, and however much he despised her, it would be useful, if not urgent, to have her on his side. So he kept providing Thérèse with a small pension and rescued her from bill collectors. But the eventual price of Thérèse's favour and his own rehabilitation turned out to be far higher than occasional driblets of cash. It could only be the sacrifice of *his* Rousseau, body and soul. Releasing the *Confessions* to the republic disappointed *conventionnels*, but releasing Rousseau's corpse bought the Girardins their freedom. Their year-long confinement was over. The Convention politely thanked *citoyen* Girardin for his prior services in maintaining Rousseau's memory. He was granted permission to attend the pantheonisation.[54]

Pantheonisation

Could Girardin be blamed if thoughts of political vandalism ran through his brain on 17 vendémiaire An III (8 October 1794), when he perused boatloads of Ermenonville worthies and representatives of the Convention rowing out to the île des Peupliers to recover 'la propriété nationale'?[55] Supervised by Lesueur, Rousseau's coffin was carefully raised and transported across the pond to the opposite shore. There musicians waited and took up a melancholy Rousseau air, 'Le saule'. As evening fell the remains were placed in a simple wagon heading for Paris; and by moonlight the modest folk of Ermenonville and its neighbouring communes lined the road to pay their respects. According to the report prepared for the Committee for Public Instruction, 'L'ombre des arbres qui le couvraient, le clair de lune qui réflétait leur feuillage mobile d'une maniere toujours variée, le silence de toute la nature, imprimaient à ce

---

54. Copy, in Girardin's hand, Committee for Public Instruction to the Committee of Public Safety, [7 vendémiaire An III/28 September 1794], *CC*, xlviii.40-41; Committee for Public Instruction to Girardin, [12 vendémiaire An III/3 October 1794], *CC*, xlviii.45-46. See also *note explicative*, *CC*, xlviii.41.

55. The place of Ermenonville in the construction of Girardin's Rousseau legend is described in two articles by Anne Ridehalgh: 'Preromantic attitudes and the birth of a legend: French pilgrimages to Ermenonville, 1778-1789', *SVEC* 215 (1982), p.231-52; and 'Rousseau as God? the Ermenonville pilgrimages in the Revolution', *SVEC* 278 (1990), p.287-308. See as well Elizabeth MacArthur, 'Textual gardens: Rousseau's Elysée and Girardin's Ermenonville', *Romance quarterly* 38 (1991), p.331-39.

spectacle un caractère religieux qui empêchait ces bonnes gens de s'approcher autrement que le chapeau à la main.'[56]

During the night of 8 October the procession camped outside Ermenonville, heading south the following morning. The deputation from the Convention, municipal officials, National Guard members, old men who had known Rousseau, mothers and their children, all accompanied the remains to the next village. Once the cortège arrived at Gonesse, a joyous patriotic atmosphere replaced the funereal mood. Flags and banners were unfurled, and the rustic hearse was decorated with flowers. From Gonesse to Montmorency (renamed Emile) the crowds grew larger: 'La marche fut souvent arrêtée par la foule qui se pressait, surtout à l'entrée des Villages.'[57] At nightfall on 9 October Rousseau's songs merged with the cheering.

The convoy spent the evening at Emile. Old acquaintances of Rousseau's reminisced and the sandy market square was strewn with flowers. Poplars were planted. Celebrants caroused all night long and at daybreak they draped garlands and poplar branches over the wagon containing Rousseau's remains. On the morning of 10 October the cortège took off once more, passing l'Ermitage. There an old man prostrated himself before the caravan; young girls dressed in white tunics and tricoloured sashes, mothers with infants at their breast, peasants and labourers accompanied the convoy. Upon reaching the gates of Paris the crowds thickened. From the entry point of La Chapelle to the place de la Révolution onlookers paid respects.[58]

Meanwhile in the hall of the Convention a concert of Rousseau's airs, martial music and M.-J. Chénier's hymn to the writer prepared deputies for the pantheonisation.[59] At the place de la Révolution a new delegation met the cortège and accompanied it to the Tuileries. In a garden pond Ermenonville's île des Peupliers had been reconstituted and a four-columned catafalque was unveiled to receive the coffin. During the evening of 10 October lights from a thousand candles illuminated the water. The *Feuille villageoise* newspaper reported that the entire scene was both magical and religious.[60] The next morning all members of the National Convention gathered in the gardens for a 'fête du peuple libre', staged by David's brother-in-law Auguste Cheval de Saint-Hubert. Politicians, musicians, botanists, artisans, mothers, war

56. Report made for the Committee for Public Instruction by the Executive Commission for Public Instruction, [c. 20 vendémiaire An III/11 October 1794], *CC*, xlviii.77.

57. Report made for the Committee for Public Instruction by the Executive Commission for Public Instruction, [c. 20 vendémiaire An III/11 October 1794], *CC*, xlviii.78.

58. Report made for the Committee for Public Instruction by the Executive Commission for Public Instruction, [c. 20 vendémiaire An III/11 October 1794], *CC*, xlviii.78.

59. *Moniteur* (22 vendémiaire An III/13 October 1794): *Réimpression*, xxix.212. For the lyrics of Chénier's hymn see *CC*, xlviii.62-63. Cologne and Aix-La-Chapelle had just fallen to the French revolutionary army of Sambre-et-Meuse; celebration of the military victories thus fused with the festivities surrounding Rousseau's reinterment (see *La Vedette ou Gazette du jour*, 22 vendémiaire An III/13 October 1794, p.2-3; and *Journal de Perlet* 748, 21 vendémiaire An III/12 October 1794, p.91-92).

60. *La Feuille villageoise* (25, 30 vendémiaire An III/16, 21 October 1794), v.65-67, vi.88-91.

orphans and those who had accompanied the cortège to Paris reassembled, bearing trophies that celebrated Rousseau's virtues. He and his new monument were reloaded onto an enormous chariot and the procession crossed the Seine. A delegation from regenerated Geneva joined it, a copy of *Du contrat social* earned a place of honour and the flags of three republics – France, the United States and Geneva – were unfurled. An American naval officer now led the procession to the Panthéon and Rousseau's music serenaded the marchers. The sarcophagus was placed on an elevated platform directly beneath the dome. Jean-Jacques-Régis de Cambacérès, president of the Convention, pronounced the eulogy.[61]

Cambacérès memorialised Rousseau as father of the Revolution, apostle of liberty and equality, and prophet of the doom of both empires and monarchies. The orator identified the pantheonisation as acquittal by the Convention of the nation's debt and of humanity's gratitude.[62] Lacking the fire and spontaneity of pre-thermidor rhetoric, Cambacérès's speech capped the contrived political mood of the three-day celebration. The ceremony concluded with a rendition of Chénier's hymn to Rousseau. Old men, mothers, deputies, young girls, Genevans and the people of Paris sang alternating verses. Thérèse Levasseur held a place of distinction, surrounded by (of all things for a Rousseau festival) a phalanx of wet-nurses! By the evening of 11 October, however, an eye-witness, the playwright Antoine-Vincent Arnault, observed that the spirit of reconciliation had outlasted its welcome. Already the amity among weary Jacobins, Thermidorians, pardoned aristocrats and ex-prisoners had broken down. They were screaming at one another. At the concluding public banquet, ex-vicomte de Ségur and *citoyen* Jean Beaudrais traded insults and worse, forcing the caterer to replenish broken dishes and glassware.[63]

What was the significance of it all? A generation ago historian Joan McDonald hypothesised that individual loyalty to Rousseau's memory was what bound revolutionaries together. The specific and detailed political theory of *Du contrat social* was of secondary importance. Because discipleship bore different messages for different people, aristocrats, Jacobins and *babouvistes* alike could select appropriate parts of the cult for themselves and take umbrage at those who used Rousseau's name to justify policies which they abhorred.[64] More recently Roger Barny and Bronislaw Baczko have nuanced McDonald's position without necessarily negating it.[65] Indeed it seems safe to say that during the eighteenth century's last decade Rousseau was an emblematic figure for antagonistic political groupings within France and Europe.

61. *Moniteur* (24 vendémiaire An III/15 October 1794): *Réimpression*, xxii.223-24.

62. *Moniteur* (24 vendémiaire An III/15 October 1794): *Réimpression*, xxii.223-24.

63. A.-V. Arnault, *Souvenirs d'un sexagénaire* (Paris 1833), iii.362-64; [11 October 1794], *CC*, xlviii.88-89.

64. McDonald, *Rousseau and the French Revolution*, p.170-73.

65. Roger Barny, 'Les aristocrates et Jean-Jacques Rousseau dans la Révolution', *Annales historiques de la Révolution française* 231-234 (1978), p.534-68; Barny, *L'Eclatement révolutionnaire du rousseauisme*; Bronislaw Baczko, 'Rousseau au Panthéon', in *Regards sur la Révolution génévoise, 1792-1798* (Geneva 1988), p.193-211.

Yet the incontrovertible fact was that he had been politicised by all of them.[66] Du Peyrou's multi-layered, all-purpose, martyr-teacher-sage, whose life story contained the message of redemption, was no longer serviceable. It was particularly difficult, if not impossible, for revolutionaries to reconcile *Du contrat social* with *La Nouvelle Héloïse*, *Emile*, *Le Devin du village* and the *Confessions*.

Instead the Thermidorians accentuated the single dimension of Rousseau's political vision, leaving it sufficiently vague in hopes of lining up various groupings behind the banner of regeneration and unity of the people. Dignified and restrained homage beneath the Panthéon's vaulted ceiling was supposed to replace the self-fulfilling and evangelical expressions of gratitude and grief that had marked both the reading of Rousseau's letters and pilgrimages to the île des Peupliers. The revolutionary Rousseau festivals were fine-tuned to serve as rigorously orchestrated political commemorations.[67]

In the post-thermidor world, of what use was the *Collection complète*, with its overlapping layers of moral didacticism? How readable still was the unselfconscious sentimentality of *La Nouvelle Héloïse*, with its once-enlightened feminism and religious non-orthodoxy? Was *Emile* still humanity's educational textbook, dangerous though it once might have seemed, or did it not now seem hopelessly utopian and elitist? Who any longer would read the *Confessions* as autobiographical liberation, rather than the quaintly self-indulgent ruminations of a grumpy eccentric? Certainly Rousseau's correspondence might continue to provide an evening's entertainment, illustrating the writer's struggles with the defunct *ancien régime*; but was it still the vehicle of moral instruction envisioned by Du Peyrou? Indeed the French reading public of the mid-1790s might prove more receptive to a mere title page of *Du contrat social*, etched in stone, than to the ringing phrases which, a generation earlier, had caused governments to condemn the work. The pantheonisation of Rousseau, in a certain sense, had domesticated the old warrior. It was a more significant cultural event than either the ostentatious apotheosis of Voltaire three years earlier or the more recent reburial of Marat.[68]

66. For her part Carol Blum insists upon the peculiarly Jacobin appropriation of rousseauvian 'virtue', centrepiece of the political philosophy of Robespierre and Saint-Just (see *Rousseau and the republic of virtue*, ch. 7 and *passim*). See also Bernard Manin's article, 'Rousseau', in *A critical dictionary of the French Revolution*, ed. François Furet and Mona Ozouf, translated by Arthur Goldhammer (Cambridge, Mass. 1989), p.841.

67. Blum suggests that the Thermidorians converted Rousseau, warrior of virtue, into Jean-Jacques, sentimental champion of the disinherited and reformer of female morals (*Rousseau and the republic of virtue*, p.278).

68. For a description of Voltaire's pantheonisation see Simon Schama, *Citizens* (New York 1989), p.561-66. On the ambiguities involved in the pantheonisation of Marat see Mona Ozouf, *L'Ecole de la France* (Paris 1984), p.94-96.

Settling accounts

As plays and concerts extolling Rousseau dominated the stages of the capital, one witness to the grand events of 20 vendémiaire perceived them with understandably mixed emotions. *Citoyen* Girardin, Rousseau's last host and fabricator of the writer's final days, was coming to terms with his own eclipse. But Girardin did not disappear quietly. While in Paris he requested and obtained an audience with members of the Committee for Public Instruction. He offered *conventionnels* the last signed Rousseau documents in his possession: some letters, four military airs and a commentary upon the musical pieces. Girardin summarised the contents of other documents he had given to Thérèse. Then his bitterness overflowed. No longer could he do anything about Rousseau's widow, a protected ward of the republic. Paul-Claude Moultou, whom he always had scorned, was long dead. But Du Peyrou, Girardin's most ancient rival for premier discipleship, was still living in Neuchâtel.

While the seigneur of Ermenonville possessed no more than a run-down estate divested of its shrine, inside his elegant Swiss townhouse Du Peyrou continued to have access to the Master, passing melancholy days perusing memoirs, letters and manuscripts in Rousseau's hand.[69] The very thought of Du Peyrou's bittersweet reveries enraged Girardin and he determined to bring them to an end. Therefore, reminding members of the Committee for Public Instruction that he alone was 'dépositeur des dernières intentions de l'auteur', Girardin invented one last tale. He said that the *trois amis* had agreed, once the *Collection complète* was published, to remit all of Rousseau's manuscripts to the library of 'un peuple libre'. In his view the repository was obvious. Therefore, the French republic bore a responsibility to liberate the treasures and display them as part of its revolutionary heritage: 'A ce titre, le peuple français a le droit plus que tout autre de réclamer aujourd'hui auprès de Du Peyrou la remise de ces manuscrits dans sa Bibliothèque nationale.'[70]

Despite patriotic posturing in the Convention, the Thermidorians were unwilling to invade Neuchâtel and tear Du Peyrou's precious collection from his hands. As early as July 1791 the intentions of Rousseau's most devoted disciple had been to deposit the writer's papers in a 'Bibliothèque publique bien assurée'.[71] Subsequently it became clear that Du Peyrou did not intend the location to be France's Bibliothèque nationale, but rather Neuchâtel's recently established *bibliothèque publique*. The town library would receive its

---

69. Urged on by Isabelle de Charrière, in April 1794 Du Peyrou reviewed his correspondence with Rousseau. Guilt over the incident at Trye a quarter-century earlier still haunted him and a re-reading of his letters at last had him determine that 'je crois avoir plus sujet de m'applaudir que de me blamer' (Du Peyrou to Isabelle de Charrière, 8 April 1794, *CC*, xlvii.217-18).

70. 'Note sur les manuscrits de J.-J. Rousseau, remise au Comité d'instruction publique par le citoyen René Girardin père', [22 vendémiaire An III/13 October 1794], *note explicative* b, *CC*, xlviii.111-12.

71. Instructions from Du Peyrou to his private secretary Guillaume-Simon Jeannin, [22 July 1791], *CC*, xlvi.343.

magnificent gift much sooner than expected, for around the time of Girardin's mid-October 1794 harangue to the Committee for Public Instruction, Du Peyrou fell very ill. Anticipating death, he sorted through his personal papers, placing aside what he would offer the *bibliothèque publique* and burning other materials. As he opened a set of letters he had ignored for thirty years, he informed Isabelle de Charrière of his plaintive mood. He threw the letters into the fire and repeated the procedure.[72] Did the destroyed materials have a connection with Rousseau? We simply do not know.

Du Peyrou died on 13 November 1794, and without incident his Rousseau papers passed on to the Neuchâtel public library. The French republic did not go empty-handed. It held the materials confiscated by the Committee for Public Instruction back in April, and on 19 October Lakanal had informed the Convention of additional papers in the Committee's possession. These included fifteen folders of scattered items and Jacques Necker's manuscript of the *Considérations sur le gouvernement de Pologne.*[73]

Thérèse Levasseur laid no claim to the redistributed Rousseau manuscripts. She preferred instead to insist upon her rights to the 24 000 *livres* once promised her by the STG, as well as the 1200 *livres* per year she had been collecting from Samuel de Tournes. On 1 November 1794, however, de Tournes informed Pierre Moultou that he no longer could supply Thérèse with her pension. Declaring bankruptcy, de Tournes suspended all payments to his creditors. Ordinarily, de Tournes informed Moultou, he would expect Thérèse to accept this turn of events. Recognising, however, that she had become a person of importance in France, he feared that she would complain to the National Convention, and the excited deputies might convert the matter into a political incident endangering Geneva's tenuous sovereignty. De Tournes therefore noted that, at considerable cost, his wife would assume half the per annum payment to Thérèse. But prior to her doing so he posed two conditions. First, Thérèse was formally to renounce her claim to the 24 000 *livres*; second, Pierre Moultou also was to declare bankruptcy and get his mother to pay Thérèse the remainder of her pension. The Moultous agreed to these conditions. To push the matter along, Etienne-Salomon Reybaz, Geneva's minister plenipotentiary to France, accepted the role of intermediary.[74]

72. Du Peyrou to Isabelle de Charrière, 31 October 1794, *CC*, xlviii.135-36.
73. *Moniteur* (1 brumaire III/22 October 1794): *Réimpression*, xxii.283. In his report Lakanal mentioned holding 'quinze cahiers écrits en entier de la main de ce grand homme; ils renferment divers morceaux qui n'ont jamais paru, et les germes des principales productions de son génie' ([28 vendémiaire An III/19 October 1794], *CC*, xlviii.126-27). These folders had been obtained by abbé Gabriel Brizard and their contents would be used in the Poinçot edition of Rousseau's collected works. At Brizard's death in January 1793 his companion Mlle Mazuyer acquired the folders and wished to sell their contents to the Committee for Public Instruction. After holding the papers for a time, the Committee decided against the purchase and returned the materials to her. They subsequently disappeared (see *note explicative* a, *CC*, xlviii.127).
74. Samuel de Tournes to Pierre Moultou, 1 November 1794, *CC*, xlviii.138-42.

By requesting that Thérèse renounce her inheritance claim to the 24 000 *livres*, de Tournes was delegitimising the convention of 21-24 September 1779 signed by Du Peyrou, Paul-Claude Moultou and Girardin. According to its terms the *trois amis* were to hold the 24 000 *livres* paid by the STG in trust, not for Thérèse, but for Jean-Jacques's children should any of them be located. All that Thérèse was entitled to was interest on the principal, judged to be 1200 *livres* per annum. If Rousseau's children failed to surface, upon Thérèse's death the writer's living relatives were to divide the 24 000 *livres*. This latter clause had led to the claims of Rousseau's cousins, supported so warmly by Girardin. Following her flight from Ermenonville in October 1779, however, Thérèse had rejected the convention of the previous September. She appealed to the earlier contract signed between 23 and 26 January 1779. By its terms the STG had promised her flatly 24 000 *livres*, payable in three years. No intermediaries were involved, no *trois amis*. While awaiting the principal, Thérèse had been entitled to collect 5 per cent interest on it: 1200 *livres* per year.

Of course the STG never was able to come up with the 24 000 *livres*. In 1783 Paul-Claude Moultou and Samuel de Tournes had agreed to share financial reponsibility in the name of the bankrupt publishers of the *Collection complète*, eventually borrowing and misinvesting the principal. Upon Moultou's death Pierre Moultou assumed his father's obligation. Irregularly, de Tournes paid Thérèse her 1200 *livres* per annum. Although Rousseau's cousins made their claims known, as long as Thérèse lived they were unable to touch any part of the principal. Until November 1794 all parties except Thérèse recognised that the convention of September 1779 superseded the contract of the previous January. But by asking Thérèse to exchange her claim to the 24 000 *livres* for a guaranteed 1200-*livre* annuity – half paid by his wife, half by P.-C. Moultou's widow – de Tournes effectively was tearing up the convention. It was the only way he could be rid of an obligation that had plagued him for more than a decade.

In delegitimising the convention of September 1779 de Tournes asked Thérèse to replace her own long-standing claim with 1200 *francs* worth of depreciating French *assignats* – not much of a bargain. Nevertheless, aware at last that she never would see the principal, Thérèse agreed to terms, provided that the annuity be exempt from taxes. She also persisted in her right to return to her original claim should Mmes de Tournes and Moultou renege on their payments.[75] On 9 February 1795 the new engagement was written.[76] Reybaz suggested that de Tournes secure approval of it from both Girardin and Théodore Rousseau, the cousin living in Paris.[77] Five years earlier both men would have denounced the deal vigorously. But times had changed. With Rousseau literally out of his hands, Girardin was a broken man. Shortly after returning from the pantheonisation he forsook Ermenonville

75. Copy in a secretary's hand sent to de Tournes, Marie-Thérèse Levasseur to Etienne-Salomon Reybaz, [23 nivôse An III/12 January 1795], *CC*, xlviii.171-72.
76. Copy in Pierre Moultou's hand, [9 February 1795], *CC*, xlviii.184-85.
77. Etienne-Salomon Reybaz to Samuel de Tournes, 21 February 1795, *CC*, xlviii.190-91.

and its gardens, themselves recently vandalised, and took refuge with a friend at Vernouillet.

Seeking to obtain Girardin's blessing for the agreement with Thérèse, de Tournes treated the ex-marquis gingerly. He coaxed Pierre Moultou into reminding Girardin of the enormous losses incurred by Moultou's father and himself for having assumed responsibility for the debts of the STG, obligations which had reached more than 30 000 *livres*, not counting the 24 000 *livres* initially set aside. De Tournes noted that leaving matters unsettled with Thérèse might have political repercussions for Geneva itself, since the Revolution had converted Rousseau's widow into 'un personnage important en France'. But the crux of the matter was financial. De Tournes admitted bankruptcy and the 24 000 *livres* had disappeared. The question of entitlement therefore was moot. Girardin was asked not to abandon his way of thinking, but simply to accept the inevitable. Indeed times had changed.[78]

Girardin never responded. Nor, apparently, did he answer a second letter sent in April.[79] Deprived of Rousseau's remains, bereft of the writer's manuscripts and shorn of his claims to special discipleship, the embittered ex-marquis had left Ermenonville for good. At Rousseau's pantheonisation Girardin had been a marginal figure and until his death in 1808 he played no further role in the evolution of the writer's reputation. Nor, for that matter, did Thérèse, whose ambivalent place in Rousseau's life story continued to haunt her. Thérèse survived until 1801, collecting the 1200-*franc* annuity from de Tournes's wife and Pierre Moultou's mother.[80] But she never was able to dissociate herself from alleged responsibility for Rousseau's unhappiness or even a nefarious role in his death. Thérèse continued to live with John Bally and mismanage her income. In 1797 she again pleaded with the French government for financial help,[81] and a year later she found herself once more publicly disavowing the Rousseau suicide thesis, insisting upon her husband's melodramatic death in her arms.[82]

Though de Tournes believed that his declaration of bankruptcy in November 1794 had released him from responsibility towards Thérèse and the STG's surviving creditors, he still needed to close the books on the past. On 1 June 1797, therefore, he, Pierre Boin and Jean-R. Prévost (representing the Moultou estate) issued a definitive financial statement. They recognised the failure of European booksellers to make good on their purchases of the *Collection complète* and estimated unsettled payments to amount to 19 606 *livres* in

---

78. Draft in de Tournes's hand, Pierre Moultou to Girardin, [4 March 1795], *CC*, xlviii.196-201.

79. Draft, Pierre Moultou to Girardin, [11 April 1795], *CC*, xlviii.223-24.

80. Compensating Thérèse for the inflation spiral over the past decade, in August 1795 Mme Moultou chipped in with a one-time gift of 6000 *francs* (Marianne Moultou to Etienne-Salomon Reybaz, 7 August 1795, *CC*, xlviii.246).

81. Marie-Thérèse Levasseur to [Nicolas-L. de Neufchâteau?], [October? 1797], *CC*, xlix.97.

82. Marie-Thérèse Levasseur to Guillaume Olivier de Corancez, 27 prairial An VI [15 June 1798], published in the *Journal de Paris* 272 (2 messidor An VI/20 June 1798), p.1145-46, *CC*, xlix.149-51.

pre-revolutionary money. In addition they noted that Grabit and veuve Barret of Lyon had failed to pay 19 373 *livres* for overstocked sets of the edition which they had purchased. Because Grabit now was out of the book business and veuve Barret was living off the charity of friends, their debts had to be considered as losses. Furthermore, the unpaid loans and interest charges of Lullin and J.-L. de Tournes had reached 46 220 *livres*. Half was owed by Samuel de Tournes and half by the Moultou heirs. Back in 1790 the value of stocked sets of the *Collection complète* had been estimated at 64 278 *livres*. Even though this amount probably was too low, no chance existed to recoup any part of it. Without hope of collecting more revenue, de Tournes and his co-signators therefore officially liberated the old Société Rousseau from its engagements.[83]

And there was one last footnote. During the winter of 1801 Rousseau's cousin Théodore paid a call on de Tournes. He mentioned that 'Rousseau le Persan' still was claiming the 24 000 *livres* originally offered by the STG for the *Collection complète*. Théodore noted that Du Peyrou had referred to the sum in the 'Discours préliminaire' prepared for his 1790 edition of the *Confessions*, Part II. He urged de Tournes to read this text. Indeed, in his 'Discours' Du Peyrou did write that the *trois amis* had preferred not to give Thérèse the 24 000 *livres*, but rather reserve the sum for Rousseau's children. Should the children not be located, the 24 000 *livres* were to go to the author's 'héritiers naturels'. But again according to Du Peyrou, Paul-Claude Moultou had made an alternative proposal, namely that the *amis* donate the 24 000 *livres* to the Paris Foundling Home for whatever charges had been incurred in rearing Rousseau's children. Though the idea never had been discussed formally, in 1790 Du Peyrou apparently was reconsidering it. He had invited a response from Girardin, the only other surviving *ami*.[84]

De Tournes considered the idea attributed to Moultou as foolish, and for Du Peyrou to have revived it publicly was irresponsible. In 1790 Du Peyrou seemingly had not understood that very little remained of the original 24 000 *livres*. A decade later nothing of it was left. Reading the 'Discours préliminaire' shortly after Thérèse's death, de Tournes needed to discredit Du Peyrou's observations, for the last thing he desired was a Rousseau cousin dragging him into a Napoleonic courtroom. He therefore prepared observations of his own which, ironically enough, restored the late Thérèse Levasseur as Rousseau's sole legitimate heir. He then noted her voluntary renunciation of what had been rightfully hers: the 24 000 *livres*. In their place, according to de Tournes, Thérèse had accepted the annuity of 1200 *francs*. De Tournes re-established Girardin as the villain of the piece, seeking to deprive Thérèse of her just due in favour of Rousseau cousins whom the writer had not even known. According to de Tournes, Du Peyrou had allowed disdain for

83. Definitive ruling of the Société Rousseau, [1 June 1797], *CC*, xlix.69-77.
84. 'Discours préliminaire', in *Seconde partie des Confessions*, iii.iv-ix.

Thérèse to overcome consideration for her future. But concern for her well-being had guided Rousseau all along:

toutes ses inquietudes se portoient sur la crainte que Therèse n'eut pas de quoi vivre après lui & que s'il avoit possedé quelque bien il en auroit disposé en sa faveur, & qu'en projettant une edition complette de ses ouvrages il pensoit autant a assurer une honnête existence a Therèse qu'a sa propre gloire, & l'on ne peut pas douter que s'il etoit dans de telles dispositions lorsque cette fille n'etoit que sa gouvernante, il n'avoit pas changé de sentiment depuis qu'elle etoit devenue sa femme.[85]

Recapitulation: forging Rousseau

Rousseau and intellectual property rights

This book has been sensitive to Michel Foucault's suggestion that the rise of modern authorship derives from the literary property claims of writers and the consequential punishment inflicted upon writers for their print transgressions.[86] In 1761 Rousseau's protector in France, *directeur de la Librairie* Malesherbes, persuaded him that authorial rights to property justified selling three manuscript versions of *La Nouvelle Héloïse* to three different publishers. As Rousseau discovered, however, the price he was to pay for official recognition of his ownership was subservience to the censorship practices of the French monarchy. This sad truth proved highly discouraging to him, but it was nothing compared to what he would endure with respect to *Du contrat social* and *Emile*, properties which he openly acknowledged the following year.

Once these two latter books were published and condemned, the police apparatus of several European states considered the texts unsalvageable and Rousseau was deemed a public menace. His publisher Marc-Michel Rey was urged to tear the name of the endangered writer from *Du contrat social*'s title page. Removal of Rousseau's authorial identity was meant to erase his ownership claim to the denounced treatise. But the pathetic ploy never materialised, and Rousseau would be forever associated with *Du contrat social*. After the second blockbuster of 1762, *Emile*, was condemned in France, Rousseau had to flee the country. He became known as Europe's most notorious writer-fugitive.

But punishment by authorities of church and state was not the sole response to Rousseau's proprietary claims to his transgressive corpus. On the contrary, late eighteenth-century publisher-booksellers simply rejected his title to property by printing, without the author's permission, edition after edition of his creations. Rousseau considered all of these piracies to be thefts and perversions

85. Samuel de Tournes's *mémoire*, [1801-1803?], *CC*, xlix.284.
86. 'Once a system of ownership for texts came into being, once strict rules concerning author's rights, author–publisher relations, rights of reproduction, and related matters were enacted – at the end of the eighteenth century and the beginning of the nineteenth century – the possibility of transgression attached to the act of writing took on, more and more, the form of an imperative peculiar to literature' (see 'What is an author?', p.148).

of his original compositions. To counter his fears of poorly printed volumes, illegitimate abridgements and adulterated texts, Rousseau foresaw a moment in the future when he might tell his story in his own edition of collected works, one authorised and including revised writings and autobiographical justifications. Moreover, the edition would be a significant piece of real property. Its sale would provide him income for his old age. Had Rousseau been able to take advantage of the French book-trade reforms of 1777/78, guaranteeing publication *privilèges* to authors and their heirs and permitting authors to resell the same work over time, he might have witnessed confirmation of his earlier ideas concerning his alleged property rights. Unfortunately he never did secure a *privilège* for his writings. Rousseau's death in 1778 ostensibly resulted in the transfer of his possessions to Thérèse Levasseur, his companion of thirty-five years.

After 2 July 1778, who owned Rousseau?

Though Rousseau believed that an authorised edition of *œuvres complètes* would properly incorporate his life and work, he doubted whether the autobiographical 'mémoires' he had composed between 1766 and 1778, offensive as they might seem to so many contemporaries, could be printed until after the deaths of those mentioned in them. Prior to his flight to England in 1766 Rousseau had left letter drafts and manuscripts with his then literary executor, Pierre-A. Du Peyrou. During his last years Rousseau distributed additional manuscripts among followers, some of whom interpreted their trusteeships as conveying rights of ownership. Finally, when Rousseau died at Ermenonville in July 1778, his last host, René-Louis de Girardin, simply expropriated what the writer had brought with him – money, personal effects, correspondence and more manuscripts. Girardin maintained that he was designated by Rousseau to use the texts left at Ermenonville for the well-being of Thérèse. For Girardin this was akin to converting unimproved property, the Rousseau corpus both published and unpublished, into a stately edifice: the authorised edition aborted during the writer's lifetime.

Girardin, and to an extent his co-editors Du Peyrou and Paul-Claude Moultou, applied a romantic interpretation of literary fellowship to their property claims as they created the *Collection complète des œuvres de J.-J. Rousseau, citoyen de Genève*. Their Rousseau was a moral messiah, they were his disciples and the *Collection complète* represented the gospel message. The *trois amis* accepted Du Peyrou's view that the most effective way to impart *rousseauisme* in the *Collection complète* was by portraying the volumes as a 'total' moral autobiography, even if there was little agreement over the meanings of the message contained in the life.

An essential question that confronted the *amis* was 'who owned Rousseau?' Indeed the ideological inheritance was to bear with it a sense of commercial property rights. Thérèse would base her title upon claims of respectable widowhood. Until the French Revolution, however, observers and disciples alike considered her to be an impediment to Rousseau's moral growth, source of the writer's paranoia and even cause of his untimely death. So Thérèse was shunted aside and made to live off the charity of the disciples. As his last host and self-appointed literary executor, Girardin insisted that Rousseau had identified him as disciple-in-chief. Girardin established Ermenonville as *rousseauisme*'s chief shrine, persuaded holders of Rousseau manuscripts to deliver all documents to him and confidently converted every one of the Master's alleged literary intentions into reflections of his own. For Girardin, primary discipleship confirmed his claims to trusteeship over Rousseau's literary property and alleged wishes, and the marquis even tried to dictate the line of inheritance accruing from sale of the manuscripts included in the *Collection complète*. Once Girardin was caught hiding an invaluable Rousseau text, Part II of the *Confessions*, Du Peyrou exploded. The marquis's arrogant and devious behaviour facilitated a rupture among the *amis*. As a consequence the *Collection complète* was gravely compromised.

The 'Collection complète' and 'l'histoire du livre'

Nevertheless, the grand work lumbered on to completion and appeared in a variety of formats. As workhorse editor, Du Peyrou arranged Rousseau's correspondence, 'mémoires' and polemics beside the author's fiction, theatre, music, and writings on politics and education. What Du Peyrou hoped would emerge was a grand moral vision, espoused by the author-warrior who had overcome despair and even madness to invite the reader to take heart from the exemplary life. Du Peyrou claimed to maintain faithfulness to Rousseau's texts; but as we have seen, he manipulated them too. Whether his portrayal of Rousseau genuinely succeeded as well-integrated 'total' moral autobiography remains an open question. It seems more likely that the vast detail contained in the *Collection complète* challenged readers to assume active interpretive roles in order to make their own sense of the life between the covers.

My narrative describing the evolution of the STG's *Collection complète des œuvres de J.-J. Rousseau* has sought to blend elements associated with *l'histoire du livre* with Anglo-American techniques of textual analysis. I am not an analytical bibliographer, however, and my application of these techniques has been admittedly artisanal. Others wishing to examine the *Collection complète* line by line will be the ones to determine the merits of the edition according to contemporary bibliographical standards.

On the other hand, it seems to me that the story of the *Collection complète* lends itself well to the interdisciplinary traditions of *l'histoire du livre*. As cultural history it illustrates the romantic confidence of disciple-editors that an author's message, embedded in printed autobiography, exists to inspire readers morally. As economic history the correspondence and balance sheets maintained by the STG and those who inherited the publisher's debts uncover an ambitious international business venture which ended badly. Mismanagement, miscalculation and poor luck proved devastating; yet at the same time the *Collection complète* was successfully pirated, indicating that in autobiographical form Rousseau remained a highly marketable commodity well into the early years of the French Revolution. As a history of social relations the saga of the *Collection complète* is an instructive tale of conflicting personal motivations. A determined widow, an abandoned disciple, a larger-than-life patron and a wealth of supporting characters expended huge blocks of their lives to assure the survival and transmission of a cultural icon. Certainly they manipulated Rousseau to suit their purposes. But as Foucault has hinted in his own highly personal contribution to *l'histoire du livre*: is not the creation of such an 'author-function' by subsequent generations an essential characteristic of print culture?[87]

87. 'The author does not precede the works, he is a certain functional principle by which, in our culture, one limits, excludes, and chooses' ('What is an author', p.159).

Bibliography

Primary sources

Manuscripts

France
Chaalis, archives of the Musée Jacquemart-André
Girardin. papers

Lyon, bibliothèque municipale
Jean-Jacques Rousseau, 'Le Devin du village', autograph manuscript.

Paris, archives du Musée de l'assistance publique
Ms. 525, subscribers' list for Rousseau's *Consolations des misères de ma vie* (Paris, Esprit 1781).

Paris, bibliothèque de l'Assemblée nationale, Palais-Bourbon
Cote 1427-29, Jean-Jacques Rousseau, 'Emile', 'brouillon' draft.
Cote 1433-38, Jean-Jacques Rousseau, 'La Nouvelle Héloïse' (maréchale de Luxembourg manuscript).
Cote 1456-57, Jean-Jacques Rousseau, 'Les Confessions' (Girardin manuscript).
Cote 1493, Jean-Jacques Rousseau, 'Rousseau juge de Jean-Jaques' (d'Angiviller manuscript).

Paris, Bibliothèque nationale de France
F.fr. 22180, no. 80, 81, 82, 87, 91, *arrêts du Conseil* of 30 August 1777; no. 175, amendment of 30 July 1778.
F.fr. 21990-94, *permission tacite* registers, 1718-1774.
F.fr. 21983-98, *permission tacite* registers, 1772-1789.
N.a.fr. 1183, Letters from Marc-Michel Rey, Jean Le Rond d'Alembert and Rousseau to Malesherbes pertaining to publication of the *Discours sur l'inégalité*, the *Lettre à M. d'Alembert* and *Emile*.
Rés. Vm⁷ 667, Certification of placement of Rousseau's music manuscripts into the Bibliothèque du roi, [10 April 1781].

Poland
Cracow, Czartoryski Library
Jean-Jacques Rousseau, 'Considérations sur le gouvernement de Pologne et sur sa réformation projetté' (Wielhorski manuscript).

Switzerland
Geneva, bibliothèque publique et universitaire
Dossier lettres: Du Peyrou/Moultou.
Ms.fr. 204, Correspondence of Du Peyrou.
Ms.fr. 221-23, Jean-Jacques Rousseau, 'Rousseau juge de Jean-Jaques' (Moultou manuscript).
Ms.fr. 225, Jean-Jacques Rousseau, 'Du contrat social', first draft (Moultou manuscript).
Ms.fr. 227, Jean-Jacques Rousseau, 'Les Confessions' (Moultou manuscript).

Geneva, Les Délices, archives of the Société Jean-Jacques Rousseau
Ms. R. 89, Jean-Jacques Rousseau, 'Discours sur les sciences et les arts' (corrected manuscript that Rousseau intended for publication).
Ms. R. 159, Documents pertaining to the production, sales, stock inventories and accounts of the *Collection complète des œuvres de J.-J. Rousseau* published by the Société typographique de Genève.
Ms. R. 160, f.145, Paul-Claude Moultou's accounting of his worth [1787].

253

Bibliography

Neuchâtel, bibliothèque publique et universitaire

Ms. R. 13, Jean-Jacques Rousseau, 'Considérations sur le gouvernement de Pologne et sur sa réformation projetée' (Girardin manuscript).

Ms. R. 14, Jean-Jacques Rousseau, 'Le Lévite d'Ephraïm', autograph draft.

Ms. R. 17, Jean-Jacques Rousseau, 'Les Confessions' (Du Peyrou manuscript).

Ms. R. 27, Jean-Jacques Rousseau, 'Pygmalion', autograph manuscript.

Ms. R. 55, Jean-Jacques Rousseau, 'Dictionnaire de musique', first complete draft.

Ms. R. 78, 79, Jean-Jacques Rousseau, 'Rêveries du promeneur solitaire' (Girardin manuscript).

Ms. R. 89-90, Rousseau's copybook of his correspondence.

Ms. R. 91-93, Drafts of Rousseau's correspondence.

Ms. R. 118, Correspondence of Du Peyrou, Girardin and others concerning publication of the Collection complète des œuvres de J.-J. Rousseau and the Confessions.

Ms. R. 284, f.71-73, Rough draft of Rousseau's will [1763?].

Ms. R. 286, Correspondence from Rousseau to P.-A. Du Peyrou.

Ms. R. 289, Correspondence from Rousseau to P.-C. Moultou.

Ms. R. 290, f.156-61, 162-67, 168-73, 174-79, 'Lettres à Malesherbes', copies that Malesherbes provided to Du Peyrou.

Ms. R. 310, Correspondence from Pierre Guy and Jean Néaulme to Rousseau.

Ms. R. 313, Correspondence from Du Peyrou to Rousseau.

Ms. R. 319, Correspondence from Moultou to Rousseau.

Ms. R. 320, Correspondence from Marc-Michel Rey to Rousseau.

USA

New York, Heineman Foundation

Jean-Jacques Rousseau, 'La Nouvelle Héloïse' (Marc-Michel Rey's working copy).

Published correspondence

Correspondance complète de Jean-Jacques Rousseau, ed. R. A. Leigh, 52 vols (Geneva, Madison, Oxford 1965-1998).

Correspondance générale de J.-J. Rousseau, ed. Théophile Dufour [and P.-P. Plan], 20 vols (Paris 1924-1934).

Jean-Jacques Rousseau/Chrétien-Guillaume de Lamoignon de Malesherbes. Correspondance, ed. Barbara de Negroni (Paris 1991).

Jean-Jacques Rousseau et Malesherbes, ed. Pierre Grosclaude (Paris 1960).

Jean-Jacques Rousseau, ses amis et ses ennemis. Correspondance, ed. G. Streckeisen-Moultou (Paris 1865).

Lettres diverses de Jean-Jacques Rousseau citoyen de Genève (Amsterdam, aux dépends de la Compagnie 1763).

Lettres inédites de Jean-Jacques Rousseau à Marc-Michel Rey, ed. J. Bosscha (Amsterdam and Paris 1858).

Works by Rousseau published individually, presented chronologically

Dissertation sur la musique moderne, in-8° (Paris, Quillau 1743).

Discours qui a remporté le prix à l'académie de Dijon, en l'année 1750, sur cette question proposé par la même académie: si le rétablissement des sciences et des arts a contribué à épurer les mœurs, par un citoyen de Genève, in-8° (Geneva, Barillot et fils [Paris, for Pissot 1751]).

Le Devin du village, intermède représenté à Fontainebleau devant leurs majestés le 18 et 24 octobre 1752 [...], engraved by Mlle Vandôme and printed by Sr Auguste, in-4° [Paris, Pissot 1753].

Discours sur l'origine et les fondements de l'inégalité parmi les hommes par Jean-Jacques Rousseau citoyen de Genève, in-8° (Amsterdam, Marc-Michel Rey 1755).

J.-J. Rousseau citoyen de Genève, à M. d'Alembert, de l'Académie française, de l'Académie royale des sciences de Paris, de celle de Prusse, de la Société royale de Londres, de l'Académie royale des belles-lettres de Suède, et de l'Institut de Bologne, sur son article 'Genève' dans le VIIe volume de l'"Encyclopédie", et particulièrement, sur le projet d'établir un théâtre de comédie en cette ville, in-8° (Amsterdam, Marc-Michel Rey 1758).

Lettres de deux amants, habitants d'une petite ville au pied des Alpes, recueillies et publiées par J.-J. Rousseau, half title *Julie, ou La nouvelle Héloïse,* 6 vols, in-12° (Amsterdam, Marc-Michel Rey 1761).

Lettres de deux amants, habitants d'une petite ville au pied des Alpes, recueillies et publiées par J.-J. Rousseau, half title *Julie, ou La nouvelle Héloïse,* 6 vols, in-12° (Amsterdam, Marc-Michel Rey [Paris, Robin] 1761).

Du contrat social, ou Principes du droit politique, par J.-J. Rousseau, citoyen de Genève, in-8° and in-12° (Amsterdam, Marc-Michel Rey 1762).

Du contrat social, ou Principes du droit politique, par J.-J. Rousseau, citoyen de Genève, édition sans cartons, à laquelle on a ajouté une lettre de l'auteur au seul ami qui lui reste dans le monde, in-12° (Amsterdam, [falsely attributed to] Marc-Michel Rey 1762).

Emile, ou De l'éducation, par J.-J. Rousseau, citoyen de Genève, 4 vols, in-8° (The Hague, Jean Néaulme [Paris, Duchesne] 1762); 4 vols, in-12° (Amsterdam, Jean Néaulme [Paris, Duchesne] 1762).

Emile, ou De l'éducation, par Jean-Jacques Rousseau, citoyen de Genève, 4 vols, in-8° (Amsterdam, Jean Néaulme 1762).

Emile, ou De l'éducation, par J.-J. Rousseau, citoyen de Genève, 4 vols, in-12° (Amsterdam [Lyon], Jean Néaulme 1762).

Jean-Jacques Rousseau, citoyen de Genève, à Christophe de Beaumont, archevêque de Paris, duc de St Cloud, pair de France, commandeur de l'ordre du St Esprit, proviseur de Sorbonne, etc., in-12° (Amsterdam, Marc-Michel Rey 1763).

Lettres diverses de Jean-Jacques Rousseau citoyen de Genève (Amsterdam 1763).

La Nouvelle Héloïse, ou Lettres de deux amants, habitants d'une petite ville au pied des Alpes, recueillies et publiées par J.-J. Rousseau, nouvelle édition, revue, corrigée et augmentée de figures en taille douce, et d'une table des matières, 4 vols, in-8° and in-12° (Neuchâtel et se trouve à Paris, Duchesne 1764).

Lettres écrites de la montagne, par J.-J. Rousseau, in-8° and in-12° (Amsterdam, Marc-Michel Rey 1764).

Lettre de M. Rousseau de Genève, à M*** (Paris, Duchesne 1764).

Dictionnaire de musique, par J.-J. Rousseau, in-4° (Paris, veuve Duchesne 1767[8]).

'Discours de M. J.-J. Rousseau de Genève, qui n'a point encore été imprimé, sur cette question: quelle est la vertu la plus nécessaire aux héros, et quels sont les héros, à qui cette vertu a manqué?', *Année littéraire* 7 (14 October 1768), p.4-27; (Amsterdam [Lausanne] 1769).

'Quatre lettres à M. le président de Malesherbes contenant le vrai tableau de mon caractère et les vrais motifs de toute ma conduite', in Jean-Antoine Roucher, *Les Mois* (1779), remarks to 'Chant XI', ii.283-307.

Fragments de Daphnis et Chloé, composé du premier acte, de l'esquisse du prologue et de différents morceaux préparés pour le second acte et le divertissement, paroles de M***, musique de J.-J. Rousseau (Paris, Jacques Esprit 1779).

Six nouveaux airs du devin du village (Paris, Jacques Esprit 1779).

Rousseau juge de Jean-Jacques, dialogues, premier dialogue, d'après le manuscrit de M. Rousseau, laissé entre les mains de M. Brooke Boothby, in-8° (Lichfield, J. Jackson, Cadell, Elmsley and Strahan 1780).

Les Consolations des misères de ma vie, ou Recueil d'airs, romances et duos, par J.-J. Rousseau, gravé sur cuivre, avec le plus grand soin, imprimé sur de beau papier, et orné d'un frontispice avec le portrait de l'auteur, in-folio (Paris, Esprit 1781).

Considérations sur le gouvernement de Pologne, et sur sa réformation projetée, par

J.-J. Rousseau, in 32° (London 1782), p.1-189, followed by the *Discours sur l'économie politique*, p.191-272.

Les Confessions [Part I] *de J.-J. Rousseau, suivies des Rêveries du promeneur solitaire*, 2 vols, in-8° and in-12° (Geneva [Société typographique de Genève] 1782).

Considérations sur le gouvernement de la Pologne et sur sa réformation projetée et lettres sur la législation de la Corse, dans lesquelles tous les souverains trouveront des choses utiles, par J.-J. Rousseau, citoyen de Genève, in-12° (The Hague and Lausanne 1783).

Les Confessions de J.-J. Rousseau. Seconde partie des Confessions de J.-J. Rousseau, 2 vols in-8° (Geneva [Barde-Manget] 1789).

Les Confessions de J.-J. Rousseau. Seconde partie des Confessions de J.-J. Rousseau, 2 vols in-8° (Paris, Poinçot and Lejay fils 1789).

Seconde partie des Confessions de J. J. Rousseau, Citoyen de Geneve, édition enrichie d'un nouveau recueil de ses lettres, 5 vols in-12° [vol. iii-vii] (Neuchâtel, Fauche-Borel 1790).

Collective editions of Rousseau's works

Œuvres diverses de M. J.-J. Rousseau de Genève, 2 vols, in-16° and in-12° (Paris, Pissot 1756).

Œuvres diverses de M. J.-J. Rousseau, nouvelle édition augmentée de sa lettre contre le projet d'établissement des spectacles à Genève, et de la réponse de M. d'Alembert, 2 vols, in-12° (Amsterdam 1761).

Œuvres diverses de M. J.-J. Rousseau citoyen de Genève, 3 vols in-8° (Amsterdam Marc-Michel Rey 1762); 9 vols, in-8° (1764).

Œuvres de M. Rousseau de Genève, nouvelle édition, revue, corrigée et augmentée de plusieurs morceaux qui n'avaient point encore paru, 9 vols, in-12° and in-8° (Neuchâtel [Paris and Amsterdam, Duchesne] 1764-1769; *Supplément formant le tome x* (Neuchâtel [Paris] 1779).

Miscellaneous works of M. J.-J. Rousseau, 5 vols (London [Becket and de Hondt] 1767).

Œuvres de J.-J. Rousseau, de Genève, nouvelle édition, revue, corrigée et augmentée de plusieurs morceaux qui n'avaient point encore paru, 11 vols, in-8° (Amsterdam, Marc-Michel Rey 1769).

Œuvres de J.-J. Rousseau, de Genève, nouvelle édition, revue, corrigée et augmentée de plusieurs morceaux qui n'avaient point encore paru, 11 vols, in-8°

(Amsterdam, Marc-Michel Rey 1772; 1773; 1776).

Collection complète des œuvres de J.-J. Rousseau, 9 vols, in-quarto (London [Brussels, J.-L. de Boubers] 1774-1776) [vols x-xii continued elsewhere in 1783].

Collection complète des œuvres de J.-J. Rousseau, avec figures en taille-douce, nouvelle édition, soigneusement revue et corrigée, 11 vols, in-8° (Neuchâtel, Samuel Fauche 1775).

Supplément aux œuvres de J.-J. Rousseau, citoyen de Genève, pour servir de suite de toutes les éditions, in-8° (Amsterdam and Lausanne, Grasset 1779).

Collection complète des œuvres de J.-J. Rousseau, citoyen de Genève, 12 vols, in-quarto and 24 vols, in-8° and in-12° (Geneva [Société typographique de Genève] [1780-]1782).

(1) *Supplément à la Collection des œuvres de J.-J. Rousseau*, 3 vols, in-4° (vol. xiii-xv) and 6 vols, in-8° and in-12° (vol. xxv-xxx) (Geneva [Société typographique de Genève] 1782).

(2) So-called *Second supplément à la Collection des œuvres de J.-J. Rousseau* [Pierre Moultou's edition of Part II of the *Confessions* and correspondence], 2 vols, in-4° (vol. xvi-xvii), and 3 vols, in-8° (vol. xxxi-xxxiii) (Geneva [Barde and Manget] 1789).

(3) *Suite de la Collection des Œuvres de J. J. Rousseau, Citoyen de Geneve* [Du Peyrou's

edition of Part II of the *Confessions* and correspondence], 5 vols, in-8° and in-12° (vol. xxv-xxix), containing the *Seconde partie des Confessions de J.-J. Rousseau, Citoyen de Genève*, édition enrichie d'un nouveau recueil de ses lettres (vol. iii-vii) (Neuchâtel, L. Fauche-Borel 1790).

Collection complète des œuvres de J.-J. Rousseau, citoyen de Genève, 30 vols in-12° (Geneva [Neuchâtel piracy] [1780-]1782). Additional piracies and counterfeit editions made by the Société typographique de Berne, 37 vols, in-12° (1783); the Société littéraire-typographique (Kehl), 34 vols, in-12° (1783-1789); Cazin (Reims), 38 vols, in-18° (1780-1791); and Sanson et compagnie (Deux-Ponts), 33 vols in-12° (1783-1784).

Œuvres posthumes de J.-J. Rousseau, ou Recueil de pièces manuscrits, pour servir de supplément aux éditions publiées pendant sa vie, 9 vols, in-8° (Geneva, [Société typographique de Genève] 1781-1782).

Œuvres posthumes de J.-J. Rousseau, ou Recueil de pièces manuscrits, pour servir de supplément aux éditions publiées pendant sa vie, 9 vols in-12° ([Neuchâtel, Société typographique de Neuchâtel] 1781-1782).

Œuvres posthumes de J.-J. Rousseau, ou Recueil de pièces manuscrits, pour servir de supplément aux éditions publiées pendant sa vie, 12 vols, in-8° (Neuchâtel, Samuel Fauche 1782).

Œuvres complètes de J.-J. Rousseau, nouvelle édition, classée par ordre de matières, et ornée de quatre-vingt-dix gravures, 38 vols, in-8° and in-4° (Paris, Poinçot 1788-1793).

Œuvres de J.-J. Rousseau, citoyen de Genève, 2 vols, in-8° (Paris An ix [1801]).

Œuvres complètes de J.-J. Rousseau, mises dans un nouvel ordre avec des notes historiques et des éclaircissements, ed. V. D. Musset-Pathay, 25 vols (Paris 1823-1826).

J.-J. Rousseau, œuvres et correspondance inédites, ed. G. Streckeisen-Moultou (Paris 1861).

Œuvres complètes, ed. Bernard Gagnebin and Marcel Raymond, 5 vols (Paris, Bibliothèque de la Pléiade 1964-1995).

Works by Rousseau published for the first time in the Collection complète des œuvres de J.-J. Rousseau ([1780-]1782), or in the Œuvres posthumes (1782)

'Les amours de milord Edouard Bomston', iii.513-30, in-4°; vi.350-76, in-8°.

Les Confessions, Part I, Books i-vi, x.1-366, in-4°; vol. xix, xx.1-208, in-8°.

Considérations sur le gouvernement de Pologne et sur sa réformation projetée, i.415-539, in-4°; ii.253-442, in-8°.

Emile et Sophie, ou Les Solitaires, v.449-514, in-4°; x.233-331, in-8°.

L'Engagement téméraire, viii.53-118, in-4°; xv.63-149, in-8°.

Essai sur l'origine des langues, viii.355-434, in-4°; vol. xvi, in-8°.

Examen de deux principes avancés par M. Rameau, in *Œuvres posthumes*, iii.335-75.

Fragments pour un dictionnaire des termes d'usage en botanique, vii.459-527, in-4°; xiv.351-428, in-8°.

Jugement sur le projet de paix perpétuelle, xii.40-52, in-4°; xxiii.62-82, in-8°.

Jugement sur la polysynodie, xii.76-90, in-4°; xxiii.118-39, in-8°.

Lettre de J.-J. Rousseau à M. le docteur Burney, followed by the *Fragments d'observation sur l'Alceste italien de M. le chevalier Gluck* and the *Extrait d'une réponse du petit faiseur à son prête-nom*, in *Œuvres posthumes*, iii.377-439.

'Lettres élémentaires sur la botanique à Mme de L***', vii.529-88, in-4°; xiv.429-518, in-8°.

'Le Lévite d'Ephraïm', vii.161-86, in-4°; xiii.239-73, in-8°.

Les Muses galantes, viii.119-56, in-4°.

La Polysynodie [from the *Ecrits sur l'abbé de Saint-Pierre*], xii.53-75, in-4°; xxiii.83-117, in-8°.

Les Prisonniers de guerre, xiv.49-83, in-4°; xxvii.69-116, in-8°.

Projet concernant de nouveaux signes pour la musique, in *Œuvres posthumes*, iii.1-21.

Projet pour l'éducation de M. de Sainte-Marie, xiv.1-24, in-4°; xxvii.1-36, in-8°.

Rêveries du promeneur solitaire, x.376-517, in-4°; xx.209-end, in-8°.

La Seconde partie des 'Mémoires', ou Rousseau juge de Jean-Jacques, en trois dialogues, vol. xi, in-4°; vol. xxi-xxii, in-8°; and in *Œuvres posthumes*, vol. x-xi, in-8°.

Eighteenth-century works alluding to Rousseau

Alembert, Jean Le Rond d', *Eloge de milord maréchal par M. d'Alembert* (1779).

–, *Lettre de M. d'Alembert à M. J.-J. Rousseau, sur l'article 'Genève' tiré du septième volume de l'"Encyclopédie", avec quelques autres pièces qui y sont relatives* (1759).

Andrieux, François-G.-J.-S., *L'Enfance de Jean-Jacques Rousseau, comédie en un acte* [1794].

Anecdotes pour servir à la vie de J.-J. Rousseau, suite du supplément à ses œuvres (1779).

Les Années de formation de F. H. Jacobi, d'après ses lettres inédites à M. M. Rey (1763-1771) avec 'Le Noble' de Mme de Charrière, ed. J. Th. de Booy and Roland Mortier, *SVEC* 45 (1966).

Arrêt de la Cour de Parlement, qui condamne un imprimé ayant pour titre, 'Emile ou de l'Education', par J.-J. Rousseau, imprimé à La Haye [...] M.DCC.LXII. à être lacéré et brûlé par l'Exécuteur de la Haute-Justice [...], 9-11 June 1762 [1762].

[Aubert de Vitry, François-Jean-Philibert], *Jean-Jacques Rousseau à l'Assemblée nationale* (1789).

Aude, Joseph, *J.-J. Rousseau au Paraclet, comédie en prose et en trois actes* (1794).

Avis de la Société typographique de Genève, sur un supplément à la Collection des œuvres de J.-J. Rousseau, en 2 volumes in-4° et 4 volumes in-8° et in-12 [1779?].

Barruel-Beauvert, Antoine-J. de, *Vie de J.-J. Rousseau, précédée de quelques lettres relatives au même sujet* (1789).

[Baudoin, François-Jean], *Recueil des pièces relatives à la motion faite à l'Assemblée nationale, au sujet de J.-J. Rousseau et de sa veuve* (1791).

Belloy, P.-L. Buirette de Dormont de, *Œuvres complètes*, 6 vols (1779-1787).

Berthier, G.-F., *Observations sur le Contrat social de J.-J. Rousseau* (1789).

[Bilhon, Jean-Frédéric-Joseph], *Eloge de J.-J. Rousseau* (1788).

[Borde, Charles], *Discours sur les avantages des sciences et des arts, prononcé dans l'assemblée publique de l'Académie des sciences et belles-lettres de Lyon, le 22 juin 1751, avec la réponse de Jean-J. Rousseau, citoyen de Genève* (1752).

Boswell on the Grand Tour: Italy, Corsica and France, ed. Frank Brady and F. A. Pottle (New York [1955]).

Bouilly, Jean.-N., *Jean-Jacques Rousseau à ses derniers moments, trait historique, en un acte et en prose, représenté pour la première fois, à Paris, par les Comédiens italiens ordinaires du roi, le 31 décembre 1790* (1791).

Bovier, Gaspard, *Journal du séjour à Grenoble de Jean-Jacques Rousseau, sous le nom de Renou*, ed. Raymond Schiltz (Grenoble 1964).

[Brard, A.-J.], *Le Reveil de J.-J. Rousseau, ou Particularités sur sa mort et son tombeau, par P.A.J.B.***D.V [...]* (1783).

Bref de N.S.P. le pape Clément XIII, à la Faculté de théologie de Paris, au sujet des censures de cette faculté contre l'Emile de Rousseau et l'Histoire du peuple de Dieu, du P. Berruyer (1764).

Brizard, Gabriel, *Prospectus des œuvres de J.-J. Rousseau, nouvelle édition, ornée de quatre-vingt-dix gravures* (1787).

[Bruny, chevalier de], *Lettre sur J.-J. Rousseau* (1780 [1779]).

Cambacérès, Jean-Jacques-Régis de, *Discours prononcé par le président de la Convention nationale, lors de la translation des cendres de Jean-Jacques Rousseau au Panthéon, le 20 vendémiaire de l'an troisième de la République* [1794].

[Champcenetz, Louis-René-Quentin de Richebourg, marquis de], *Réponse aux lettres sur le caractère et les ouvrages de*

J.-J. Rousseau, bagatelle que vingt libraires ont refusé de faire imprimer (1789).

Charrière, Isabelle de, *Œuvres complètes* [*d'Isabelle de Charrière*], ed. J.-D. Candaux, C. P. Courtney *et al.*, 10 vols (Amsterdam 1979-1984).

–, 'De Rousseau' [1788-1789], in *Œuvres complètes*, x.125.

–, *Eclaircissements relatifs à la publication des Confessions de Rousseau*, [1790], in *Œuvres complètes*, x.183-94.

–, 'Eloge de Jean-Jacques Rousseau' [1790], in *Œuvres complètes*, x.199-211.

–, *Plainte et défense de Thérèse Levasseur* [1789], in *Œuvres complètes*, x.173-76.

Chas, François, *J.-J. Rousseau justifié, ou Réponse à M. Servan, ancien avocat-général au Parlement de Grenoble* (1783).

–, *Réflexions philosophiques et impartiales sur J.-J. Rousseau et Mme de Warens* (1786).

Chénier, Marie-Joseph, 'Hymne à J.-J. Rousseau […] chanté au Panthéon le 20 vendémiaire An 3ᵉ de la République', *La Décade philosophique* 17 (20 vendémiaire An III), iv.164-66.

'Déclaration de J. J. Rousseau, relative à M. le Pasteur Vernes, Accompagnée des notes responsives fournies par ce dernier', *Suite de la Collection des Œuvres de J. J. Rousseau, Citoyen de Geneve* (Neuchâtel 1790), xxvii.5-85. [*Seconde partie des Confessions de J. J. Rousseau, Citoyen de Genève*, v.5-85].

Décret de la Convention nationale du 15ᵉ jour de brumaire An second de la République française […] *relatif à l'érection d'une statue de J.-J. Rousseau en bronze* [1794].

[Delacroix Jacques-V.], *Eloge de Jean-Jacques Rousseau, par M.D.L.C. avocat* (1778).

Delon, Alexandre, *Discours sur les 'Confessions' de Jean-Jacques Rousseau* (1784).

[Désorgues, Théodore], *Hymne à Jean-Jacques Rousseau* [1794].

[Desriaux, Philippe], *L'Ombre de J.-J. Rousseau, comédie en deux actes et en prose, par M. L**** (1787).

Diderot, Denis, *Essai sur la vie de Sénèque le philosophe, sur ses écrits, et sur les règnes de Claude et de Néron* (1779).

–, *Essai sur les règnes de Claude et de Néron, et sur les mœurs et les écrits de Sénèque, pour servir d'introduction à la lecture de ce philosophe*, 2 vols (1782).

[Doppet, François-Amédée], *Mémoires de Mme de Warens, suivis de ceux de Claude Anet, publiés par un C.D.M.D.P. pour servir d'apologie aux Confessions de J.-J. Rousseau* (1786).

[Dubrail], *Grande dispute au Panthéon, entre Marat et Jean-Jacques Rousseau* [1794].

Du Peyrou, Pierre-Alexandre, 'Dédicace aux mânes de Jean-Jacques Rousseau', in *Collection complète des œuvres de J.-J. Rousseau, citoyen de Genève* (Geneva [Société typographique de Genève] [1780-]1782), i.3-7.

–, 'Discours préliminaire' to the *Seconde partie des Confessions de J.-J. Rousseau, citoyen de Genève* […] (Neuchâtel, Fauche-Borel 1790), iii.i-xxiii. [Also cited as in the *Suite de la Collection des Œuvres* […], xxv.i-xxiii.]

–, *Lettre à M.*** relative à M. J.-J. Rousseau* (1765) [containing the 'Lettre de Goa'] (anonymous publication).

–, *Lettre à Monsieur *** relative à M. J.-J. Rousseau*, […] *avec la Réfutation de ce libelle par le Professeur de Montmollin* (1765) (anonymous publication).

–, *Pièces relatives à la publication de la suite des 'Confessions' de J.-J. Rousseau* (1790) (anonymous publication).

–, *Recueil des pièces relatives à la persécution suscitée à Motiers-Travers contre M. J.-J. Rousseau* (1765) (anonymous publication).

–, *Seconde lettre relative à M. J.-J. Rousseau, adressée à milord comte de Wemyss* […] [1765] (anonymous publication).

Dusaulx, Jean, *De mes rapports avec J.-J. Rousseau, et de notre correspondance, suivie d'une notice très importante* (1798).

[Duvernet, Théophile], *La Vie de Voltaire, par M**** (1786).

Epinay, Louise-Florence d', *Histoire de Mme de Montbrillant*, ed. Georges Roth, 3 vols (Paris 1951).

[Eymar, Ange-Marie], *Motion relative à J.-J. Rousseau, par A. M. Eymar, député de Forcalquier, à l'Assemblée nationale, Paris, le 29 novembre 1790* (1790).

Fête champêtre, célébrée à Montmorency, en l'honneur de J.-J. Rousseau […] (1791).

F[ochier], L., *Séjour de J.-J. Rousseau à Bourgoin, notice par L. Fxxx* (1860), p.30-47.

Formey, J.-H.-Samuel, *Anti-Emile* (1762).

–, *Emile chrétien, consacré à l'utilité publique* (1764).

–, *L'Esprit de Julie, ou Extrait de la Nouvelle Héloïse, ouvrage utile à la société et particulièrement à la jeunesse* (1763).

[Foulquier, François-Joseph de], *Lettre sur la mort de J.-J. Rousseau écrite par un de ses amis, aux auteurs du J.^{al} de Paris, Paris le 12 juillet 1778* [1778].

Gautier, Joseph, *Observations sur la lettre de M. Rousseau de Genève à M. Grimm* (1752).

Ginguené, Pierre-L., *Lettres sur les 'Confessions' de J.-J. Rousseau* (1791).

–, *Pétition à l'Assemblée nationale, contenant demande de la translation des cendres de J.-J. Rousseau au Panthéon français, IIe séance, du 27 août 1791* [1791].

[Girardin, René-Louis de], 'Lettre à Sophie comtesse de *** par René Girardin, sur les derniers moments de J.-J. Rousseau à Ermenonville, juillet 1778', appendix to Jean-Antoine Roucher, *Les Mois* (1779), ii.307-11.

Helvétius, Claude-Adrien, *Lettres à M. D[e] B[ure] sur la réfutation du livre De l'esprit d'Helvétius, par J.-J. Rousseau* (1779).

Hume, David, *A concise and genuine account of the dispute between Mr Hume and Mr Rousseau* (1766), translated by J.-B.-A. Suard, *Exposé succinct de la contestation qui s'est élevée entre M. Hume et M. Rousseau avec les pièces justificatives* (1766).

Isnard, Achille, *Observations sur le principe qui a produit les révolutions de France, de Genève et d'Amérique dans le dix-huitième siècle* (1789).

[Ivernois, François d'], *Tableau historique et politique des révolutions de Genève dans le dix-huitième siècle* [...] (1782).

J.-J. Rousseau dans l'île de St-Pierre, pièce représentée àu Théâtre de la nation en décembre 1791.

J.-J. Rousseau raconté par les gazettes de son temps, d'un décret à l'autre (9 juin 1762 – 21 décembre 1790), ed. Pierre-Paul Plan (Paris and Geneva 1912).

Jean-Jacques, ou Le réveil-matin des représentants de la nation française (1789).

Jean-Jacques Rousseau des Champs-Elisées à la nation française [1791].

La Borde, J.-B. de, *Essai sur la musique ancienne et moderne*, 4 vols (1780).

[La Croix, Pierre-Firmin de], *Jean-Jacques Rousseau, citoyen de Genève, à Jean-François de Montillet, archevêque et seigneur d'Auch, primat de la Gaule novempopulanie, et du royaume de Navarre, conseiller du roi en tous ses conseils* (1764).

–, *Lettre de J.-J. Rousseau de Genève, qui contient sa rénonciation à la société civile, et ses derniers adieux aux hommes, adressé au seul ami qui lui reste dans le monde* (1762) (anonymous publication).

[Lakanal, Joseph], *Rapport sur J.-J. Rousseau, fait au nom du Comité d'instruction publique, par Lakanal, dans la séance du 29 fructidor, imprimé par ordre de la Convention nationale et envoyé aux départements, aux armées et à la République de Genève* [1794].

[La Tour de Franqueville, Marie-Anne Alissan de], *Jean-Jacques Rousseau vengé par son amie, ou Morale pratico-philosophico-encyclopédique des coryphées de la secte* (1779).

–, *Précis pour M. J.-J. Rousseau, en réponse à l'Exposé succinct' de M. Hume, suivi d'une lettre de Mme D*** à l'auteur de la 'Justification de M. Rousseau'* (1767).

–, 'La vertu vengée par l'amitié, ou Recueil de lettres sur J.-J. Rousseau par Mme de ***', in *Supplément à la Collection des œuvres de J.-J. Rousseau* (Geneva [Société typographique de Genève] 1782), iii.xv.309-32, in-4°.

[Lebègue de Presle, Achille-Guillaume], *Relation ou notice des derniers jours de M. Jean-Jacques Rousseau, circonstances de sa mort, et quels sont les ouvrages posthumes qu'on peut attendre de lui* [...] *avec une addition relative au même sujet, par J.-H. de Magellan, gentilhomme portugais* [...] (1778).

[Le Cat, Claude-Nicolas], *Réfutation du discours du citoyen de Genève, qui a remporté le prix à l'académie de Dijon, en l'année 1750, par un académicien de la même ville* (1751).

Lefébure, Louis-F.-H., *Bévues, erreurs et méprises de différents auteurs célèbres, en matières musicales* (1789).

[Lenormant, Charles-François], *J.-J. Rousseau aristocrate* (1790).

Lettre de Jean-Jacques Rousseau à l'Assemblée nationale [1789].

Mandement de M. l'archevêque de Paris, portant condamnation d'un livre qui a pour titre: Emile, ou De l'éducation, par J.-J. Rousseau, citoyen de Genève (1762).

Manuel, [Louis-]Pierre, *La Police de Paris dévoilée* (1793).

[Maréchal, Pierre-Sylvain], *Le Tombeau de J.-J. Rousseau, stances* (1779).

[Marignan de], *Eclaircissements donnés à l'auteur du 'Journal encyclopédique' sur la musique du 'Devin du village'* (1781).

Mercier, Louis-S., *De J.-J. Rousseau, considéré comme l'un des premiers auteurs de la Révolution*, 2 vols (1791).

[Métra, François], *Correspondance littéraire secrète*, 19 vols (1775-1793).

[Moultou, Paul-C.], 'Avant-propos', in *Collection complète des œuvres de J.-J. Rousseau, citoyen de Genève* (Geneva [Société typographique de Genève] [1780-]1782), i.1-2, in-4°.

Olivier de Corancez, Guillaume, *De J.-J. Rousseau, extrait du 'Journal de Paris', des n⁰ˢ 251, 256, 258, 259, 260 et 261, de l'An VI* [1798].

Palissot de Montenoy, Charles, *Les Philosophes, comédie en trois actes, en vers, représentée pour la première fois par les Comédiens français ordinaires du roi, le 2 mai 1760* (1760).

Petit, Michel-Edme, *Eloge de J.-J. Rousseau, citoyen de Genève* (1792).

[Petit de Bachaumont, Louis de, attributed to], *Mémoires secrets pour servir à l'histoire de la République des lettres en France depuis M.DCC.LXII jusqu'à nos jours, ou Journal d'un observateur*, 36 vols (1777-1787).

Pétition à l'Assemblée nationale, contenant demande de la translation des cendres de J.-J. Rousseau au Panthéon français [...] 27 août 1791 [...] [1791].

Private papers of James Boswell from Malahide Castle, in the collection of Lt Colonel Ralph Heyward Isham, ed. Geoffrey Scott and F. A. Pottle, [Mount Vernon, N.Y. 1928].

Projet de souscription pour un livre intitulé: le véritable Emile consacré à l'utilité publique, rédigé par M. Formey (1763).

'Ptivar', *La Vérité, ou J.-J. Rousseau montrant à Robespierre le livre des destins* [1794].

Recueil des écrits de J.-J. Rousseau, proposé par souscription, à Genève, chez la Société typographique, in-4° et in-8°, avec un portrait de l'auteur [1779].

Recueil des écrits de J.-J. Rousseau, sur la copie de Genève, proposé par Souscription, in-12, de la Grandeur des Théâtres de Molière, Racine, Crébillon, & c [1780]. Reprinted in the *Journal helvétique* (February 1780), p.103-107.

Recueil des pièces relatives à la motion faite à l'Assemblée nationale, au sujet de J.-J. Rousseau et de sa veuve (1791).

Roucher, Jean-Antoine, *Les Mois, poème en douze chants*, 2 vols (1779).

[Saint-Chamond, Claire-Marie Mazarelli, marquise de La Vieuville de], *Jean-Jacques à M. S... sur des réflexions contre ses derniers écrits* (1784).

Servan, Antoine-Joseph-Michel, *Réflexions sur les 'Confessions' de J.-J. Rousseau, sur le caractère et le génie de cet écrivain, sur les causes et l'étendue de son influence sur l'opinion publique, enfin sur quelques principes de ses ouvrages, insérées dans le 'Journal encyclopédique' de l'année 1783* (1783).

[Staël-Holstein, Anne-L.-Germaine de], *Lettres sur les ouvrages et le caractère de J.-J. Rousseau* (1788; Geneva 1979).

[Stanislas I, king of Poland/Joseph de Menoux], *Réponse au discours qui a remporté le prix de l'académie de Dijon, sur cette question: si le rétablissement des sciences et des arts a contribué à épurer les mœurs, par un citoyen de Genève* (1751).

Voltaire, F. M. Arouet dit, *Le Docteur Pansophe, ou Lettres de M. de Voltaire* (1766).

–, *Sentiment des citoyens* [1764] (anonymous publication).

Periodicals

L'Ami du peuple (Paris 1789-1793).
Annales politiques, civiles et littéraires du dix-huitième siècle (London, Paris and Brussels 1777-1792).
Année littéraire (Paris 1754-1791).
Courrier de l'Europe (London 1776-1792).
Courrier du Bas-Rhin (Cleves 1767-1809?).
Gazette d'Amsterdam (Amsterdam 1688-1795).
Gazette de Berne and *Supplément* (Berne 1689-1787).
Gazette de Leyde (Leiden 1677-1811).
Gazette de littérature, des sciences et des arts (Paris 1783-1789).
Gazette littéraire de l'Europe (Paris 1764-1766; Amsterdam 1766-1784).
Journal de Lausanne (Lausanne 1786-1792).
Journal de la montagne (Paris 1793-1794).
Journal de Paris and *Supplément* (Paris 1777-1840).
Journal encyclopédique (Liège and Bouillon 1756-1794).
Journal helvétique (Neuchâtel 1738-1769).
Lloyd's evening post (and British chronicle) (London 1757-1805).
London chronicle (London 1757-1823).
Mercure de France (Paris 1724-1791)
Le Monde comme il est (Amsterdam and Paris 1760).
Le Moniteur universel, reimpression (Paris 1789-1868).
Révolutions de Paris (Paris 1789-1794).
St James's chronicle or British evening post (London 1761-1866).

Other contemporary works

Buffon, Georges-Louis Leclerc, comte de, *Histoire naturelle, générale et particulière*, 15 vols, in-4° (1749-1767).
Catalogue des livres françois de Marc-Michel Rey, Libraire (Amsterdam 1754).
Girardin, René-Louis de, *De la composition des paysages, ou Des moyens d'embellir la nature autour des habitations, en joignant l'agréable à l'utile* (1777), ed. Michel-H. Conan (Paris 1979), translated by Daniel Malthus, *An essay on landscapes* (1783; New York 1982).
[–], *Promenade ou itinéraire des jardins d'Ermenonville* (1788), in *De la composition des paysages* (Paris 1979), p.119-94.
[Malesherbes, Chrétien-Guillaume de Lamoignon de], *Mémoires sur la librairie;*
mémoire sur la liberté de la presse, ed. Roger Chartier (Paris 1994).
Servan, Antoine-Joseph-Michel, *Commentaire sur un passage du livre de M. Necker, ou Eclaircissements demandés à messieurs les commis des postes, préposés à décacheter les lettres* (1784).
–, *Discours sur l'administration de la justice criminelle* (1767).
Voltaire, F. M. Arouet dit, *Œuvres complètes de Voltaire*, 70 vols in-8° and 92 vols in-12° ([Kehl], Société littéraire typographique 1784-1789).
Voltaire, lettres inédites à son imprimeur Gabriel Cramer, ed. Bernard Gagnebin (Geneva 1952).

Secondary works

Adams, Thomas R. and Nicolas Barker, 'A new model for the study of the book', in *A Potencie of life: books in society. The Clark lectures*, ed. Nicolas Barker (London 1993), p.5-43.
Altman, Janet Gurkin, 'The letter-book as a literary institution 1539-1789', *Yale French studies* 71 (1986), p.17-62.
Arnault, Antoine-Vincent, *Souvenirs d'un sexagénaire*, vol. iii (1833).
Attridge, Anna, 'The reception of *La Nouvelle Héloïse*', *SVEC* 120 (1974), p.227-67.
Aubert, F., 'Catalogue des manuscrits de Jean-Jacques Rousseau qui se trouvent à Genève', *Annales de la Société Jean-Jacques Rousseau* 24 (1935), p.179-250.

Autobiography: essays theoretical and critical, ed. James Olney (Princeton 1980).

Ayers, Eleanor Hall, 'Histoire de l'impression et de la publication de la *Lettre à d'Alembert* de J.-J. Rousseau', *Publications of the Modern Language Association of America* 37 (1922), p.527-65.

Baczko, Bronislaw, 'Rousseau au Panthéon', in *Regards sur la Révolution génévoise, 1792-1798* (Geneva 1988), p.193-211.

–, *Rousseau. Solitude et communauté*, translated from the Polish by Claire Brendhel-Lamhout, Collection civilisations et sociétés 30 (Paris and The Hague 1974).

Barber, Giles, 'The financial history of the Kehl Voltaire', in *The Age of the Enlightenment: studies presented to Theodore Besterman*, ed. W. H. Barber *et al.* (London and Edinburgh 1967), p.152-70.

–, *Studies in the booktrade of the European Enlightenment* (London 1994).

Barbier, A.-A., *Notice bibliographique sur les diverses éditions des ouvrages de J.-J. Rousseau*, 4th edn, augmented by Louis Barbier and J.-J. Quérard (Paris 1836).

–, *Notice des principaux écrits relatifs à la personne et aux ouvrages de J.-J. Rousseau*, 4th edn (Paris 1836) (anonymous publication).

Barny, Roger, 'Les aristocrates et Jean-Jacques Rousseau dans la Révolution', *Annales historiques de la Révolution française* 231-34 (1978), p.534-68.

–, *L'Eclatement révolutionnaire du rousseauisme* (Paris 1988).

–, *Prélude idéologique de la Révolution française. Le rousseauisme avant 1789* (Paris 1985).

–, *Rousseau dans la Révolution. Le personnage de Jean-Jacques et les débuts du culte révolutionnaire (1789-1791)*, SVEC 246 (1986).

Battaglia, Otto Forst de, 'Un peu de lumière sur les *Considérations*', *Annales de la Société Jean-Jacques Rousseau* 17 (1926), p.97-119.

Belin, J.-P., *Le Commerce des livres prohibés à Paris de 1750 à 1789* (Paris 1913).

Benjamin, Walter, 'The work of art in the age of mechanical reproduction', in *Illuminations*, ed. Hannah Arendt, translated by Harry Zohn (New York 1969), p.217-51.

Berkvens-Stevelinck, Christiane, 'L'édition française en Hollande', in *Histoire de l'édition française*, vol. ii *Le Livre triomphant, 1660-1830* (Paris 1990), p.403-11.

Biographie universelle ancienne et moderne, ed. Louis-G. Michaud, 45 vols (Paris 1843-1865).

Biou, Jean, *Roman et lumières au XVIIIᵉ siècle* (Paris 1970).

Birn, Raymond, 'A certain place for memory: Rousseau, *Les Confessions* and the first edition of the *Discours sur l'origine de l'inégalité*', in *Le Livre et l'historien. Etudes offertes en l'honneur du professeur Henri-Jean Martin*, ed. Frédéric Barbier *et al.* (Geneva 1997), p.557-70.

–, 'Fashioning an icon: Jean-Jacques Rousseau and the *Mémoires secrets*', in *The 'Mémoires secrets' and the culture of publicity in eighteenth-century France*, ed. Jeremy D. Popkin and Bernadette Fort (Oxford 1998), p.93-105.

–, 'Lettre sur le commerce de la librairie' and 'Luneau de Boisjermain', in *Dictionnaire de Diderot*, ed. Roland Mortier and Raymond Trousson (Paris 1999), p.283-84, 300.

–, 'Malesherbes and the call for a free press', in *Revolution in print: the press in France, 1775-1800*, ed. Robert Darnton and Daniel Roche (Berkeley and Los Angeles 1989), p.50-66.

–, 'Marc-Michel Rey's enlightenment', in *Le Magasin de l'univers, the Dutch republic as the centre of the European book trade*, ed. C. Berkvens-Stevelinck *et al.* (Leiden 1992), p.23-32.

–, 'Les "Œuvres complètes" de Rousseau sous l'ancien régime', *Annales de la Société Jean-Jacques Rousseau* 41 (1997), p.229-62.

–, *Pierre Rousseau and the philosophes of Bouillon*, SVEC 29 (1964).

–, 'The profits of ideas: *privilèges en librairie* in eighteenth-century France', *Eighteenth-century studies* 4 (1971), p.131-69.

–, 'Religious toleration and freedom of expression', in *The French idea of freedom: the old regime and the declaration of rights of 1789*, ed. Dale Van Kley (Stanford 1994), p.265-99, 407-18.

–, 'Rousseau and literary property', *Leipziger Jahrbuch zur Buchgeschichte* 3 (1993), p.13-37.

–, 'Rousseau et ses éditeurs', *Revue d'histoire moderne et contemporaine* 41 (1993), p.127-36.

–, 'Rousseau senza frontiere', *Rivista storica italiana* 107 (1995), p.575-613.

Bloom, Edward A., 'Samuel Johnson on copyright', *Journal of English and Germanic philology* 47 (1948), p.165-72.

Blum, Carol, 'Jean-Jacques Rousseau in the 1780s: popularisation of a radical folk hero', *SVEC* 265 (1989), p.1659-61.

–, *Rousseau and the republic of virtue: the language of politics in the French Revolution* (Ithaca 1986).

Bollème, Geneviève, *et al.*, *Livre et société dans la France du XVIIIᵉ siècle*, 2 vols (Paris and The Hague 1965-1970).

Bonnell, Thomas F., 'Bookselling and canon making: the trade rivalry over the English poets, 1776-1783', *Studies in eighteenth-century culture* 19 (1989), p.53-69.

Bonnet, Jean-Claude, 'L.-S. Mercier et les *Œuvres complètes* de Jean-Jacques Rousseau', *SVEC* 370 (1999), p.111-24.

Braudy, Leo, *The Frenzy of renown: fame and its history* (New York 1986).

Brewer, Daniel, *The Discourse of enlightenment in 18th-century France* (Cambridge 1993).

Brewer, John, *The Pleasures of the imagination: English culture in the eighteenth century* (New York 1997).

Brissart-Binet, Charles-A., *Cazin, sa vie et ses éditions* (Paris 1863).

Buffenoir, Henri, 'Concours ouverts sous la Révolution pour un monument en l'honneur de J.-J. Rousseau', *Mercure de France* 155 (1922), p.93-119.

–, 'L'image de J.-J. Rousseau dans les sociétés de la Révolution à Paris', *La Révolution française* 70 (1917), p.504-17.

Burt, E. S., 'The meeting place of autobiography and censorship: Rousseau's *Lettres à Malesherbes*', *Studies in eighteenth-century culture* 17 (1987), p.289-308.

Calemard, Jean, 'L'édition originale d'*Emile*', *Bulletin du bibliophile* 5 (1926), p.111-18.

Champion, Edme, *J.-J. Rousseau et la Révolution française* (Paris 1909).

Chartier, Roger, 'The chimera of the origin: archeology, cultural history, and the French Revolution', in *Foucault and the writing of history*, ed. Jan Goldstein (Cambridge, Mass. and Oxford 1994), p.167-86.

–, *The Cultural origins of the French Revolution*, translated by Lydia G. Cochrane (Durham and London 1991).

–, 'Figures of the author', in *The Order of books: readers, authors, and libraries in Europe between the fourteenth and eighteenth centuries*, translated by Lydia G. Cochrane (Cambridge 1994), p.25-59.

–, 'L'homme de lettres', in *L'Homme des Lumières*, ed. Michel Vovelle (Paris 1996), p.159-209.

Chouillet, Jacques, 'La présence de J.-J. Rousseau après sa mort dans les écrits de Diderot', in *Cahiers de Varsovie* 10 (1982), p.177-88.

Collins, A. S., *Authorship in the days of Johnson: being a study of the relations between author, patron, publisher, and public 1726-1780* (London 1927).

Conlon, P. M., *Ouvrages français relatifs à Jean-Jacques Rousseau, 1751-1799. Bibliographie chronologique* (Geneva 1981).

–, *Le Siècle des Lumières. Bibliographie chronologique*, 21 vols to date (Geneva 1983–).

The Construction of authorship: textual appropriation in law and literature, ed. Martha Ann Woodmansee and Peter Jaszi (Durham 1994).

The Consumption of culture 1600-1800, ed. Ann Bermingham and John Brewer (London and New York 1995).

Courtney, C. P., *Isabelle de Charrière (Belle de Zuylen): a biography* (Oxford 1993).

Courtois, Louis J., 'Chronologie critique de la vie et des œuvres de Jean-Jacques Rousseau', *Annales de la Société Jean-Jacques Rousseau* 15 (1923), p.vii-366.

Cranston, Maurice, *Jean-Jacques: the early life and work of Jean-Jacques Rousseau 1712-1754* (Chicago 1982).

–, *The Noble savage: Jean-Jacques Rousseau 1754-1762* (Chicago 1991).

–, *The Solitary self: Jean-Jacques Rousseau in exile and adversity* (Chicago 1997).

Crocker, Lester G., *Jean-Jacques Rousseau*, vol. i *The Quest 1712-1758* (New York and London 1968); vol. ii *The Prophetic voice 1758-1778* (New York and London 1973).

Darnton, Robert, *The Business of enlightenment: a publishing history of the 'Encyclopédie' 1775-1800* (Cambridge, Mass. 1979).

–, *The Corpus of clandestine literature in France, 1769-1789* (New York and London 1995).

–, *The Forbidden best-sellers of pre-revolutionary France* (New York and London 1995).

–, 'The high Enlightenment and the low-life of literature', in *The Literary underground of the old regime* (Cambridge, Mass. 1982), p.1-40, 211-23.

–, 'Readers respond to Rousseau: the fabrication of romantic sensitivity', in *The Great Cat massacre and other episodes in French cultural history* (New York 1984), p.215-56, 279-82.

The Darnton debate: books and revolution in the eighteenth century, ed. Haydn T. Mason, *SVEC* 359 (1998).

Dawson, Robert L., *The French booktrade and the 'permission simple' of 1777, SVEC* 301 (1992).

De Crue, F., *L'Ami de Rousseau et des Necker. Paul Moultou à Paris en 1778* (Paris 1926).

Dedeck-Héry, Ernestine, *J.-J. Rousseau et le projet de constitution pour la Corse* (Philadelphia 1932).

Dictionnaire de Jean-Jacques Rousseau, ed. Frédéric-S. Eigeldinger and Raymond Trousson (Paris 1996).

Dictionnaire des journaux, 1600-1789, ed. Jean Sgard, 2 vols (Paris 1991).

Dorigny, Marcel, 'Les Girondins et Jean-Jacques Rousseau', *Annales historiques de la Révolution française* 231-234 (1978), p.569-83.

–, 'Louis-Sébastien Mercier lecteur de Rousseau en 1791. Rousseau Giron-din?', *Etudes Jean-Jacques Rousseau* 3 (1989), p.55-68.

Dubosq, Yves-Zacharie, *Le Livre français et son commerce en Hollande de 1750 à 1780 (d'après des documents inédites)* (Amsterdam 1925).

Dufour, Théophile, *Recherches bibliographiques sur les œuvres imprimées de J.-J. Rousseau, suivies de l'inventaire des papiers de Rousseau conservés à la bibliothèque de Neuchâtel*, introduction by Pierre-Paul Plan, 2 vols (Paris 1925; New York 1971).

Echeverria, Durand, 'The pre-revolutionary influence of Rousseau's *Contrat social*', *Journal of the history of ideas* 33 (1972), p.543-60.

Ecrire. Publier. Lire. Les correspondances (problématique et économie d'un 'genre littéraire'), ed. Jean-Louis Bonnat and Mireille Bossis (Nantes 1982).

Eigeldinger, Frédéric S., 'Des manuscrits de Rousseau dans une grande enveloppe jaune', *Revue de la Société suisse des bibliophiles* 26, no. 2 (October 1983), p.81-86.

–, '*Des pierres dans mon jardin*'. Les années neuchâteloises de Jean-Jacques Rousseau et la crise de 1765 (Paris and Geneva 1992).

–, 'Histoire d'une œuvre inachevée: *Emile et Sophie, ou Les solitaires*', *Annales de la Société Jean-Jacques Rousseau* 40 (1992), p.153-83.

Ellrich, Robert J., 'The cultural meaning of the anti-Rousseau tradition', *Romance quarterly* 38 (1991), p.309-17.

Fajn, Max, 'Marc-Michel Rey: boekhandelaar op de bloe[m]mark (Amsterdam)', *Proceedings of the American philosophical society* 117 (1974), p.260-68.

Favret, Mary, *Romantic correspondence* (Cambridge 1993).

Feather, John, 'The publisher and the pirates: British copyright law in theory and practice, 1710-1775', *Publishing history* 22 (1987), p.5-32.

–, *Publishing, piracy, and politics* (London 1994).

Foster, Elizabeth A., *Le Dernier séjour de J.-J. Rousseau à Paris, 1770-1778*, Smith College studies in history (Northampton, Mass. 1920-1921).

Foucault, Michel, 'What is an author?', in *Textual strategies: perspectives in post-structuralist criticism*, ed. Josué V. Harari (Ithaca 1979), p.147-59.

Foxon, David, *Pope and the early eighteenth-century book trade. The Lyell lectures, Oxford, 1975-1976*, revised and ed. James McLaverty (Oxford 1991).

François, Alexis, 'La correspondance de J.-J. Rousseau dans la querelle littéraire du XVIIIe siècle', *Revue d'histoire littéraire de la France* 33 (1926), p.355-69.

Françon, Marcel, 'La condamnation de l'*Emile*', *Annales de la Société Jean-Jacques Rousseau* 31 (1946-1949), p.209-45.

Fusil, C.-A., *La Contagion sacrée* (Paris 1932).

Gagnebin, Bernard, 'L'édition originale de l'*Emile*', *Bulletin du bibliophile* 3 (1953), p.107-30.

–, 'L'étrange accueil fait aux *Confessions* de Rousseau au XVIIIe siècle', *Annales de la Société Jean-Jacques Rousseau* 38 (1969-1971), p.105-26.

–, 'L'héritage littéraire de Rousseau', in *Rousseau after 200 years: proceedings of the Cambridge bicentennial colloquium*, ed. R. A. Leigh (Cambridge 1982), p.151-81.

–, 'Notices bibliographiques', in Jean-Jacques Rousseau, *Œuvres complètes*, ed. Bernard Gagnebin and Marcel Raymond (Paris 1964-1995), i.1883-908; ii.1961-94; iii.1851-90; iv.1853-92; v.1807-33.

Gallas, K. R., 'Autour de Marc-Michel Rey et de Rousseau', *Annales de la Société Jean-Jacques Rousseau* 17 (1926), p.73-90.

–, 'La condamnation de l'*Emile* en Hollande', *Annales de la Société Jean-Jacques Rousseau* 17 (1926), p.53-72.

Gillet, Louis, 'La collection Girardin au musée de Chaalis. Le reliquaire de Jean-Jacques', *Revue des deux mondes* (1 November 1925), p.134-61.

Girardin, Fernand de, *Iconographie de Jean-Jacques Rousseau. Portraits, scènes, habitations, souvenirs* (Paris 1909).

Girardin, Stanislas, *Lettre de Stanislas Girardin à M. Musset-Pathay, sur la mort de J.-J. Rousseau* (Paris 1824).

Gobel, Gundula and Albert Soboul, 'Audience et pragmatisme du rousseauisme (les almanachs de la Révolution 1788-1795)', in *Objet et méthodes de l'histoire de la culture*, ed. Jacques Le Goff *et al.* (Paris and Budapest 1982), p.97-121.

Gobet, Philippe, 'Mme de Charrière et Jean-Jacques Rousseau', *Annales de la Société Jean-Jacques Rousseau* 1 (1905), p.67-93.

Goldgar, Anne, *Impolite learning: conduct and community in the Republic of Letters* (New Haven 1995).

Goodman, Dena, 'Epistolary property: Michel de Servan and the plight of letters on the eve of the French Revolution', in *Early modern conceptions of property*, ed. John Brewer and Susan Staves (New York and London 1996), p.339-64.

–, *The Republic of Letters: a cultural history of the French Enlightenment* (Ithaca 1994).

Goulemot, Jean-Marie, 'Rousseau et les figures de l'intellectuel', *Saggi e ricerche di letteratura francese* 28 (1989), p.57-82.

Grazia, Margareta de, *Shakespeare verbatim: the reproduction of authenticity in the 1790 apparatus* (Oxford 1991).

Griffin, Dustin, *Literary patronage in England, 1650-1800* (Cambridge 1996).

Grosclaude, Pierre, *Malesherbes. Témoin et interprète de son temps* (Paris 1961).

Guéhenno, Jean, *Jean-Jacques Rousseau*, translated by John and Doreen Weightman, 2 vols (London and New York 1966).

Guenot, Hervé, 'De l'île des Peupliers au Panthéon. La translation des cendres de Rousseau. 11 octobre 1794', *Etudes Jean-Jacques Rousseau* 3 (1989), p.101-25.

–, 'Jean-Jacques: Crispin? Diogène? Socrate? la représentation théâtrale de Rousseau (1755-1819)', *Etudes Jean-Jacques Rousseau* 1 (1987), p.93-124.

Guillemin, Henri, *Les Philosophes contre Jean-Jacques. 'Cette affaire infernale'. L'affaire J-J. Rousseau–Hume* (Paris 1942).

Guyot, Charly, 'L'accueil fait en Suisse au *Contrat social*', in *Etudes sur le 'Contrat social'* (Paris 1964), p.381-93.

–, *Un ami et défenseur de Rousseau. Pierre-Alexandre Du Peyrou* (Neuchâtel 1958).

–, *De Rousseau à Mirabeau. Pèlerins de Môtiers et prophètes de 89* (Neuchâtel 1936).

–, *Plaidoyer pour Thérèse Le Vasseur* (Neuchâtel 1962).

Habermas, Jürgen, *The Structural transformation of the public sphere: an inquiry into a category of bourgeois society*, translated by Thomas Burger (Cambridge, Mass. 1989).

Hanley, William, 'The policing of thought: censorship in eighteenth-century France', *SVEC* 183 (1980), p.265-95.

Hesse, Carla, 'Enlightenment epistemology and the laws of authorship in revolutionary France, 1777-1793', *Representations* 30 (1990), p.109-37.

–, *Publishing and cultural politics in revolutionary Paris, 1789-1810* (Berkeley and Los Angeles 1991).

Higgin[s], D., 'Rousseau and the Pantheon: the background and implications of the ceremony of 20 vendémiaire Year III', *Modern language review* 50 (1955), p.274-80.

Hoeveler, Diane L., *Romantic androgyny: the woman within* (University Park, Penn. 1990).

Huizinga, J. H., *The Making of a saint: the tragi-comedy of Jean-Jacques Rousseau* (London 1976).

Hulliung, Mark, *The Autocritique of enlightenment: Rousseau and the philosophes* (Cambridge, Mass. 1994).

Jimack, Peter D., *La Genèse et la rédaction de l'"Emile" de J.-J. Rousseau*, *SVEC* 13 (1960).

–, 'Some eighteenth-century imitations of Rousseau's *Emile*', *SVEC* 284 (1991), p.83-105.

Jourdan, Annie, 'Le culte de Rousseau sous la Révolution. La statue et la panthéonisation du citoyen de Genève', *SVEC* 324 (1994), p.57-77.

Katz, Wallace, 'Le rousseauisme avant la Révolution', *Dix-huitième siècle* 3 (1971), p.205-22.

Kernan, Alvin, *The Death of literature* (New Haven 1990).

–, *Printing technology, letters, and Samuel Johnson* (Princeton 1987).

Kirsop, Wallace, 'Les mécanismes éditoriales', in *Histoire de l'édition française*, vol. ii *Le Livre triomphant, 1660-1830* (Paris 1990), p.15-34.

Labrosse, Claude, *Lire au XVIIIe siècle. 'La Nouvelle Héloïse' et ses lecteurs* (Lyon 1985).

Lecercle, Jean, 'Les Confessions. Texte ou document?', *Œuvres et critiques* 3 (1978), p.23-37.

–, 'Rousseau et ses publics', in *Jean-Jacques Rousseau et son œuvre. Problèmes et recherches* (Paris 1964), p.283-302.

Lefebvre, Philippe, 'Jansénistes et catholiques contre Rousseau. Essai sur les circonstances religieuses de la condamnation de l'*Emile* à Paris', *Annales de la Société Jean-Jacques Rousseau* 38 (1966-1968), p.129-48.

Leigh, Ralph A., 'Une balle qu'il eût fallu saisir au bond. Frédéric-Samuel Ostervald et l'édition des *Œuvres* de Rousseau (1778-1779)', in *Aspects du livre neuchâtelois*, ed. Jacques Rychner and Michel Schlup (Neuchâtel 1986), p.89-96.

–, 'The Geneva edition and the *Confessions*', in *Unsolved problems in the bibliography of Jean-Jacques Rousseau*, ed. J. T. A. Leigh (Cambridge 1991), p.121-33.

–, 'Jean-Jacques Rousseau and Mme de Warens: some recently discovered documents', *SVEC* 57 (1969), p.165-75.

–, 'Les manuscrits disparus de J.-J. Rousseau. Quelques observations et quelques fragments retrouvés ou complétés', *Annales de la Société Jean-Jacques Rousseau* 34 (1956-1958), p.31-81.

–, 'La mort de J.-J. Rousseau. Images d'Epinal et roman policier', *Revue d'histoire littéraire de la France* 78 (1978), p.187-98.

–, 'Rousseau, his publishers and the *Contrat social*', *Bulletin of the John*

Rylands University Library of Manchester 66 (1984), p.204-27.

–, 'Rousseau's English pension', in *Studies in 18th-century French literature presented to Robert Niklaus* (Exeter 1975), p.109-22.

–, *Unsolved problems in the bibliography of Jean-Jacques Rousseau*, ed. J. T. A. Leigh (Cambridge 1991).

Lejeune, Philippe, *Le Pacte autobiographique* (Paris 1975).

Link-Heer, Ursula, 'Facetten des Rousseauismus mit einer Auswahlbibliographie zu seiner Geschichte', *Zeitschrift für Litteraturwissenschaft und Linguistik* 63 (1986), p.127-63.

MacArthur, Elizabeth, 'Textual gardens: Rousseau's Elysée and Girardin's Ermenonville', *Romance quarterly* 38 (1991), p.331-39.

Macdonald, Frederika, *Jean-Jacques Rousseau: a new criticism*, 2 vols (London 1906).

Manin, Bernard, 'Rousseau', in *A critical dictionary of the French Revolution*, ed. François Furet and Mona Ozouf, translated by Arthur Goldhammer (Cambridge, Mass. 1989), p.829-43.

Martin, Angus, V. G. Mylne and R. Frautschi, *Bibliographie du genre romanesque français 1751-1800* (London 1977).

Martin, Henri-Jean, 'La librairie française en 1777-1778', *Dix-huitième siècle* 11 (1979), p.87-112.

–, 'La prééminence de la librairie parisienne', in *Histoire de l'édition française*, vol. ii *Le Livre triomphant, 1660-1830* (Paris 1990), p.331-57.

Martin-Decaen, A., *Le Marquis René de Girardin (1735-1808). Le dernier ami de Jean-Jacques Rousseau* (Paris 1912).

Maza, Sarah, *Private lives and public affairs: the 'causes célèbres' of prerevolutionary France* (Berkeley and Los Angeles 1993).

–, 'Stories in history: cultural narratives in recent works in European history', *The American historical review* 101 (1996), p.1493-515.

McDonald, Joan, *Rousseau and the French Revolution* (London 1965).

McEachern, Jo-Ann E., *Bibliography of the writings of Jean-Jacques Rousseau to 1800*, vol. i *Julie, ou La nouvelle Héloïse* (Oxford 1993); vol. ii *Emile, ou De l'éducation* (Oxford 1989).

–, 'L'édition originale de l'*Emile*', *Bulletin du bibliophile* (1987), p.20-30.

–, 'Eighteenth-century continental books: some problems of bibliographical description', *Text* 3 (1987), p.355-66.

–, '*La Nouvelle Héloïse* et la censure', in *Rousseau and the eighteenth century: essays in memory of R. A. Leigh*, ed. Marian Hobson, J. T. A. Leigh and Robert Wokler (Oxford 1992), p.83-99.

–, '*La Nouvelle Héloïse*: some bibliographical problems', *Eighteenth-century fiction* 1 (1989), p.305-17.

McNeil, Gordon H., 'The cult of Rousseau and the French Revolution', *Journal of the history of ideas* 6 (1945), p.197-212.

Mély, Benoît, *Jean-Jacques Rousseau. Un intellectuel en rupture* (Paris 1985).

Minois, Georges, *Censure et culture sous l'ancien régime* (Paris 1995).

Monglond, André, *Le Préromantisme français*, vol. i *Le Héros préromantique* (Paris 1965); vol. ii *Le Maître des âmes sensibles* (Paris 1966).

Monin, H., 'Les œuvres posthumes et la musique de J.-J. Rousseau aux *Enfans trouvés*', *Revue d'histoire littéraire de France* 20 (1915), p.48-55.

Mornet, Daniel, 'Les enseignements des bibliothèques privées', *Revue d'histoire littéraire de la France* 17 (1910), p.449-96.

–, 'L'influence de J.-J. Rousseau au XVIIIᵉ siècle', *Annales de la Société Jean-Jacques Rousseau* 8 (1912), p.33-67.

–, *Les Origines intellectuelles de la Révolution française, 1715-1787* (Paris 1933).

–, 'Le texte de la *Nouvelle Héloïse* et les éditions du XVIIIᵉ siècle', *Annales de la Société Jean-Jacques Rousseau* 5 (1909), p.67-80.

Morton, Brian N., 'Beaumarchais et le prospectus de l'édition de Kehl', *SVEC* 81 (1971), p.133-47.

Mounier, Jacques, *La Fortune des écrits de Jean-Jacques Rousseau dans les pays de langue allemande de 1782 à 1813* (Paris 1980).

Moureau, François, 'Les inédits et la campagne de presse de 1778', *Dix-huitième siècle* 12 (1980), p.411-23.

Muir, P. H., 'The Kehl edition of Voltaire', *The Library* 3 (September 1948), Fifth Series, p.85-100.

Ozouf, Mona, *L'Ecole de la France* (Paris 1984).

Palmer, R. R., *The Age of the democratic revolution*, 2 vols (Princeton 1959-1964).

Peoples, Margaret Hill, 'La querelle Rousseau-Hume', *Annales de la Société Jean-Jacques Rousseau* 18 (1927-1928).

Perrin, Jean-François, 'Ceci est mon corps. J.-J. Rousseau et son "édition générale"', *SVEC* 370 (1999), p.85-94.

Pizzinger, Alda Maria, 'The relationship between Jean-Jacques Rousseau and his publishers', Ph.D. dissertation, New York University, 1953.

Pomeau, René, *Voltaire en son temps*, vol. iii with Christiane Mervaud, *De la cour au jardin, 1750-1759* (Oxford 1991); vol. iv *'Ecraser l'infâme', 1759-1770* (Oxford 1994); vol. v *'On a voulu l'enterrer', 1770-1791* (Oxford 1994).

Quérard, J.-M., *La France littéraire, ou Dictionnaire bibliographique des savants, historiens et gens de lettres de la France* [...], 12 vols (Paris 1827-1864).

–, *Les Supercheries littéraires dévoilées*, 3 vols (Paris 1869-1870).

Reddick, Allen, *The Making of Johnson's Dictionary* (Cambridge 1990).

Reichenburg, Marguerite, *Essai sur les lectures de Rousseau* (Philadelphia 1932).

Revault d'Allonnes, M., 'Rousseau et le jacobinisme. Pédagogie et politique', *Annales historiques de la Révolution française* 231-234 (1978), p.584-607.

The Rhetorics of life writing in early modern Europe, ed. Thomas F. Mayer and D. R. Woolf (Ann Arbor 1995).

Ridehalgh, Anne, 'Preromantic attitudes and the birth of a legend: French pilgrimages to Ermenonville, 1778-1789', *SVEC* 215 (1982), p.231-52.

–, 'Rousseau as God? the Ermenonville pilgrimages in the Revolution', *SVEC* 278 (1990), p.287-308.

Roche, Daniel, 'La censure' and 'La police du livre', in *Histoire de l'édition française*, vol. ii *Le Livre triomphant, 1660-1830* (Paris 1990), p.88-109.

–, 'Les primitifs du rousseauisme. Une analyse sociologique et quantitative de la correspondance de J.-J. Rousseau', *Annales. Economies, sociétés, civilisations* 26 (1971), p.151-72.

Roddier, Henri, *J.-J. Rousseau en Angleterre au XVIIIe siècle* (Paris 1950).

Rogers, Pat, 'Pope and his subscribers', *Publishing history* 3 (1978), p.7-36.

Rose, Mark, *Authors and owners: the invention of copyright* (Cambridge 1993).

Rose, R. B., 'The marquis René-Louis de Girardin: the perfect Rousseau revolutionary', *Australian journal of French studies* 20 (1992), p.131-52.

Rosenblatt, Helena, *Rousseau and Geneva: from the First discourse to the Social contract, 1749-1762* (Cambridge 1997).

Rosselet, Claire, *Catalogue de la correspondance de J.-J. Rousseau (lettres expédiées et reçues) conservée à la bibliothéque de la ville de Neuchâtel* (Neuchâtel 1963).

Roussel, Jean, *Jean-Jacques Rousseau en France après la Révolution, 1795-1830* (Paris 1972).

–, 'Le phénomène de l'idéntification dans la lecture de Rousseau', *Annales de la Société Jean-Jacques Rousseau* 39 (1972-1977), p.65-78.

Saunders, David, *Authorship and copyright* (London 1992).

Saussure, Hermine de, *Etude sur le sort des manuscrits de J.-J. Rousseau* (Neuchâtel 1974).

–, *Rousseau et les manuscrits des 'Confessions'* (Paris 1958).

Schama, Simon, *Citizens* (New York 1989).

Schinz, Albert, 'Histoire de l'impression et de la publication du *Discours sur l'inégalité* de J.-J. Rousseau', *Publications of the Modern Language Association of America* 28 (1913), p.253-90.

–, *Jean-Jacques Rousseau et le libraire Marc-Michel Rey. Les relations personnelles* (Geneva 1916).

Schlobach, Jochen, 'Un reportage sur Rousseau en 1763', *Dix-huitième siècle* 16 (1984), p.211-42.

Sénelier, Jean, *Bibliographie générale des œuvres de Jean-Jacques Rousseau* (Paris 1949).

Sgard, Jean, 'Des collections aux œuvres complètes, 1756-1798', *SVEC* 370 (1999), p.1-12.

–, 'Morts parallèles', *Dix-huitième siècle* 11 (1979), p.15-26.

Simon, Julia, *Mass enlightenment* (Albany, N.Y. 1995).

Soboul, Albert, 'Classes populaires et rousseauisme sous la Révolution', *Annales historiques de la Révoluton française* 34 *(1962), p.*421-38.

–, 'Jean-Jacques Rousseau et le jacobinisme', in *Etudes sur le 'Contrat social'. Actes des journées d'étude organisées à Dijon pour la commémoration du 200ᵉ anniversaire du 'Contrat social'* (Paris 1964), p.405-24.

Sozzi, Lionello, 'Interprétations de Rousseau pendant la Révolution', *SVEC* 64 (1968), p.187-223.

Spink, John Stephenson, *Jean-Jacques Rousseau et Genève* (Paris 1934).

Starobinski, Jean, *Jean-Jacques Rousseau: transparency and obstruction*, translated by Arthur Goldhammer (Chicago 1988).

Stewart, Philip, 'Half-title or *Julie* beheaded', *The Romanic review* 86 (1995), p.31-44.

–, 'Rousseau, Boucher, Gravelot, Moreau', *LIT* 5 (1994), p.261-83.

Sturrock, John, *The Language of autobiography* (Cambridge 1995).

Suchy, Joseph, 'Les *Confessions* à la mort de Rousseau, un témoignage sur une "pré-réception". Deux lettres peu connues de Denis Fonvisine', *Œuvres et critiques* 3 (1978), p.126-27.

Swenson, James, *On Jean-Jacques Rousseau considered as one of the first authors of the Revolution*, Stanford 2000.

Tatin, Jean-Jacques, 'La dissémination du texte Rousseau. Le *Contrat social* dans les recueils de *Pensées de J.-J. Rousseau*', *Littérature* 69 (1988), p.19-27.

Taylor, Samuel S. B., 'Rousseau's contemporary reputation in France', *SVEC* 27 (1963), p.1545-74.

Temmer, Marc J., *Samuel Johnson and the three infidels* (Athens, Ga. 1988).

Théry, Robert, 'Histoire, description et analyse de l'exemplaire du *Discours sur l'inégalité* acquis par le musée', *Etudes Jean-Jacques Rousseau* 4 (1991), p.231-61.

Trénard, Louis, 'La diffusion du *Contrat social*, 1762-1832', in *Etudes sur le 'Contrat social'. Actes des journées d'étude organisées à Dijon pour la commémoration du 200ᵉ anniversaire du 'Contrat social'* (Paris 1964), p.425-58.

Trousson, Raymond, *Isabelle de Charrière* (Paris 1994).

–, 'Isabelle de Charrière et Jean-Jacques Rousseau', *Bulletin de l'Académie royale de langue et littérature françaises* 63 (1985), p.5-57.

–, *Jean-Jacques Rousseau*, vol. ii *Le Deuil éclatant du bonheur* (Paris 1989).

–, *Rousseau et sa fortune littéraire*, 2nd edn (Paris 1977).

–, 'Rousseau, sa mort et son œuvre dans la littérature périodique en 1778', *Revue internationale de philosophie* 32 (1978), p.177-96.

Trousson, Raymond and Frédéric-S. Eigeldinger, *Dictionnaire de Jean-Jacques Rousseau* (Paris 1996).

Underwood, George A., 'Rousseauism in two early works of Mme de Staël', *Modern philology* 13 (1915), p.417-32.

Vercruysse, Jeroom, 'Marc-Michel Rey, imprimeur philosophe ou philosophique?', *Literaturgeschichte als geschichtlicher Auftrag: in memoriam Werner Krauss* (Berlin 1978), p.149-56.

–, 'Marc-Michel Rey, libraire des Lumières', in *Histoire de l'édition française*, vol. ii *Le Livre triomphant, 1660-1830* (Paris 1990), p.413-17.

Voltaire imprimé tout vif. Un choix d'éditions suisses, 1723-1778, ed. J.-P. Candaux and Silvio Corsini (Geneva and Lausanne 1994).

Walter, Eric, 'Les auteurs et le champ littéraire', *Histoire de l'édition française*, vol. ii *Le Livre triomphant, 1660-1830* (Paris 1990), p.499-518.

Warner, James H., 'A bibliography of eighteenth-century English editions of J.-J. Rousseau, with notes on the early diffusion of his writings', *Philological quarterly* 13 (1934), p.225-47.

Wirz, Charles, 'Rousseau. Les éditions, les recherches bibliographiques', *Revue d'histoire littéraire de la France* 79 (1979), p.351-73.

Index

Page numbers in bold type refer to entries or significant mentions in the STG edition of the *Collection complète*.

Mr Hume and Mr Rousseau, translated by J.-B.-A. Suard as the *Exposé succinct de la contestation qui s'est élevée entre M. Hume et M. Rousseau avec les pièces iustificatives*, 63-64, 170, 189n

Ivernois, François d', 74, 108, 129, 132-33, 134, 135-36, 137, 149, 151, 155, **177**, 192-93, 226; *Tableau historique et politique des révolutions de Genève*, 155
Ivernois, François-Henri d', 151, **181**
Ivernois, Isabelle d', **172**

Jessop, Edmund, **180**
Journal de la montagne, 236
Journal de Lausanne, 220-21, 223, 225
Journal de Paris, 50, 57-58, 65, 89, 90, 91, 92, 93, 131, 132, 147, 154, 167, 190, 223, 228
Journal des savants, 13
Journal encyclopédique, 147, **189**-90

Keith, George, count-marshal of Scotland, 98n, 132, **169**-70, 173, **175**, **179**, **185**-86, 187, 203
Kendrick, William, 31
Kirchberger, Niklaus, **170**

La Borde, Jean-Benjamin de, *Essai sur la musique ancienne et moderne*, 145-46
La Combe, François, 138n
La Condamine, Charles-Marie de, 41
La Croix, Pierre-Firmin de, **174**
La Fontaine, Jean de, 9n
La Harpe, Jean-François de, 153
Lakanal, Joseph, 237, 245
Laliaud, Henri, 135
Lambert, Michel, 3
La Porte, Joseph de, 44
Larnage, Suzanne-Françoise de, **183**
La Rochefoucauld et de La Roche-Guyon, Louis-Alexandre, duc de, 84
La Tour de Franqueville, Marie-Anne Alissan de, **190**-91, 213; *Errata de l'Essai sur la musique ancienne et moderne*, **191**n; *Lettre à l'auteur de la justification de J.-J. Rousseau dans la contestation qui lui est survenue avec M. Hume*, **191**n; *Jean-Jacques vengé par son amie*, **191**n; *Réflexions sur ce qui s'est passé au sujet de la rupture de J.-J. Rousseau et de M. Hume*, **191**n; *La Vertu vengée par l'amitié*, **191**n

La Tourette, Marc-Antoine Claret de, **187**
Lebègue de Presles, Achille-Guillaume, 57, 69-70, 70n, 98, 98n, 100, 107, 108, 121; *Relation ou notice des derniers jours de mons. Jean Jacques Rousseau*, 57
Lefébure, Louis-François-Henri, 147, 190
Leigh, Ralph A., 58n, 80n, 151, 164-65, 190, 190n
Le Jay, Edme-Jean, 84
Le Marchand, François, 89-90, 93-96
Lenieps, Toussaint-Pierre, 48
Le Noir, Jean-Charles-Pierre, 65, 90-91
Le Roy (bookseller in Caen), 194
Le Roy, Amable, 136, 192, 195
Leroy, Charles-Georges, **164**
Lesueur, Jacques-Philippe, 237-38, 240
Le Tourneur, Pierre-P.-F., 193n
Levasseur, Marie-Thérèse, 3, 4, 5, 33, 35, 45, 46, 50, 56-58, 59-61, 63, 65-73, 78, 79, 83-84, 89-91, 93-109, 113, 116, 119-23, 127, 131-32, 134, 135, 137, 142, 145-46, 148, 198, 202, 203-11, 218, 227, 230-40, 242, 244-49, 250-51
Levebure, Simon, 205, 207
Linguet, Simon-Nicolas-Henri, 153
Linnaeus (Linné), Carl von, **187**
Louis, dauphin of France, **184**
Louis XV, king of France, 13n, 25n, 28
Louis XVI, king of France, 122, 155, 200
Lullin and Company (bankers), 197-99, 202, 205, 208
Lullin, Gabriel, 136, 193, 196, 248
Luneau de Boisjermain, Pierre-J.-F., 9n
Luxembourg, Charles-François-Frédéric de Montmorency-Luxembourg, maréchal-duc de, 16, **170**
Luxembourg, Madeleine-Angélique de Neufville-Villeroy, maréchale-duchesse de, 2, 23n, 30, 33, 37, 40, 41, 135, 142, 144, 147, 200, 238

Madin, Pierre, 233
Mailly (bookseller in Dijon), 194
Malesherbes, Chrétien-Guillaume de Lamoignon de, 2, 3, 12, 13-17, 20-28, 30, 33, 36-38, 40-42, 41n, 117, 129, 138-39, **140**-45, 200, 213, 216, 238, 249; *Mémoires sur la librairie*, 11n; 'Mémoire sur la liberté de la presse', 214n
Malesherbes, Marie-Françoise de Lamoignon de, 142
Manget, Gaspard-Joël, 220-25, 227-28

Printed and bound by CPI Group (UK) Ltd, Croydon, CR0 4YY

23/04/2025

14660996-0001